T0338873

Dense Cities
Architecture for Living Closer Together

Spricht man gegenüber Architekten, Fachplanern, Politikern und Nutzern das Wort „Dichte" aus, ist den ersten Reaktionen häufig gemeinsam, dass Dichte eher quantitativ – zwischen „Bevölkerungsdichte" und „baulicher Dichte" – verstanden wird und man Übereinstimmung und Ablehnung gleichermaßen erfährt. Übereinstimmung in der Vorstellung, dass angesichts der in jeder Hinsicht knapper werdenden Ressourcen über neue Formen des Zusammenlebens nachgedacht werden muss. Ablehnung in der Vorstellung, dass dieses Zusammenleben auch ein Zusammenrücken bedeutet. Ähnlich wie in Roland Barthes Vorlesung „Wie zusammen leben" („Comment vivre ensemble"), in der er das Phantasma artikuliert, „alleine leben zu wollen und zugleich, ohne Widerspruch dazu, zusammenleben zu wollen",[1] scheinen auf der Ebene des städtischen Miteinanders somit verschiedene Handlungsstränge nebeneinander zu existieren. Diese erfordern jedoch gänzlich andere Lesarten und Lesbarkeiten von Dichte als die durch Kennzahlen und wenige Parameter festgelegten Möglichkeiten städtischer Planung. Was fehlt, ist eine Auseinandersetzung mit den qualitativen Aspekten von Dichte, die ihre Legitimation nicht bloß dem Umstand verdankt, eine naheliegende Alternative zu Zersiedelung zu bieten.

When the word "density" is brought up to architects, district planners, politicians, and occupants, their initial reactions will frequently be similar in that density is usually understood as pertaining to quantity—somewhere between "population density" and "building density"—and the replies will usually reflect consensus or opposition in equal measure. Consensus when it comes to the idea that new forms of coexistence must be contemplated in view of the increasing scarcity of resources in all respects. And opposition based upon the idea that this reconceptualized coexistence means shifting closer together. Similar to Roland Barthes's lecture "Comment vivre ensemble" (How to Live Together), where he articulates the phantasm of "wanting to live alone while simultaneously, without an inherent contradiction, wanting to live together,"[1] various lines of action seem to concurrently exist side by side in the realm of urban togetherness. They, however, necessitate completely different readings and interpretations of density than those offered by an urban-planning potential determined by ratios and parameters. What is missing is an exploration of the qualitative aspects of density that draw their legitimacy from more than just the mere circumstance of providing an easy alternative to urban sprawl.

HANS GANGOLY

Ansatzpunkt der vorliegenden Ausgabe von *GAM* ist daher die Überlegung, den Begriff „Dichte" programmatisch durch vielfältige Lektüren von Dense Cities in theoretischen Manifesten, historischen Analysen, urbanen Entwicklungskonzepten und architektonischen Entwurfsansätzen zu entfalten, die geeignet scheinen, die Diskussion über neue Formen des städtischen Miteinanders zwischen Architekten, Fachplanern und Nutzern jenseits von Kennzahlen neu anzuregen.

Die Notwendigkeit näher zusammenzurücken, steht außer Zweifel. Nicht nur aus ökonomischen Gründen, wenn in Zeiten mangelnder Finanzkraft der Länder und Kommunen die Infrastruktur der zersiedelten Landschaft langfristig nicht gesichert werden kann, sondern auch aus ökologischen Gründen. Mehr als die Hälfte des Energieverbrauchs wird für Wohnraum und für den motorisierten Individualverkehr aufgewandt. Wenn man sich vergegenwärtigt, dass für die aktuelle Produktion von neuem Wohnraum mehr Energie aufgewendet werden muss als für 50 Jahre Betrieb desselben, dann ist völlig klar, dass die einzig entscheidende Frage die nach dem Standort der Immobilie ist. Das ist zunächst die wichtigste Entscheidung. Seit dem Jahr 2007 leben mehr als die Hälfte der Weltbevölkerung in Städten und bis zum Jahr 2050 werden es mehr als 70 Prozent sein. Dennoch ist die Stadt der Zukunft keine smarte, supereffiziente Retortenstadt auf der grünen Wiese, sondern kann auch die bestehende europäische Stadt sein, die repariert wird, die Anpassungen an geänderte gesellschaftliche Bedürfnisse und geänderte Nutzerstrukturen erfährt und die im Zuge dessen dort, wo sinnvoll, verdichtet wird. Daher muss die Frage nach den räumlichen Bedingungen in einer dichteren Stadt mit urbanen Entwurfsansätzen verbunden werden, die Formen definieren, in denen wir auch näher zusammenrücken wollen.

In dieser Hinsicht bildet die funktionale und auch soziale Durchmischung der Stadt, die sich vornehmlich in den Erdgeschosszonen und im öffentlichen Raum manifestiert, einen zentralen qualitativen Aspekt der städtischen Dichte. Denn der öffentliche Raum, seine Gestaltung und die Möglichkeiten seiner Aneignung ist entscheidend für die Akzeptanz von Dichte. Je dichter eine Stadt wird, umso bedeutsamer wird auch die Aufenthaltsqualität dieser öffentlichen Räume, die als Handlungsräume die Chance auf atmosphärische Dichte als Ausdruck einer urbanen Lebenswelt bieten. Eine wichtige architektonische Aufgabe besteht hier insofern darin, die Übergänge vom Öffentlichen ins Private angemessen zu gestalten. Denn die Gestaltungsqualität von Plätzen, Straßenräumen und Grünanlagen lässt sich nicht von den sie definierenden, begrenzenden und prägenden Bebauungen trennen. Der öffentliche Raum benötigt eine architektonische Fassung; die Rolle der Architektur geht hier über die Gestaltung von Gebäudehüllen und über die Entwicklung neuer intelligenter Typologien weit hinaus. *GAM.08 Dense Cities* stellt die Frage, wie diese aktive Rolle der Architektur bei der Entwicklung eines „living closer together" aussehen und ausgestaltet werden kann. Welche Optionen können entwickelt werden, um den verschiedenen sozialen Gruppen ein hochqualitatives, vielfältiges und anpassungsfähiges urbanes Lebensumfeld zu schaffen?

Die Beiträge des ersten Teils – „Manifestos" – stellen unterschiedliche Positionen der architektonischen Auseinandersetzung mit dem Thema Dichte

The point of departure for the current issue of *GAM* is therefore the notion of seeing the concept of "density" programmatically unfold through multifarious texts on "dense cities." Taking the form of theoretical manifestos, historical analyses, urban development concepts, and architectural design approaches, these contributions are those deemed appropriate for newly fostering discussion—between architects, district planners, and residents—about new forms of urban togetherness above and beyond set parameters.

There is beyond doubt a need to move closer together. Not only for economic reasons, being that the infrastructure of sprawling landscapes cannot be weathered in the long term in these times of insufficient spending power within states and municipalities, but also for ecological reasons. More than half of energy consumption results from living space and motorized private transport. If we try to envision how more energy is expended for the current production of new living space than for fifty years of upholding these living quarters, then it is no wonder that the only decisive criterion to be taken into account is the location of real estate. Initially, this is the most important decision to be made. Since the year 2007 more than half of the world's population has been living in cities, and by the year 2050 this number will have risen to upward of 70 percent. All the same, the city of the future will not be a smart, super-efficient artificial city in a green zone but, more likely, an existing European city that has been revamped, that experiences adaptation to modified societal needs and altered occupant-related structures, and that is densified in the process in ways that make sense. Therefore, the issue of spatial conditions in a densified city must be associated with urban design approaches that define forms which make us want to move closer together.

In this respect, the functional and also social blending within a city that has predominately manifested in ground-level zones and public space represents a pivotal qualitative aspect of urban density. This is because public space, its configuration, and the possibilities it presents for appropriation prove decisive for the acceptance of density. The more dense a city becomes, the more important is the quality of life within these public spaces, which in their role as spaces of agency offer an opportunity for atmospheric density to emerge as an expression of an urban lifeworld. So it follows that a vital architectural task consists in appropriately designing the transitions at the juncture of public and private space. For the design quality of plazas, street expanses, and green spaces cannot be separated from the building developments that define, delineate, and influence them. Public space requires an architectural framework; the role of architecture here moves far beyond the design of structural shells and also beyond the development of new, intelligent typologies.

---

1   Vgl. Roland Barthes: *Wie zusammen leben. Simulationen einiger alltäglicher Räume im Roman*, Vorlesung am Collège de France 1976–1977, Frankfurt am Main 2007.

1   See Roland Barthes, *Comment vivre ensemble: Cours et séminaires au Collège de France (1976–1977)* (Paris, 2002).

GAM.08 Dense Cities fields the question as to how this active role played by architecture might look when planning and manifesting a state of "living closer together." Which options might be developed in order to create a highly qualitative, multifaceted, and adaptable urban living environment for society's different groups?

The contributions to the first section of this issue—"Manifestos"—introduce different positions in the architectural exploration of the topic "density," ranging from design concepts, ecological factors, and new technologies to the sociopolitical dimension of urban planning. Thus it becomes clear within the first section of *GAM.08 Dense Cities* that urban density in the scope of mid-sized European cities can in no way be equated with the negatively connoted hyperdensity of megacities within Asia or South America. Instead, this urban density fosters potential, protects resources, and facilitates sustainable coexistence.

Helmut Tezak's photo series signalizes the transition from architectural manifestos to more concrete and localizable principles or, more precisely, to historical and analytical configurations of spatial proximity. Just as Tezak illustrates the concept of density in a photographic essay on the City of Graz, the text contributions in the second section—"Configurations"—are likewise concerned with the question of the de facto constitution or fabric of dense cities, here through concrete case studies and analyses that specifically focus on the creation of European city centers and related densification processes, as well as on their sociopolitical ramifications.

The third section of *GAM.08*—"Contexts"—is in turn dedicated to those multilayered contexts that are taken as reference points in discourse on urban density and its spatial configurations: urbanist models of theory and planning, conceptual history, the sustainability debate, research on crowding, filmic documentaries about cities. Here density manifests as a relative reference value that renders possible open concepts of architectural design.

Finally, the fourth section—"Potentials"—establishes an outlook on the issue of what density may effectuate within urban-spatial development, and on the extent to which we can invoke urban expansion or retrospective densification as a quality feature within urban planning. Compiled through the related contributions are various different architectural strategies which, by means of an increase in density, not only "repair" sprawling areas but also create new networks, mixed utilizations, dialogues, and thus also a sustainable urban landscape.

On this note, *GAM.08* goes beyond simply mirroring the complexity and multifacetedness of dense cities. It moreover thematically explores a rich, elaborate myriad of designs that, based upon a historically and analytically substantiated framework, establish clear positions on the elaboration of urban densification.

Translation Dawn Michelle d'Atri

zwischen gestalterischen Konzepten, ökologischen Faktoren, neuen Technologien und der sozialpolitischen Dimension der Stadtplanung vor. Damit wird in diesem ersten Teil von *GAM.08 Dense Cities* klar, dass städtische Dichte im Rahmen mittelgroßer europäischer Städte keineswegs mit der negativ-besetzten Hyperdichte von Megacities Asiens oder Südamerikas gleichzusetzen ist, sondern vielmehr Potenziale eröffnet, wie Ressourcen gespart und ein nachhaltiges Zusammenleben ermöglicht werden können.

Helmut Tezaks Fotoserie signalisiert den Übergang von architektonischen Manifesten zu konkreteren und lokalisierbaren Prinzipien, oder genauer historischen und analytischen Konfigurationen der räumlichen Nähe. So wie Tezak den Begriff Dichte in einem fotografischen Essay zur Stadt Graz veranschaulicht, beschäftigen sich auch die Beiträge des zweiten Teils – „Configurations" – mit der Frage der tatsächlichen Konstitution oder Beschaffenheit von Dense Cities, also mit konkreten Fallstudien und Analysen, insbesondere zur Entstehung und den Verdichtungsprozessen europäischer Stadtzentren und deren gesellschaftspolitischen Auswirkungen.

In Folge ist der dritte Teil von *GAM.08* – „Contexts" – jenen vielschichtigen Kontexten gewidmet, denen der Diskurs über städtische Dichte und ihre räumlichen Konfigurationen ihre Bezüge entnehmen: urbanistische Theorie- und Planungsmodelle, Begriffsgeschichte, Nachhaltigkeitsdebatte, Crowding-Forschung, filmische Stadtdokumentationen. Dichte erscheint hier als eine relative Bezugsgröße, die offene Konzepte des architektonischen Entwurfs ermöglicht.

Schließlich eröffnet der vierte Teil – „Potentials" – eine Perspektive auf die Frage, was Dichte für die stadträumliche Entwicklung bewirken kann, und inwieweit wir Stadterweiterung oder Nachverdichtung als ein Qualitätsmerkmal der Stadtentwicklung nutzen können. Die Beiträge versammeln unterschiedliche architektonische Strategien, die durch eine Erhöhung der Dichte nicht nur zersiedelte Gebiete „reparieren", sondern auch neue Netzwerke, Mischnutzungen, Dialoge und damit eine nachhaltige Stadtlandschaft schaffen.

In diesem Sinne spiegelt *GAM.08* nicht nur die Komplexität und Vielschichtigkeit von Dense Cities wider, sondern thematisiert auch eine facettenreiche Vielfalt von Entwürfen, die basierend auf einem historisch und analytisch fundierten Rahmen klare Positionen zur Ausgestaltung von urbaner Verdichtung eröffnen.

Why Are We Interested in Density?

Firstly, in terms of carbon emissions, it has been proved that the dispersed city, consisting of individual houses, is a bigger source of carbon emissions than the compact city, not only for the energy required for each house, but also for the emissions derived from the individual transport. Public transport is unaffordable because the population does not reach a critical mass.

Warum interessieren wir uns für Dichte? In Bezug auf den CO_2-Ausstoß ist erstens nachgewiesen worden, dass die aus einzelnen Häusern bestehende zersiedelte Stadt mehr Kohlendioxidemissionen produziert als die verdichtete Stadt. Dies geschieht nicht allein aufgrund des Energiebedarfs für jedes Haus, sondern auch wegen der Emissionen aus dem Individualverkehr.

A+T RESEARCH GROUP • AURORA FERNÁNDEZ PER • JAVIER MOZAS • JAVIER ARPA

Secondly, road surfaces increase proportionally to the dispersion and convert rural land into asphalt landscapes.

The proportion of asphalt needed to serve individual houses is, according to some studies carried out, of one square meter of road per one square meter of gross floor area, and the tons of material needed for road constructions and buildings could achieve in many cases the same proportion of 1:1.

Finally, the compact city promotes interaction between citizens and uses, not only as neighbors but at a bigger scale, sharing facilities, amenities, and public spaces.

In the last ten years, we have been measuring and comparing all that can be quantified, but we have avoided getting to the bottom of the matter, to the bottom of the wishing well that housing usually represents for its residents.

Do we really desire the dwellings that we publish?

Do we really want to live in the compact city?

If we were to ask ourselves what the desired house really was, most of us would recognize that we have an ideal photo in mind.

It would be even more embarrassing, if we were to ask ourselves where we live at present, in which type of house, in which part of the city and what plans we have for the future.

Suddenly, density ceases to be a concept, something vital for the planet, a ratio for judging plans.

Suddenly, density becomes an uncomfortable subject which deeply affects our decisions.

We know that the dense city has to be built, but while building the city, we can't forget the home.

The home for the user who will put his or her name on the letterbox.

If we asked at the beginning of this statement what density was, you can be sure that we were not referring to hyperdensity.

For us, density is the good balance of population and uses, the sustainable way of living together, the successful performances of the buildings.

Since we need to live in dense cities to save resources, this need must be converted into desire, and we will achieve this by turning housing into home and each home into our home.

For us the definition of density would be: *Density is home*.

So, if you believe in dense cities, make every dwelling a desirable home.

Der öffentliche Verkehr ist zu teuer, da die Bevölkerungszahl keine kostendeckende Größe erreicht. Zweitens nehmen die Straßenflächen proportional mit der Zersiedelung zu und verwandeln den ländlichen Raum in Asphaltlandschaften.

Laut einiger Studien erfordert die Versorgung einzelner Häuser ein Verhältnis von einem Quadratmeter Straße zu einem Quadratmeter Bruttogeschossfläche. Die Tonnen an Material, die für den Bau der Straßen und der Gebäude benötigt werden, könnten in vielen Fällen das gleiche Verhältnis von 1:1 erreichen.

Schließlich fördert die verdichtete Stadt die Interaktion zwischen Bewohnern und Nutzungen nicht nur auf der Ebene von Nachbarschaften, sondern auch im größeren Maßstab, indem städtische Einrichtungen, Freizeitanlangen und öffentliche Räume gemeinsam genutzt werden.

In den letzten zehn Jahren haben wir alle erdenklichen quantitativ bestimmbaren Größen gemessen und verglichen, jedoch haben wir es vermieden, der Sache auf den Grund zu gehen und zu den Wünschen und Träumen vorzustoßen, mit denen die Bewohner ihre Behausung üblicherweise verbinden.

Sehnen wir uns wirklich nach den Wohnungen, die wir publizieren?

Wollen wir wirklich in der verdichteten Stadt leben?

Wenn wir uns fragen würden, was das ersehnte Haus wirklich wäre, würden die meisten von uns erkennen, dass wir ein idealisiertes Bild im Kopf haben. Noch peinlicher wäre es, wenn wir uns zudem fragten, wo wir derzeit leben, in welcher Art von Haus, in welchem Teil der Stadt und welche Pläne wir für die Zukunft haben.

Plötzlich hört Dichte auf, ein Konzept zu sein, etwas Lebenswichtiges für den Planeten, eine Kennzahl für die Bewertung von Plänen. Dichte wandelt sich vielmehr zu einem unbequemen Thema, das unsere Entscheidungen grundlegend beeinflusst.

Wir wissen, dass die dichte Stadt gebaut werden muss, aber während wir die Stadt bauen, dürfen wir das Haus nicht vergessen. Das Haus für den Bewohner, der seinen Namen am Briefkasten anbringt. Wenn wir zu Beginn dieser Stellungnahme darüber nachgedacht haben, was Dichte bedeutet, haben wir sicherlich nicht an *Hyperdensity* gedacht. Für uns bedeutet Dichte die Ausgewogenheit zwischen Bewohnern und Nutzungsinteressen, einen nachhaltigen Weg des Zusammenlebens, eine gelungene Performance der Gebäude.

Da wir in dichten Städten leben müssen, um Ressourcen zu sparen, muss sich diese Notwendigkeit in etwas Wünschenswertes verwandeln und wir werden das erreichen, indem wir Behausungen in ein Heim und jedes Haus in unser Zuhause verwandeln.

Für uns wäre die Definition von Dichte: *Dichte ist ein Zuhause*.

Wenn Sie also an verdichtete Städte glauben, machen Sie aus jeder Wohnung ein wünschenswertes Zuhause.

Übersetzung Claudia Wrumnig

In the last ten years, we have been measuring and comparing all that can be quantified, but we have avoided getting to the bottom of the matter, to the bottom of the wishing well that housing usually represents for its residents.
Do we really desire the dwellings that we publish?
Do we really want to live in the compact city?
If we were to ask ourselves what the desired house really was, most of us would recognize that we have an ideal photo in mind.

1–13   Beispiele von Orten mit unterschiedlicher Dichte; Konzept und Zusammenstellung im Rahmen des Forschungsprojektes „Dichte". Examples of places of different degrees of density.
Concept and compilation within the framework of the research project "Dichte" (density). © Michael Heinrich, München Munich

19 Thesen zur Dichte

I. Die Dichtekategorien repräsentieren jeweils einen bestimmten zeitlichen Abschnitt und dadurch die jeweiligen Wertvorstellungen dieser Zeit.

19 Theses on Density. I. Each category of density represents a certain segment of time and thus reflects the respective ideals of this period.

DIETMAR EBERLE • SUSANNE FRANK

10 Grundsätze zur Stadtbau- kunst heute[1]

Die folgenden 10 Grundsätze zur Stadtbaukunst sind inhaltlich zugespitzt, um die drängendsten Probleme unserer Städte deutlich zu machen. Denn trotz aller Beteuerungen, die multifunktionale, fußläufige und schöne Stadt zu wollen, wird allzu oft durch einseitige Betrachtung eines bestimmten Aspektes der Stadt das Gegenteil produziert: Verkehrsplaner planen Verkehr, Ökonomen planen Wirtschaftsimpulse, Soziologen planen soziale Maßnahmen, Architekten planen Einzelhäuser – doch Stadt entsteht keine.

10 Principles of the Civic Art Today[1]. The following 10 civic art principles have been sharpened in terms of content in order to make the most pressing problems faced by our cities obvious. For despite all claims of wanting multifunctional, pedestrian-friendly, and beautiful cities, precisely the opposite is too often produced thanks to one-sided consideration of a certain city facet: transport planners plan traffic, economists plan economic impulses, sociologists plan social measures, architects plan single-unit structures—without a city emerging.

CHRISTOPH MÄCKLER • WOLFGANG SONNE

Genau hier setzt die Stadtbaukunst an: denn der Stadtbaukunst geht es nicht allein um das Gestalterisch-Künstlerische, sondern um das Gestalterisch-Künstlerische im Zusammenspiel mit den anderen die Stadt bestimmenden Faktoren. In dieser Hinsicht vertritt die Stadtbaukunst ein umfassendes und anspruchsvolles Konzept; eines, das die rein soziologisch-politologisch-ökonomisch-ökologisch operierenden Stadtplaner ebenso herausfordert wie die rein autistisch-ästhetisch denkenden Architekten.

1. Stadttheorie. Komplexität statt Reduktion. Stadtbaukunst muss alle Aspekte der Stadt umfassen und ihnen Gestalt geben. Städte lassen sich nicht auf einzelne Aspekte und deren Bewältigung durch einzelne Disziplinen reduzieren.

2. Stadtbild. Städtebau statt Fachplanung. Das Stadtbild entsteht aus der bewussten Anordnung und Gestaltung städtischer Bauwerke und bedarf eines auf dauerhafte Schönheit bedachten Städtebaus. Die Vernachlässigung des überkommenen Stadtbildes in der Stadtplanung, die durch die Trennung der unterschiedlichen Planungsbereiche verursacht wird, verhindert die Entwicklung umfassend qualitätvoller Lebensorte.

3. Stadtarchitektur. Gebautes Ensemble statt individualistischer Eventarchitektur. Städtische Architektur muss Ensembles mit ausdrucksreichen Fassaden bilden und ein gegliedertes Ganzes von zusammenhängender Textur und Substanz schaffen. Ausschließlich individualistische Eventarchitektur löst den städtischen Zusammenhang und die Verständlichkeit des öffentlichen Raums auf.

Die Identität der Stadt entsteht durch ihre langfristige Geschichte sowie die Pflege ihrer Denkmäler, ihres Stadtgrundrisses und ihrer Baukultur.

4. Stadtgeschichte. Langfristige Stadtkultur statt kurzfristiger Funktionserfüllung. Städtebau ist eine kulturelle Tätigkeit, die auf historischer Erfahrung und Bildung aufbaut. Vorgeblich wissenschaftliche Modelle und spontan verfasste Leitbilder wie beispielsweise die „verkehrsgerechte Stadt" verkennen den langfristigen und umfassenden Charakter der Stadt.

5. Stadtidentität. Denkmalpflege statt Branding. Die Identität der Stadt entsteht durch ihre langfristige Geschichte sowie die Pflege ihrer Denkmäler, ihres Stadtgrundrisses und ihrer Baukultur. Individualistisches Bran-

It is here that civic arts comes into play: for civic arts is not only concerned with design-related and artistic aspects, but also with how these aspects interact with other factors that show determinative impact on a city. In this regard, civic art advocates an integral and ambitious concept, one that challenges city planners who are operating on a purely sociological-politological-economic-ecological level as well as architects who are thinking solely in individual-aesthetic terms.

1. Urban Theory: Complexity not Reduction. Civic art must encompass all aspects of a city and give it form. Cities cannot be reduced to individual aspects or their problems be solved through individual disciplines.

2. Cityscape: Urban Design not Sectoral Planning. A cityscape takes form through the purposeful arrangement and design of urban structures and requires urban design that fosters long-term beauty. A neglect of the traditional cityscape during the urban-planning process, as caused by the separation of the different planning sectors, inhibits the development of residential areas of all-around quality.

3. Urban Architecture: Architectural Ensemble not Individualistic Event Architecture. It is important that urban architecture builds ensembles with expressive façades and creates an articulate whole comprised of coherent texture and substance. Just individualistic event architecture disintegrates the cohesive urban context and the perspicuity of public space.

4. Urban History: Long-Term City Culture not Short-Term Functional Fulfillment. Urban planning represents a cultural activity that builds upon historical experience and development. Ostensibly scientific models and spontaneously drafted guiding principles, such as the "traffic-friendly city," undermine the comprehensive, long-term character of cities.

5. Urban Identity: Monument Preservation not Branding. The identity of a city is lent shape through its long-running history as well as through the preservation of its monuments, its original layout, and its building culture. Individualistic branding denies a city its existing distinctive features and promotes a loss of identity in this age of globalization.

1   Die „10 Grundsätze zur Stadtbaukunst" wurden auf der ersten Konferenz zur Schönheit und Lebensfähigkeit der Stadt in Düsseldorf im März 2010 diskutiert und anschließend von Christoph Mäckler (Professor für Städtebau, TU Dortmund) und Wolfgang Sonne (Professor für Geschichte und Theorie der Architektur, TU Dortmund) verfasst und vom Deutschen Institut für Stadtbaukunst an der TU Dortmund im April 2010 herausgegeben. Die „10 Grundsätze" wurden u.a. in *Die Welt* vom 3.8.2010, in *Ach!* 41, Juli/August 2010 und in: Christoph Mäckler/Wolfgang Sonne (Hg.), *Konferenz zur Schönheit und Lebensfähigkeit der Stadt 1*, Sulgen 2011, publiziert.

1   The "10 Principles of the Civic Art" were introduced at the first Conference for Beautiful and Viable Cities held in Düsseldorf in March 2010 and later written up by Christoph Mäckler (professor for urban planning, TU Dortmund University) and Wolfgang Sonne (professor for history and architectural theory, TU Dortmund University) before subsequently being published by the German Institute of Civic Arts in April 2010. The "10 Principles" were also published in the *Die Welt* newspaper on August 3, 2010, in the magazine *Ach!* 41 (July/August 2010), and in the following volume: Christoph Mäckler and Wolfgang Sonne (eds.), *Konferenz zur Schönheit und Lebensfähigkeit der Stadt 1* (Sulgen, 2011).

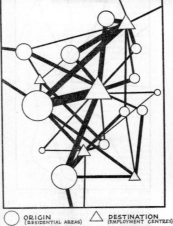

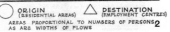

ORIGIN (RESIDENTIAL AREAS)　DESTINATION (EMPLOYMENT CENTRES)
AREAS PROPORTIONAL TO NUMBERS OF PERSONS
AS ARE WIDTHS OF FLOWS 2

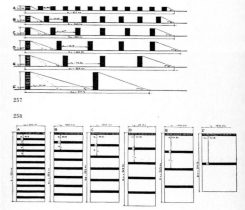

3

4

5

6

2　　Stadttheorie: Komplexität statt Reduktion　Urban Theory: Complexity not Reduction

3　　Stadtarchitektur: Gebautes Ensemble statt individualistischer Eventarchitektur
　　　Urban Architecture: Architectural Ensemble not Individualistic Event Architecture

4　　Stadtbild: Städtebau statt Fachplanung　Cityscape: Urban Design not Sectoral Planning

5　　Stadtgeschichte: Langfristige Stadtstruktur statt kurzfristige Funktionserfüllung
　　　Urban History: Long-Term City Culture not Short-Term Functional Fulfillment

6　　Stadtidentität: Denkmalpflege statt Branding　Urban Identity: Monument Preservation not Branding

7   Stadtpolitik: Stadtbürger als Gestalter statt anonymer Immoblilienwirtschaft
      Urban Politics: City Residents as Designers not Anonymous Real-Estate Industry

8   Stadtgesellschaft: Stadtquartier statt Siedlung
      Urban Society: City District not Housing Complex

9   Stadtverkehr: Stadtstraßen statt Autoschneisen
      Urban Transportation: City Streets not Automobile Thoroughfares

10   Stadtökonomie: Einzelhandel und Kleingewerbe statt Ketten
      Urban Economy: Local Retail Stores not Chains

11   Städtische Umwelt: Nachhaltig Bauen statt schnell Verpacken
      Urban Environment: Sustainable Building not Quick Packaging

6. Urban Society: City District not Housing Complex and Industrial Estate. The city district, with its functional mix and architecturally expressed spaces, represents the basic element of a city that is founded upon a diversity of lifestyles. Monofunctional settlements as well as shopping malls and industrial parks adjacent to the city destroy its urbanity and impede residents' ability to identify with their city.

7. Urban Politics: City Residents as Designers not Anonymous Real-Estate Industry. Urban building should first and foremost be borne by responsible citizens as future city users and be founded upon equitable access to a parceled land market. Institutional real-estate developers as well as public housing associations or property funds without long-term interest in a city's quality do not contribute to the construction of quality buildings.

8. Urban Economy: Local Retail Stores not Chains. The urban economy needs to be more strongly supported by a diversified range of inner-city retail stores and trade. All large chains and subsidiaries of large companies weaken the urban economy and obliterate city-based and self-determined employment opportunities.

9. Urban Transportation: City Streets not Automobile Thoroughfares. City streets are multifarious and well-designed spaces of agency, which are conductive not only to different kinds of transport but also to shopping, taking walks, maintaining social contacts, political manifestation, and leisure activities. Monofunctional automobile thoroughfares and pedestrian zones contribute to the destruction of a city.

10. Urban Environment: Sustainable Building not Quick Packaging. The sustainability of the urban environment comes about through widespread, sound longevity and urbanity. A reduction of vital energy-saving measures to oil-based thermal-insulation packaging and solitary energy houses exacerbates tomorrow's environmental issues.

Translation Dawn Michelle d'Atri

ding verleugnet die bestehenden Eigenheiten des Ortes und leistet dem Identitätsverlust im Zeitalter der Globalisierung Vorschub.

6. Stadtgesellschaft. Stadtquartier statt Wohnsiedlung und Gewerbepark. Das Stadtquartier mit Funktionsmischung und architektonisch gefassten Räumen bildet das Grundelement der auf vielfältigen Lebensweisen beruhenden Stadt. Monofunktionale Siedlungen sowie Einkaufs- und Gewerbeparks vor der Stadt zerstören die Urbanität und verhindern die Identifikation der Stadtgesellschaft mit ihrer Stadt.

7. Stadtpolitik. Stadtbürger als Gestalter statt anonymer Immobilienwirtschaft. Städtisches Bauen soll vor allem von verantwortungsbewussten Bürgern als künftigen Nutzern getragen werden und auf einem gleichberechtigten Zugang zu einem auf der Parzelle gegründeten Bodenmarkt beruhen. Institutionelle Bauträger wie öffentliche Wohnungsbaugesellschaften oder Immobilienfonds ohne langfristiges Interesse an der Qualität des Ortes schaffen keine guten Stadtbauten.

8. Stadtökonomie. Einzelhandel statt Ketten. Die Stadtökonomie sollte stärker vom diversifizierten innerstädtischen Einzelhandel und Gewerbe getragen werden. Allein Großketten und ausgelagerte Großbetriebe machen die Stadtökonomie krisenanfälliger und vernichten urbane und selbstbestimmte Arbeitsplätze.

9. Stadtverkehr. Stadtstraßen statt Autoschneisen. Stadtstraßen sind vielfältige und wohlgestaltete Aufenthaltsräume, die neben den verschiedenen Arten des Verkehrs auch dem Einkaufen, dem Spazieren, dem sozialen Kontakt, der politischen Manifestation und dem Vergnügen dienen. Monofunktionale Autoschneisen und Fußgängerzonen zerstören die Stadt.

10. Städtische Umwelt. Nachhaltig bauen statt schnell verpacken. Die Nachhaltigkeit der städtischen Umwelt entsteht durch umfassende und solide Dauerhaftigkeit und Urbanität. Die Reduktion der notwendigen Energieeinsparungsmaßnahmen auf ölbasierte Wärmedämmverpackungen und solitäre Energiehäuser schafft die Umweltprobleme von morgen.

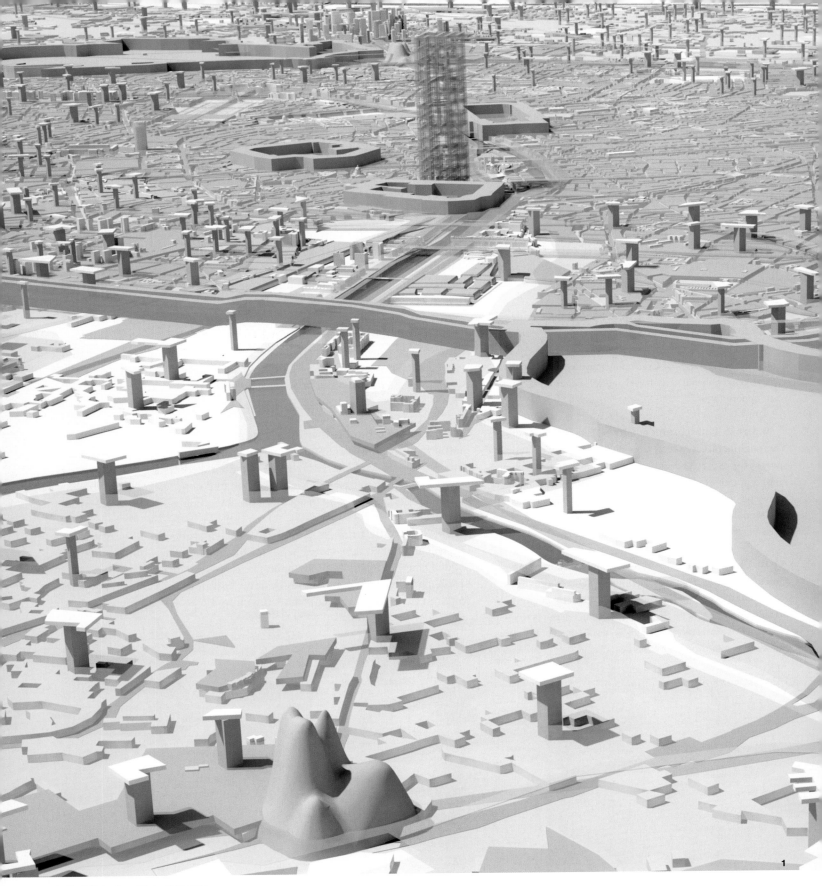

1 Groß-Paris Grand Paris © MVRDV

Be More![1]

Grand. What makes a city great today? Some major cities are currently facing a dramatic reality: they almost unavoidably cause chain reactions such as pollution, traffic congestion, monotony and poverty. The greatness of a city is therefore measured in terms of quality (rather mediocre today) in relation to its size. Yet some qualities such as prosperity, variety, freedom, specialty, and cleanliness can be reunited under or in responsibility.

Größe. Was macht eine Stadt heute großartig? Einige wichtige Städte sind derzeit mit einer dramatischen Realität konfrontiert: fast zwangsläufig verursachen sie Kettenreaktionen wie Umweltverschmutzung, Verkehrsüberlastung, Eintönigkeit und Armut. Die Großartigkeit einer Stadt wird daher in Bezug auf eine (meist mittelmäßige) Qualität in Relation zu ihrer Ausdehnung gemessen. Und dennoch kann die Verbindung von Attributen wie Wohlstand, Vielfalt, Freiheit, Einzigartigkeit und Sauberkeit immer auch ein Indiz für eine gewisse Verantwortlichkeit sein.

WINY MAAS

At the same time, other complementary qualities would define the city's ambition and ability to be unique, attractive, fun, spectacular, exemplary, etc., in terms of social, political and environmental aspects, urban development and architecture.

Exemplary. What role must a city take on to be exemplary? At the advent of this new millennium, the world has never been so dense! The global population is continually on the rise and consumes increasing amounts. Who would like to live more comfortably, who can afford to, who can demand more? Such a world is practically screaming for more space, for its production needs, water and energy resources, oxygen, various environmental offsets and for its safety, to keep at bay the increasing risks of accidents. Everyone wants space. Is it still possible to meet this demand given the current situation (spatial, economic, cultural and technological)? Where, when and how can we innovate? Is it possible to close the gap between our resources and our requirements? And above all, how can we make up for this difference?

Dense Space: Capa-City. It is probable that the major role of future cities is to generate space for this gap. And the more space the better. The world could continue to grow, to ensure its reserves like a real response to its responsibility.

Density ensures diversity between the city and the landscape. The space gained can be used to redefine the conditions of landscapes. Density allows an increase in our capacities. In a nutshell, a city's density brings about the synergy of its components in environmental, economic, sociological, cultural and architectural terms.

> Density ensures diversity between the city and the landscape. The space gained can be used to redefine the conditions of landscapes. Density allows an increase in our capacities.

Controversy. Such a transformation is mostly based on the Kyoto and Copenhagen Protocols that redefine the most effective spatial paradigms. However, there is still too much opposition between the protection of our cities, which limits the scope of action, and the means of meeting Kyoto and Copenhagen objectives. Too many people are still rejecting density, dreaming of a house with a garden in the inner suburbs of a city. Can we find an appropriate development method? Can we combine the aforementioned intentions and these dreams?

Competition. In this post-Kyoto era, it is clear that we must act responsibly and take part in stabilizing the climate and our environment. Yet in

Gleichzeitig drücken andere, sich ergänzende Qualitäten den Ehrgeiz und die Fähigkeit einer Stadt aus, attraktiv, fröhlich, spektakulär oder vorbildlich zu sein und zwar in Bezug auf soziale, politische und ökologische Aspekte, die Stadtentwicklung und ihre Architektur.

Vorbildlich. Welche Rolle muss eine Stadt übernehmen, um vorbildlich zu sein? Am Beginn des neuen Jahrtausends war die Welt so dicht wie noch nie! Die Weltbevölkerung wächst stetig und verbraucht immer größere Rohstoffmengen. Wer würde gerne bequemer leben, wer kann es sich leisten, wer kann mehr beanspruchen? Eine solche Welt schreit praktisch nach mehr Raum für ihren Produktionsbedarf, Wasser- und Energieressourcen, Sauerstoff, verschiedene ökologische Entlastungen und nach Sicherheit, um das zunehmende Unfallrisiko in Grenzen zu halten. Jeder will Raum. Ist es überhaupt noch möglich, diesem Bedarf angesichts der aktuellen räumlichen, wirtschaftlichen, kulturellen und technologischen Lage nachzukommen? Wo, wann und wie können wir Erneuerungen durchführen? Ist es möglich, die Lücke zwischen unseren Ressourcen und unseren Bedürfnissen zu schließen? Und vor allem, wie können wir diese Ungleichheit überwinden?

Dichter Raum: Capa-City. Wahrscheinlich ist die Hauptaufgabe der Städte der Zukunft, Raum für diese Lücke schaffen zu müssen. Und je mehr Raum, desto besser. Die Welt könnte weiter wachsen und ihre Reserven als eine reale Antwort auf ihre Verantwortlichkeit einsetzen.

Dichte sorgt für mehr Diversität zwischen Stadt und Landschaft. Der gewonnene Platz kann dazu verwendet werden, die Situation der Landschaften neu zu definieren. Dichte ermöglicht ein Mehr an Kapazitäten. Kurz gesagt macht die Dichte einer Stadt Synergien zwischen ihren Bestandteilen in ökologischer, ökonomischer, soziologischer, kultureller und architektonischer Hinsicht möglich.

Kontroverse. Eine solche Umgestaltung ist von den Kyoto- und Kopenhagen-Protokollen motiviert, in denen die wirksamsten räumlichen Paradigmen neu definiert werden. Allerdings herrscht noch ein zu großer Widerspruch zwischen dem Schutz unserer Städte, der den Handlungsspielraum einschränkt, und den Maßnahmen zur Erfüllung der Ziele von Kyoto und Kopenhagen. Zu viele Menschen lehnen Dichte immer noch ab und träumen von einem Haus mit Garten in den Vororten einer Stadt. Können wir eine geeignete Planungsmethode entwickeln? Können wir einen Konsens zwischen den oben genannten Absichten und diesen Träumen herstellen?

1   This article was originally published in *L'Architecture d'Aujourd'hui* 378 (June/July 2010), pp. 109–11.

1   Dieser Beitrag wurde erstmals in *L'Architecture d'Aujourd'hui* 378 (Juni/Juli 2010), S. 109–111 veröffentlicht.

Configurations

1 Giovanni Battista Nolli, Plan von Rom plan of Rome, 1748

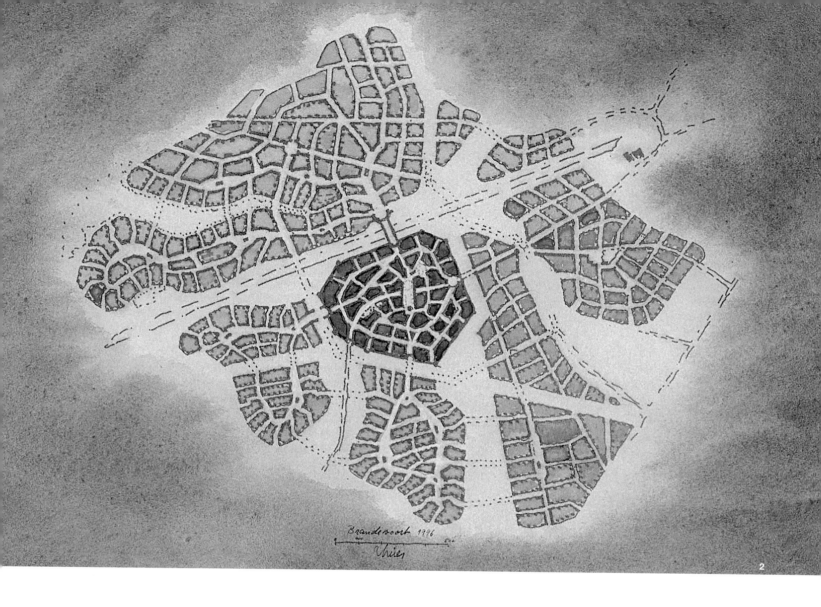

Die angewandten Kunstsparten Architektur und Städtebau arbeiten mit einem Regelwerk sachlicher Theoreme, die nicht von jeder Generation neu erfunden werden müssen. Die Inszenierung von Raumsequenzen in einer städtebaulichen Struktur kann aus einem gigantischen Fundus schöpfen.

temples to completion. The architectural language of classical antiquity continued to survive a further two thousand years on all continents, right up to the present time. This was only possible because the canon of the elements in architecture, sculpture and painting had developed up to a point where it gained universal validity. Despite regional peculiarities and individual artistic temperaments, the rules of design allowed for optimal adaptation and variation. With the revolution in the arts at the beginning of the twentieth century and the movement towards unrestricted freedom of personal expression, the validity of the classical repertoire appeared to become questionable, or at least, it was seriously put to the test. The unsettling thing about today's world of artistic expression is the mania for uniqueness that keeps museums and galleries on tenterhooks. Architecture and urban design are not spared this.

In past times, the art of composition using pictorial means could be taught. Theoretical approaches were based on a tradition that had given rise to products that lasted hundreds of years. They had gained general recognition and one did not have to be the representative of a philosophical tendency in order to find access to them or even to understand them. What can I teach students nowadays about the form of the modern building? They have seen a lot of things in the built world, discovered fantastic leaps of joy in modern construction. They want to be just as revolutionary and unique. How can a teacher rein in such a comprehensible desire to create one's own world wonder? It is a question of opening their eyes for critical viewing and understanding, of showing them the anomalies such ego trips can lead to. It is a thankless task to teach the virtues of restraint.

In this essay I want to try to awaken hope for a dignified future city. It should avoid superficial spectacle and offer contemplative niches that make life on the streets enjoyable again. It might seem arrogant that in the following I attempt to do this with the aid of my own projects, but every one of our works carries within it the intention of finding a typological solution to its problem. We deal with our themes in the domain of urban design in such a manner as to distance ourselves from all spectacular effects. We would like to move towards "normal" solutions that protect life with quiet and comfort and leave room for daydreams, solutions that are so filled with poetry that mistakes can be endured painlessly. The discipline attached to the planning may often appear strict and artificial, from a single mold as it were, but it always leaves gaps for inconsistencies and planning uncertainties—even outright failure.

My dream of the ideal town[2] is not an unattainable paradise. There are enough models of breathtaking beauty like Pienza, Dinkelsbühl, and Bruges. It is not an aberrant desire to wish to have this beauty in one's daily life. As ugliness is not a condition that can be dealt with by laws and prohibitions, we have to endure it in this liberal society. We hope that the free

choice of place of residence will some time in the future put an end to inhospitableness.

The applied arts of architecture and urban design work with a set of objective theorems that do not have to be reinvented by every generation. The staging of spatial sequences in an urban architectural structure can draw upon a gigantic store of knowledge. Their geometrical parameters are infinitely variable; the opportunities for innovation based on a secured repertoire are boundless. The adherence to rules that are tried and true is not tainted the way copying is. Making use of the experiences of history does not brand one as an epigone or an eclectic. A profound knowledge of history enables us to confront emanations of the times critically and to hold alternative models up to the modern city.

Translation Fiona Greenwood Fincannon

auf ein Weltwunder eigener Machart? Es geht darum, die Augen zu öffnen für ein kritisches Sehen und Verstehen, vor Augen zu führen, zu welchen Anomalien derlei Egotrips führen können. Die Tugend der Zurückhaltung zu lehren ist ein undankbares Unterfangen.

Ich will in dem vorliegenden Beitrag versuchen, die Hoffnung auf eine würdevolle zukünftige Stadt zu wecken. Sie soll das oberflächliche Spektakel meiden und besinnliche Nischen anbieten, die das Leben auf der Straße wieder genießbar machen. Dass dies anhand von eigenen Projekten geschieht, mag anmaßend anmuten. Doch jede unserer Arbeiten trägt in sich die Absicht, zu ihrer Problematik eine typenhafte Lösung zu finden. Wir behandeln unsere Themen im Bereich des Städtebaus fern aller spektakulären Effekte. Wir möchten zu „normalen" Lösungen vorstoßen, die das Leben in aller Stille und Geborgenheit schützen und Räume für Tagträume offen lassen. Lösungen, die so mit Poesie erfüllt sind, dass Fehler ohne Schmerzen geduldet werden. Ihre Planungsdisziplin mag oft streng und künstlich, gleichsam wie aus einem Guss aussehen, sie hat aber immer Schlupflöcher für Ungereimtheiten und Planungsunsicherheiten – bis hin zu grobem Versagen.

Mein Traum von der idealen Stadt ist kein unerreichbares Paradies. Es gibt ausreichend Vorbilder von berauschender Schönheit wie Pienza, Dinkelsbühl, Brügge. Es ist kein verbotenes Ansinnen, sich diese Schönheit für sein tägliches Leben herbeizuwünschen. Da Hässlichkeit kein Zustand ist, dem mit Gesetzen und Verboten beizukommen wäre, müssen wir sie in dieser liberalen Gesellschaft dulden. Wir hoffen, dass die freie Wahl des Aufenthaltsortes der Unwirtlichkeit irgendwann den Garaus macht.

Die angewandten Kunstsparten Architektur und Städtebau arbeiten mit einem Regelwerk sachlicher Theoreme, die nicht von jeder Generation neu erfunden werden müssen. Die Inszenierung von Raumsequenzen in einer städtebaulichen Struktur kann aus einem gigantischen Fundus schöpfen. Ihre geometrischen Parameter sind unendlich variierbar; die Innovationsmöglichkeiten am gesicherten Repertoire sind grenzenlos. Der Imitation von erprobten Regeln haftet nicht der Makel des Kopierens an. Sich der Erfahrungen der Geschichte zu bedienen, brandmarkt einen nicht als Epigonen oder Eklektiker. Die profunde Kenntnis der Geschichte befähigt uns, den Zeiterscheinungen kritisch gegenüberzutreten und der modernen Stadt entgegenzuhalten.[2]

---

2   The theme of the composition of urban spaces will be explained with the aid of typological projects that I have compiled since 1965. In the last twelve years, Christoph Kohl has been by my side; without his help, I would not have been able to cope with the abundance of themes including the realizations.

2   Beim Thema der Komposition von Stadträumen, die ich seit 1965 erarbeitet habe, stand mir in den vergangenen zwölf Jahren Christoph Kohl zur Seite, ohne dessen Hilfe ich die Fülle der Themen bis hin zur Realisierung nicht hätte bewältigen können.

1 Ausschnitt Detail *The City of the Captive Globe* © OMA by Madelon Vriesendorp, 1972 (veröffentlicht in: published in Rem Kohlhaas, *Delirious New York*, 1978, 1994, S. p. 295)

Archipelago Urbanism

The European City is built. And the era of the large-scale urban master plans has come to an end. At least we—architects, urban designers, and planners—are told so. And true, Western societies are aging and shrinking. Overall. If we take the premise *cum grano salis* for granted, since there are regional differences between urban areas with a stable development, even growth in hotspots, such as the "global cities" and their agglomerations,[1] whilst other areas on the old continent suffer already from decades of depopulation and disurbanization.[2]

Der Archipel-Urbanismus. Die Europäische Stadt ist gebaut. Und die Ära der groß angelegten städtebaulichen Masterpläne ist zu Ende. Zumindest wird das uns – also den Architekten, Städtebauern und Stadtplanern – immer wieder vorgehalten. Und tatsächlich, westliche Gesellschaften sind im Begriff, immer schneller zu altern und zu schrumpfen. Global betrachtet. Und nur, wenn wir diese Prämisse *cum grano salis* verstehen, denn es gibt durchaus regionale Unterschiede zwischen Stadtgebieten mit stabiler Entwicklung, sogar Wachstum in städtischen Hotspots wie den „Global Cities"[1] und ihren Ballungsräumen, während andere Gegenden auf dem alten Kontinent bereits seit Jahrzehnten unter Bevölkerungsrückgang und Entstädterung[2] leiden.

OLE W. FISCHER

Seen from this perspective the task of urbanism has shifted from the design of entire new cities or quarters to the repair, cultivation, and adaptation of the existing. However, strategies are rare: one of the few examples is the concept of the city as an archipelago, developed by Oswald Mathias Ungers for Berlin.

Berlin in the late 1970s: destroyed in WW II, divided thereafter, cut off from its hinterland by the wall, deprived of political as well as economic significance, the districts of West Berlin faced shrinking. Against this background of the walled-in post-industrial city and under the premise of a statistically projected drop in population of another 10 percent over the next decade, Ungers convened a Cornell University summer school studio in Berlin (West) in 1977. Together with Rem Koolhaas, Peter Riemann, Hans Kollhoff and Arthur Ovaska he published 11 theses on "cities within the city" as "green archipelago."[3] Instead of imposing (another) overall master plan on Berlin, or indulging in fantasies about turning around depopulation by means of urban planning, the group around Ungers offered an alternative reading of the existing city as a compound of multiple contrasting, even opposing urban "enclaves." They exemplified these differentiated urban structures with the various settlements that were merged into Greater Berlin in 1920 or as manifestations of historic plans, such as the baroque Friedrichstadt, the reformist Siemensstadt, the postwar Gropiusstadt or the modernist Siedlungen, etc.[4] Ungers' team proposed a twofold dialectical strategy for shrinking: first, a series of punctual interventions, densifications, and complementary additions of the as-found fragmented "city enclaves" according to associative references, each offering a particular history, ideology, civic community and lifestyle. Examples include the radial "fan" of Karlsruhe, Leonidov's linear city for Magnitogorsk, the dialectic of the Manhattan grid vs. Central Park, or the baroque chessboard of Mannheim. Second, these stabilized "islands" of exacerbated difference stand in strong contrast to the "green" that replaces the defunct and depopulated areas that are given up. These intermediate green spaces would allow for agriculture, urban gardening, and the upcoming forest as well as suburban houses, but also provide the infrastructure to interconnect the "islands" of the archipelago.

The term "archipelago" describes a group of islands—originally the Greek Islands in the Aegean—that are not only interconnected by proximity and similarity, but also share the sea in between.[5] Ungers chose the insular geographic metaphor to differentiate between the smaller scale of the formally, structurally, and programmatically clearly delineated "cities" against the vast urbanized territory of Greater Berlin, respectively its Western sectors. He recognized the loss of population and (economic) pressure on the land as an advantage, as an opportunity to break down the anonymity of the (potentially endless) urban mass into distinct cities with increased quality of

So betrachtet hat sich die Aufgabe des Städtebaus gewandelt: vom Entwurf gänzlich neuer Städte und Quartiere hin zur Reparatur, Pflege und Anpassung des bereits Bestehenden. Strategien dafür sind dennoch rar: eine der wenigen Ausnahmen bildet die Vorstellung von der Stadt als Archipel, wie sie Oswald Mathias Ungers für Berlin entwickelt hat.

Berlin in den späten 1970er Jahren: im Zweiten Weltkrieg zerstört, im Anschluss geteilt und dadurch vom Umland abgeschnitten, ihrer wirtschaftlichen und politischen Bedeutung beraubt, sahen sich die Stadtteile Westberlins mit dem Phänomen der Schrumpfung konfrontiert. Vor diesem Hintergrund der eingeschlossenen, postindustriellen Stadt und ausgehend von einem statistisch prognostizierten Rückgang der Bevölkerung um weitere 10% über das nächste Jahrzehnt, veranstaltete Ungers im Jahre 1977 eine Sommerakademie der Cornell Universität in Westberlin. Im Anschluss veröffentlichte er gemeinsam mit Rem Koolhaas, Peter Riemann, Hans Kollhoff und Arthur Ovaska elf Thesen zur „Stadt in der Stadt" als „grüner Archipel".[3] Anstatt Berlin einen (weiteren) großangelegten Masterplan überzustülpen, oder sich der Fantasie hinzugeben, den Bevölkerungsrückgang durch stadtplanerische Mittel aufhalten und umkehren zu können, bietet die Gruppe um Ungers eine alternative Lektüre der existierenden Stadt als Verbund von zahlreichen unterschiedlichen, sogar gegensätzlichen städtischen „Enklaven". Beispielhaft für diese differenzierten städtischen Strukturen nennen sie die zahlreichen älteren Ansiedelungen und Stadtkerne, welche 1920 zu „Groß-Berlin" zusammengeschlossen wurden, oder die physischen Zeugen der historischen Planstädte, wie die barocke Friedrichsstadt, die reformistische Siemensstadt, die Gropiusstadt der Nachkriegszeit oder die Siedlungen der Moderne etc.[4] Die Gruppe um Ungers schlug eine dialektische Doppelstrategie vor, um der Schrumpfung zu begegnen: Erstens durch eine Serie von punktuellen Eingriffen, Verdichtungen und Erweiterungen der vorgefundenen fragmentierten Stadtenklaven auf Basis assoziativer Referenzbeispiele, von denen jedes für eine spezifische Geschichte, Ideologie, Form der Gemeinschaft und des Lebensstils steht. Beispiele beinhalten die Karlsruher „Fächerstadt", Leonidovs „lineare Stadt" für Magnitogorsk, die Dialektik zwischen dem Straßenraster Manhattans und dem Central Park, oder das barocke „Schachbrett" der Mannheimer Innenstadt. Zweitens stehen diese stabilisierten „Inseln" der verschärften Unterschiede im

1   See Saskia Sassen, *The Global City: New York, London, Tokyo* (Princeton, 1991).

2   See Philipp Oswalt (ed.), *Shrinking Cities* (Ostfildern-Ruit 2005/2006) and *Arch+ 173: Shrinking Cities Reinventing Urbanism* (2005).

3   Oswald Mathias Ungers et. al., *Die Stadt in der Stadt – Berlin das grüne Stadtarchipel: ein stadträumliches Planungskonzept für die zukünftige Entwicklung Berlins* (Köln, 1977). For English translation see O.M. Ungers, Rem Koolhaas, Peter Riemann, Hans Kollhoff, Arthur Ovaska, "Cities within the city – Proposals by the Sommer Akademie for Berlin", in *Lotus* 19 (1978), pp. 82–97.

4   Ungers (1978), ibid., p. 88.

5   The etymology emphasizes the water above the land, since archipelago stems from Greek ἀρχι (arkhi) as first or primary and πέλαγος (pélagos), which means sea.

1   Vgl. Saskia Sassen: *The Global City: New York, London, Tokyo*, Princeton 1991.

2   Vgl. Philipp Oswalt (Hg.): *Shrinking Cities*, Ostfildern-Ruit 2005/2006 und *Arch+ 173: Shrinking Cities Reinventing Urbanism* (2005).

3   Oswald Mathias Ungers et. al.: *Die Stadt in der Stadt – Berlin das grüne Stadtarchipel. Ein stadträumliches Planungskonzept für die zukünftige Entwicklung Berlins*, Köln 1977. Für die englische Übersetzung vgl. O. M. Ungers, Rem Koolhaas, Peter Riemann, Hans Kollhoff, Arthur Ovaska: „Cities within the city – Proposals by the Sommer Akademie for Berlin", in: *Lotus* 19 (1978), S. 82–97.

4   Ungers: *Die Stadt in der Stadt*, (wie Anm. 3), These 6 (ohne Seiten), vgl. ders.: „Cities within the city" (wie Anm. 3), S. 88.

starken Kontrast zum „Grün“, das die nutzlosen, entvölkerten Stadtteile ersetzt, welche aufgegeben werden. Diese grünen Zwischenflächen würden nicht nur zusätzlichen Raum für Landwirtschaft, Urban Gardening, den aufschießenden Wald oder Einfamilienhäuser schaffen, sondern auch die Infrastruktur bereitstellen, um die „Inseln“ des Archipels miteinander zu verbinden.

Der Begriff „Archipel“ bezeichnet eine Inselgruppe – ursprünglich die der griechischen Inseln im Ägäischen Meer – welche nicht nur durch Nähe und Ähnlichkeit verbunden sind, sondern auch durch das zwischen den Inseln liegende Meer bestimmt werden.[5] Ungers wählte diese insulare geografische Metapher, um zwischen dem kleineren Maßstab der formal, strukturell und programmatisch klar abgegrenzten „Städte“ und dem großflächigen urbanisierten Territorium von Groß-Berlin – oder genauer gesagt den westlichen Sektoren – zu differenzieren. Er erkannte den Rückgang der Bevölkerung und das Nachlassen des (ökonomischen) Drucks auf das Land als einen Vorteil, als eine Chance, die Anonymität der (potenziell endlosen) urbanen Masse in eigenständige Städte herunterzubrechen, um die Lebensqualität in ihnen zu erhöhen. Und mit derselben Metapher der „Stadt in der Stadt“ argumentierte Ungers für architektonische Eingriffe im städtischen Maßstab, für eine Neubetrachtung von Form, Morphologie und Typologie, wie auch von Dichte und klaren Grenzen gegenüber dem „Anderen“ der Stadt, was nichts anderes ist als das Grün. Jedoch auf den zweiten Blick wird jedoch klar, dass auch das „grüne Meer“ selbst eine Art Insel darstellt: Die den Text begleitenden Pläne zeigen Berlin auf einem Rasternetz, wie es figürlich von der politischen Linie der Mauer begrenzt wird und als klar definierte Form oder Küstenlinie hervortritt. So gesehen, werden die „Stadt-Enklaven“ im „grünen Meer“ zu Inseln innerhalb einer Insel, wenn man den insularen Status Westberlins als eine Enklave der DDR mitbetrachtet.

In diesem Punkt wirkt Ungers Lektüre von Berlin eher rückwärtsgewandt als neu: Sie geht zurück auf die Vorstellung der (Europäischen) Stadt als Insel, beispielhaft illustriert durch die von Stadtmauern eingefasste griechische *Polis*, Thomas Morus' Vision von *Utopia* als mondsichelförmigem Eiland oder Frederick Law Olmsteds Central Park in New York: Allen gemeinsam ist die Differenzierung zwischen der Stadt und ihrem Gegensatz – das Ländliche, Suburbane, Grüne. Wie bereits Pier Vittorio Aureli hervorgehoben hat, bezeichnen die Begriffe für Stadt – *Polis* oder *Civitas* – eine klar abgegrenzte, politische Einheit, während Urbanisierung oder Urbanismus auf eine andere etymologische Linie verweisen, welche auf das Lateinische *urbs* zurückgeht, das eine bloße Ansammlung von Menschen und Strukturen bezeichnet, die – unterstützt von der Infrastruktur des römischen

Ungers chose the insular geographic metaphor to differentiate between the smaller scale of the formally, structurally, and programmatically clearly delineated "cities" against the vast urbanized territory of Greater Berlin, respectively its Western sectors. He recognized the loss of population and (economic) pressure on the land as an advantage, as an opportunity to break down the anonymity of the (potentially endless) urban mass into distinct cities with increased quality of living.

5 Die Etymologie hebt die Bedeutung des Wassers gegenüber dem Land hervor, denn Archipelago stammt vom Griechischen ἄρχι *(arkhi)* als Erstem oder Grundlegendem und πέλαγος *(pélagos)*, was Meer bedeutet.

living. And with the same metaphor of "cities within the city" he argued for architectural interventions on an urban scale, for a reconsideration of form, morphology, and typology as well as density and clear edges against the cities' "Other," which is the green. Yet, at a second glance, the "green sea" itself turns out to be an island: the plans accompanying the proposal show Berlin defined by the political figurative line of the wall on a square grid, as a clearly defined shape or coastline. From this perspective, the "city enclaves" in the "green sea" come to be islands within an island, if we consider the insular status of West Berlin as an enclave in the GDR.

In this respect Ungers' reading of Berlin seems to be more rearguard than new: it goes back to the idea of the (European) city as an island, exemplified by the walled-in polis, Thomas More's vision of *Utopia* as a crescent formed island, or Frederick Law Olmsted's Central Park New York: they all share the differentiation of the city to what it is not—the rural, the suburban, the green. As Pier Vittorio Aureli has pointed out, the city as *polis* or *civitas* denotes a limited, political entity whereas the urbanization or urbanism deriving from the Latin *urbs* has a different heritage of the mere aggregation of people and structures, that—supported by infrastructure and the Roman grid—is potentially despotic, limitless, and formless.[6] Despite avoiding the neoromantic imagery of the European city and its perimeter block, Ungers'

Despite avoiding the neoromantic imagery of the European city and its perimeter block, Ungers' proposed breakdown to distinct "city enclaves" seems to refer to pre-modern times when cities were still walled in and strictly separated from their surroundings.

proposed breakdown to distinct "city enclaves" seems to refer to pre-modern times when cities were still walled in and strictly separated from their surroundings. However, the concept of the archipelago undermines this obvious dialectic of figure and ground: besides the group of islands, it features the states of transitions between land and water, respectively suggests the water as part of the islands. Therefore, the redefined nuclei of urban fragments establish relationships in-between and span a space of the landscape. Ungers took this understanding of the Berlin landscape as archipelago from Karl Friedrich Schinkel,[7] who together with the landscape architect Peter Joseph Lenné rearranged the Havel river- and lakeland between Berlin an Potsdam for Friedrich Wilhelm IV by framing spaces and establishing connections with individual buildings respectively insular enclaves within an interconnected field of parks and water. Yet this romantic adaption of the Greek archipelago was not limited to the reworking of the royal parks and

Rasters – potenziell despotisch, unbegrenzt und formlos ist.[6] Obwohl Ungers auf die neoromantische Bildsprache der Europäischen Stadt und ihrer Blockrandbebauung verzichtet, scheint seine Untergliederung in einzelne „Stadtklaven" auf jene vormodernen Zeiten zu verweisen, als Städte noch von einer Mauer umfasst und klar von der Außenwelt abgetrennt waren. Und dennoch, das Konzept des Archipels unterläuft diese allzu offensichtliche Dialektik zwischen Figur und Grund: denn neben der Inselgruppe selbst zeichnet sich der Archipel durch Übergänge zwischen Land und Wasser aus, oder suggeriert vielmehr, dass das Wasser ein Teil der Inseln ist. Demzufolge bilden die neu definierten Stadtkerne Beziehungen untereinander aus und spannen einen eigenen Raum in der Landschaft auf. Ungers übernahm diese Vorstellung der Berliner Landschaft als einem Archipel von Karl Friedrich Schinkel,[7] der gemeinsam mit dem Landschaftsarchitekten Peter Joseph Lenné die Fluss- und Seenlandschaft der Havel zwischen Berlin und Potsdam im Auftrag von Friedrich Wilhelm IV. neu gestaltete, indem sie Freiräume rahmten und Beziehungen zwischen den einzelnen Gebäuden bzw. inselförmigen Enklaven innerhalb der vernetzten Park- und Wasserlandschaft herstellten. Schinkels romantische Übersetzung des griechischen Archipels im Sinne einer „Einheit von Fragmenten" war jedoch nicht auf die Neugestaltung der königlichen Parks und Schlösser, wie z.B. Glienicke, Charlottenhof, Babelsberg, Cecilienhof, Pfaueninsel und Sacrow beschränkt, sondern eine ähnliche Strategie zeigt sich auch in seinen Projekten für Berlin, wo er den Stadtraum durch „Solitäre" – freistehende Bauten – neu ordnete: In bewusster Abweichung von den barocken Rastern der königlichen Stadterweiterungen und des barocken königlichen Stadtschlosses platzierte Schinkel seine Einzelobjekte insular, ja fast körperlich, um interne Beziehungen herzustellen und den öffentlichen Raum zu rahmen, wie beispielsweise seine Gebäudegruppe aus Altem Museum, Friedrichswerderscher Kirche und der Bauakademie, die über die neugestaltete Schlossbrücke und Lennés Lustgarten über die Spree verbunden wurden. Und wieder eröffnet sich hier eine Referenz auf die Antike, doch hier ganz bewusst auf die skulpturale Positionierung der griechischen Tempel, wie sie die Akropolis in Athen beispielhaft verkörpert, auf der die monumentalen Volumina sogenannte „field conditions" erzeugen, indem sie einen relationalen Raum mit teilweisen Überdeckungen schaffen, der sich erst in der Zeit durch die physische Bewegung des Betrachters entlang der topografischen Promenade entfaltet.

Die Vorstellungen der „field conditions", des relationalen Raumes und der Differenzierung zwischen einer Reihe von permanenten, mit Intensität aufgeladen Strukturen, und den eher

6   Pier Vittorio Aureli, *The Possibility of an Absolute Architecture* (Cambridge, 2011). See especially chapter 1: "Toward the Archipelago". I take a different reading of Ungers' project as well as of the relationship of the formal to the political.

7   Ungers (1978), ibid., p. 94.

6   Vgl. Pier Vittorio Aureli: *The Possibility of an Absolute Architecture*, Cambridge 2011. Besonders Kapitel 1 „Toward the Archipelago". Hier wird jedoch eine andere Interpretation von Ungers Projekt vertreten, die sich vor allem in Bezug auf den Zusammenhang von Formalem und Politischem unterscheidet.

7   Vgl. Ungers: „Die Stadt in der Stadt" (wie Anm. 3), These 9 (ohne Seiten).

fließenden, temporären und verbindenden Nutzungen des „Grünraumes", die sich aus der Strategie, die Stadt als Archipel zu lesen, ergeben, taucht heute unter den Namen *Landscape Urbanism* oder *Ecological Urbanism* wieder auf.[8] Doch im Unterschied zu diesen gegenwärtigen Ansätzen, die mithilfe ökologischer und landschaftsgestalterischer Instrumente die urbanistischen Probleme des 21. Jahrhunderts angehen, um die Kluft zwischen Natur, Kultur und Infrastruktur zu überbrücken und gleichzeitig nachhaltige städtische Lebensräume für Menschen, Flora und Fauna zu schaffen, verherrlicht das „grüne Archipel" für Berlin gerade nicht das Natürliche und die Landschaft in dieser zeitgenössisch politisch-korrekten Art und Weise. Ungers zeichnet das „grüne Meer" zwischen den fragmentierten „Stadtinseln" eher als eine Übergangszone, die Raum für (Verkehrs-)Infrastruktur, Supermärkte und automobile Drive-In-Angebote, Produktionsstätten, freistehende Einfamilienhäuser und Freizeiteinrichtungen oder temporäre Nutzungen – wie urbane Landwirtschaft, Schrebergärten oder Wohnwagensiedlungen – schaffen sollte.[9] Obwohl Ungers Konzept auch eher traditionelle Landschaftselemente wie öffentliche Parks, Sportplätze, Wiesen oder Wälder beinhaltete, darf das „Grün" in Ungers' Konzept des Archipels nicht im ökologischen Sinn, sondern eher im Sinne individualisierter Programmelemente einer immer heterogener werdenden Gesellschaft verstanden werden. Mehr noch, das „Grün" dient als dialektische Ergänzung zu den politischen, kollektiven und kommemorativen Räumen der unterschiedlichen Stadtenklaven, als ein Versuch, die Collage der suburbanen und periurbanen Gebiete in die (schrumpfende) Stadt wiedereinzugliedern.

Diese analoge Schlussfolgerung vom Dauerhaften und Formalen der Stadt hin auf das Sozio-Politische und Historische – während die temporäre Dimension der städtischen Infrastruktur für das Ökonomische, Individuelle und (Re-)Produktive in einer Gesellschaft steht – ist ein Topos des postmodernen Denkens und zeigt Parallelen zum theoretischen Werk von beispielsweise Aldo Rossi.[10] Oder aber zu zeitgenössischen Interpretation von Pier Vittorio Aureli, der für eine „absolute Architektur" plädiert und der die aus den 1980er Jahren stammende These von der Autonomie der Architektur wiederaufnimmt, welche die Trennung der Form von Gesellschaft und Kultur mit politischem Inhalt auflud.[11] Die Opposition der geschlossenen architektonischen Form gegen die betriebswirtschaftlich expansive Logik

castles of Glienicke, Charlottenhof, Babelsberg, Cecilienhof, Pfaueninsel and Sacrow as a "union of fragments," but Schinkel showed a similar approach for his projects in the city of Berlin, where he rearranged urban space with solitary volumes: in deliberate difference to the baroque grid of the royal urban extensions and the baroque royal city palace, Schinkel positioned singular architectural objects, insular and almost corporeal, to establish relations and frame public spaces, such as his group of Altes Museum (Old Museum), Friedrichswerdersche Kirche (Friedrichswerder Church), Bauakademie (Building Academy), connected by the Schlossbrücke (Palace Bridge) and Lenné's Lustgarten (Pleasure Garden) as well as the Spree river. Again there is a reference to Greek antiquity, but here intentionally to the sculptural positioning of Greek temples as exemplified in the Acropolis of Athens, where the monumental volumes create a field condition and relational space of partial disclosure that unfolds temporarily with the physical movement of the observer along the topographical promenade.

The notion of field condition, of relational space and of the differentiation between multiple permanent structures charged with intensity versus the more fluid, temporal, and connective uses of the "green" imbedded in the strategy of reading the city as an archipelago resurfaces today as landscape urbanism or ecological urbanism.[8] Yet in contrast to these contemporary approaches to engage with the instruments of landscape and environmental design the problems of urbanization for the 21st Century, to bridge the gap between nature, culture, and infrastructure and to construct urban spaces as sustainable habitats for humans as well as for flora and fauna, the "green archipelago" of Berlin did not envision the natural or the landscape in such a contemporary political correct manner. Ungers depicted the "green sea" between the fragmented "city islands" rather as an intermediate zone for infrastructure (traffic), supermarkets and drive-in amenities, production, detached houses and temporary uses—including urban farming, family allotments, and mobile homes—or leisure activities.[9] Despite the use of more traditional landscape features such as public parks, athletic grounds, pasture or forest, the "green" in Ungers' concept of the archipelago has to be understood as a space allowing for "individualized" programs of a more and more differentiated society. More, the "green" serves as a dialectical complement to the political, collective, and commemorative space of the distinct multiple city enclaves, as an attempt to reintegrate the collage of suburban and periurban areas back into the (shrinking) city.

This analogical conclusion from the more permanent and formal of the city to the socio-political and historical sphere,—whilst the temporal dimension of urban (infra-)structure stands for the economic, individualistic and (re)productive in society—is a topos of postmodern thinking and shows parallels to the theoretic work of for example Aldo Rossi.[10] Or to the recent interpretation of Pierre Vittorio Aureli, who advocates for an "absolute architecture" and reassessed the autonomy argument of the 1980s, which warranted

8   Vgl. Charles Waldheim (Hg.): *The Landscape Urbanism Reader*, New York 2006, und Mohsen Mostafavi/Gareth Doherty (Hg.): *Ecological Urbanism*, Cambridge 2010.

9   Ungers: „Die Stadt in der Stadt" (wie Anm. 3) These 8 (ohne Seiten).

10 Aldo Rossi: *L'architettura della città*, Padua 1966. Für die englische Übersetzung vgl. ders.: *The Architecture of the City*, Cambridge 1982, für die deutsche Übersetzung vgl. ders.: *Die Architektur der Stadt*, Düsseldorf 1973.

11 Im Gegensatz zur autonomen Architektur der 1980er Jahre, vertreten von Peter Eisenman, deklariert er die „Autonomie des Projekts" und stellt konzeptuelles Denken in den Vordergrund (zusammen mit den Überlegungen zu den Bedingungen architektonischen Handelns, beziehungsweise zu den

8   See Charles Waldheim (ed.), *The Landscape Urbanism Reader* (New York, 2006); and Mohsen Mostafavi and Gareth Doherty (eds.), *Ecological Urbanism* (Cambridge, 2010).

9   Ungers (1978), ibid., p. 91.

10 Aldo Rossi, *L'architettura della città* (Padua, 1966), for the English translation see: idem, *The Architecture of the City* (Cambridge, 1982)

the separation of form from society and culture with political content.[11] The opposition between the finite architectural form and the economic-managerial expansive logic of urbanization (of integration *and* closure) would be already a political act, since Aureli defines the political—with nod to Carl Schmitt—as "agonism through separation and confrontation."[12] However with Aureli this relationship remains primarily representational,[13] while Ungers assigned the differentiated strong architectural form with a political and economic dimension in and for the city that lies beyond its semiotic or structural meaning. Although he rejects utopianism for the sake of as-found reality of the existing city,[14] Ungers is well aware of its social, economic, and political factors. If urban expansion is the result of growth of population, production, and consumption, shrinking shows the opposite effects of a city beyond capitalism: here the motor of real estate speculation has come to a halt, if supply exceeds demand by far (without the "fantasy" of a comeback) which devalues ownership and land permanently. The group around Ungers delivered the proposal to the hands of the Berlin Senator for Housing, since in the late 1970s the social-democratic municipal government of the city state of West Berlin was still in the position of a strong public hand, supported by federal transfer money and semi-public building cooperatives that implemented much of the IBA Berlin in the 1980s. The idea to restructure the city into a group of contrasting enclaves and green intermediate zones—in other words: a de facto destruction of private and public property as well as architectural interventions on an urban scale—ask for institutional land ownership, resettlement of inhabitants, and large investments into the repair of the existing "enclaves" and its additions. Here, Ungers probably had the project "Red Vienna" of the 1920s in mind,[15] where a social-democratic municipality implemented a series of "superblocks" as insular interventions into the existing (feudal respectively capitalist) urban fabric. Instead of the gross of the worker housing of the Weimar Republic, which was built as Siedlungen at the periphery of the industrial cities, the superblocks in Vienna are surgical operations inside the city's districts, and with their extensive public programs (health, sports, childcare, education, clubs and amenities) and shared courtyards, introduced a communal form of urban living. In addition, the search for strong forms and monumentality realized with tradition-

der Urbanisierung (von gleichzeitigem Ein- *und* Ausschluss) würde bereits selbst einen politischen Akt darstellen, da Aureli – in Anlehnung an Carl Schmitt – das Politische als „Feindschaft, herbeigeführt durch Trennung und Konfrontation"[12] definiert. Doch verbleibt diese Beziehung bei Aureli primär auf der Ebene der Repräsentation,[13] während Ungers die differenzierte, starke architektonische Form mit politischer und wirtschaftlicher Bedeutung in und für die Stadt auflädt, welche jenseits semiotischer oder strukturalistischer Interpretationen liegt. Obwohl sich Ungers gegen den Utopismus zugunsten einer objektiven Wirklichkeit der existierenden Stadt ausspricht,[14] ist er sich der sozialen, wirtschaftlichen und politischen Faktoren bewusst. Wenn die Ausbreitung der Städte vom Wachstum der Bevölkerung und dem Anstieg von Produktion und Konsum angetrieben wird, dann repräsentiert die Schrumpfung die gegenteiligen Auswirkungen einer Stadt jenseits des Kapitalismus: in ihr ist der Motor der Immobilienspekulation zu einem Halt gekommen, wenn das Angebot die Nachfrage bei Weitem übersteigt (und zwar ohne die „Fantasie" einer wirtschaftlichen Erholung), womit Land und Besitz dauerhaft entwertet sind. Die Gruppe um Ungers legte den Entwurfsvorschlag dem Berliner Senator für Bauen und Wohnungswesen vor, da in den späten 1970er Jahren die sozialdemokratische Stadtverwaltung des Stadtstaates Westberlin noch immer in der Position einer starken öffentlichen Hand war, unterstützt durch Mittel aus dem bundesdeutschen Finanzausgleich und der halböffentlichen Baugenossenschaften, die in den 1980er Jahren halfen, den größten Teil der IBA Berlin umzusetzen. Die Idee, die Stadt in eine Gruppe kontrastierender Enklaven und grüner Zwischenzonen umzustrukturieren – mit anderen Worten: eine faktische Zerschlagung von öffentlichem und privatem Eigentum wie auch architektonische Eingriffe im städtebaulichen Maßstab –, verlangen implizit nach institutionellem Landbesitz, nach der Umsiedlung von Einwohnern, sowie nach hohen Investitionen in die Reparatur bestehender „Enklaven" und deren Ergänzungen. Dabei hatte Ungers vermutlich das Projekt des „Roten Wien" aus den 1920er Jah-

11 In difference to autonomous architecture of the 1980s à la Peter Eisenman he conceptualizes the "autonomy of the project" with emphasis on conceptual thinking (and the reflections of the very conditions of architectural action respectively its limitations by socio-economic conditions), yet at the same time insists on the "political" (or "critical") meaning of form per se: "the general project of the city that manifests itself through the exceptional and 'insular' form of architecture." See Pierre Vittorio Aureli, *The Possibility of an Absolute Architecture* (Cambridge, 2011), p. xiv; for an extensive discussion of autonomy in architecture see the forthcoming Ole W. Fischer "Architecture, Capitalism and Criticality" in Crysler/Cairns/Heynen (eds.), *Handbook of Architectural Theory* (London, 2012), pp. 56–69.

12 Aureli (2011), idem, pp. ix–x.

13 Aureli (2011), idem, p. 31: "Inasmuch as the formal is defined in terms of limits rather than self-sufficiency, it is fundamental relational. In its finitude and specificity, it implies the existence of something outside itself. In being concerned with 'itself,' it necessarily concerns the 'other.' For this reason, the formal is against totality and generic conceptions of multiplicity. The formal is thus a veritable representation of the political, since the political is the agonistic space of real confrontation, of the others. As such, the formal is a partisan idea."

14 Ungers (1978), ibid. p. 96, "There is no need for a new Utopia but rather to create a better reality."

15 See Oswald Mathias Ungers (ed.), *Die Wiener Superblocks* (Berlin, 1969) and *Arch+ 181/182: Lernen von O. M. Ungers* (2006), pp. 148–149, see also: Aureli (2011), p. 200f: Aureli points out the relevance of the Viennese Superblocks as a historical case study of Ungers' "city within the city" concept, however in difference to the interpretation of the Superblock (and Ungers' reading of it) proposed here, Aureli takes the confined architectural form of the block typology itself already as political act.

einhergehenden Einschränkungen durch sozio-ökonomische Bedingungen). Gleichzeitig jedoch besteht er auf der „politischen" (oder „kritischen") Bedeutung der Form an sich: „The general project of the city that manifests itself through the exceptional and 'insular' form of architecture". Pier Vittorio Aureli: *The Possibility of an Absolute Architecture* (Anm. 6), S. xiv. Für eine ausführliche Diskussion zur Autonomie in der Architektur vgl. „Architecture, Capitalism and Criticality" in: Crysler/Cairns/Heynen (Hg.): *Handbook of Architectural Theory*, London 2012, S. 56–69 (im Erscheinen).

12 Pier Vittorio Aureli: *The Possibility of an Absolute Architecture* (wie Anm. 6), S. ix–x.

13 Vgl. ebd., S. 31: „Inasmuch as the formal is defined in terms of limits rather than self-sufficiency, it is fundamental relational. In its finitude and specificty, it implies the existence of something outside itself. In being concerned with ‚itself‘, it necessarily concerns the ‚other‘. For this reason, the formal is against totality and generic conceptions of multiplicity. The formal is thus a veritable representation of the political, since the political is the agonistic space of real confrontation, of the others. As such, the formal is a partisan idea."

14 Ungers: „Die Stadt in der Stadt" (wie Anm. 3), These 10: „Was gebraucht wird, ist nicht eine neue Utopie, sondern der Entwurf für eine bessere Realität", vgl. ders., „Cities within the City" (wie Anm. 3), S. 96.

ren vor Augen,[15] in dem eine sozialdemokratische Stadtverwaltung eine Reihe von großformatigen Gemeindebauten als insulare Interventionen in die bestehende (feudale bzw. kapitalistische) Stadtstruktur integrierte. Im Unterschied zur Masse der Arbeiter-Wohnhäuser der Weimarer Republik, die als Siedlungen an der Peripherie der Industriestädte errichtet wurden, stellten die Großblöcke der Wiener Gemeindebauten operative Eingriffe in die bestehenden Stadtteile dar und waren mit ihren umfangreichen öffentlichen Programmen (Gesundheitsversorgung, Sport, Kinderbetreuung, Bildung, Vereine und andere öffentliche Dienstleistungen) und gemeinschaftlichen Innenhöfen ein Schritt zu einer kommunalen Form des städtischen Lebens. Zudem machte das Streben nach starken Formen und Monumentalität, realisiert mit traditionellen Typologien und konventionellen Bautechniken, die Gemeindebauten zu einem potenziellen Bezugspunkt für Ungers Konzept der „Stadt in der Stadt" und der „Enklave".

Diese Vorstellung eines großen architektonischen Konglomerates im Maßstab und von der Komplexität einer städtischen Enklave, die wie eine Maschine eines (alternativen) urbanen Lebensstils wirkt – im Fall der Wiener Gemeindebauten einer kommunalen, sozialdemokratischen, proletarischen Kultur –; dieses Konzept eines Gebäudes oder einer Gruppe von Bauten als „Stadt in der Stadt" steht auch im Zentrum von Rem Koolhaas' Suche nach einer metropolitanen Architektur. Doch was für Ungers einst einen alternativen „Gegensatz zum ständigen Wachstum und unbegrenzter Ausdehnung"[16] des konventionellen Nachkriegsstädtebaus zu bieten schien, wurde bei Koolhaas und den nachfolgenden Projekten von OMA zu einer Abkehr vom (modernen) Urbanismus und einer affirmativen Hinwendung zur kapitalistischen Spekulation und den kollektiven (Konsum-) Sehnsüchten als den treibenden Kräften der Großstadt: Es lässt sich eine konstante gedankliche Linie von den „Voluntary Prisoners of Architecture" (1972) über die Bewunderung des Waldorf-Astoria und des Downtown Athletic Club in *Delirious New York* (1978) bis zu den „Large-Box"-Projekten der 1980er-Jahre (Zeebrugge Sea Terminal, 1989; Bibliothèque Nationale de France Paris, 1989 etc.), und weiter zu dem Manifest „Bigness" in *S,M,L,XL* (1995), sowie den aktuellen Großbauprojekten, wie der Seattle Public Library (2004) und den CCTV Headquarters in Beijing (2009) ziehen. Mit Koolhaas, auch wenn man seinen Einfluss auf Ungers und die Entwicklung des Archipel-Konzeptes für Berlin kaum verleugnen kann, wurde die Lektüre der Stadt als dialektisch, zersplittert und differenziert in

The idea to restructure the city into a group of contrasting enclaves and green intermediate zones, — in other words: a de facto destruction of private and public property as well as architectural interventions on an urban scale — ask for institutional land ownership, resettlement of inhabitants, and large investments into the repair of the existing "enclaves" and its additions.

15 Vgl. Oswald Mathias Ungers (Hg.): *Die Wiener Superblocks*, Berlin 1969, und *Arch+ 181/182: Lernen von O. M. Ungers* (2006), S. 148–149. Vgl. auch Aureli: *The Possibility of an Absolute Architecture* (wie Anm. 6), S. 200 f. Aureli verweist hier auf die Relevanz der Wiener „Superblocks" als Fallstudien für Ungers „Städte in der Stadt"-Konzept. Anders als in Ungers hier geschilderter Interpretation der „Superblocks", liest Aureli die beschränkende architektonische Form der Block-Typologie als politischen Akt.

16 Ungers: „Die Stadt in der Stadt" (wie Anm. 3), *These* 10, vgl. ders. „Cities within the City" (wie Anm. 3), S. 96.

al typologies and conventional building technology make them a potential reference point for Ungers' notion of "cities within the city" and the "enclave."

This notion of the large architectural compound on the scale and complexity of an urban enclave functioning as a machine for an (alternative) urban lifestyle—in case of the Viennese superblocks, a communal, social-democratic, and proletarian culture—this concept of a building or group of buildings as "cities within the city" is at the heart of Rem Koolhaas' search for a metropolitan architecture. Yet what for Ungers seemed to be an "alternative to constant growth and unlimited enlargement"[16] of conventional postwar urban planning, turned with Koolhaas and the subsequent work of OMA into a point of retreat from (modern) urbanism and affirmative embrace of the capitalist speculation and collective desires as the driving forces of the metropolis: there is a constant line of thought from the early "Voluntary Prisoners of Architecture" (1972) to the admiration for the Waldorf-Astoria and the Downtown Athletic Club in *Delirious New York* (1978) to the large box projects of the 1980s (Zeebrugge Sea Terminal, 1989; Bibliothèque Nationale de France Paris, 1989, etc.) on to the manifesto for "Bigness" in *S,M,L,XL* (1995) and to the more recent large scale projects such as the Seattle Public Library (2004) and the CCTV Headquarters in Beijing (2009). With Koolhaas, though one cannot deny his intellectual influence on Ungers

> However, it is exactly the pluralism of "built ideologies" as self-sufficient enclaves next to each other and the mechanical repetition of avant-garde moves that annihilate any meaning and empty form of the political, economic, or social content that it once carried.

and the evolution of the archipelago concept for Berlin, the reading of the city as dialectic, fragmented, and differentiated was radicalized in *Delirious New York* to the "culture of congestion." But he turned away from the city to the scale of the vertically stacked multi-hybrid building, detached from the ground. Instead of the contextual delineated city fragments or rather the specific insular enclaves, which stand in dialectic tension with each other and the in-between space of the "green," Koolhaas proposes the abstract matrix of the homogenous horizontal grid of urbanization in combination with radical differentiated architectural forms on each block. However, it is exactly the pluralism of "built ideologies" as self-sufficient enclaves next to each other and the mechanical repetition of avant-garde moves that annihilate any meaning and empty form of the political, economic, or social content that it once carried. Whilst both Ungers and Koolhaas were analyzing depopulating cities in the 1970s (New York and Berlin) in order to react to the failure of modernist urbanization with "cities within the city," in the 1990s, Koolhaas shifted his attention to the rapidly urbanizing areas in Asia, Africa, and South America. In the non-European centers of urban growth

Delirious New York zur „Kultur der Verstopfung" radikalisiert. Doch wandte er sich von der Stadt ab, um sich dem Maßstab des vertikal gestapelten, multifunktionalen Hochhauses, losgelöst vom Boden, zuzuwenden. Anstatt der aus dem Kontext herausgearbeiteten Stadtfragmente, oder vielmehr der spezifischen insularen Enklaven, die in dialektischer Spannung untereinander und zum umgebenden Raum des „Grüns" stehen, schlägt Koolhaas eine abstrakte Matrix aus dem homogenen horizontalen Raster der Urbanisierung in Kombination mit radikal ausdifferenzierten architektonischen Formen jedes einzelnen Blocks vor. Aber es ist genau dieser Pluralismus der „gebauten Ideologien" als selbstgefällige Enklaven in unmittelbarer Nachbarschaft und die mechanische Wiederholung avantgardistischer Gesten, welche jegliche Bedeutung auslöschen und welche die Formen ihrer politischen, wirtschaftlichen oder sozialen Inhalte entleeren, die sie einst besaßen. Während sowohl Ungers wie auch Koolhaas in den 1970er Jahren von Entvölkerung betroffene Städte (New York und Berlin) analysierten, um auf das Scheitern der modernen Stadtplanung mit dem Konzept der „Stadt in der Stadt" zu reagieren, wandte sich Koolhaas in den 1990er Jahren der raschen Verstädterung in Asien, Afrika und Südamerika zu. In den außereuropäischen Zentren urbanen Wachstums fand Koolhaas Belege, um den Tod der Europäischen Stadt durch die postmoderne Wirklichkeit einer generischen Mischung zwischen Suburbia, Infrastruktur und multihybriden Komplexen zu verkünden. Die Objekte der Stadt ohne Eigenschaften haben die Dichte von verschiedenen kontrastierenden Nutzungen und sich im Widerspruch befindenden Aktivitäten des (ehemaligen) städtischen Raums in das Innere ihrer endlosen Interieurs aufgesaugt, losgelöst (oder „lobotomiert") von ihrer äußerlichen Erscheinung und dem sie umgebenden (öffentlichen) urbanen Raum: „Die Stadt gehört der Vergangenheit an. Wir können das Theater jetzt verlassen."[17]

Das gegenwärtige Interesse an Ungers ist Teil einer größeren Revision der „Architektur seit 1968", wie Publikationen, Ausstellungen und ein vermehrtes Interesse praktizierender Architekten an der Arbeit dieser Generation zeigen.[18] Dies scheint der natürliche Lauf der Dinge zu sein: nachdem die Architekturhistoriker in den 1980er und 1990er Jahren intensiv die Moderne

17   Rem Koolhaas: „Die Stadt ohne Eigenschaften" in: *Arch+ 132* (1996), S. 27.

18   Vgl. hierzu auch das bereits erwähnte Buch von Aureli: *The Possibility of an Absolute Architecture* (wie Anm. 6) als auch Aurelis *The Project of Autonomy. Politics and Architecture Within and Against Capitalism*, New York 2008. Vgl. auch K. Michael Hays: *Architecture's Desire. Reading the late avant-garde*, Cambridge 2010; Reinhold Martin: *Utopia's Ghost. Architecture and Postmodernism, again*, Minneapolis 2010; Jorge Otero-Pailos: *Architecture's Historical Turn. Phenomenology and the Rise of the Postmodern*, Minneapolis 2010; Mark Crinson und Claire Zimmerman (Hg.): *Neo-avant-garde and Postmodern. Postwar Architecture in Britain and Beyond*, New Haven 2010; Anthony Vidler: *James Frazer Stirling. Notes from the Archive*, New Haven 2010; ders.: *Histories of the Immediate Present. Inventing Architectural Modernism*, Cambridge 2008, vgl. hier Kapitel 5: „Postmodernism or Posthistoire?"; Felicity D. Scott: *Architecture or Techno-Utopia. Politics after Modernism*, Cambridge 2007; John D. McMorrough: *Signifying Practices. The Pre-texts of Post-modern Architecture*, Dissertation, Harvard University 2007 (unveröffentlicht); als auch Monographien, wie beispielsweise zu Robert Venturi: Aron Vinegar und Michael J. Golec (Hg.): *Relearning from Las Vegas*, Minneapolis 2009, und Martino Stierli:

analysiert und in den letzten zehn Jahren die Architekturproduktion der Nachkriegszeit bis in die späten 1960er Jahre durchgearbeitet haben, scheint es plausibel, jetzt den nächsten Schritt zu wagen und sich mit der jüngeren Vergangenheit – der sogenannten Postmoderne – auseinanderzusetzen. Dennoch sollte der Prozess der Historisierung nicht als Selbstzweck verstanden werden. Worum es geht, ist die Frage, inwieweit das Konzept des „Archipels" als Modell für zeitgenössische städtebauliche Problemstellungen dienen kann.[19] Ironischerweise wurden die Vorschläge von Ungers und seinem Team nie realisiert. Stattdessen nahm die Stadtentwicklung von Berlin eine andere historische Route: Es kam gar nicht zu dem prognostizierten Bevölkerungsrückgang, stattdessen wurde Wohnraum knapp, was den politischen Willen anheizte, ein groß angelegtes Bauprogramm für die Innenstadtbezirke von West-Berlin aufzulegen, das unter der Bezeichnung IBA (Internationale Bauausstellung) Berlin von 1984/87 bekannt wurde. Die Renovierung und Aufwertung der bestehenden Wohnblöcke aus dem späten 19. Jahrhundert, oftmals in Mieterbeteiligungsverfahren, wurde durch den Bau neuer Mietwohnungen von renommierten Architekten (darunter Ungers, Koolhaas, Kollhoff und Ovaska) ergänzt, welche unter dem Dogma der „kritischen Rekonstruktion" auf traditionellen städtischen Blockrandtypologien basierten. Die Renaissance der Innenstadt als einem (oft subventionierten) Ort zum Wohnen wurde zu einem Modell für andere europäische Städte, und, nach dem Fall der Mauer in den Jahren 1989/90, auch auf die östlichen Sektoren Berlins ausgedehnt. Heute ist die Kehrseite der „Hipness" der Innenstadtbezirke Berlin-Mitte und Prenzlauer Berg der suburbane Sprawl im Speckgürtel der Einzugsgebiete, der in den letzten zwei Jahrzehnten aufgeschossen ist. Anstatt der Auslichtung und Differenzierung von kontrastierenden „Inseln" innerhalb der alten Stadt, welche durch die „Grünareale" verbunden werden sollten, kam es zu einer allgemeinen Verdichtung der Stadtstruktur, die mehr oder weniger der „kritischen Rekonstruktion" folgte, während die klare Grenze zwischen (West-) Berlin und einem einst feindlichen Territorium zu einem suburbanen Brei verwischt wurde.

Trotzdem bleibt die kritische Lektüre von Berlin als einem „grünen Archipel" eine wichtige Alternative sowohl zum gegenwärtigen Ruf nach preußischer Ordnung und der Rekonstruktion der historischen steinernen Stadt, als auch als Gegenmaßnahme zu anti-urbanen Ressentiments, die von einer Auflösung der Form, des architektonischen Inhalts und urbanen Raumes träumen, zugunsten von fließenden Übergängen, Netzwerken,

he found evidence to declare the death of the European city by the postmodern reality of a generic mix between suburbia, infrastructure, and multi-hybrid complexes. The objects of the generic city sucked in the density of various contrasting programs and conflicting activities of (former) civic space into their endless interiors, detached (or "lobotomized") from their outside appearance and their surrounding exterior (public) urban space: "The city is no longer. We can leave the theater now."[17]

The current interest in Ungers is part of a larger revision of "architecture since 1968," as publications, exhibitions, and growing interest of practicing architects in the work of that generation show.[18] This might be the natural cause of things: after architectural historians analyzed the modern movement intensively in the 1980s and 1990s and have worked through architectural production of the post-war period up to the late 1960s over the last decade, it seems plausible to go one step further and scrutinize the recent past that we have been calling the "postmodern." Yet the process of historization should not be an end in itself. What is at stake is the question to what extend the notion of the "archipelago" may serve as a model to address contemporary urban design problems.[19] Ironically, the proposal of Ungers and his team was never implemented. Rather, the urban development in Berlin took a different historical route: the predicted population drop did not occur, instead there was a housing shortage that fueled the political will to start a large scale building program for the inner city districts of West Berlin that became known as the IBA (international building exhibition) Berlin in 1984/87. The repair and upgrading of existing late nineteenth century housing blocks, often participatory models with renters, was complemented with the design of new apartment houses by well-known architects (including Ungers, Koolhaas, Kollhoff and Ovaska) under the dogma of "critical reconstruction" based on traditional urban perimeter block typologies. The renaissance of the inner city as a place to live (often subsidized) became a model for other European cities and, after the fall of the wall in 1989/90, was carried over to the Eastern sectors of Berlin. Today the "hipness" of the inner city quarters Berlin Mitte and Prenzlauer Berg is paralleled by the affluent suburban sprawl in the commuter belt that shot up in the last two decades. Instead of the cutting back and differentiation of contrasting "islands" within the old city connected by areas of "green," the urban structure witnessed an overall densi-

17 Rem Koolhaas, "The generic city," in Rem Koolhaas, Bruce Mau (eds.), *S,M,L,XL* (New York, 1995), p. 1264.

18 See also the aforementioned book by Pierre Vittorio Aureli, *The Possibility of an Absolute Architecture* (Cambridge, 2011) as well as Aureli's *The Project of Autonomy: Politics and Architecture Within and Against Capitalism* (New York, 2008). See also K. Michael Hays, *Architecture's Desire: Reading the late avant-garde* (Cambridge, 2010); Reinhold Martin, *Utopia's Ghost: Architecture and Postmodernism, again* (Minneapolis, 2010); Jorge Otero-Pailos, *Architecture's Historical Turn: Phenomenology and the Rise of the Postmodern* (Minneapolis, 2010); Mark Crinson and Claire Zimmerman (eds.), *Neo-avant-garde and Postmodern: Postwar Architecture in Britain and Beyond* (New Haven, 2010); Anthony Vidler, *James Frazer Stirling: notes from the archive* (New Haven, 2010); idem, *Histories of the Immediate Present: Inventing Architectural Modernism* (Cambridge, 2008) see here chapter 5: "Postmodernism or Posthistoire?"; Felicity D. Scott, *Architecture or Techno-Utopia: Politics after Modernism* (Cambridge, 2007); John D. McMorrough, *Signifying Practices: The Pre-texts of Post-modern Architecture* (Ph.D. Thesis Harvard University, 2007, unpublished); as well as monographic studies, such as on Robert Venturi (Aron Vinegar; Michael J. Golec [eds.], *Relearning from Las Vegas* [Minneapolis, 2009] as well as: Martino Stierli, *Las Vegas im Rückspiegel: die Stadt in Theorie, Fotografie und Film* [Zurich, 2010] or on Oswald Mathias Ungers: Jaspar Cepl, *Oswald Mathias Ungers: Eine intellektuelle Biographie* [Cologne, 2007]). A catalogue by the Deutsches Architekturmuseum Frankfurt of 2004 seems to indicate a turning point: the collection of essays hovers between a postmodern class-reunion and critical revision, see Ingeborg Flagge/Romana Schneider (eds.), *Post-Modernism Revisited* (Frankfurt am Main, 2004).

Las Vegas im Rückspiegel. Die Stadt in Theorie, Fotografie und Film, Zürich 2010 oder zu Oswald Mathias Ungers: Jaspar Cepl: *Oswald Mathias Ungers. Eine intellektuelle Biographie*, Köln 2007. Ein Katalog des Deutschen Architekturmuseums Frankfurt von 2004 scheint auf einen Wendepunkt zu verweisen: Der folgende Sammelband bewegt sich zwischen einem postmodernen Klassentreffen und kritischer Revision, vgl. Ingeborg Flagge/ Romana Schneider (Hg.): *Post-Modernism Revisited*, Frankfurt am Main 2004.

19 Vgl. Kees Christiaanse: „Ein grüner Archipel. Ein Berliner Stadtkonzept ‚revisited'", in: *DISP 156* (2004), S. 21–29.

19 See Kees Christiaanse, "Ein grüner Archipel. Ein Berliner Stadtkonzept ‚revisited'," in *DISP 156* (2004), pp. 21–29.

fication following more or less "critical reconstruction", whilst the clear edge of (West) Berlin against the once hostile territory blurred into suburbia.

Nevertheless, the critical reading of Berlin as "green archipelago" remains vibrant as an alternative to recent calls for Prussian order and reconstruction of the historic petrified city as well as to opposing anti-urban resentments of the dissolution of form, architectural matter, urban space in favor of flows, networks, plug-ins and augmented reality. Beyond Ungers' realism to start from the existing (or predicted) conditions the concept of the archipelago carries a strong commitment to life in the city as controversial, competitive and contrasting, if not conflict-prone, but for the sake of a liberal public sphere. The accentuation of existing city enclaves, their readjustment and dialectic intensification against the backdrop of the "green" is supposed to provide "habitats" for different urban milieus and to reconcile individual life styles with shared common spaces. The city as archipelago allows for the vicinity of contrasting elements, for the divergent cities in the city, for the union of fragments: "The project for critical antithesis and for divergent multiplicity is the profound sense and characteristic of Berlin."[20] Yet in contrast to the late 1970s and the unique conditions of walled-in Berlin, the concept of the archipelago has to be reframed to address the problems of today's European urban areas: due to fundamental changes over the last two decades—political, economic, social, cultural—that are summarized as globalization, privatization and post-industrial society, numerous areas of small, medium, and large cities as well as of metropolitan regions have fallen out of their "use." Many of these areas have been planned with respect to the modernist dogma of zoning and have been conceptualized, optimized, and built strictly mono-functional. With the loss of their primary use they have been deprived of their *raison d'être* and sunken into oblivion, that is, they turned into "junkspace" in a much more literal sense than Koolhaas would have ever thought when he phrased the term to ridicule the global spread of generic cheap air-conditioned retail and transit indoor spaces as the fallout of the modern age.[21] In our Western societies, we tend to consume space—that is infrastructure, buildings and land—in a similar way to goods and services, and turn them into "trash" in ever-shorter circles. Often, these "wasted" areas are "disposed"—or "renatured" respectively "revitalized," if one takes the more euphemist terms for demolition at hand.

Going back to the idea of the archipelago, it is worth noting that in geology the term refers to a common principle or formative process of insular chains or clusters, such as volcanic activity of a "hot spot" or subduction zone or alternatively erosion or, respectively, land elevation. Translated into the field of "city design" (to emphasize the architectural perspective of urbanism) this metaphor addresses the reciprocity of mass as well as void, of buildings as well as landscape, of space as well as program, of the visual as well as the unseen. These are entangled entities, like the sea and the islands, and hence share an internal logic: what was the original reason, its use, program, design, structure, ownership, users etc. How did this site relate to the surrounding city fabric, which stages and transformations did it go through and why? Similar observations can be drawn from "useless" or "wasted" urban areas, since they often carry (underneath their rough skin)

Plug-Ins und digital erweiterter Realität. Abgesehen von Ungers' Realismus, von den gegebenen (oder prognostizierten) Verhältnissen auszugehen, beweist das Konzept des Archipels ein starkes Bekenntnis für ein Leben in der Stadt als kontrovers, konkurrierend und kontrastierend, wenn nicht sogar konfliktanfällig, alles um einer liberalen Öffentlichkeit willen. Die Akzentuierung der bereits bestehenden Stadt-Enklaven, ihre Umgestaltung und dialektische Intensivierung gegen den Hintergrund des „Grüns" soll Lebensräume für unterschiedliche städtische Milieus schaffen und dabei individualisierte Lebensstile mit einer gemeinschaftlichen Öffentlichkeit versöhnen. Das Stadt-Archipel ermöglicht eine Koexistenz von kontrastierenden Elementen auf engem Raum, divergierende Städte innerhalb der Stadt, eine Union der Fragmente: „Das Konzept der kritischen Gegensätze der divergierenden Vielfalt ist Inhalt und die Eigenart von Berlin."[20] Aber im Gegensatz zu den späten 1970er Jahren und den außerordentlichen Bedingungen eines von Mauern umschlossenen Berlins muss das Konzept des Archipels neu gefasst werden, um die gegenwärtige Probleme der Europäischen Städte zu adressieren: Aufgrund von gravierenden Veränderungen der letzten beiden Jahrzehnte – politischer, wirtschaftlicher, sozial und kultureller Natur –; Veränderungen, die man unter den Begriffen Globalisierung, Privatisierung und post-industrielle Gesellschaft zusammenfassen kann, sind viele Gebiete in den kleinen, mittelgroßen und großen Städten sowie in Metropolregionen aus ihrer „Nutzung" gefallen. Viele dieser Gebiete wurden unter Berücksichtigung des modernistischen Glaubens an Flächennutzung und Zonierung geplant und wurden daher strikt nach mono-funktionalen Kriterien konzipiert, optimiert und gebaut. Mit dem Verlust ihrer Hauptfunktion wurden diese Gebiete ihrer Existenzberechtigung beraubt und gerieten damit in Vergessenheit, das heißt, sie wurden zu „Junkspace" in einem wesentlich direkteren Wortsinn, als es Koolhaas jemals für möglich gehalten hätte, als er den Begriff prägte, um die globale Ausbreitung von generischer, billiger, klimatisierter Innenarchitektur der Kommerz- und Verkehrsbauten als „Fallout" des modernen Zeitalters zu verspotten.[21] In unseren westlichen Gesellschaften tendieren wir dazu, Räume – also Infrastruktur, Gebäude und Land – ähnlich zu konsumieren wie Gebrauchsgüter und Dienstleistungen und sie in immer rascheren Zyklen in „Müll" zu verwandeln. Oft werden diese „verbrauchten" Räume sogar „entsorgt" – oder „renaturiert" bzw. „revitalisiert", wenn man die etwas euphemistischeren Begriffe für Abriss und Zerstörung heranziehen möchte.

Um aber nochmals auf das Konzept des Archipels zurückzukommen, sei an dieser Stelle darauf hingewiesen, dass in der Geologie der Begriff Archipel auf ein gemeinsames Prinzip oder auf einen formativen Prozess von insularen Ketten oder Clustern

20 Ungers (1978), ibid., p. 95.

90   21 Rem Koolhaas, "Junkspace," in *October, V 100* (2002), pp. 175–190.

20 Ungers: „Die Stadt in der Stadt" (wie Anm. 3), These 9 vgl. ders.: „Cities within the City" (wie Anm. 3), S. 95.

21 Vgl. Rem Koolhaas: „Junkspace", in: *October V, 100* (2002), S. 175–190.

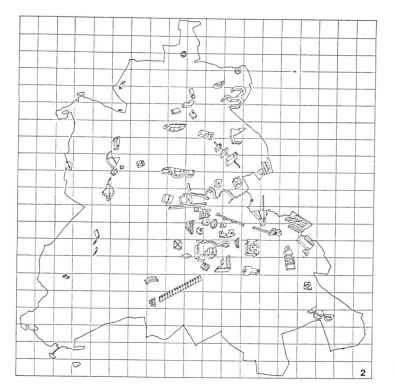

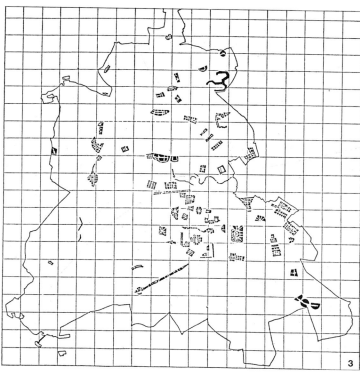

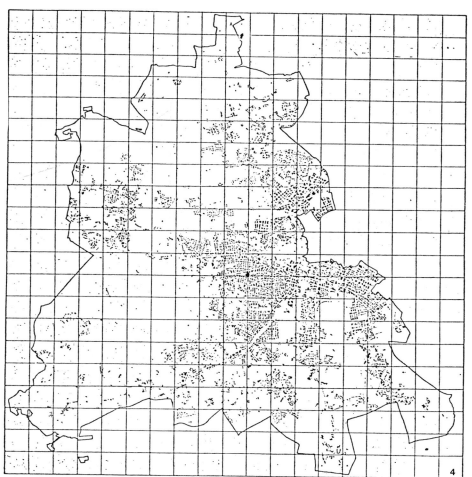

2–4   Ungers Archipel (aus: *Lotus 19*, 1978)
       Ungers' Archipelago (from: *Lotus 19*, 1978)
(2)   Diagramm der Berliner Bebauung
       Chart of housing structure in Berlin
(3)   Plan urbaner Inseln Plan of urban island
(4)   Städte in der Stadt Towns in the town
Mit freundlicher Genehmigung des With courtesy of
Ungers Archiv für Architekturwissenschaft UAA Köln

disguised or latent similarities, specific coherences and internal relations. The conceptual frame of the archipelago enables to detect the formative principles and understand them as immanent systems, not only on the planning scale of entire cities or metropolitan regions, but also on the architectural scale of "city design." Because the transformation and re-adoption of industrial, military, or infrastructural brown sites, the amendment of leftover pieces and fallows in urbanized areas, the filling in of gaps and empty lots of the historical core of the city to the periphery, or of densifications in suburban areas asks for an architectural scale. While in the 1970s the cores and production areas of large European and American cities were in decline, today the cycle of speculation, consumption and crisis has reached suburbia:[22] Ungers' dialectic between densified and stabilized city fragments against the "green" may go far beyond the literal sense and include the field condition of non-urban conditions of sprawl. Punctual interventions could implement "islands" of urban life into the vast "green sea" of detached houses and infrastructure, since the absence of—or distance to—urban amenities such as collective space, nods of public transport, public and private service providers and retail as well as culture and education remain a crucial factor. The notion of the archipelago addresses the programmatic as well as architectural scale, allows for the reconfiguration of parts to islands of density, intensity and social as well as ideological encounter and exchange between the contrast islands as much as with the suburban isotropic condition.

In difference to the visual, material, or typological "contextualism" the archipelago approach searches for "internal" logic of a specific site and existing structures. This does not end with retrospective research: while Ungers emphasized the formal, dialectic and associative of the existing city, the new

The new model of the archipelago city favors the group, the composite, the accumulation or aggregate, in short: structures where the members share common causes, histories, interdependencies or simply environment and proximity with each other.

reading of the archipelago city that asks for the forming forces and offers as an alternative to notions of the closed form of the traditional European city, to the grand master plan, to stylistic patterns or to urban utopias. The new model of the archipelago city favors the group, the composite, the accumulation or aggregate, in short: structures where the members share common causes, histories, interdependencies or simply environment and proximity with each other. The new archipelago reading recognizes conditions and contingencies in order to strengthen, highlight, question, criticize and overwrite them, to make them comprehensible to the contemporary observer. The conceptual frame of the archipelago unfolds hidden correlations,

hinweist, wie z.B. die vulkanische Aktivität eines „Hot Spot" oder einer Subduktionszone oder andererseits die Erosion bzw. Hebung des Landes. Wenn man diese geologische Metapher nun in das Feld des „Städtebaus" übersetzt (und damit eine architektonische Perspektive auf den Urbanismus hervorhebt), bezeichnet sie sowohl die Gegenseitigkeit von Masse und Leere, von Gebäuden und Landschaft, von Raum und Programm, als auch von Sichtbarem und Unsichtbarem. Alle diese Gegensätze bilden verschränkte Einheiten, wie das Meer und die Inseln, und sind über eine interne Logik verbunden: Was war ihr Ursprung, ihre Funktion, ihr Programm, ihr Entwurfsansatz, ihre Struktur, ihr Besitzer, ihre Benutzer etc.? Auf welche Weise bezog sich dieser Ort auf die städtische Umgebung, welche Stadien und Veränderungen hat er erlebt und aus welchem Grund? – Ähnliche Fragen kann man sich zu den „wertlosen" oder „verbrauchten" Stadtgebieten stellen, da sie oft (vor allem unter der rauen Oberfläche) versteckte oder latente Ähnlichkeiten, spezifische Zusammenhänge und interne Verbindungen tragen. Der konzeptionelle Rahmen des Archipels ermöglicht es uns, die formativen Prinzipien aufzuspüren und als immanente Systeme besser zu verstehen – und zwar nicht nur im Maßstab der Planung für ganze Städte oder Metropolregionen, sondern auch im architektonischen Maßstab des „Städtebaus". Denn die Umwidmung und Wiederaneignung von industriellen, militärischen und infrastrukturellen Flächen, die Annahme von Reststücken und Brachen in urbanen Gebieten, das Auffüllen von Lücken und verödeten Flächen, vom historischen Kern der Stadt bis in die Peripherie, oder das Verdichten in suburbanen Gegenden verlangt nach einem architektonischen Maßstab. Während in den 1970er Jahren die Kerngebiete und industrielle Produktionsflächen der europäischen und amerikanischen Ballungsräume im Niedergang waren, hat der Kreislauf von Spekulation, Konsum und Krise heute Suburbia erreicht.[22] Ungers Dialektik zwischen verdichteten, stabilisierten Stadtfragmenten gegenüber dem „Grün" mag weit über den wörtlichen Sinn hinausgehen und die „field condition" von nichturbaner Zersiedelung miteinschließen. Punktuelle Eingriffe könnten „Inseln" des städtischen Lebens in das überdimensionale „grüne Meer" an freistehenden Einfamilienhäusern und Infrastruktur induzieren, da das Nichtvorhandensein von – bzw. die große Distanz zu – städtischen Angeboten, wie zum Beispiel zu kollektiv nutzbaren Räumen, zu Knotenpunkten des öffentlichen Verkehrsnetzes, zu öffentlichem und privatem Dienstleistungsangebot, zu Einkaufsmöglichkeiten, als auch zu Kultur und Bildung noch immer ein Problem darstellt. Die Vorstellung des Archipels verhandelt sowohl die programmatische als auch die architektonische Dimension, ermöglicht eine Neukonfigurierung von Einzelteilen zu Inseln der Dichte, der Intensität und des sozialen sowie ideologischen

22   See for example the series of workshops for the upcoming exhibition "Foreclosed: Rehousing the American Dream" at the MoMA New York City (scheduled February 2012).

22   Vgl. zum Beispiel die Workshop-Serie der aktuellen Ausstellung „Foreclosed. Rehousing the American Dream" im MoMA New York City (ab Februar 2012).

Austauschs und Kontakts sowohl zwischen den kontrastierenden Inseln, als auch mit den umgebenden suburbanen isotropen Bedingungen.

Im Gegensatz zu einem bildlichen, materiellen oder typologischen „Kontextualismus" sucht der Ansatz des Archipels nach einer inhärenten Logik eines spezifischen Ortes und seiner bestehenden Strukturen. Das endet nicht mit retrospektiver Forschung: während Ungers das Formale, Dialektische und Assoziative der bestehenden Stadt untersucht hat, fragt die neue Lesart der Stadt als Archipel nach den formgebenden Kräften und stellt eine Alternative zur geschlossenen Form der traditionellen Europäischen Stadt, zum großen Masterplan, zu stilistischen Mustern oder städtischen Utopien dar. Das neue Modell des Stadt-Archipels begünstigt die Gruppe, den Verbund, die Ansammlung oder das Zusammengesetzte – Strukturen, die gemeinsame Anliegen, Geschichten, Abhängigkeiten oder einfach die Umgebung oder räumliche Nähe miteinander teilen. Der neue Archipel-Ansatz lässt uns Bedingungen und Abhängigkeiten erkennen, damit man sie stärken, auf sie aufmerksam machen, sie infrage stellen, kritisieren oder überschreiben kann, um sie dem heutigen Betrachter verständlich vor Augen zu führen. Der konzeptuelle Rahmen des Archipels entfaltet unsichtbare Zusammenhänge, führt neue Verbindungen ein, akzeptiert aber auch die Existenz von Brüchen, Kanten, Unterteilungen und Fragmenten sowie von unvorhergesehenen „anderen" Räumen. Das Archipel rückt immaterielle als auch materielle Aspekte in den Vordergrund: die Frage des Außenräumlichen, der Übergangszonen, der Oberflächen und der Bilder ebenso wie die von Programmen, Eigentumsrecht und möglichen Formen der Aneignung. Inseln struktureller Ordnung, klar abgegrenzte Räume mit hoher Dichte und spezifische Orte, die auf geschichtsträchtigem Boden aufbauen, kontrastieren mit der improvisatorischen, fragmentarischen, flüchtigen und chaotischen Natur der heutigen Städte und urbanen Landschaften. Da Städte immer schon Orte der räumlichen Nähe, der Interaktion, des Austauschs, der Zusammenkunft und Konfrontation, des Konfliktes zwischen Öffentlichem und Privatem waren, strebt das neue Konzept des Archipels nach relationalen Räumen für eine heutige Öffentlichkeit, die genauso ein Einheit aus Fragmenten darstellt, und auch die nichtmenschlichen Akteure der Natur mit einbezieht.[23] Nach dem teilweisen Rückzug des Staates aus den Bereichen Planung, Wohnungsbau und Bodenmarkt spricht der konzeptionelle Rahmen des Archipels erneut Probleme der Partizipation, der Politik und des Eigentums an und fragt nach dem Zugang zu kulturellen, sozialen und wirtschaftlichen Angeboten und dem Recht auf die Stadt.

Übersetzung Petra Eckhard

introduces new coherences, but accepts the fractures, edges, partitions and fragments as well as contingent "other" places. The archipelago focuses on immaterial as much as material aspects: questions of exterior, transitions, surfaces and images as well as program, ownership and potential forms of appropriation. Islands of structural order, clearly framed spaces of high density and specific places built on historic ground alternate with the improvisational, fragmentary, ephemeral and chaotic nature of contemporary cities and urban landscapes. Since the cities have been the spaces of proximity, interaction, exchange, encounter and confrontation, of conflict between private and public, the new notion of the archipelago asks for relational spaces for a contemporary public that is a union of fragments, including the non-human actors of ecology.[23] After the partial retreat of the state from planning, housing, and land market, the conceptual frame of the archipelago readdresses questions of participation, politics and ownership, and asks for the access to cultural, social and economic amenities and the right to the city.

23   Vgl. Bruno Latour: *Die Hoffnung der Pandora. Untersuchungen zur Wirklichkeit der Wissenschaft*, Frankfurt 2000.

23   See Bruno Latour, *Pandora's hope: an essay on the reality of science studies* (Cambridge, 1999).

1   Das Reisverkostungs-Festival „Mostra d'Arrossos del món" auf der Rambla del Raval   Rice tasting festival "Mostra d'Arrossos del món" on Rambla del Raval   © FOCIVESA

Contexts

1 Europa bei Nacht. Online unter: http://geology.com/articles/satellite-photo-earth-at-night.shtml © Bearbeitung und Darstellung der Satellitenaufnahme Studio Secchi-Viganó
Europe by night. Accessible online at: http://geology.com/articles/satellite-photo-earth-at-night.shtml © Elaboration and photo-interpretation of the satellite image Studio Secci-Viganó

The Return to Density

A return to reflection on density. This is what we are observing today. I use the term "return" because we all still remember how, during the 1990s, "density" was at the center of the debate as one of the crucial perspectives for understanding the contemporary city. Dealing with density without considering the importance of the discourse fostered during the past twenty years of practice pertaining to the city would therefore risk missing the point. According to Foucault, "the new lies not in what is said, but in the event of its return."[1]

Die Wiederkehr der Dichte. Gegenwärtig lässt sich eine Wiederkehr der Überlegungen zur Dichte beobachten. Ich gebrauche den Begriff „Wiederkehr" bewusst, da wir alle uns noch daran erinnern können, wie „Dichte" während der 1990er Jahre im Zentrum der Debatte als einer der Schlüsselbegriffe für ein Verständnis der Stadt der Gegenwart verwendet wurde. Demzufolge würde jegliche Auseinandersetzung mit Dichte, welche ihre Bedeutung für den architektonischen Diskurs während der vergangenen 20-jährigen Verwendung des Begriffs außer Acht lässt, am Kern der Sache vorbeigehen. Laut Foucault liegt aber „das Neue nicht in dem, was gesagt wird, sondern im Ereignis seiner Wiederkehr".[1]

PAOLA VIGANÒ

The event of its return can be better understood if we reconsider this moment in time and clarify what we have learned from that period.

Sustainable Density. From the 1990s onward, density—one of the main issues tied to urbanism—has been reappearing in broader debates in the fields of sustainable development and urban planning. As opposed to the criticism of high population density, on which modern urbanism was once built (fundamentally based on hygienic reasons and overcrowding—the housing questions—and other policies countering the excessive concentration of the proletariat in cities), at the end of the twentieth century densities began to be observed from new perspectives, incorporating the emerging theme of sustainability, the environmental question, that of energy consumption and the pollution caused by the automobile. In 1990, the EEC published the *Livre vert sur l'environnement urbain*, which indicates that "the strategies that delineate mixed usages and denser development are those capable of bringing people closer to their workplace and the services required for daily living."[2] Here, densifying, meaning the process of reaching higher densities and creating compact cities, is proposed as a way of safeguarding the environment, practically turning the initial understanding of density (as proposed by modern urbanism) on its head. The fear of density—manifested in the terror of urban congestion that had produced theories, reflections, dispersion of industries, decentralization of dwellings and services, in turn generating the fear of the dissolution of the city and the disappearance of the same—was countered at the beginning of the 1990s by a new faith in density spurred by a *mixité* of things and people.

The idea of the compact city contains the figure of concentration,[3] of opposition between city and countryside, and, at the same time, the division of work. "Physical aspects of the city and the territory via the figure of concentration are thus placed in a relation of meaning with relations involving manufacture and production along with social relations."[4] It is worth remembering that a fundamental part of modern urbanism is opposed to the figure of concentration and has provided alternative approaches;[5] yet its strength is such as to be considered an innate characteristic of the city, and this has long been placing a veil on transformation heading in the opposite direction. "Figure," here, is used in the literary sense: acting, as in rhetoric, in the formation of a discourse on the modern and contemporary city and its design.

Low Density. In the 1990s, scholars and architects not only spoke of density in relation to the emergence of the debate on sustainability and to the first positions taken up by the European Union: the very territory itself, marked by profound transformations, revealed the forming of a diffuse and fragmented urban structure which manifests itself differently depending on

Wenn wir die Vergangenheit neu denken und uns bewusst machen, was wir aus dieser Zeit gelernt haben, können wir das Ereignis seiner Wiederkehr besser begreifen.

Nachhaltige Dichte. Seit den 1990er Jahren taucht Dichte als eines der wesentlichen Themen des Urbanismus in den Debatten zur Stadtplanung und zur nachhaltigen Entwicklung immer wieder auf. Im Gegensatz zur Kritik an hoher Bevölkerungsdichte, auf der einst der moderne Urbanismus aufbaute – und sich insbesondere auf Überbevölkerung und mangelnde Hygiene bezog, die politische Maßnahmen erforderten, um die Unterbringung des wuchernden städtischen Proletariats zu regulieren – kam es am Ende des 20. Jahrhunderts zu neuen Betrachtungsweisen von Dichte, die das Thema der Nachhaltigkeit, die Umweltfrage, den Energieverbrauch und die Luftverschmutzung durch den Automobilverkehr in die Debatte integrierten. Im Jahre 1990 veröffentlichte die Europäische Kommission das *Grünbuch über die städtische Umwelt* (*Livre vert sur l'environnement urbain*), das vermerkt, dass „die Strategien, die für Mischnutzungen und eine größere Dichte entscheidend sind, auch jene Strategien sind, die Menschen näher an ihren Arbeitsplatz und an Einrichtungen des täglichen Bedarfs heranbringen".[2] Hier wird Verdichtung, also der Prozess, eine höhere Dichte und kompakte Städte zu erreichen, als eine Maßnahme zum Umweltschutz verstanden, was die ursprünglichen Vorstellungen zur Dichte, wie sie vom modernen Urbanismus propagiert wurden, auf den Kopf stellt. Die Angst vor Dichte, wie sie das Schreckensbild von urbaner Überbevölkerung ausdrückte, das Theorien und Reflexionen, eine räumliche Verteilung von Industrieanlagen, die Zersiedelung von Wohnbauten und des Dienstleistungssektors, sowie schließlich die Angst vor der Auflösung und gar dem Verschwinden der Stadt zur Folge hatte, wurde zu Beginn der 1990er Jahre von einem neuen Zutrauen in die Dichte als Kraft einer Vermischung von Dingen und Menschen abgelöst.

Die Idee der kompakten Stadt umfasst die Denkfigur der Konzentration,[3] den Gegensatz zwischen Stadt und Land und gleichzeitig die Arbeitsteilung. „Durch die Figur der Konzentration werden die materiellen Aspekte der Stadt und des Stadtgebiets in einen semantischen Zusammenhang mit Fertigungs- und Produktionslinien als auch mit sozialen Verhältnissen gebracht".[4] In diesem Zusammenhang sei an die Tatsache erinnert, dass sich ein wesentlicher Teil der modernen Stadtplanung gegen die Denkfigur der Konzentration gerichtet und folglich

---

1   Michel Foucault, *L'ordre du discours* (Paris, 1971). Cited from the English translation: "The Order of Discourse," in *Untying the Text: A Post-Structuralist Reader*, ed. Robert Young (Boston and London, 1981), pp. 51–78, esp. p. 58.

2   Commission Européenne, *Livre vert sur l'environnement urbain* (Brussels, 1990), p. 60.

3   See Bernardo Secchi, *Prima lezione di urbanistica* (Bari, 2000).

4   Ibid., p. 19.

5   On the design of a "reverse city," see my book *La città elementare* (Milan, 1999). See also *Les Annales de la recherche urbaine* 67 (1995).

1   Michel Foucault: *Die Ordnung des Diskurses*, Frankfurt am Main 1991, S. 20.

2   Commission Européenne: *Livre vert sur l'environnement urbain*, Brüssel 1990, S. 60.

3   Vgl. Bernardo Secchi: *Prima lezione di urbanistica*, Bari 2000.

4   Ebd., S. 19.

alternative Ansätze entwickelt hat;[5] dennoch liegt ihre Stärke darin, als ein gleichsam naturgegebenes Kennzeichen der Stadt zu gelten und dies hat lange Zeit einen Schleier über Entwicklungen gebreitet, die in die gegenteilige Richtung liefen. „Figur" wird hier also im übertragenen Sinne als Denkfigur verwendet: wie in der Rhetorik spielt sie auch für die Ausprägung eines Architekturdiskurses über die moderne und zeitgenössische Stadt und ihre Gestaltung eine zentrale Rolle.

Niedrige Dichte. In den 1990er Jahren haben Wissenschaftler und Architekten über Dichte nicht nur in Bezug auf die Nachhaltigkeitsdebatte und erste Stellungnahmen der Europäischen Union gesprochen; vielmehr entfaltete sich auf dem urbanen Territorium, das von gravierenden Veränderungen geprägt war, selbst die Formierung einer diffusen und fragmentierten urbanen Struktur, die sich je nach Region unterschiedlich ausprägte. Sie weist eine feine Strukturform in vielen Regionen Südeuropas von Norditalien bis Portugal auf, die das Ergebnis von schrittweisen, individuellen und diffusen Operationen ist; in Nordeuropa, im Ruhrgebiet oder in Dänemark, wo jeder urbane oder ländliche Teil das Resultat von Funktionstrennung und Segmentierung der Verkehrsinfrastruktur ist, bildete sich eher eine grobe Strukturform. Die Großstadt aus Fragmenten, oder „patchwork metropolis",[6] bringt Interpretationen hervor, die diesen neuen Raumtypus mit Neologismen wie *città diffusa*[7] oder einige Jahre später als *Zwischenstadt*[8] vorstellten. Hier kehrt sich der Gegenstand der Dichte um: es ist die Dichte eines offenen Raumes, die vielfältige Möglichkeiten zur Reflexion und Vorstellung eines neuen städtischen Raumes liefert. Wie ich an anderer Stelle bereits ausgeführt habe,[9] spielten die durch Zersiedelung gekennzeichneten Gebiete eine wichtige Rolle für die Entstehung eines Diskurses über die gegenwärtige Stadt, indem sie einen neuen Gegenstand für die Forschung und für neue Planungsgrundlagen anregten. Seine Beschreibung hat „intellectual territories"[10] hervorgebracht, deren Entwurf als ein erster Schritt zur Etablierung neuer zentraler Themen im Städtebau und der Regionalplanung als auch zur Integration neuer räumlicher Dimensionen, Themen und Landschaften angesehen werden muss.

the region. It shows a fine grain in many regions of southern Europe, from northern Italy to Portugal, which is the outcome of incremental, individual, and diffuse operations; it has a coarse grain in northern Europe, in the regions of the Ruhr, or in Denmark, where each urban or rural patch is the result of functional separation and mobility infrastructure segmentation. The metropolis of fragments, the "patchwork metropolis,"[6] generates interpretations that introduce this new type of space using neologisms like *città diffusa*[7] or, some years later, that of *Zwischenstadt*.[8] Here the subject of density is reversed: it is the density of open space that provides new possibilities for reflection and for imagining a new type of urban space. As I have already pointed out,[9] the territories of dispersion have played an important role in the formation of a discourse on the contemporary city, proposing a new object for research and project design. Their description has produced "intellectual territories"[10] the invention of which must be considered a first step in establishing new key themes for urbanism and regional design, along with new scales, subjects, and landscapes.

Variations of Density.
If the compact city, the diffuse city, and the territories of dispersion are categories of analysis that also indicate different lifestyles, images, and social relations, we must consider that a continuous flow of hybridization runs from one to the other, generally redefining the contemporary ways of living together in terms of different "idiorhythms." This concept was used by Roland Barthes in his lectures on "How to live together" at the Collège de France in the late 1970s to reflect on shared and individual spatial configurations and rhythms.[11] In dense cities, spaces for idiorhythms typical to the territories of dispersion are evermore sought after and formed, while in the looser structure of dispersed urbanity simulacra of urban centrality are inserted with ever greater insistence. This hybridization does not mean a homogenization of space, but rather a continuous process of adaptation that will affect dense and loose territories, intersecting forms of recycling, as well as experimentation with the notion of density.

> In dense cities, spaces for idiorhythms typical to the territories of dispersion are evermore sought after and formed, while in the looser structure of dispersed urbanity simulacra of urban centrality are inserted with ever greater insistence.

5 Zum Design einer „Reverse City" vgl. Paola Viganò: *La città elementare*, Mailand 1999. Vgl. auch *Les Annales de la recherche urbaine*, 67 (1995).

6 Willem Jan Neutelings: „Fragmentatie in de periferie: de ‚tapijtmetropool'", *Archis* 3 (1990), S. 16–21.

7 Vgl. Francesco Indovina (Hg.): *La città diffusa*, Venedig 1990; Bernardo Secchi: „La periferia", *Casabella* 583 (1991), S. 20–22.

8 Vgl. Thomas Sieverts: *Zwischenstadt*, Braunschweig 1997.

9 Vgl. Paola Viganò: *I territori dell'urbanistica*, Rom 2010.

10 Greig Crysler: *Writing Spaces, Discourses of Architecture, Urbanism and the Built Environment, 1960–2000*, New York/London 2003, S. 195.

6 Willem Jan Neutelings, "Fragmentatie in de periferie: de 'tapijtmetropool,'" *Archis* 3 (1990), pp. 16–21.

7 See Francesco Indovina (ed.), *La città diffusa* (Venice, 1990); Bernardo Secchi, "La periferia," *Casabella* 583 (1991), pp. 20–22.

8 See Thomas Sieverts, *Zwischenstadt* (Braunschweig, 1997).

9 See Paola Viganò, *I territori dell'urbanistica* (Rome, 2010), p. 171.

10 Greig Crysler, *Writing Spaces: Discourses of Architecture, Urbanism, and the Built Environment, 1960–2000* (New York and London, 2003), p. 195.

11 See Roland Barthes, *Comment vivre ensemble: Notes de cours et de séminaires au Collège de France, 1976–1977* (Paris, 2002).

In fact, the 1990s mark a fertile period for the exploration of projects featuring two main approaches: the first one recovered the urban block that had been extensively investigated during the 1980s, starting from the Italian tradition of urban studies and the experience of the Berlin IBA; the second approach moves within the very hypothesis of the hybridization of different conditions and urban spaces. The *Europan* archive (which details European competitions for young architects and urbanists since 1989) surely represents an important deposit of ideas that have nurtured a part of the debate on forms of density, but also the ironic exercises of MVRDV in *FARMAX* articulated—explicitly and in a simplified manner—that one should not be afraid of density, be it high or low.[12] The 1990s have initiated the rewriting of spatial relations between individuals and have thus produced a new discourse that questions the type of space, of which the Modern Movement constitutes an epilogue (i.e., the space of hygienism) and where the criticism of density is one of the main subjects.

Density in Discourse. The return to a reflection on density is in fact the return to a discourse that is heavily charged from an ideological point of view. It is a topic toward which we are asked to declare ourselves and which invites us to take a position: Should we argue for or against high density; for or against the diffuse city or the territories of dispersion? To go beyond this ideological question, we suggest taking some precautions.

Can we accept that density equals sustainability?

In mainstream urbanism, density is considered a guarantee of sustainable design. However, this position is not fully convincing and seems oversimplified, even misleading, and points to unacceptable shortcuts. For example, simply by using the equation "sustainable = density = urban block," we pass, too rapidly, from the general ambition for a sustainable city to a unique and peculiar urban type and living environment.

The discussion about density should not lose its openness toward a variety of urban configurations and types, toward a possibility of spatial choices. The fundamental debate about how we want to live together cannot be flattened by simplified ideological assumptions. Today, the problem is to face and deal with the transformations of the city as well as the contemporary needs and desires of its populations: in the wake of growing inequalities,

> The discussion about density should not lose its openness toward a variety of urban configurations and types, toward a possibility of spatial choices. The fundamental debate about how we want to live together cannot be flattened by simplified ideological assumptions.

Variationen der Dichte. Wenn die kompakte Stadt, die *città diffusa* und die Zersiedlungszonen nun Analysekategorien bilden, die auf unterschiedliche Lebensweisen, Bilder und soziale Beziehungen hinweisen, müssen wir bedenken, dass ein kontinuierlicher, wechselseitiger Prozess der Hybridisierung stattfindet, der unser gegenwärtiges Zusammenleben im Sinne von unterschiedlichen „Idiorhythmen" neu definiert. Dieses Konzept wurde von Roland Barthes in seiner Vorlesung „Wie zusammmen leben" am Collège de France in den späten 1970er Jahren verwendet, um auf gemeinsame und individuelle räumliche Konfigurationen und Rhythmen hinzuweisen.[11] In Städten mit hoher Dichte werden Räume für Idiorhythmen, wie sie für zersiedelte Gebiete typisch sind, immer mehr nachgefragt und geschaffen, während in die eher lose Struktur der urbanen Zersiedelung Simulakra einer städtischen Zentralität mit immer größerem Nachdruck eingebettet werden. Diese Hybridisierung zieht nun aber keineswegs eine Homogenisierung des Raums nach sich, sondern vielmehr einen kontinuierlichen Adaptionsprozess, der sich sowohl auf dichte wie auf weniger dichte Gebiete auswirkt, indem er Experimente mit urbanen Formen wie auch deren Recycling mit dem Konzept der Dichte verbindet

Tatsächlich bezeichnen die 1990er Jahre eine ertragreiche Forschungsperiode, die vorrangig zwei Ansätze verfolgte: Der erste Ansatz widmete sich der Rückgewinnung des städtischen Blocks, der schon während der 1980er Jahre beginnend mit der italienischen Tradition der Stadtforschung und der Praxis der IBA Berlin umfassend untersucht wurde. Der zweite Ansatz verfolgte die These der Hybridisierung von unterschiedlichen Bedingungen und Stadträumen.

Das Archiv von *Europan* (seit 1989 Veranstalter von Architektur-Wettbewerben für junge Architekten und Stadtforscher) stellt sicherlich einen wichtigen Ideenfundus dar, der einen Teil der Debatten um Formen von Dichte genährt hat; gleichzeitig waren es aber auch die in *FARMAX* publizierten ironischen Projekte von MVRDV, die in expliziter und vereinfachter Form aufzeigten, dass man sich vor hoher oder niedriger Dichte nicht fürchten müsse.[12] Die 1990er Jahre haben eine Ära eingeleitet, in der Raumbeziehungen zwischen den Menschen neu gedacht wurden, und haben somit einen neuen Diskurs geschaffen, der die Art von Raum untersucht, aus dem die modernistische Bewegung lediglich einen Epilog (den Raum der Hygienebewegung) konstituierte und wo die Kritik von Dichte eines der zentralen Themen bildet.

---

12 In their book on density, MVRDV argue that there is a space of invention inside regulations not fully exploited yet. In relation to density, the extremes of high and low density are addressed to show their relation with infrastructure and livability. Wini Maas, Jacob van Rijs, Richard Koek, and MVRDV (eds.), *FARMAX: Excursions on Density* (Rotterdam, 1998).

11 Vgl. Roland Barthes: *Comment vivre ensemble. Notes de cours et de séminaires au Collège de France, 1976–1977*, Paris 2002.

12 In ihrem Buch über Dichte argumentieren MVRDV, dass es innerhalb von Verordnungen einen Ort der Innovation gibt, der noch nicht zur Gänze erforscht wurde. Wini Maas/Jacob van Rijs/Richard Koek/MVRDV (Hg.): *FARMAX: Excursions on Density*, Rotterdam 1998.

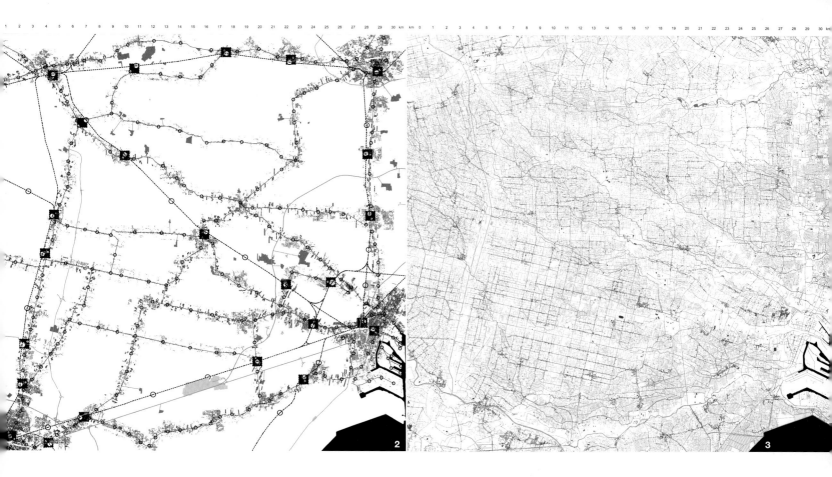

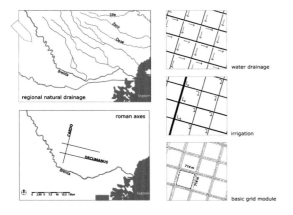

regional natural drainage

roman axes

CARDO

DECUMANUS

Brenta

0 2,50 5 7,5 10 12,5 15km

water drainage

irrigation

714 m

714 m

basic grid module

4

2 High Inten(City): Infrastruktur mit Verkehrskanälen ohne
   Autoverkehr in der Region Venetien. Online unter:
   http://www.regione.veneto.it High Inten(City):
   Infrastructure using car-free channels in the Veneto Region.
   Accessible online at: http://www.regione.veneto.it

3 Low Inten(City): Infrastruktur mit Verkehrskanälen ohne
   Autoverkehr in der Region Venetien. Online unter:
   http://www.regione.veneto.it Low Inten(City): Infrastructure
   using car-free channels in the Veneto Region. Accessible
   online at: http://www.regione.veneto.it

4 Römische Landaufteilung für Bewässerung und Landwirtschaft
   in der Region Venetien Roman rationalization of the water and
   agriculture systems in the Veneto Region © Studio Secchi-Viganó

Today this extended urban realm is changing as new projects continue to modify its isotropic structure, i.e., a structure which provides equal conditions of inhabitability in all directions, with a series of variations which are the result of a long territorial accumulation process. Important mobility projects, all conceived through the idea of a new hierarchy of accessible places, will insert fractures, decrease permeability, and diminish the actual connectivity of the road and water network.

Dichte im Diskurs. Die Wiederkehr der Überlegungen zur Dichte ist eigentlich die Wiederkehr zu einem Diskurs, der ideologisch schwer beladen ist. Es ist ein Thema, dem wir uns widmen sollen und das uns dazu einlädt, Position zu beziehen: Sollen wir uns für oder gegen eine hohe Dichte aussprechen? Für oder gegen die *città diffusa* oder die zersiedelten Gebiete? Um jenseits dieser ideologischen Frage zu gelangen, sollte man unserer Meinung nach Vorsicht walten lassen. Können wir akzeptieren, dass Dichte mit Nachhaltigkeit gleichgesetzt wird? In der traditionellen Stadtforschung wird Dichte als Garant für nachhaltiges Design betrachtet. Diese Annahme ist jedoch nicht gänzlich überzeugend und wirkt stark vereinfacht, wenn nicht sogar irreführend, weist sie doch eine nicht annehmbare Verkürzung auf. Denn durch das Gleichsetzen der Parameter „Nachhaltigkeit = Dichte = Blockbebauung" richtet sich unser generelles Streben nach einer nachhaltigen Stadt zu schnell auf einen einzelnen und speziellen Stadtbautypus und auf ein besonderes Lebensumfeld.

Die Debatte über die Dichte sollte ihre Offenheit gegenüber einer Vielzahl von urbanen Konfigurationen und Typen und gegenüber einer räumlichen Wahlmöglichkeit nicht verlieren. Die zentrale Diskussion darüber, wie wir zusammenleben möchten, darf nicht durch vereinfachende ideologische Annahmen ihren Tiefgang verlieren. Heute besteht das Problem nämlich darin, sich sowohl mit den Veränderungen der Stadt als auch mit den gegenwärtigen Bedürfnissen und Wünschen ihrer Einwohner auseinanderzusetzen: im Zuge der wachsenden Ungleichheiten, der Umweltkrisen, der Problematik erzwungener oder verhinderter Mobilität entsteht eine neue urbane Frage. Die folgenden drei Fallstudien sollen dazu dienen, jenseits dieser vereinfachten Gegensätze zu gelangen.

Stadt hoher Intensität/Stadt geringerer Intensität: Die Rolle des öffentlichen Verkehrs im zersiedelten Stadtgebiet von Venedig. Im Zeitalter des Klimawandels ist Venedig – gemeinsam mit anderen Gebieten wie der Deltaregion und der Themsemündung in London – eine der extremsten Städte Europas. Erstens ist sie extrem, weil sich dort die Folgen des Klimawandels am dramatischsten manifestieren. Wie viele Städte der Niederlande muss sich auch Venedig Problemen wie dem ansteigenden Meeresspiegel, Überschwemmungen des Landesinneren oder Dürrekatastrophen stellen. Zweitens ist diese Region extrem im Sinne ihrer urbanen Struktur,[13] die sich im Laufe vieler Jahre entwickelt hat. Der Großraum Venedig ist ein Gebiet, das zwar als urban definiert werden kann, dessen

13   Bernardo Secchi/Paola Viganò: „The project of Isotropy", X Venice Biennale, 2006; Paola Viganò: „Water and Asphalt: The Project of Isotropy in the Metropolitan Region of Venice", *AD* 78 (2008), S. 34–39; Lorenzo Fabian/Paola Viganò: *Extreme City: Climate Change and the Waterscape*, Venedig 2010.

Konfiguration sich jedoch von einem klassischen Stadtraum stark unterscheidet. Es ist eine Stadt mit vielen Qualitäten, weil sie mit unterschiedlichen offenen Räumen verbunden ist: landwirtschaftlichen Nutzflächen, Naturräumen, Räumen der Industrieproduktion und Räumen des Wohnens. Es ist eine Stadt, die ein Integrationsmodell (inklusive der Landwirtschaft) vorschlägt, das gerade heute hinsichtlich der Frage von enormer Bedeutung ist, wie sich ein Stadtraum vorstellen ließe, der als Raum für die Nahrungsmittelproduktion konzipiert ist. Die räumliche Nähe von großen landwirtschaftlichen und natürlichen Ressourcen in diesem Gebiet könnte zusammen mit der isotropen Verteilung von sozialen Einrichtungen vielleicht wichtige Fragen zur Nachhaltigkeit beantworten. Heute ist dieser erweiterte Stadtraum einem konstanten Wandel unterworfen, da neue Projekte nach wie vor seine isotrope Struktur verändern – eine Struktur, die die gleichen Bedingungen der Bewohnbarkeit in alle Richtungen mit einer Serie von durch territoriale Aneignungsprozesse bedingten Variationen verbindet. Wichtige Mobilitätsprojekte, die alle von der Idee einer neuen Hierarchie der zugänglichen Orte geleitet sind, werden Bruchstellen ausbilden, welche die Durchlässigkeit verringern und die tatsächlichen Verbindungsmöglichkeiten im Straßenverkehrs- und Wassernetzwerk reduzieren.

Die Frage, die hinter unseren Arbeiten zur Metropolregion Venedigs steht, lautet: Wie können wir diese grandiose tragfähige Grundstruktur nutzen und verbessern? Es ist eine Struktur, die auf den jahrtausendelangen Investitionen zur Erhaltung des Wasser- und Straßensystems basiert, die das Gebiet gänzlich organisiert haben, und zwar hinsichtlich der Beschaffenheit des Untergrundes, den trockenen und durchlässigen Gebieten im Norden und den tiefer gelegenen Überflutungsgebieten im Süden, wo Be- und Entwässerungsvorrichtungen installiert wurden. Heute unterstützt die lange Geschichte der Beherrschung des Wassers ein „horizontales" und diffuses Stadtgefüge.

Wenn man aber alle Szenarien des Klimawandels in Venedig durchspielt, scheint das Problem der Dichte nicht wirklich prioritär. Die Probleme der Wasserversorgung und der Mobilität erfordern einen integrativen Ansatz, der den großen räumlichen Maßstab mit der Vielzahl von möglichen Lösungsansätzen verbindet. Eine Referenz auf die „Geddes Section"[14] zeigt die Notwendigkeit einer übergreifenden Perspektive, d.h. für ein Verständnis eines Gebietes, das sich von den Bergen zur Lagune und dem Meer erstreckt, und das dazu in der Lage ist, urbane, soziale und ökologische Themen zusammenzuführen. Das bedeutet, sich mit einigen radikalen Verän-

environmental crises, problems of mobility, forced or inhibited, a new urban question arises. The following three case studies might help to go beyond these simple oppositions.

High Intense City/Low Intense City: The New Role of Public Transport in the Diffuse Venice Metropolitan Area. In the age of climate change, the metropolitan region of Venice is, together with the delta region and the Thames estuary in London, one of the extreme cities in Europe. First, it is extreme because it is a place where the consequences of climate change might be most dramatic. Like many cities in the Netherlands, Venice must also face problems such as rising sea levels, inland flooding, or drought.

Second, this region is extreme[13] in terms of the urban structure which developed there in the *longue durée*. The metropolitan region of Venice is a space that can be defined as urban but whose configuration is very different from a traditional urban setting. It is a city of many qualities because it is connected to various open spaces: agricultural land, naturally created areas, spaces for industrial production, and spaces of living. It is a city that proposes a model of integration, agriculture included, which is today particularly significant when considering the question of how to conceive of an urban environment that is modeled as a space for food production. In this region the proximity between great agricultural and natural resources, along with the isotropic distribution of welfare facilities, might provide important answers to questions related to sustainability.

Today this extended urban realm is changing as new projects continue to modify its isotropic structure, i.e., a structure which provides equal conditions of inhabitability in all directions, with a series of variations which are the result of a long territorial accumulation process. Important mobility projects, all conceived through the idea of a new hierarchy of accessible places, will insert fractures, decrease permeability, and diminish the actual connectivity of the road and water network.

The question behind our research on the metropolitan region of Venice is: How can we exploit and enhance this amazing supporting structure? It is a structure founded upon the investments made over thousands of years in the water and road systems, which have completely organized the territory in relation to the condition of its subsoil, the dry and permeable areas in the north, and the low wet plain in the south, where special irrigation and drainage devices have been installed. Today, a long history of water rationalization supports a "horizontal" and diffuse urban field.

Considering all of the possible effects of climate change in Venice, density does not seem to be the most crucial issue. For the problems of water and mobility, we need an integrated approach that connects the great territorial scale to the wide range of possible solutions. Quoting the "Geddes Section"[14] is a way of reconsidering the need for a transversal perspective, i.e., for understanding the territory from the mountains to the lagoon and the sea, while being capable of merging urban, social, and ecological issues.

14 Geddes schlug die „Valley Section", einen Schnitt von den Bergen bis ins Tal, als didaktisches Hilfsmittel zur Analyse von wirtschaftlichen und sozialen Beziehungen zwischen Stadt und Land vor. Vgl. Patrick Geddes: *Cities in Evolution*, London 1915.

13 Bernardo Secchi and Paola Viganò, "The project of Isotropy," X Venice Biennale, 2006; Paola Viganò, "Water and Asphalt: The Project of Isotropy in the Metropolitan Region of Venice," *AD* 78 (2008), pp. 34–39; Lorenzo Fabian and Paola Viganò, *Extreme City: Climate Change and the Waterscape* (Venice, 2010).

14 Geddes proposed the valley section as explanatory device of city and countryside economic and social relations. See, for example, Patrick Geddes, *Cities in Evolution* (London, 1915).

This means reflecting on some radical modifications along the section that might start from the dispersed and isotropic structure: for example, one could reconnect the water system and collect water in the hundreds of gravel pits situated in the dry areas; one could reforest the fragile spring area, or retrofit the reclaimed areas in the southern wet part.

To decrease the CO_2 emissions in the diffuse city, densification is not enough as the quantities required are unrealistic; on the contrary, the challenge will be to use the existing network of public transport to support it: reusing old and abandoned railway lines, reinstalling tramways where they were at the beginning of the twentieth century, and inserting new ones that might easily intercept the manufacturing activities aligned along the main roads. Tramways will be the backbone of a "high-intensity city" while also supporting the "low-intensity city" just behind the former, close to agriculture, water, and nature. The two cities share the same *loco*. In this scenario, the significant number of surfaces dedicated to cars will be the starting point for a requalification project for the *città diffusa*. Similar projects can have a deep impact on the territory and point to the rationality of the isotropic model: an economic, political, and ecological rationality that risks being undervalued if we are blinded by ideological discourse in favor of the compact city.

Porous City: 100 Percent Recycling Grand Paris. In 2008, ten international, multidisciplinary teams started to work on "Grand Paris," the Parisian agglomeration: requested was a reflection on the twenty-first-century, post-Kyoto metropolis as well as an understanding of the specific condition of the Paris region and a vision for its future. In this frame, our study revealed a space of exclusion, of enclaves, fractures, and barriers in many parts of the Paris *banlieue*. In response, our team proposed a project which would foster a city that is porous, permeable, and connected in all its parts.

The lack of permeability and porousness corresponds to isolated areas, ghettos, strips of housing with gardens separated by stretches of infrastructure, or underused public parks. The five strategies proposed deal with the water risk and biodiversity, with isotropic mobility entrusted to public transport, with the unveiling of *loci* significant for the various populations of Grand Paris, and the reduction of energy consumption through recycling. All of these strategies head in the direction of introducing new porousness and connections by taking advantage of what is already there.

In a metropolis largely formed by *pavillonnaires*, i.e., isolated houses with gardens, punctuated by large public building projects, the greatest amount of energy consumption is caused by heating the dwellings. The scenario is built starting from the assumption of achieving energy self-sufficiency in the Île-de-France in 2050: a result that can only become possible by combining the drastic reduction of consumption and the production of renewable energy locally. The study also shows that the idea of concentrating the efforts on new construction will have only marginal effects on the reduction of energy consumption and the emission of CO_2 into the atmosphere. Demolition and reconstruction will not be the most effective procedures seen from an energy point of view, because the grey energy contained in the existing buildings will be lost.

Numerous studies have shown that renewing, recovering, or reusing a building implies the consumption of a lower amount of grey energy as com-

derungen im Schnitt durch dieses Gebiet auseinanderzusetzen, indem man mit der Analyse der dispersiven und isotropischen Struktur beginnt: Beispielsweise könnte man das Wassersystem wieder neu verbinden und das Wasser in den unzähligen Kiesgruben sammeln, wie man sie in den trockenen Gebieten findet; man könnte das fragile Quellgebiet aufforsten oder aber das eingedeichte Gebiet im Süden modernisieren.

Um die CO_2-Emissionen in der *città diffusa* herabzusetzen, wird Verdichtung nicht genügen, da die erforderliche Größenordnung unrealistisch ist. Im Gegenteil besteht die Herausforderung darin, das existierende öffentliche Verkehrsnetz zu verwenden, um sie zu unterstützen: Die Wiederinbetriebnahme von alten oder aufgelassenen Bahnstrecken, die Wiedereinführung von Straßenbahnlinien in ihren ursprünglichen Netzen zu Anfang des 20. Jahrhundert, sowie die Schaffung von neuen Linien, die sich an den Vertriebs- und Produktionsstandorten entlang der Hauptstraßen ausrichten. Straßenbahnen werden so zur Grundlage einer „Stadt hoher Intensität", während sie gleichzeitig hinter derselben auch die „Stadt niedrigerer Intensität" unterstützen, die sich nahe den Regionen der Landwirtschaft, des Wassers und der Natur befindet. Die beiden Stadttypen teilen sich denselben Ort. In diesem Szenario wird der beträchtliche Teil der Flächen für die Automobilnutzung einen ersten Ansatz für ein Umnutzungsprojekt der *città diffusa* bilden. Ähnliche Projekte können einen großen Einfluss auf das Gebiet haben und die Rationalität des isotropischen Modells aufzeigen: eine Rationalität im wirtschaftlichen, politischen und ökologischen Sinn, die Gefahr läuft, unterbewertet zu werden, wenn wir vom ideologischen Diskurs der kompakten Stadt geblendet sind.

Die poröse Stadt: 100 Prozent Recycling Grand Paris. Im Jahre 2008 begannen zehn internationale multidisziplinäre Teams ihre Arbeit zu „Grand Paris", dem Ballungsraum von Paris: Ziel war sowohl eine Auseinandersetzung mit der Post-Kyoto-Stadt des 20. Jahrhunderts als auch eine Erforschung der Besonderheiten der Pariser Region, auch im Hinblick auf ihre zukünftige Entwicklung. Innerhalb dieses Bezugsrahmens zeigte unsere Studie, dass viele Vororte von Paris durch Räume der Ausgrenzung, Enklaven, räumliche Bruchstellen und territoriale Barrieren geprägt sind. Als Reaktion darauf schlug unser Team ein Projekt vor, das einen porösen, durchlässigen und verzweigten Stadtraum begünstigt.

Das Fehlen von Durchlässigkeit und Porösität manifestiert sich in isolierten Vierteln, Ghettos, Wohnsiedlungen mit Gärten, die von Infrastrukturflächen getrennt werden oder in wenig genutzten öffentlichen Parkanlagen. Die fünf vorgeschlagenen Strategien beschäftigen sich mit einer Risikoanalyse zum Thema Wasser und zum Verlust von Biodiversität, mit isotroper Mobilität, die dem öffentlichen Verkehr anvertraut wird, mit der Sichtbarmachung von Orten, die für unterschiedliche Bevöl-

5 Groß-Paris: Recycling und *Mixité* im Industriegebiet
Grand Paris: Recycling and *mixité* in the industrial area
© Équipe Studio 09, Studio Secchi-Viganó

6 Das Stadtprojekt: Zac la Courrouze, Rennes
The urban project: Zac la Courrouze, Rennes
© Studio Secchi-Viganó

7 Großraum Paris: Synergien zwischen Aktivitäten und
dem Stadtgefüge: Vermischen und Verdichten Grand Paris:
Synergies among activities and the tissues: Mixing and
densifying © Équipe Studio 09, Studio Secchi-Viganó

8–11 Durchmischung der Typologien in Zac la Courrouze,
Rennes Mixité of typologies in Zac la Courrouze, Rennes
© Studio Secchi-Viganó

12 Die Beziehung zu Landschaftselementen:
die kontrastreiche Landschaft von Rennes
The relation to landscape features: The
contrasted landscape of Zac la Courrouze,
Rennes © Studio Secchi-Viganó

13 Die Beziehung zu Landschaftselementen:
erhaltener Baumbestand innerhalb der
„Agorà"-Typologie im Bezirk *Bois Habité*
(Zac la Courrouze, Rennes) The relation
to landscape features: Trees saved inside
the „Agorà" typology in the *Bois Habité*
sector (Zac la Courrouze, Rennes)
© Studio Secchi-Viganó

14 Varietät der Typologien: Die „maisons
en hauteur" im Bezirk *Bois Habité* (Zac la
Courrouze, Rennes) Typological Variety:
The "maisons en hauteur" in the *Bois
Habité* district (Zac la Courrouze, Rennes)
© Studio Secchi-Viganó

kerungsschichten im Großraum Paris relevant sind und schließlich mit der Reduzierung des Energieverbrauchs durch Recycling. Diese Strategien zielen darauf ab, neue Porösität und Verbindungsstränge zu schaffen, indem sie Vorteile aus dem ziehen, was bereits besteht. In einer Metropole, die hauptsächlich aus *pavillonnaires*, d.h., freistehenden Wohnhäusern mit Gärten besteht, die ab und zu von großen öffentlichen Wohnbauten durchzogen werden, entsteht der größte Anteil des Energieverbrauchs durch die Beheizung der Wohnungen. Dieses Szenario ist auf der Vision gegründet, im Jahre 2050 in der Region Île-de-France Energieautarkie zu erreichen: ein Ziel, das nur dann realisiert werden kann, wenn man eine drastische Senkung des Energieverbrauchs erzielen und Energie aus erneuerbaren lokalen Energiequellen gewinnen kann. Die Studie zeigt außerdem, dass eine Fokussierung auf neu zu bauende Strukturen nur geringe Auswirkungen auf eine Senkung des Energieverbrauchs und eine Reduktion der Abgabe von CO_2-Emissionen in die Atmosphäre haben wird. Abriss und Neuaufbau werden aus Sicht des Energieverbrauchs nicht die effektivsten Verfahren sein, da die in den Gebäuden bereits vorhandene graue Energie verloren geht. Unzählige Studien haben bewiesen, dass die Erneuerung oder Wiedernutzung eines Gebäudes immer einen niedrigeren Wert an grauer Energie mit sich bringt als bei neuen Gebäuden. Sehr oft ist ersteres auch am wirtschaftlichsten.

Die innovativste Strategie zur Verbesserung der Energieeffizienz der Gebäude ist daher die Umstrukturierung der bereits existierenden Baussubstanz. Je umfassender und radikaler der Ansatz ist, desto besser. Dabei geht es nicht einfach darum, die Stadt auf der bestehenden Stadt weiter zu bauen, sondern eher darum, eine Position der radikalen Wiederverwendung einzunehmen. Kurz gesagt bedeutet das: 100 Prozent Recycling.

Das ist auch das Szenario, das wir für Grand Paris[15] im Sinn hatten, denn das Projekt sollte die Nachfrage nach neuen Wohnungen in den Jahren von 2009–2030 abfedern, indem die vorhandene Stadtbebauung einschließlich der Industrie neu qualifiziert und strukturiert wurde und dadurch zu einer neuen Durchmischung beitragen konnte. Das angepeilte Ziel, Energieautarkie zu erreichen, war jedoch unmöglich; trotz einer Reduktion des Energieverbrauches ließ sich innerhalb der Grenzen der Île de France keine Unabhängigkeit im Energiebereich erzielen. Nichtsdestotrotz kann diese Perspektive Aufschluss über die Grade der Porösität der unterschiedlichen urbanen Schich-

pared to new buildings. Very often this first option is also the most economical.

The most innovative strategy for improving the energy performance of the buildings is hence to restructure the existing fabric. The more extensive and radicalized the approach, the better. It is not merely a matter of building the city on top of the existing city, but that of assuming a position of radical reuse. Summed up, this means: 100 percent recycling.

This is the scenario that we imagined for Grand Paris,[15] absorbing the demand for new dwellings from 2009 to 2030 in a project focused on re-qualifying and restructuring the existing city, also including the areas of production in a new *mixité*. The objective to be reached was energy self-sufficiency, which proved impossible; despite a reduction of energy consumption, Île de France failed to reach energy autonomy within its boundaries. Nevertheless, observing the city from this point of view reveals the degrees of porosity of the different tissues, their readiness to be revamped, adapted, modified in conserving the grey, hidden energy already accumulated on site.

The difficulties entailed by reworking the existing fabric in-depth are evident. We still lack theories that can support the effort of 100 percent recycling. The theories that informed the aggressive and triumphant strategy of tabula rasa will certainly not do, but not even those of de-growth, which often look backwards rather than investigate new forms of the city.

The freestanding house and collective dwellings have been hosting the most varied of activities, as well as the aging family homes along with various other types of nuclei; in the areas of production, the porosity of fractures should be read along with the residual, the abandoned, imagining the synergies that extreme forms of proximity and functional mixture might generate. In the post-Kyoto metropolis, the reduction of CO_2 emissions and the reduction of energy consumption imply the radical reuse of the existing city as well as the mobilization of its inhabitants.

Recycling means not only considering the different life cycles of the urban space, but also being prepared to abandon or conclude a cycle while imagining what new cycle might start: commercial centers changing formats, industrial declining areas, aging neighborhoods provide the opportunity to reconceive the spatial structure of the region, where a public space on a metropolitan scale can support a variety of evolving situations. Incor-

> The difficulties entailed by reworking the existing fabric in-depth are evident. We still lack theories that can support the effort of 100 percent recycling.

15   STUDIO 09 Bernardo Secchi/Paola Viganò gemeinsam mit A. Calò, D. Ming Chang, T. Cos, N. Fonty, A. Pagnacco; L. Fabian, E. Giannotti, P. Pellegrini, IUAV; Ingenieurbüro Hausladen GMBH; MIT und P-REX/Clemson und P-REX, A. Berger, C. Brown; MOX, A. Quarteroni, P. Secchi, C. D'Angelo, F. Nobile, F. Della Rossa; PTV France. European Master in Urbanism (EMU). Vgl. Bernardo Secchi/Paola Viganò: *La ville poreuse*, Genf 2011.

15   STUDIO 09 Bernardo Secchi, Paola Viganò with A. Calò, D. Ming Chang, T. Cos, N. Fonty, A. Pagnacco; L. Fabian, E. Giannotti, P. Pellegrini, IUAV; Ingenieurbüro Hausladen GMBH; MIT and P-REX/Clemson and P-REX, A. Berger, C. Brown; MOX, A. Quarteroni, P. Secchi, C. D'Angelo, F. Nobile, F. Della Rossa; PTV France. European Master in Urbanism (EMU). See also Bernardo Secchi and Paola Viganò, *La ville poreuse* (Geneva, 2011).

Concerning density, we have to be aware that the risk of reducing the debate to purely quantitative considerations or to one single option—the city of blocks, the "normal city"—is real. The notion that we are all heading toward an urban future is also a questionable assumption.

tungen geben, über ihr Potenzial zum Umbau, zur Adaption oder Funktionsänderung zugunsten einer Konservierung von versteckter, grauer Energie, die sich bereits in der Bausubstanz befindet.

Die Probleme, die eine Neugestaltung der bestehenden Struktur mit sich bringt, sind offensichtlich. Noch immer fehlt es an Theorien, die die Bestrebungen von 100 Prozent Recycling untermauern könnten. Die Theorien, die der aggressiven und siegreichen Strategie der tabula rasa zugrunde liegen, sind hier nur wenig hilfreich, aber auch jene einer Kritik des unbegrenzten Wachstums, die sich lieber der Geschichte als neuen Stadtformen widmen, sind nicht von Nutzen.

Das freistehende Wohnhaus und die Siedlungsbauten haben Raum für die unterschiedlichsten Aktivitäten gelassen, wie auch die in die Jahre gekommenen Einfamilienhäuser neben zahlreichen weiteren Grundtypologien; in den Bereichen der Produktion lässt sich die Porösität der Brüche im Zusammenhang mit den Resten, mit dem Verlassenen lesen, um sich so die Synergien vor Augen zu führen, die extreme Ausprägungen der räumlichen Nähe und funktionale Vermischungen erzeugen können. In der Post-Kyoto-Stadt impliziert eine Veringerung der CO_2-Emissionen und des Energieverbrauchs nicht nur die radikale Wiederverwendung der vorhandenen Stadt, sondern auch die Mobilisierung ihrer Bewohner.

Recycling bedeutet nicht nur die Berücksichtigung der verschiedenen Lebenszyklen im urbanen Raum, sondern auch die Bereitschaft, einen Lebensabschnitt als beendet zu erkennen und gleichzeitig bereit zu sein, sich zukünftige Abschnitte vorzustellen: Einkaufszentren, die ihr Format wechseln, Gebiete mit rückläufiger industrieller Entwicklung und alternde Stadtteile bieten die Gelegenheit, die räumliche Struktur eines Gebietes neu zu denken, wo öffentlicher Raum auf der Metropolenebene also das Potenzial besitzt, eine Vielzahl von Entwicklungsmöglichkeiten zu unterstützen. Es ist wichtig, diese Vorstellungen in die Debatte über Dichte zu integrieren: Man kann die massiven Veränderungen im Großraum Paris nicht nur durch die Linse einer neuen Dichte oder eines neuen Verdichtungsprozesses betrachten, sondern muss sich auch darüber klar werden, welche Art von öffentlicher Struktur wir für die großen Einheiten wollen, die wir weiter verwenden. Daher bildet Dichte hier nicht ein Grundprinzip, sondern vielmehr ein Werkzeug.

Schlusswort. Nachhaltigkeit bedeutet mehr als Dichte: das Stadtprojekt von La Courrouze in Rennes, welches 2003 initiiert wurde, versteht Dichte als das Medium, durch das ein neuer Teil der Stadt weiter verwendet und neu konfiguriert wird. Das Design folgt der bereits vorhandenen Biodiversität und einer neuen Diversität, die aus schlechten Böden entsteht, welche von verdichteten Böden und ehemals betonierten Flächen verursacht wurden. Eine typologische Vielfalt ergibt sich

aus der Verbindung mit Elementen der Landschaft: es geht darum, dass eine gewisse Lebensweise nicht über eine Typologie des Wohnens definiert wird. So macht es beispielsweise einen enormen Unterschied, ob man im Wald oder im Stadtzentrum von La Courrouze wohnt. Das Vorhandensein eines starken öffentlichen Verkehrsnetzes, das Wassermanagement etc. weisen auf den Grundgedanken hin, der dieses Projekt antreibt. Diesen Grundgedanken möchte ich hier als Schlussfolgerung zitieren: Ein neues Projekt der Koexistenz entsteht gerade. Dazu brauchen wir keine befriedete Vorstellung von Natur oder vom öffentlichen Raum, sondern vielmehr einen Raum, in dem Begegnungen stattfinden können. In La Courrouze haben wir versucht, mit dem zu arbeiten, was vor Ort vorhanden war: nur wenig fruchtbarer Boden und eine Übergangszone zwischen den Bedingungen von Feuchtgebieten und trockenem Land entlang einer neuen, vom Wassermanagement generierten Topografie. Das Ergebnis zielt nicht darauf ab, traditionelle grüne Flächen innerhalb des öffentlichen Raums zu positionieren, sondern vielmehr darauf, einen Raum der natürlichen Dynamiken hervorzubringen, der sich im Laufe der Zeit erweitern kann. Gemeinsam mit einer kontrastreichen Landschaft aus konstruierten Formen und unterschiedlichen Wohnbauten ist es ein Raum, der der städtischen Erfahrungswelt Kontinuität verleiht.

Was die Dichte betrifft, müssen wir uns im Klaren darüber sein, dass eine reale Gefahr darin besteht, die Diskussion auf eine rein quantitative Ebene oder auf einen einzigen Lösungsansatz – die urbanen Blöcke, die „normale Stadt" – zu reduzieren. Die Vorstellung, dass wir alle auf eine urbane Zukunft zusteuern, ist allerdings genauso fragwürdig. Wenn wir alle in Städten leben würden, würden viele Gebiete schrumpfen. Eine starke Polarisierung und ein mögliches Verschwinden von weiten Gebieten und ihrem sozialen Kapital sind die Folgen von Metropolisierung. Aktuelle Debatten über Dichte müssen diese Argumente und Diskurse miteinbeziehen, um eine produktive Neukonzeptionalisierung zu erreichen.[16]

Übersetzung Petra Eckhard

porating these terms into the discussion about density is crucial: the large-scale transformation occurring in Grand Paris cannot not be only approached from the angle of a new density, or densification process, but must effect a decision about what kind of public structure we want for the large entities we are recycling. Density, therefore, it is not a founding principal, but a tool.

Conclusion. Sustainability is more than density: the urban project of La Courrouze in Rennes, initiated in 2003, regards density as the medium through which a new part of city is recycled and reconfigured. The design is guided by the already existing biodiversity and by the new one created from poor soils deriving from compacted soils and former concrete platforms. A typological variety is organized in relation to landscape features: the idea is that a type of living is not just defined by the type of dwelling. For instance, living in a forest or in downtown La Courrouze are two fundamentally different experiences. The presence of a strong public transport network, the water management, et cetera, lead to the main concept informing the project. It is the concept I would like to cite in conclusion: a new project of coexistence is emerging. We do not need a pacified idea of nature or of public space, but a place in which encounters become possible. In La Courrouze we tried to work with what we had on site: a very scarce, fertile soil and a transition between dry and wet conditions along the new topography that was designed by water management. The result does not aim at establishing traditional green patches inside public space, but at creating a place of natural dynamics that can improve over time. Together with a contrasting landscape of constructed forms and various types of housing, it is a space that lends continuity to the urban experience.

Concerning density, we have to be aware that the risk of reducing the debate to purely quantitative considerations or to one single option—the city of blocks, the "normal city"—is real. The notion that we are all heading toward an urban future is also a questionable assumption. If we all became urban, many territories would shrink. Strong polarization and a possible abandonment of vast territories and their social overhead capital are the consequences of metropolitanization. Current discussion about density must consider all these arguments and discourses in order to attain a fertile reconceptualization.[16]

---

16 Dies war auch das erklärte Ziel von „Inside Density", einer Konferenz, in der umfassende Überlegungen zur Dichte – hinsichtlich der Intensität, der Durchmischung und in Bezug auf Zeitkonzepte – angestellt wurden. Vgl. Hilde Heynen/David Vanderburgh: *Inside Density*, Brüssel 2003.

16 This was also the goal of *Inside Density*, a colloquium in which an attempt was made to develop a wide reflection about density in term of intensity, mixity, and time-related concepts. Hilde Heynen and David Vanderburgh, *Inside Density* (Brussels, 2003).

1 Shanghai © bricoleurbanism

Der Begriff *Dichte*

Dichte ist ein in der städtebaulichen Debatte derzeit sehr verbreitetes Thema. Die Themensetzung der vorliegenden GAM-Ausgabe steht in einer Linie mit etlichen weiteren Bezugnahmen:

The Concept of *Density*. Density is currently a very prevalent topic within urban-development discourse. The thematic focus of this year's GAM issue correlates with quite a few other references to density:

NIKOLAI ROSKAMM

Im Juni 2011 ist das Heft der schweizerischen *Archithese Dichte/Density* erschienen, das Deutsche Institut für Urbanistik in Berlin hat im September 2009 die Tagung „Qualifizierte städtebauliche Dichte – Lernen aus neuen Stadtquartieren" veranstaltet, der spanische Verlag a+t ediciones gibt seit einigen Jahren eine Buchreihe mit dem Titel *Density* heraus, im Rahmen des ETH-Netzwerkes für Stadt und Landschaft wurde das Forschungsprojekt „Chancen und Potenziale städtischer Dichte" durchgeführt und der Sammelband *Städtische Dichte*[1] veröffentlicht. Für den städtebaulichen und stadtplanerischen Bereich lässt diese (unvollständige) Auflistung von jüngeren diskursiven Dichteereignissen das enorme aktuelle Interesse am Thema erkennen. Ebenso findet der Begriff auch in der aktuellen stadtsoziologischen Debatte große Beachtung (zumindest was den deutschsprachigen Bereich betrifft), auch hier kann von einer regelrechten Renaissance der Dichte gesprochen werden.[2] Auffällig ist es nun, dass auf den Kongressen, in den Sammelbänden und in den Sondereditionen, die den Begriff im Titel führen, nur wenig Explizites über den Begriff Dichte selbst zu erfahren ist. Natürlich wird Dichte in den entsprechenden Einführungen und Einleitungen zum Thema gemacht und dabei regelmäßig auf die Kompliziertheit, Widersprüchlichkeit und Unschärfe des Terminus verwiesen,[3] dieser Hinweis wird dann aber selten genauer ausgeführt. Dabei ist Dichte auch für sich ein durchaus interessantes Analyseobjekt: In vielen Disziplinen ist Dichte nicht nur irgendein Ausdruck oder eine austauschbare Kategorie, sondern wirklich ein *Begriff*, ein Begriff mit eigener Geschichte, mit speziellen Eigenschaften und mit spezifischen Funktionen. Meiner These nach ist es lohnens-

> Meiner These nach ist es lohnenswert, über die Verwendung dieses Dichtebegriffs grundsätzlicher nachzudenken: darüber, wie Dichte konstruiert wird und auch darüber, was mit Dichte konstruiert wird.

wert, über die Verwendung dieses Dichtebegriffs grundsätzlicher nachzudenken: darüber, wie Dichte konstruiert wird und auch darüber, was mit Dichte konstruiert wird. Zu diesem Zweck soll hier (zumindest schlaglichtartig) ein kritisch-historischer Überblick über die Herkunft des Begriffs gegeben werden, über die zahlreichen Diskurse, in denen Dichte eine entscheidende Rolle gespielt hat (und weiterhin spielt) und über die Kontexte, in denen diese Diskurse stattgefunden haben. Ziel dieser Genealogie[4] ist es,

---

1   Vittorio Magnago Lampugnani/Thomas K. Keller/Benjamin Buser (Hg.): *Städtische Dichte*, Zürich 2007.

2   Vgl. Helmuth Berking: „Städte lassen sich an ihrem Gang erkennen wie Menschen – Skizzen zur Erforschung der Stadt und der Städte", in: Helmuth Berking/Martina Löw (Hg.): *Die Eigenlogik der Städte*, Frankfurt am Main 2008, S. 15–31; Martina Löw: *Soziologie der Städte*, Frankfurt am Main 2008.

3   Vgl. Hartmut Häußermann: „Phänomenologie und Struktur städtischer Dichte", in: Lampugnani/Keller/Buser (Hg.), Zürich 2007, S. 19–31; Robert Kaltenbrunner: „Urbane Kondensation", in: *Archithese* 3 (2011), S. 32–37.

4   Mit dem Begriff „Genealogie" wird eine auf Nietzsche und Foucault zurückgehende Praxis diskursiv-analytischer Kritik bezeichnet, auf der auch mein Forschungsansatz aufbaut. Das Ziel einer genealogischen Analyse besteht in der Befreiung des untersuchten Gegenstandes aus seiner für selbstverständlich gehaltenen Verankerung, die verschleiert, welche jeweiligen politischen, sozialen oder psychologischen Machtinteressen, Normen und Mechanismen in ihm am Werk sind. Nachgewiesen werden soll dabei insbesondere auch die Kontingenz eines Phänomens. Die Durchführung einer Genealogie ist besonders dann lohnend, wenn ihr Gegenstand zum Ausgangszeitpunkt der Analyse einen Status der Unantastbarkeit oder Selbstverständlichkeit besitzt. Vgl. Eva von Redecker: *Zur Aktualität von Judith Butler*, Wiesbaden 2011, S. 41–45.

In June 2011 the Swiss journal *Archithese* was published with the title *Dichte/Density*, the Deutsche Institut für Urbanistik in Berlin organized a conference in September 2009 under the heading "Qualifizierte städtebauliche Dichten: Lernen aus neuen Stadtquartieren" (Qualified Urban-Development Densities: Learning from New City Districts), the Spanish publisher a+t ediciones has for several years now been annually publishing a book series entitled Density, and in the scope of ETH's Network City and Landscape the research project "Chancen und Potenziale städtischer Dichte" (Opportunities and Potentials of Urban Density) was initiated and the anthology *Städtische Dichte*[1] (Urban Density) published. For the urban-development and urban-planning field, this (incomplete) list of recent discursive, density-related thematic explorations illustrates the enormous interest in density at present. Similarly, the term is also attracting significant attention in current urban-sociological debate (at least in the German-speaking countries) so that, here too, it may be considered an actual Renaissance of density.[2] Noticeable, however, is how only very little explicit information can be found on the concept of density itself at the congresses, in the anthologies, or in the special editions bearing this term as a title. Of course density is thematized in the respective prefaces and introductions to the topic, but while the concept's complexity, contradictoriness, or vagueness is regularly referenced,[3] this allusion is rarely explored in more detail. Yet density is itself an interesting subject for analysis: in many disciplines, density is not just an expression used or an interchangeable category; it is truly a *concept*, a concept with its own history, with particular characteristics, and with specific functions. In my line of thinking, contemplating the application of the concept of density in a more fundamental way is a worthwhile undertaking: exploring the ways in which density is construed and also what is constructed with density. To this aim, a critical-historical overview of the provenance of this term will be attempted (or at least spotlighted) here, with the many discourses where density has played (and continues to play) a decisive role and the contexts in which these discourses have unfolded likewise highlighted. The objective of this genealogy[4] is to better understand and evaluate not only

---

1   Vittorio Magnago Lampugnani, Thomas K. Keller, and Benjamin Buser (eds.), *Städtische Dichte* (Zurich, 2007).

2   Helmuth Berking, "Städte lassen sich an ihrem Gang erkennen wie Menschen: Skizzen zur Erforschung der Stadt und der Städte," in Helmuth Berking and Martina Löw (eds.), *Die Eigenlogik der Städte* (Frankfurt am Main, 2008), pp. 15–31. Martina Löw, *Soziologie der Städte* (Frankfurt am Main, 2008).

3   See Hartmut Häußermann, "Phänomenologie und Struktur städtischer Dichte," in Lampugnani et al., *Städtische Dichte*, pp. 19–31. Robert Kaltenbrunner, "Urbane Kondensation," *Archithese* 3 (2011), pp. 32–37.

4   The term "genealogy" signifies a practice of discursive-analytical critique that harks back to Nietzsche and Foucault and upon which my research approach is founded. The objective of a genealogical analysis lies in the liberation of the examined subject from an entrenchment that is taken for granted, a state which disguises the political, social, or psychological power interests, norms, and mechanisms that are respectively at play within the subject. In the process, the contingency of a phenomenon is meant to be

the concept of density itself but rather also the once again so popular stagings thereof.[5]

Initially, density was a concept originating from philosophy or, more specifically, physics (prior to modern times, these two fields of knowledge were considered one unit and treated as such). Since the day of Isaac Newton, physical density has been defined as a quotient of mass and volume (in terms of material matter) and has enjoyed a fixed position as analytical parameter for empirically measureable material properties. Also, starting in the early nineteenth century, population density emerged as a second concept of density in scientific discourse and everyday language use. Population density can be considered the original concept behind what would later become a growing number of further expressions of density, for all instances of this multiplicity of densities can be traced back to population density itself and were developed from this point of reference (such as "building density," see below). Population density is defined as the relationship between a number of people and a unit of area (in relation to a concrete location). Differences can be discerned between a physical concept of density and a social-scientific/spatial one: the former is "contextlessly definable," while the latter remains unqualifiable without information on the "situative point of reference."[6] Thus considered alone, the social-scientific concept of density is "contentless"[7] and, taken by itself, represents a category without independent meaning, an observation without consequence, a container devoid of content. Yet this changes when density is posited in the context of its application. Since density does not "exist in and of itself," it is constituted by the "interreferentiality of certain units," thus becoming a metaphor that is charged with meaning and a transparent slate for "underlying conceptions of value."[8] In other words: when density is used—as a component of analyses, theories, programs—then the contentless container becomes filled, with positions, narratives, explanations, interpretations. Density is a construct that is construed through context. Hence, reflection on this approach allows, on the one hand, density to be interpreted as a container with which content may be transported. On the other hand, when the various practices for appropriating density are examined, our view is shifted to the normative origins that underlie (both overt and covert) density-related discourse.

im Ergebnis nicht nur den Dichtebegriff selbst, sondern auch die aktuell wieder so populär gewordenen Inszenierungen von Dichte besser verstehen und einordnen zu können.[5]

Ursprünglich ist Dichte ein Begriff der Philosophie oder genauer der Physik (beide Wissensbereiche wurden bis in die Neuzeit als eine Einheit verstanden und betrieben). Seit Isaac Newton wird die physikalische Dichte definiert als Quotient aus Masse und Volumen (bezogen auf einen materiellen Stoff) und hat einen festen Platz als analytische Kenngröße für empirisch messbare stoffliche Eigenschaften. Daneben etablierte sich seit Beginn des 19. Jahrhunderts mit der Bevölkerungsdichte ein zweiter Dichtebegriff im wissenschaftlichen Diskurs und im alltäglichen Sprachgebrauch. Die Bevölkerungsdichte kann als Ursprungsbegriff der sich später verbreitenden großen Anzahl von weiteren Dichteausdrücken bezeichnet werden, da sich all jene Dichte-Spielarten auf die Bevölkerungsdichte rückbeziehen lassen und aus einem solchen Bezug heraus auch entwickelt wurden (etwa die „bauliche Dichte", siehe weiter unten). Definiert wird Bevölkerungsdichte als das Verhältnis einer Anzahl von Menschen zu einer Flächeneinheit (bezogen auf einen konkreten Ort). Zwischen dem physikalischen und dem sozialwissenschaftlichen/räumlichen Dichtebegriff lassen sich Unterschiede festmachen: Ersterer ist „kontextfrei definierbar", während letzterer ohne Angaben der „situativen Bezugsgrößen" ohne Aussage bleibt.[6] Isoliert betrachtet ist der sozialwissenschaftliche Dichtebegriff also „inhaltsleer",[7] für sich alleine genommen bleibt er eine Kategorie ohne selbstständigen Bedeutungsgehalt, eine Ausführung ohne Folge, ein Behälter ohne Inhalt. Das ändert sich allerdings, wenn Dichte in den Kontext ihrer Verwendung gestellt wird. Da Dichte nicht „aus sich selbst heraus existiert", wird sie aus dem „aufeinander Bezogensein bestimmter Einheiten" konstituiert, und dabei zur Metapher, beladen mit Bedeutungen und transparent für „dahinter stehende Wertvorstellungen".[8] Anders gesagt: Beim Gebrauch von Dichte – als Bestandteil von Analysen, Theorien, Programmen – wird der inhaltsleere Behälter aufgefüllt: mit Haltungen, Erzählungen, Erklärungen, Interpretationen. Dichte ist ein Konstrukt, das mit Kontext konstruiert ist. Die Betrachtung dieser Gebrauchspraxis macht damit einerseits Dichte als einen Behälter lesbar, mit dem Inhalte transportiert werden. Andererseits wird, wenn die verschiedenen Praxen der Dichteverwendung in Augenschein genommen werden, der Blick auf die normativen Ursprünge gelenkt, die den mit Dichte bestrittenen Diskursen (offen oder versteckt) zugrunde liegen.

Die Gebrauchspraxis der Dichte besteht aus einem komplexen In- und Nebeneinander der quantifizierenden und qualifizierenden Verwendungen des Begriffs. Auf der einen Seite gibt es die (quantitative) Zahlenangabe von Dichte. Eine solche Nennung stellt eine Fiktion dar: in der Realität wird man einen Dichtewert in aller Regel nicht beobachten können. Zweitens ist die quantitative Dichteangabe eine Reduktion: Um zu einer Vergleichsmöglichkeit zu kommen, wird der jeweilige Dichtewert immer auf die Ziffer Eins reduziert (also auf *einen* Quadratmeter, *einen* Hektar oder

verified in particular. The requirement for developing a genealogy is that the research subject be invested with a status of inviolability or implicitness from the outset. See Eva von Redecker, *Zur Aktualität von Judith Butler* (Wiesbaden, 2011), pp. 41–45.

5   An extensive history and analysis of the term can be found in this publication: Nikolai Roskamm, *Dichte: Eine transdisziplinäre Dekonstruktion* (Bielefeld, 2011).

6   Claus Heidemann, *Städtebauliche Verdichtung* (Dortmund, 1975), p. 23.

7   Erika Spiegel, "Dichte," in Hartmut Häußermann (ed.), *Großstadt: Soziologische Stichworte* (Opladen, 2000), p. 39.

8   Irene Gerberding-Wiese, *Dichtewerte und Freiflächenzahl im Städtebau* (Aachen, 1968), pp. 1–2.

5   Die ausführliche Begriffsgeschichte und -analyse kann nachgelesen werden bei: Nikolai Roskamm: *Dichte. Eine transdisziplinäre Dekonstruktion*, Bielefeld 2011.

6   Claus Heidemann: *Städtebauliche Verdichtung*, Dortmund 1975, S. 23.

7   Erika Spiegel: „Dichte", in: Hartmut Häußermann (Hg.): *Großstadt. Soziologische Stichworte*, Opladen 2000, S. 39.

8   Irene Gerberding-Wiese: *Dichtewerte und Freiflächenzahl im Städtebau*, Aachen 1968, S. 1f.

einen Quadratkilometer). Drittens ist die quantitative Dichteverwendung auch eine Abstraktion: die beschriebene Realität wird mit dem Dichtewert auf eine vermittelnde Darstellungsebene gehoben. Schon die quantitative Dichteverwendung ist damit eine auf verschiedene Arten konstruierte Gebrauchsform. Auf der anderen Seite lässt sich eine qualitative Anwendungsebene unterscheiden. Zur (qualitativen) Metapher wird Dichte, wenn sie nicht als konkreter Zahlenwert angegeben wird, sondern wenn von *der* Dichte die Rede ist. Formulierungen wie „die Dichte der europäischen Stadt" oder die „zu hohe Dichte in den Arbeitervierteln der industrialisierten Stadt des 19. Jahrhunderts" sind Beispiele für Verwendungen des Begriffs, hinter denen sich komplexe und normative Begründungskonstruktionen verbergen, die mit dem Begriff metaphorisch zum Ausdruck gebracht werden. Wenn nicht von „Dichte", sondern von „der Dichte" (respektive nicht über „Dichte", sondern über „die Dichte") gesprochen wird, dann drückt sich damit regelmäßig eine Personifizierung des Begriffs und/oder die Behauptung einer eigenen Materialität von Dichte aus. Entscheidend ist es nun, dass die beiden Verwendungsformen – der qualitative Gebrauch und der quantitative Gebrauch von Dichte – in einem engen Wechselverhältnis zueinander stehen. Die quantitative Dichteangabe wird durch die metaphorische Tradition inhaltlich mit Bedeutung aufgewertet, die metaphorische Dichtenennung gewinnt durch die Berechenbarkeit ihres quantitativen Gegenstücks an (natur)wissenschaftlichem Gehalt und Seriosität. Dichte, so könnte man es formulieren, ist eine *potenziell berechenbare Metapher*.

Als Ursprungsdiskurs des Begriffs „Bevölkerungsdichte" kann die Debatte bezeichnet werden, die durch *An Essay on the Principle of Population* (1798), die berühmte Schrift des anglikanischen Pfarrers Thomas Robert Malthus, ausgelöst wurde.[9] Kern dieser die neuzeitliche Bevölkerungswissenschaft als Teil der Nationalökonomie fundierenden Schrift ist das sogenannte Bevölkerungsgesetz, mit dem Malthus behauptete, dass die Ernährungsfähigkeit der Erdbevölkerung arithmetisch, die Vermehrung der Bevölkerung dagegen exponentiell wachse. Daraus leitete Malthus die Gefahr eines baldigen Weltunterganges ab, wenn es nicht gelänge, die „überzählige Bevölkerung" – also die sozial schwachen Schichten – zu verringern. Über das Für und Wider dieses „Gesetzes" ergab sich eine lang andauernde Diskussion, in der der Begriff „Bevölkerungsdichte" bald einen wichtigen Bezugspunkt bildete. In dieser Debatte entwickelte sich ein Bewertungssystem, mit welchem dem Gebrauch der Kategorie Bevölkerungsdichte ein normatives Fundament gegeben wurde. Erst das Einbinden der Dichteangabe in solch ein normatives System, in dem eine niedrige (zu niedrige), richtige (optimale) oder hohe (zu hohe) Bevölkerungsdichte konstruiert wird, ermöglichte es, die (für sich alleine) inhaltslose Dichteangabe einzuordnen und richtunggebend zu verwenden. Die jeweilige Codierung von Bevölkerungsdichte, also die Frage, ob hohe Bevölkerungsdichte als etwas Positives oder als etwas Negatives zu bewerten ist, wurde dabei zur Gretchenfrage des gesamten Diskurses. Auf der einen Seite gab es eine negative Codierung, mit der „hohe Dichte" im malthussianischen Sinne als naturgegebenes nationales Grundproblem konstruiert wurde. Auf der anderen Seite wurde genau das Gegenteil behauptet und eine hohe Bevölkerungsdichte (mehr oder

The approach to density follows a complex intertwining and coexistence of quantification and qualification of the term's applications. For one, there is density expressed as (quantitative) numerical figures. Such mention represents a fictionalization: in reality it is not really possible for a density value to be observed. Secondly, the quantitative indication of density is a reduction: so as to have an opportunity for comparison, the respective density value must always be reduced to the number one (meaning, to *one* square meter, *one* hectare, *one* square kilometer). Thirdly, the quantitative application of density is also an abstraction: the described reality is elevated through the density value to a communicable representational level. The quantitative application of density thus already, in many ways, becomes a construed form of usage. All of the above may be contrasted with a qualitative application level. Density becomes a (qualitative) metaphor when it is not specified as a concrete numerical value but is instead referenced as *the* density. Phrasing like "the density of the European city" or "the density was too high in the working districts of nineteenth-century industrialized cities" are examples for the term's usage, behind which are concealed complex and normative constructions of argumentation that may metaphorically find expression through this term. When we speak not of "density" but of "the density," then what is being formulated is usually a personification of the concept and/or the assertion of an individualized materiality of density. Decisive is now for the two usage forms—the qualitative application and the quantitative application of density—to enter into a close reciprocal relationship. The quantitative mention of density is enhanced with meaning (in terms of content) by the metaphorical tradition, and the metaphorical mention of density in turn acquires (natural) scientific substance and soundness through the calculability of its quantitative counterpart. Density is, as we might put it, a *potentially calculable metaphor*.

What might be identified as the first discourse on the "population density" concept is the debate incited by *An Essay on the Principle of Population* (1798), a famed essay by the Anglican clergyman Thomas Robert Malthus.[9] At the basis of this written work, which considered modern demography as a foundational part of the national economy, is the so-called "principle of population," which Malthus used to assert that the power for producing subsistence for the earth's population grows by arithmetic progression while the growth of the population on the other hand increases exponentially. From this Malthus extrapolated the danger of an impending doomsday should it not be possible to reduce the "surplus population," that is, the socially weak classes. A long, extensive discussion ensued on

9   Thomas Robert Malthus: *An Essay on the Principle of Population as It Affects the Future Improvement of Society, with Remarks on the Speculations of Mr. Godwin, Mr. Condorcet, and other Writers*, London 1798.

9   Thomas Robert Malthus, *An Essay on the Principle of Population as It Affects the Future Improvement of Society, with Remarks on the Speculations of Mr. Godwin, Mr. Condorcet, and other Writers* (London, 1798).

the pros and cons of this "principle," in which the phrase "population density" was soon to form one of the more important points of reference. Through this debate an evaluation system was created by which a normative fundament was fostered for the use of the category population density. Not until density is qualified within such a normative system—where population density is construed as low (too low), fitting (optimal), or high (too high)—is it possible to classify the contentless (when viewed alone) qualification of density and apply it in an innovative way. The respective codification of population density—that is, the question as to whether high population density should be assessed as something positive or as something negative—ended up being the litmus test of the entire discourse. On one side, there was a negative codification with which "high density" was interpreted, in a Malthusian sense, as a fundamental, naturally arising problem of national scope. But on the other, the exact opposite was claimed, whereby high population density was (more or less clearly) considered a positive, progress-guaranteeing element and a prerequisite for (or cause of) cultural and economic progress. The stance advocated by reformed socialists in Germany at the turn of the twentieth century (with a positive assessment of "high density") virtually became symbolic for a reformist faith in progress,[10] just as the assessment of high density as something negative ended up becoming the epitome of a politically conservative basic attitude.

A second source of discourse on density is geography. The first explicit instances of population density being mentioned or charted are connected in terms of time and content with the inception of scientific geography in the nineteenth century. By the end of this century a widespread methodological debate on the concept had started, with density rising to the fore of theoretical discourse on geography and cartography.[11] Taking center stage here was the question as to the "correct" usage pertaining to population density, including its precise definition and the most sensible methods for presenting it (for instance in the second section of Friedrich Ratzel's *Anthropogeographie*[12]). Yet more specifically, these debates revolved around significantly more than just methodological issues: the geographical conception of density is based on the classical meta-narrative of geography, which later came to be known as "natural determinism." Population density was understood as a direct mirror of "natural conditions" and the "correctly" drafted population-density map was stylized as a blueprint for a society ordained

minder deutlich) als positives, Fortschritt garantierendes Element und als Voraussetzung (oder Ursache) für kulturelles und wirtschaftliches Vorankommen konstruiert. Die von den deutschen Reformsozialisten um die Wende zum 20. Jahrhundert vertretene Haltung (die Bewertung von „hoher Dichte" als etwas Positives) wurde geradezu zum Erkennungszeichen für einen reformerischen Fortschrittsoptimismus,[10] genauso wie sich die Bewertung von hoher Dichte als etwas Negatives zum Inbegriff einer politisch konservativen Grundhaltung entwickelte.

Eine zweite Quelle der Dichtediskurse ist die Geografie. Die ersten expliziten Nennungen und Darstellungen von Bevölkerungsdichte sind zeitlich und inhaltlich mit der Entstehung der wissenschaftlichen Geografie im 19. Jahrhundert verbunden. Ende des 19. Jahrhunderts setzte eine breite methodische Debatte über den Begriff ein und Dichte wurde zum Zentrum der geografischen und kartografischen Theoriediskurse.[11] Im Mittelpunkt stand dabei die Frage nach der „richtigen" Verwendung der Bevölkerungsdichte, ihrer genauen Definition und sinnvollsten Darstellungsmethoden (etwa im zweiten Teil von Friedrich Ratzels *Anthropogeographie*[12]). Genau genommen ging es in diesen Debatten jedoch um weit mehr als nur um methodische Fragestellungen: Die geografische Dichtekonzeption basiert auf der klassischen geografischen Metaerzählung, die später als „Naturdeterminismus" bezeichnet worden ist. Bevölkerungsdichte wurde als direktes Abbild der „natürlichen Verhältnisse" konstruiert und die „richtig" erstellte Bevölkerungsdichtekarte zur Blaupause der naturdeterminierten Gesellschaft stilisiert.[13] Ende des 19. Jahrhunderts taucht im geografischen Kontext dann erstmals der Begriff „Volksdichte" auf und kündigt

> Bevölkerungsdichte wurde als direktes Abbild der „natürlichen Verhältnisse" konstruiert und die „richtig" erstellte Bevölkerungsdichtekarte zur Blaupause der naturdeterminierten Gesellschaft stilisiert.

eine Verschiebung des inhaltlichen Schwerpunktes in den geografischen Debatten an. „Volksdichte" wurde dabei weniger als Quotient von „Bevölkerung zur Fläche" definiert, sondern vielmehr als Quotient des Verhältnisses von „Volk zu Raum".[14] Vor allem bei Ratzel zeigte sich damit die Hinwendung zu einer „politischen Geographie",[15] die in den 1920er Jahren zur Geopolitik transformiert wurde und in der der Begriff „Volksdichte" weiter an

10   See Gustav Schmoller, *Grundriss der Allgemeinen Volkswirtschaftslehre*, section one (1901; repr., Munich, 1919). Franz Oppenheimer, "Das Bevölkerungsgesetz des T.R. Malthus und der neueren Nationalökonomie," in Franz Oppenheimer, *Gesammelte Schriften*, vol. 1, *Theoretische Grundlegungen* (1901; repr., Berlin, 1995), pp. 281–384.

11   See Max Eckert, *Die Kartenwissenschaft*, vol. 2 (Berlin and Leipzig, 1925), p. 153. Herbert Wilhelmy, *Kartographie in Stichworten* (Kiel, 1966), p. 120.

12   See Friedrich Ratzel, *Anthropogeographie, Teil 2: Die geographische Verbreitung des Menschen* (Stuttgart, 1891).

10   Vgl. Gustav Schmoller: *Grundriss der Allgemeinen Volkswirtschaftslehre*, Erster Teil, München 1919 [1901]; Franz Oppenheimer: „Das Bevölkerungsgesetz des T.R. Malthus und der neueren Nationalökonomie", in: Franz Oppenheimer, *Gesammelte Schriften*, Band I, *Theoretische Grundlegungen*, Berlin 1995 [1901], S. 281–384.

11   Vgl. Max Eckert: *Die Kartenwissenschaft*, Bd. 2, Berlin/Leipzig 1925, S. 153; Herbert Wilhelmy: *Kartographie in Stichworten*, Kiel 1966, S. 120.

12   Vgl. Friedrich Ratzel: *Anthropogeographie, Teil 2: Die geographische Verbreitung des Menschen*, Stuttgart 1891.

13   Etwa bei Alfred Hettner: „Über die Untersuchung und Darstellung der Bevölkerungsdichte", in: *Geographische Zeitschrift*, 7, 9 (1901), S. 498–514; siehe auch Ute Wardenga: *Geographie als Chorologie*, Stuttgart 1995.

14   Dabei wurden gleichzeitig und von derselben völkischen Seite die (eigentlich widersprüchlichen) Diskurse „Volk ohne Raum" und „Raum ohne Volk" propagiert, und zwar beides Mal unter Bezugnahme auf Dichte. Vgl. auch Siegfried Grundmann: „Bevölkerungslehre im und vor dem ‚Dritten Reich'", in: Rainer Mackensen (Hg.): *Bevölkerungslehre und Bevölkerungspolitik im „Dritten Reich"*, Opladen 2004, S. 319–335.

15   Friedrich Ratzel: *Politische Geographie*, München/Berlin 1923 [1897].

Diesen Zusammenhang entwickelt Durkheim mithilfe der Unterscheidung in die Begriffe „moralische" und „materielle Dichte". Die „moralische Dichte" wird dabei inszeniert als abstrakte, übergreifende Solidarität, als das soziale Band, welches die Gesellschaft zusammenhält. Durkheims „materielle Dichte" hingegen bildet das heute in den Sozial- und Planungswissenschaften übliche Spektrum ab: bauliche Dichte, Einwohnerdichte, Kommunikationsdichte und Verkehrsdichte.

by nature.[13] Thus emerging for the first time in the late nineteenth century in the context of geography was the concept of "Volksdichte" introducing a shift in focus of content within geographical discourse. Here "Volksdichte" was to be defined not as the quotient of "people to area" but rather as the quotient of the relationship "nation to space."[14] Especially Friedrich Ratzel's efforts displayed an orientation toward a "political geography,"[15] which in the 1920s was transformed to geopolitics and where the phrase "Volksdichte" continued to assume a central and prominent position. A increasing radicalization of these discourses played out, with Karl Haushofer for instance extending the concept of density as a shibboleth for German expansionism;[16] the latter was meant to be enriched by the quantitative-qualitative creation of the term "Volksdichte" as a quasi scientific explanatory category.

A third line of discourse, one that likewise goes back to the nineteenth century, can be traced within sociology. The constructions and usage of the term density in this field can be identified as originating with Émile Durkheim, who in his early work *Über soziale Arbeitsteilung* (The Division of Labor in Society)[17] invoked density as the reason behind societal progress. This correlation was honed by Durkheim in that he differentiated between the concepts of "moral density" and "material density." In his book, "moral density" is staged as reflecting abstract, comprehensive solidarity, as the social glue that holds society together. Durkheim's "material density," in turn, describes a spectrum typical for today's social and planning sciences: building density, resident density, communications density, and traffic density. Though Durkheim's theory postulates that "moral density" and "material density" correlate in their respective forms, it also explicitly zeroes in on the advantage presented by "material density" (as opposed to "moral density") in being empirically ascertainable and observable.[18] Yet according to Durkheim's hypothesis—and this discourse on density is not far afield from its relatives in geography and national economics—not only do both forms of density behave in the same way; they are also mutually dependent. So in the case of Durkheim as well, a causal relationship is construed through den-

13 For instance in Alfred Hettner, "Über die Untersuchung und Darstellung der Bevölkerungsdichte," *Geographische Zeitschrift* 7, no. 9 (1901), pp. 498–514. Also see Ute Wardenga, *Geographie als Chorologie* (Stuttgart, 1995).

14 Here the (actually quite contradictory) discourses "people without space" and "space without people" were simultaneously propagated from the same camp, in both instances while making reference to density. See also Siegfried Grundmann, "Bevölkerungslehre im und vor dem 'Dritten Reich,'" in Rainer Mackensen (ed.), *Bevölkerungslehre und Bevölkerungspolitik im "Dritten Reich"* (Opladen, 2004), pp. 319–35.

15 Friedrich Ratzel, *Politische Geographie* (1897; repr., Munich and Berlin, 1923).

16 See Karl Haushofer, "Vergleich des Lebens-Raumes Deutschlands mit dem seiner Nachbarn unter besonderer Berücksichtigung der wehrgeographischen Lage der Vergleichs-Staaten," in Hans-Adolf Jacobsen (ed.), *Karl Haushofer: Leben und Werk*, vol. I (Boppard am Rhein, 1979), pp. 524–37.

17 See Émile Durkheim, *Über soziale Arbeitsteilung* (1893; repr., Frankfurt am Main, 1992).

18 Ibid., p. 318.

sity. However—and this is a decisive turning point—Durkheim soon thereafter categorically reversed his own position on density in his work *The Rules of Sociological Method*. Behind this about-face was a fundamental reversal in the thought patterns of this founding father of French sociology: with his new credo, which was now pressing to the foreground, that "a social fact cannot be explained except by another social fact,"[19] Durkheim clearly distances himself from his earlier work and advances to become a founder of the constructivist line of development in the discipline of sociology. Interesting here is not only the fact that Durkheim has explicitly reversed his own conception of density, but also that we cannot find any kind of reference to this revocation in the many explorations of density in contemporary urban sociology. Rather, the original Durkheimian causal approach has been assiduously carried forth in the urban-sociological context, most notably by Louis Wirth. In his famous essay "Urbanism as a Way of Life,"[20] Wirth cites density as a component of his well-known definition of the city: for Wirth, density—next to large numbers and heterogeneity—counts among the main elements that make up a city. In the process, Wirth adopts Durkheim's causal construction (which he specifically references) and takes it even further: he considers density not only the cause of societal progress, but also the reason for a generally tolerant mindset among metropolitan residents. Wirth's essay thus takes on significance as a milestone for the urban-sociological understanding of density, though less because of his own definition of density and more because of the application of the term to the definition of "city" and the related debate.[21]

The fourth central discursive root for the concept of density can be found in discussions on modern city planning. In this setting, density functions as a—if not *the*—key concept, and it has done so from the very beginning. In the constitutional writings of Freiherr Lorenz von Stein, which may be considered the precursor to urban-development discourse, density plays a decisive role. According to von Stein, it is "law" that the "import of air and light in housing directly correlates with density of population" so that the "responsibility of sanitary residential housing" must "grow at the same pace" as "the density of population increases." This sentence appeared "as a fundament in the history of residential housing."[22] Reinhard

zentraler und exponierter Stelle zu finden war. Bei der zunehmenden Radikalisierung dieser Diskurse wurde von Karl Haushofer das Dichtekonzept zu einem Kampfbegriff des deutschen Expansionismus ausgebaut,[16] dem mit der quantitativ-qualitativen Begriffsschöpfung „Volksdichte" eine quasi naturwissenschaftliche Begründungskategorie an die Hand gegeben werden sollte.

Eine dritte und ebenso bis ins 19. Jahrhundert zurückreichende Diskurslinie kann in der Soziologie nachgezeichnet werden. Der Ursprung der dortigen Konstruktion und Verwendung des Begriffs findet sich bei Émile Durkheim, der in seinem Frühwerk *Über soziale Arbeitsteilung*[17] Dichte als Ursache für gesellschaftlichen Fortschritt implementiert. Diesen Zusammenhang entwickelt Durkheim mithilfe der Unterscheidung in die Begriffe „moralische" und „materielle Dichte". Die „moralische Dichte" wird dabei inszeniert als abstrakte, übergreifende Solidarität, als das soziale Band, welches die Gesellschaft zusammenhält. Durkheims „materielle Dichte" hingegen bildet das heute in den Sozial- und Planungswissenschaften übliche Spektrum ab: bauliche Dichte, Einwohnerdichte, Kommunikationsdichte und Verkehrsdichte. Durkheims These besagt nun, dass sich „moralische Dichte" und „materielle Dichte" in ihrer jeweiligen Ausformung entsprechen und zielt dabei explizit auf den Vorteil ab, dass „materielle Dichte" (im Gegensatz zur „moralischen Dichte") empirisch erheb- und beobachtbar ist.[18] Nach Durkheims Theorie – und damit ist dieser Dichtediskurs nicht weit entfernt von seinen geografischen und nationalökonomischen Verwandten – verhalten sich die beiden Dichtearten jedoch nicht nur gleichförmig, sie bedingen sich auch gegenseitig. Auch von Durkheim wird mit Dichte also ein kausales Verhältnis konstruiert. Allerdings, und das ist ein entscheidender Punkt, hat Durkheim wenig später in seiner Schrift *Die Regeln der soziologischen Methode* seine eigene Dichtetheorie selbst explizit widerrufen.[19] Hintergrund für diese Kehrtwende ist ein grundlegender Richtungswechsel im Denken des Gründervaters der französischen Soziologie: Mit seinem nun in den Vordergrund gerückten Credo, dass „Soziales nur durch Soziales" zu erklären sei, setzt sich Durkheim deutlich von seinem Frühwerk ab und avanciert zu einem Begründer der konstruktivistischen Entwicklungslinie der soziologischen Disziplin. Interessant ist dabei nicht nur, dass Durkheim sein eigenes Dichtekonzept explizit widerruft, sondern auch, dass man in den zahlreichen Dichterezeptionen der zeitgenössischen Stadtsoziologie auf diesen Widerruf keinerlei Hinweis findet. Der ursprüngliche Durkheimsche Kausalansatz wurde im stadtsoziologischen Kontext vielmehr fleißig weitertransportiert. Und zwar vor allem von Louis Wirth. Im seinem berühmten Aufsatz „Urbanism as a Way of Life"[20] verwendet Wirth Dichte als einen Bestandteil seiner bekannten Stadtdefinition: Dichte gehört für Wirth – neben der Größe und der Heterogenität – zu den drei Bausteinen, aus denen sich Stadt zusammensetzt. Wirth übernimmt dabei Durkheims Kausalkonstruktion (auf die er sich explizit bezieht) und erweitert sie noch: Dichte ist bei Wirth nicht

19 See Émile Durkheim, *The Rules of Sociological Method and Selected Texts on Sociology and Its Method*, ed. Steven Lukes (1895; repr., New York, 1982), p. 162.

20 Louis Wirth, "Urbanism as a Way of Life," *The American Journal of Sociology* 44, no. 1 (1938), pp. 1–24.

21 On the appropriation of density in current urban-sociological discourse, see Nikolai Roskamm, "Lost in Spatial Turn," in *Lokalistische Stadtforschung, kulturalisierte Städte: Zur Kritik einer "Eigenlogik der Städte,"* ed. Jan Kemper and Anne Vogelpohl (Münster, 2011). Nikolai Roskamm, "Das Konstrukt 'Dichte' und die 'europäische Stadt,'" in Oliver Frey and Florian Koch (eds.), *Die Zukunft der europäischen Stadt* (Wiesbaden, 2010), pp. 71–85.

22 Lorenz von Stein, *Die Verwaltungslehre, Dritter Theil, Das Gesundheitswesen* (Stuttgart, 1882), p. 227.

16 Vgl. Karl Haushofer: „Vergleich des Lebens-Raumes Deutschlands mit dem seiner Nachbarn unter besonderer Berücksichtigung der wehrgeographischen Lage der Vergleichs-Staaten", in: Hans-Adolf Jacobsen (Hg.): *Karl Haushofer – Leben und Werk*, Bd. I. Boppard/R. 1979, S. 524–537.

17 Vgl. Émile Durkheim: *Über soziale Arbeitsteilung*, Frankfurt am Main 1992 [1893].

18 Ebd., S. 318.

19 Vgl. Émile Durkheim: *Die Regeln der soziologischen Methode*, Frankfurt am Main 1984 [1895], S. 195 f.

20 Louis Wirth: „Urbanism as a Way of Life", in: *The American Journal of Sociology*, 44, 1 (1938), S. 1–24.

nur Ursache von gesellschaftlichem Fortschritt, sondern auch Ursache für eine allgemeine tolerante Einstellung der Großstadtbewohner. Wirths Aufsatz wird damit zu einem Meilenstein für das stadtsoziologische Verständnis von Dichte, allerdings weniger durch die von ihm vorgenommene Dichtedefinition, als durch die Verwendung des Begriffs für die Definition von „Stadt" und die daran anschließende Debatte.[21]

Die vierte zentrale diskursive Wurzel des Begriffs Dichte ist in den Debatten des modernen Städtebaus zu finden. In diesem Umfeld fungiert Dichte als ein, wenn nicht als *der* disziplinäre Schlüsselbegriff, und zwar bereits von Anfang an. Schon in den staatsrechtlichen Schriften von Freiherr Lorenz von Stein, die als Vorläufer des städtebaulichen Diskurses gesehen werden können, spielt Dichte eine tragende Rolle. Stein formuliert, es sei „Gesetz", dass die „Bedeutung der Wohnung für Luft und Licht in geradem Verhältniß zur Dichtigkeit der Bevölkerung" stehe, so dass „die Aufgabe des gesundheitlichen Wohnungswesens in demselben Grade" wachse, in welchem „die Dichtigkeit der Bevölkerung zunimmt". Dieser Satz erscheine „als Grundlage der Geschichte des Wohnungswesens".[22] Ähnlich sieht es auch Reinhard Baumeister, dessen Schrift *Stadt-Erweiterungen in technischer baupolizeilicher und wirtschaftlicher Beziehung*[23] häufig als das erste ausgearbeitete Werk einer Städtebautheorie genannt wird. Baumeister bezeichnet eine hohe Dichte als Ursache sämtlicher städtischer Problemlagen: der Gesundheitspflege, der „sozialen Frage" und der Bodenspekulation (1911).[24]

Dichte wurde im städtebaulichen und stadtplanerischen Kontext ebenso wie in den anderen Disziplinen als *Ursache* für soziale Entwicklungen kontextualisiert, allerdings mit einer ausschließlich negativen Codierung. Hohe Dichte war im Städtebau für sehr lange Zeit (bis weit in die 1960er Jahre) Ursache und Merkmal für beinahe sämtliche von den Städtebauern als Übel wahrgenommenen städtischen Realitäten. Hauptsächliches Ziel der städtebaulichen Zunft war es dabei, allgemeingültige städtebauliche Regeln aufzustellen und durchzusetzen, um solche Missstände zu vermeiden respektive abzubauen.

Folgerichtig wurde es daher bald zu einer zentralen Strategie, Dichte durch Verordnungen und Gesetze zu reglementieren. Und zu diesem Zweck wurde ein (neben der Bevölkerungsdichte) zweites Dichtekonstrukt geschaffen: die bauliche Dichte. Die bauliche Dichte, definiert als das Verhältnis von Nutzfläche zu Grundstücksfläche, bot für die städtebauliche Debatte vor allem zwei Vorteile: Zum einen ließ sie sich exakt ermitteln und unterstrich damit den angestrebten naturwissenschaftlichen Charakter der stadtplanerischen Normvorgaben. Zum anderen bezog sich die bauliche Dichte auf bereits bezogenes Terrain: Die Regelung der baulichen Dichte konnte mit Recht als angestammter städtebaulicher Zuständigkeitsbereich in Anspruch genommen werden. Aus diesem Grunde etablierte sich in der Disziplin eine arbeitsteilige Dichteverwendung: Die Bevölkerungsdichte wurde vor allem als Analyse-

Baumeister took a similar view, with his work *Stadt-Erweiterungen in technischer baupolizeilicher und wirtschaftlicher Beziehung* (Urban-Expansion Related to Technical Building Inspection and Economics)[23] being frequently cited as the first elaborate piece on urban-development theory. In 1911 Baumeister claimed that high density was at the root of all problematic urban issues: health care, the "social question," and land speculation.[24]

Density in an urban-development and urban-planning context has been contextualized, as in other disciplines as well, as a *reason* behind certain social developments (however, exclusively with negative codification). In city planning, high density had long (all the way up to the 1960s) been held responsible for, and considered the earmark of, nearly all urban realities that represented eyesores for urban planners. At the time, the principle objective of the urban-development clique was to define and implement rules meant to avoid such abuse of urban space and to dismantle the structures in question. So the natural consequence was to soon establish a central strategy for regimenting density by means of ordinances and laws. To this end, a second construct of density (in addition to population density) was engendered: building density. Defined as the relationship between area available for use and total land area of the lot, building density provided those involved in the urban-development debate with two main advantages. First of all, it could be precisely determined and thus underlined the desired scientific character of the standardized urban-development norms. Secondly, building density was related to known terrain: the regulation of building density could justifiably be utilized as a traditional urban-development domain. For this reason, an appropriation of density based upon division of labor developed within the discipline: population density was predominately implemented as an instrument for analysis, while building density was considered a functional instrument and tool. The urban deficiencies that were (putatively) definable by the category of population density were then supposed to be remedied by a regimentation of building density.[25]

Taking this even further was the fourth Congrès Internationaux d'Architecture Moderne in its *Charter of Athens*. In this document, developed under the aegis of Le Corbusier, density is granted a considerable measure of attention.[26] Here, too, it becomes obvious that the question of density in an urban-development context reflects not dissonance between conservative and reformist positions (such as those characterizing the issue of national economy) but rather a situation of inclusive

21 Zu den Dichteverwendungen in den aktuellen Diskursen der Stadtsoziologie vgl. Nikolai Roskamm: „Lost in Spatial Turn", in: Jan Kemper/Anne Vogelpohl (Hg.): *Lokalistische Stadtforschung, kulturalisierte Städte: Zur Kritik einer „Eigenlogik der Städte"*, Münster 2011; Nikolai Roskamm: „Das Konstrukt ‚Dichte' und die ‚europäische Stadt'", in: Oliver Frey/Florian Koch (Hg.): *Die Zukunft der europäischen Stadt*, Wiesbaden 2010, S. 71–85.

22 Lorenz von Stein: *Die Verwaltungslehre, Dritter Theil, Das Gesundheitswesen*, Stuttgart 1882, S. 227.

23 Reinhard Baumeister: *Stadt-Erweiterungen in technischer baupolizeilicher und wirtschaftlicher Beziehung*, Berlin 1876.

24 Vgl. Reinhard Baumeister: *Bauordnung und Wohnungsfrage*, Berlin 1911.

23 Reinhard Baumeister, *Stadt-Erweiterungen in technischer baupolizeilicher und wirtschaftlicher Beziehung* (Berlin, 1876).

24 See Reinhard Baumeister, *Bauordnung und Wohnungsfrage* (Berlin, 1911).

25 The separation of the concept of structural density from the concept of population density is explained very well in Baumeister, *Stadt-Erweiterungen* (note 24). On this, also see Nikolai Roskamm, *Dichte*, pp. 236–44 (note 5).

26 See Le Corbusier, *An die Studenten: Die "Charte d'Athènes"* (1933; repr., Reinbek, 1962), pp. 84–85.

consensus within the discipline. In the *Charter of Athens* all cases are cited in which high density had been staged as the central urban-development evil over the preceding decades. New, however, was the fact that not only the regimentation of building density is challenged but also specifically the limitation on resident density (to be set by urban developers). This proposal, called an "administrative act heavy with consequences,"[27] stands for a new qualitative step in the history of density discourse: thought through to the end is the demand for regulatory determination of population density, an approach that vehemently encroaches on individual's right to self-determination and that should be considered an example of the affinity for totalitarian positions,[28] as is occasionally encountered within urban-development discourse. So this is perhaps not really surprising when we see where each planning approach was specifically formulated: in the 1930s and 1940s, the determination (and also an attempt at the creation) of "correct" densities of population for entire regions (especially in the occupied areas of Eastern Europe) came to occupy a central sphere of activity within National Socialist spatial planning.[29] Yet following the Second World War, the conditions for dictating population density through government authorities had significantly deteriorated. Therefore, this train of thought was soon dismissed within urban-development discourse and replaced by the concept of building density. Nevertheless, the pivotal position of the density concept remained secure within this discipline—as opposed to within discourse on geography and the national economy, where density played a considerably less important role after 1945. What might be viewed as the apex and (tentative) terminus of classical urban-development discourse on density (at least for the German context) is the West German building legislation of the 1960s. Introduced for the first time in 1962 with the *Baunutzungsverordnung* (Federal Land Utilization Ordinance) were generally applicable maximum limits, based upon urban-development considerations, for building density. This meant that the classical urban-development model of the segmented and relaxed (or "undensified") city was cast into law (where it still remains today, almost unchanged).

At the same time, however, a counterposition was developing in the 1960s and 1970s, which was for example apparent in the critical debate on the pros and cons of such generalized ceilings on density.[30] Resulting from this internal criticism, on

27   Ibid.

28   See Hartmut Häußermann, Dieter Läpple, and Walter Siebel, *Stadtpolitik* (Frankfurt am Main, 2008), pp. 72–77.

29   See Ariane Leendertz, *Ordnung schaffen: Deutsche Raumplanung im 20. Jahrhundert* (Göttingen, 2008) and Nikolai Roskamm, *Dichte*, pp. 179–95 (note 5).

30   See Gerhard Boeddinghaus, *Die Bestimmung des Maßes der baulichen Nutzung in der städtebaulichen Planung* (Aachen, 1969). Herbert Hübner, "Richtwerte und Werturteile," *Bauwelt* 51–52 (1969), pp. 270–72. Klaus Borchard, "Städtebauliche Orientierungswerte," in Akademie für Raumforschung und Landesplanung (ed.), *Handwörterbuch der Raumforschung und Raumordnung* (Hanover, 1970), pp. 3181–202.

instrument eingesetzt, während die bauliche Dichte als fachliches Instrument und Werkzeug betrachtet wurde. Die durch die Kategorie Bevölkerungsdichte (vermeintlich) bestimmbaren städtischen Missstände sollten durch die Reglementierung der baulichen Dichte behoben werden.[25]

Noch weiter gegangen ist der vierte Congrès Internationaux d'Architecture Moderne in seiner *Charta von Athen*. In diesem unter der Federführung von Le Corbusier entwickelten Dokument wird Dichte ein überaus exponierter Platz eingeräumt.[26] Auch hier zeigt es sich, dass die Frage der Dichte im Städtebau nicht ein Trennpunkt zwischen konservativen und reformerischen Positionen gewesen ist (wie etwa in der Nationalökonomie), sondern einen übergreifenden disziplinären Konsens repräsentierte. Zunächst werden in der *Charta von Athen* alle Register wiederholt, mit denen in den Jahrzehnten zuvor hohe Dichte als das zentrale städtebauliche Übel inszeniert worden war. Neu ist jedoch, dass nicht nur die Reglementierung der baulichen Dichte, sondern explizit auch eine (von Städtebauern festzulegende) Beschränkung der Einwohnerdichte gefordert wird. Dieser als „folgenschwerer Akt der Verwaltung"[27] bezeichnete Vorschlag steht für eine neue qualitative Stufe in der Geschichte der Dichtediskurse: Zu Ende gedacht ist die Forderung nach behördlicher Festlegung der Einwohnerdichte ein Ansatz, der ganz vehement in das Selbstbestimmungsrecht des Einzelnen eingreift und der als Beispiel für die im städtebaulichen Diskurs nicht selten anzutreffende Affinität zu totalitären Positionen[28] zu betrachten ist. Daher ist es vielleicht auch nicht überraschend, wenn man sieht, wo jener Planungsansatz explizit ausgearbeitet wurde: in den 1930er und 1940er Jahren wurde die Ermittlung (und auch der Versuch der Herstellung) von „richtigen" Bevölkerungsdichten ganzer Regionen (insbesondere in den besetzten Gebieten in Osteuropa) ein zentrales Betätigungsfeld der nationalsozialistischen Raumplanung.[29] Nach dem Zweiten Weltkrieg hatten sich

Der Blick in die Geschichte hat nun gezeigt, dass Dichte in vielen bedeutenden Diskursen der Sozial- und Planungswissenschaften eine tragende Rolle spielt oder gespielt hat.

die Voraussetzungen, Bevölkerungsdichte behördlich zu diktieren, allerdings deutlich verschlechtert. Im städtebaulichen Diskurs wurde diese Denkrichtung daher auch bald aufgegeben und wieder auf das Konzept der baulichen Dichte zurückgegriffen. Die zentrale Stellung des Dichtebegriffs blieb der Disziplin jedoch erhalten – im Gegensatz zu den Diskursen der Geografie und der Nationalökonomie, wo Dichte nach 1945 eine wesentlich geringere

25   Nachvollziehen lässt sich die Trennung des Konzepts der „baulichen Dichte" vom Konzept der Bevölkerungsdichte gut bei Baumeister 1911 (Anm. 24); vgl. dazu Nikolai Roskamm: *Dichte*, S. 236–244 (wie Anm. 5).

26   Vgl. Le Corbusier: *An die Studenten, Die „Charte d'Athènes"*, Reinbek 1962 [1942, 1933], S. 84 f.

27   Ebd.

28   Vgl. Hartmut Häußermann/Dieter Läpple/Walter Siebel: *Stadtpolitik*, Frankfurt am Main 2008, S. 72–77.

29   Vgl. Ariane Leendertz: *Ordnung schaffen. Deutsche Raumplanung im 20. Jahrhundert*, Göttingen 2008 und Nikolai Roskamm: *Dichte*, S. 179–195 (wie Anm. 5).

Rolle spielte. Als Höhe- und vorläufiger Endpunkt des klassischen städtebaulichen Dichtediskurses kann (zumindest für den deutschen Kontext) die westdeutsche Baugesetzgebung der 1960er Jahre bezeichnet werden. Mit der *Baunutzungsverordnung* wurden 1962 erstmals allgemein gültige, städtebaulich begründete Obergrenzen für die bauliche Dichte eingeführt und damit das klassische Städtebauleitbild der gegliederten und aufgelockerten (also „entdichteten") Stadt in Gesetzesform gegossen (wo es bis heute nahezu unverändert zu finden ist).

Gleichzeitig entwickelte sich in den 1960er und 1970er Jahren jedoch eine Gegenposition, und zwar nicht zuletzt in der kritischen Debatte über das Für und Wider solcher allgemeinen Dichte-Obergrenzen.[30] Aus dieser internen Kritik auf der einen Seite und aus dem Widerstand der von den stadtplanerischen Maßnahmen Betroffenen (vor allem gegen die Flächensanierungen jener Zeit) auf der anderen Seite entstand dann im städtebaulichen Diskurs die eindrucksvolle Neucodierung von Dichte: Dichte gilt seitdem nicht mehr als Metapher für soziales Elend, Seuchengefahr und umstürzlerische Massenansammlungen, sondern als Garant für städtisches Leben und/oder für ökologischen Städtebau. Diese Neucodierung wurde erstaunlich schnell zum allgemeinen disziplinären Konsens verfestigt, allerdings ohne sich dabei in der Planungsgesetzgebung niederzuschlagen.[31]

Eine Sonderstellung in der Diskursgeschichte des Begriffs Dichte im städtebaulichen Kontext hat schließlich das sogenannte Leitbild der „Urbanität durch Dichte". Und zwar deshalb, weil es genau genommen gar nicht existiert hat. Die übliche Erzählung in der städtebaulichen Geschichtsschreibung lautet, dass der Schweizer Ökonom Edgar Salin den Terminus „Urbanität durch Dichte" in die deutsche Fachdebatte eingeführt und ihr damit „eine neue Richtung" gegeben habe.[32] Bei genauerer Betrachtung entpuppt sich diese Berichterstattung jedoch als wenig stichhaltig. Salin hat in seinem berühmten und lesenswerten Vortrag über Urbanität[33] nämlich weder den Begriff Dichte in den Mund genommen, noch hat er Urbanität als mögliches Planungsziel propagiert (im Gegenteil warnt Salin eindrücklich vor solch einem Ansinnen). Mehr noch: auch in der damit bezeichneten Periode (also den 1960er und frühen 1970er Jahren) findet sich der Slogan „Urbanität durch Dichte" nirgendwo; verwendet wurde er erst in den 1980er Jahren, dann allerdings nicht als Leitbild, sondern als nachträgliche Kritik der vorgängigen Städtebau-Phase.[34] Wenn zu einem Leitbild die Eigenschaft gehört, dass es in dieser Funktion auch verwendet worden ist, dann kommt man zu dem Schluss, dass der Slogan „Urbanität durch Dichte" schlicht und einfach gar kein Leitbild gewesen ist. Zudem stellt sich die Frage, ob der inhaltliche Gehalt des Slogans wirklich dafür geeignet ist, die entsprechende Städtebauphase zu beschreiben. Und auch hier sind Zweifel angebracht: der soziale Wohnungsbau der 1960er Jahre, dem das Leitbild der „Urbanität durch Dichte" ja angeblich zugrunde gelegen haben soll, steht nämlich gar nicht in

the one hand, and from resistance (especially against the large-scale redevelopment going on at the time) on the part of residents impacted by the urban-development measures, on the other, was an impressive recodification of density within urban-development discourse: since then, density has no longer been a metaphor for social misery, threat of epidemics, and subversive mass congregations, but has rather been considered a guarantor for urban life and/or for ecological urban development. This recoding became anchored as universal consensus within the discipline astonishingly quickly, however without becoming established within urban-planning legislation.[31]

A special position with the history of discourse for the concept of density in an urban-development context is occupied by the so-called model of "Urbanität durch Dichte" (urbanity through density). And this is because, strictly speaking, it never actually existed. The standard narrative within urban-development historiography reads that Swiss economist Edgar Salin introduced the terminology "Urbanität durch Dichte" into German debate on the topic, thus having given it "a new direction."[32] But upon closer examination, this reporting turns out to lack validity. For in his renowned lecture on urbanity,[33] which is well worth reading, Salin mentions neither the term density nor does he propagate urbanity as a possible planning objective (on the contrary, Salin expressly warns again any such suggestion). What is more, nowhere can the slogan "Urbanität durch Dichte" be found during the designated period (namely, the 1960s and early 1970s); it first displayed usage in the 1980s, though not as a model but as a retrospective critique of the antecedent urban-development phase.[34] When the existence of a model implies that it has also been used in this function, then we must inevitably conclude that the slogan "Urbanität durch Dichte" was simply not a model at all. Moreover, we must question whether the slogan's substance (in terms of content) is even suited to describing the related urban-planning phase. And here, too, misgivings are justified: social housing development in the 1960s, said to have been supposedly based upon the model of "Urbanität durch Dichte" does not even stand in the tradition of the densely built Gründerzeit city; rather, it is based on the (actual) model of the scattered and structured city together with its demand for (as compared to Gründerzeit urban reality) extremely low rates of density.[35]

The fact that the narrative of the "Urbanität durch Dichte" model, so often cited today, ends up lacking credibility upon closer examination is more than just a side note in our consid-

30 Vgl. Gerhard Boeddinghaus: *Die Bestimmung des Maßes der baulichen Nutzung in der städtebaulichen Planung*, Aachen 1969; Herbert Hübner: „Richtwerte und Werturteile", in: *Bauwelt*, 51/52 (1969), S. 270–272; Klaus Borchard: „Städtebauliche Orientierungswerte", in: Akademie für Raumforschung und Landesplanung (Hg.): *Handwörterbuch der Raumforschung und Raumordnung*, Hannover 1970, S. 3181–3202.

31 Siehe auch: Nikolai Roskamm: „Der morsche Kern", in: *Planerin* 5/2011, S. 4–7.

32 Kaltenbrunner: „Urbane Kondensation", S. 32 (wie Anm. 3).

33 Vgl. Edgar Salin: „Urbanität", in: *Neue Schriften des Deutschen Städtetages*, 6 (1960).

34 Etwa bei Dietrich Kautt: *Wolfsburg im Wandel städtebaulicher Leitbilder*. Tübingen 1983, S. 308. Hier wird „Urbanität durch Dichte" vermutlich erstmalig als „Leitbild" bezeichnet.

31 Also see Nikolai Roskamm, "Der morsche Kern," *Planerin* (May 2011), pp. 4–7.

32 Kaltenbrunner, "Urbane Kondensation," p. 32 (note 3).

33 See Edgar Salin, "Urbanität," *Neue Schriften des Deutschen Städtetages* 6 (1960).

34 For instance in Dietrich Kautt, *Wolfsburg im Wandel städtebaulicher Leitbilder* (Tübingen, 1983), p. 308. It is here that "urbanity through density" was probably first called a "model."

35 On this, also see Nikolai Roskamm, *Dichte*, pp. 299–315 (note 5).

erations. Here, in fact, some of the fundamental characteristics of the density concept clearly stand out. Density has been and still remains a key concept for various disciplines in the social and planning sciences. And this key concept indeed is, to start off with, a contentless container—a container that must be filled with content in order to come by its (a) function. Precisely this metaphor can, in my opinion, also explain the inconsistencies among the many different appropriations of density, which are justifiably detected again and again: it is presumably only possible to arrive at such strongly deviating claims, as is the case in so many discourses on density, when something starts out devoid of content. And this contentlessness by all means sets density apart from other key concepts within urban development. It goes without saying that other concepts—like urbanity, ecology, sustainability, or the garden city—are always ultimately defined by the context in which they are applied. Yet from the outset they also connote a certain programmatic nature, one that is absent in the case of density prior to it being placed into some kind of context and thereby being imbued with meaning.

This glimpse into history has now shown that density plays, or has played, a key role in many important discourses within the social and planning sciences. In these various mentions—in the Malthusian overpopulation discourse, in Ratzel's and Haushofer's narrative on "a people without space," in Durkheim's societal theory, and in the many models of urban development—density is meant to make the respectively asserted fundamental truths justifiable and empirically ascertainable. Hence the conclusion of the genealogy sketched here is, for one, that density may be perceived as a common currency within the pivotal spatial discourses of modernity and that, moreover, it obviously still today represents an important reference point for such foundational analyses and explanations. Nevertheless, caution must be exercised when exploring these explanations, as is for instance illustrated by the unmasking as myth of the repeatedly invoked model of "Urbanität durch Dichte." And with this diagnosis at the latest, the relevance of the reflections put forth here for the Renaissance of density, as mentioned early on in this essay, within urban-development and architectural discourse becomes clear. We may note in conclusion that, when considering present-day productions of density, it is certainly worthwhile to become aware of the complex implicit and explicit historical references attached to the concept of density. For it is only in this way that the many snares can be avoided which indwell constructions of density, especially when the term is introduced as a societal or urban-theoretical causality or is staged as a universally valid instrument of planning.

Translation Dawn Michelle d'Atri

der Tradition der dicht bebauten Gründerzeitstadt, sondern basiert vielmehr auf dem (tatsächlichen) Leitbild der aufgelockerten und gegliederten Stadt mitsamt dessen Forderung nach (im Vergleich zur gründerzeitlichen städtischen Realität) äußerst geringen Dichtewerten.[35]

Dass die heute ständig reproduzierte Erzählung vom Leitbild der „Urbanität durch Dichte" bei genauerer Betrachtung so wenig belastbar ist, ist dabei mehr als nur eine Randnotiz. Vielmehr treten hier nochmals einige der grundlegenden Eigenschaften des Dichtebegriffs deutlich hervor. Dichte war und ist in vielen Disziplinen der Sozial- und Planungswissenschaften ein Schlüsselbegriff. Und dieser Schlüsselbegriff ist tatsächlich erst einmal ein inhaltsleerer Behälter – ein Behälter, der mit Inhalt aufgefüllt werden muss, um seine (eine) Funktion zu erhalten. Genau damit kann meines Erachtens auch die zu Recht immer wieder konstatierte Widersprüchlichkeit bei den zahlreichen Dichteverwendungen erklärt werden: Vermutlich ist es nur bei etwas selbst Inhaltslosem möglich, zu derart widersprechenden Aussagen zu kommen, wie das in so vielen Dichtediskursen festzustellen ist. Und diese Inhaltslosigkeit unterscheidet Dichte durchaus von anderen städtebaulichen Schlüsselbegriffen. Natürlich werden auch Begriffe wie Urbanität, Ökologie, Nachhaltigkeit oder Gartenstadt letztlich immer durch ihren Gebrauchskontext definiert. Sie implizieren jedoch von vornherein auch eine gewisse Programmatik. Und diese Programmatik fehlt bei der Dichte, bevor man den Begriff in irgendeinen Kontext gestellt und dadurch mit Bedeutung aufgeladen hat.

Der Blick in die Geschichte hat nun gezeigt, dass Dichte in vielen bedeutenden Diskursen der Sozial- und Planungswissenschaften eine tragende Rolle spielt oder gespielt hat. In diesen Diskursen – im Malthusschen Überbevölkerungsdiskurs genauso wie in Ratzels und Haushofers Erzählung vom „Volk ohne Raum", in Durkheims Gesellschaftstheorie und in den vielen Leitbildern des Städtebaus – sollten mit Dichte die jeweilig behaupteten Grundwahrheiten begründbar und empirisch erfassbar gemacht werden. Das Ergebnis der hier skizzierten Genealogie ist also, dass zum einen Dichte als eine gemeinsame Währung der zentralen Raumdiskurse der Moderne betrachtet werden kann und dass sie zum anderen offenbar bis heute einen wichtigen Bezugspunkt für solche Grundlegungen und Erklärungsangebote abgibt. Gegenüber diesen Erklärungsangeboten, das zeigt nicht zuletzt die Enttarnung des so kontinuierlich repetierten Leitbildes der „Urbanität durch Dichte" als eine Legende, ist jedoch Vorsicht walten zu lassen. Und spätestens mit dieser Diagnose dürfte dann auch die Relevanz der hier vorgenommenen Betrachtung für die anfangs dargestellte aktuelle Renaissance der Dichte im städtebaulichen und architektonischen Diskurs deutlich werden. Für die gegenwärtigen Inszenierungen von Dichte, so lässt sich abschließend festhalten, ist es jedenfalls lohnend, sich die komplexen impliziten und expliziten geschichtlichen Bezüge des Begriffs bewusst zu machen. Denn nur so können die vielfältigen Fallstricke gemieden werden, die den Dichtekonstruktionen vor allem dann immanent sind, wenn der Begriff als gesellschafts- oder stadttheoretische Kausalität eingeführt oder als allgemeingültiges planerisches Instrument in Szene gesetzt wird.

35   Auch hierzu siehe: Roskamm: *Dichte*, S. 299–315 (wie Anm. 5).

1 Bebauungsgrad 0,5, FAR 4 Degree of development 0.5, FAR 4

Energy Parameters. Decisive for the energy-related assessment of a building is, on the one hand, embodied energy demand, and on the other, operational energy demand. For the area of embodied energy, the lowest energy expenditure for a three-story structure was ascertained based upon the relevant factors.[7] In the range of one to three stories, a reduction of the specific energy value becomes apparent, yet this development reverses in buildings with four or more stories, since the specific energy value tendentially increases the higher the building is (fig. 7). Such developments can be better understood by noting that in structures with, for example, less than three stories all expenditures for roof and foundation constructions are calculated at the expense of comparatively low gross floor area. The fact that a rise in embodied energy is seen in relation to the number of stories a building has can be explained by the higher demands placed on statics, framing, and façade, such as is felt in the case of higher wind loads. Furthermore, higher demands will inevitably be placed on building-mechanical systems like ventilation, elevators, and fire safety measures. These in turn generate a decreased ratio between useable floor area and gross floor area due to shafts and escape staircases of larger dimensions. Degrees of roof thickness can also increase as a result of the necessary installations. All specific embodied-energy values were calculated based upon a building life span of fifty years.

In the context of operating energy, parallel tendencies can be detected (fig. 8), where a lower number of stories can imply higher energy expenditures, for example because of a poor surface to volume (S/V) ratio. As building height increases, heightened operating and maintenance costs are to be expected thanks to stronger demands on building-mechanical systems like ventilation and elevators. Since operating energy will in future lose significance as compared to embodied energy thanks to continual optimizations, for this study the ratio between the two was defined as 33 percent embodied energy to 67 percent operating energy.

The relation between urban density and transport energy demand was evaluated based upon investigations conducted by Kenworthy and Laube[8] which provide an extensive database on the correlation between energy consumption via passenger transport and population density by example of a broad spectrum of cities. However, it is important to note that the transport values were assessed in the year 1990, and this area has in years since surely been subjected to strong shifts, thanks to both technological progress and sociopolitical developments.

zunehmender Gebäudehöhe der spezifische Energiekennwert tendenziell wieder steigt (Abb. 7). Diese Entwicklungen lassen sich dadurch erklären, dass beispielsweise unter drei Geschossen sämtliche Aufwendungen für Dach- und Fundamentkonstruktionen zulasten verhältnismäßig geringer Bruttogeschossflächen gerechnet werden. Dass es zu einem Anstieg der Herstellungsenergie in Abhängigkeit zur Geschossanzahl über drei Geschossen kommt, lässt sich aufgrund der höheren Anforderungen an Statik, Rohbau und Fassade – wie beispielsweise durch höhere Windlasten – erklären. Des Weiteren sind erhöhte Anforderungen an Gebäudetechnikausrüstung wie mechanische Lüftungsanlagen, Aufzüge und Brandschutzeinrichtungen zu erwarten. Diese wiederum verursachen ein schlechteres Nutzflächen- zu Bruttogeschossflächenverhältnis aufgrund größer dimensionierter Schächte und Fluchtstiegenhäuser. Auch Deckenstärken können aufgrund der notwendigen Installationen zunehmen. Sämtliche spezifischen Herstellungsenergiekennwerte wurden auf eine Lebensdauer des Gebäudes von 50 Jahren kalkuliert.

Im Bereich der Betriebsenergie lassen sich parallele Tendenzen feststellen (Abb. 8), wobei es bei niedrigeren Geschossanzahlen zu höheren energetischen Aufwendungen beispielsweise durch schlechte A/V-Verhältnisse kommen kann. Bei zunehmender Gebäudehöhe sind steigende Betriebs- und Wartungsaufwendungen durch höhere Anforderungen an Gebäudetechnik wie Lüftungs- und Aufzugsanlagen zu erwarten. Da die Betriebsenergie aufgrund ständiger Optimierungen gegenüber der Herstellungsenergie künftig an Bedeutung verlieren wird, wurde für die

> Betrachtet man die energetischen Absolutwerte, so zeigt sich, dass der Gesamtenergiebedarf bei höherem Bebauungsgrad mit steigender Dichte weniger stark zunimmt als bei geringerem Bebauungsgrad.

durchgeführten Untersuchungen ein Verhältnis von 33% Herstellungsenergie zu 67% Betriebsenergie definiert.

Der Zusammenhang zwischen urbaner Dichte und Verkehrsenergiebedarf wurde anhand der Untersuchungen von Kenworthy und Laube bewertet,[8] welche eine umfangreiche Datenbank der Abhängigkeit des Energieverbrauchs durch Personenverkehr zur Bevölkerungsdichte zahlreicher Städte bereitstellen. Allerdings muss festgehalten werden, dass die Verkehrswerte auf Basis des Jahres 1990 erhoben wurden, diese aber zwischenzeitlich sowohl aufgrund technologischer Fortschritte als auch gesellschaftspolitischer Entwicklungen vermutlich einem starken Wandel unterworfen waren. Es könnte bereits zu einer wesentlichen Abflachung des Verlaufes der Energiebedarfskurve gekommen sein, da einerseits westliche Länder ein gesteigertes Ökologiebewusstsein entwickelt haben und auf immer effizientere Fahrzeugflotten setzen, andererseits asiatische Länder einen wirtschaftlichen Aufschwung durchleben, und daher mit einer Zunahme des Verkehrsaufkommens zu rechnen ist. Da für den Bereich Verkehr schließlich keine

7   See G. J. Treloar et al., "An analysis of the embodied energy of office buildings by height," *Facilities* 19, no. 5/6 (2001), pp. 204–14; Lu Aye et al., "Optimising Embodied Energy in Commercial Office Development," *COBRA* (1999), RICS Foundation, pp. 217–23.

8   See Kenworthy and Laube, *An International Sourcebook* (note 5), pp. 421–526, esp. 551.

8   Vgl. Kenworthy/Laube: *An International Sourcebook*, S. 421–526, 551 (wie Anm. 5).

Werte für die Herstellungsenergie verfügbar sind, wurden 20% des Betriebsenergiebedarfs angenommen (Abb. 9).

Im Bereich der gebäudeintegrierten Energieproduktion (Abb. 3) wurden eigenständige Untersuchungen mittels Simulationen durchgeführt, deren Ergebnisse zeigen, dass bei steigender Dichte der Einfluss der gegenseitigen Verschattung der Gebäude auf den Energieertrag – im Gegensatz zum Verhältnis von Kollektorfläche zu Geschossfläche – nur von untergeordneter Bedeutung ist. Für PV-Anlagen wurde, mit einem Wirkungsgrad von 15% und unter Berücksichtigung der Herstellungsenergie der Module, ein spezifischer Energieertrag von 132 kWh/m².a angesetzt. Turbinen der Windkraftanlagen mit Rotordurchmessern von 100 m liefern bei jährlicher durchschnittlicher Windgeschwindigkeit von 5 m/s und unter Berücksichtigung der Herstellungsenergie einen Ertrag von 14 kWh/m².a.[9] Die Herstellungsenergie wurde in beiden Fällen mit einem Erntefaktor von 5 berechnet, wodurch sich der Ertrag um 20% verringerte. Der Primärenergiefaktor für Strom wurde mit 3 angenommen und als Belegungsgrad der aktivierbaren Flächen wurden 66% gewählt.

Zur Bewertung des Einflusses der Lebensmittelproduktion auf den Gesamtflächenbedarf einer Stadt wurde ein Zehntel der derzeit durchschnittlich notwendigen fruchtbaren Landfläche von 2.600 m²/P angenommen.[10] Diese massive Reduktion ist auf das „Vertical Farm"-Konzept zurückzuführen, welches durch Stapelung der Anbauflächen nach dem Prinzip konventioneller Gewächshäuser entwickelt und bereits in Seoul realisiert wurde.[11] Der Produktionsertrag ist äquivalent zur Deckung des täglichen Kalorienbedarfs einer Person, dies bedeutet aber nicht, dass eine vollständig ausgewogene Ernährung gewährleistet ist.

Die Einbeziehung der angeführten Parameter zur Erstellung des energetischen Gesamtbildes einer Stadt ermöglicht eine duale Betrachtungsweise des optimalen Grades urbaner Dichte, einerseits aus dem Blickwinkel des Gesamtenergiebedarfs und andererseits aus der Perspektive des Gesamtflächenbedarfs.

Zusammenhang zwischen Gesamtenergie- und Gesamtflächenbedarf sowie räumlicher Dichte einer Stadt. Die Ergebnisse der Untersuchungen zeigen, dass der niedrigste Gesamtenergiebedarf, unabhängig vom Frei- bzw. Grünraumanteil einer Stadt, in den Bereich einer Bebauungsdichte von FAR 2 bis 3 fällt. Dies entspricht in Abhängigkeit zum jeweiligen Bebauungsgrad einer durchschnittlichen Anzahl von vier bis zwölf Geschossen. Betrachtet man die energetischen Absolutwerte, so zeigt sich, dass der Gesamtenergiebedarf bei höherem Bebauungsgrad mit steigender Dichte weniger stark zunimmt als bei geringerem Bebauungsgrad. Diese Tatsache lässt sich durch die geringere Geschossanzahl höherer Bebauungsgrade bei konstanter Bebauungsdichte erklären (Abb. 11).

Schaut man sich den Gesamtflächenbedarf der untersuchten Stadtmodelle an – bestehend aus urbanisiertem Stadtteil, welcher der Summe aus Bauland, Frei- und Verkehrsflächen entspricht, sowie dem Landflächenbe-

This may already imply that a significant flattening of the energy demand curve has been evolving, especially considering, for one, that Western countries have acquired a stronger awareness of ecology which includes a focus on increasingly efficient vehicle fleets, but also that Asian countries are experiencing an economic upswing which makes it probable that traffic volume is on the rise. Since no up-to-date embodied-energy figures are available for transportation, a value of 20 percent of the operating energy demand has been assumed for this study (fig. 9).

In the area of building-integrated energy production (fig. 3), independent experiments using simulations have been conducted, the results of which show that when density grows, the influence of the reciprocal shadowing of the buildings on energy gain—as opposed to the ratio between collector surface to floor space—is only of secondary importance. For PV systems—with a coefficient of performance (COP) of 15 percent and also taking the embodied energy of the module into consideration—a specific energy yield of 132 kWh/m².a was estimated. Turbines in wind power plants with blade diameters of 100 meters yield 14 kWh/m².a at an annual average wind speed of 5m/s and allowing for embodied energy.[9] In both cases, embodied energy has been calculated with a harvesting factor of 5, which causes a 20 percent reduction in energy yielded. The primary energy factor for electricity was assumed to be 3 and a utilization factor of 66 percent was taken for activable spaces.

In evaluating the influence of food production on the total land area use of a city, one tenth of the fertile land area currently necessary on average, 2,600 m²/P, has been assumed.[10] This massive reduction is attributable to the "vertical farm" concept that was developed by stacking cultivation acreage according to the principle of conventional greenhouses, as has already been realized in Seoul.[11] The production output is equivalent to what is needed to cover the daily caloric requirements of a single person, though without implying that a completely balanced diet would be ensured.

Integrating the aforementioned parameters for creating the energy-related overall picture of a city opens a dual approach to viewing the optimal level of urban density: on the one hand, from the vantage point of total energy demand and, on the other, from the perspective of total land area use.

Correlation between Total Energy Demand and Total Land Area Use as well as Spatial Density of a City. The re-

9   Vgl. Sinisa Stankovic/Neil Campell/Alan Harries: *Urban Wind Energy*, London 2009, S. 34.

10   Vgl. Dickson Despommier: *The Vertical Farm. Feeding the World in the 21ˢᵗ Century*, New York 2010, S. 82.

11   Vgl. Fabian Kretschmer: „Ackerbau im Hochhaus", in: *Der Standard*, 26.5.2011, S. 10.

9   See Sinisa Stankovic, Neil Campell, and Alan Harries, *Urban Wind Energy* (London, 2009), p. 34.

10   See Dickson Despommier, *The Vertical Farm: Feeding the World in the 21ˢᵗ Century* (New York, 2010), p. 82.

11   See Fabian Kretschmer, "Ackerbau im Hochhaus," *Der Standard*, May 26, 2011, p. 10.

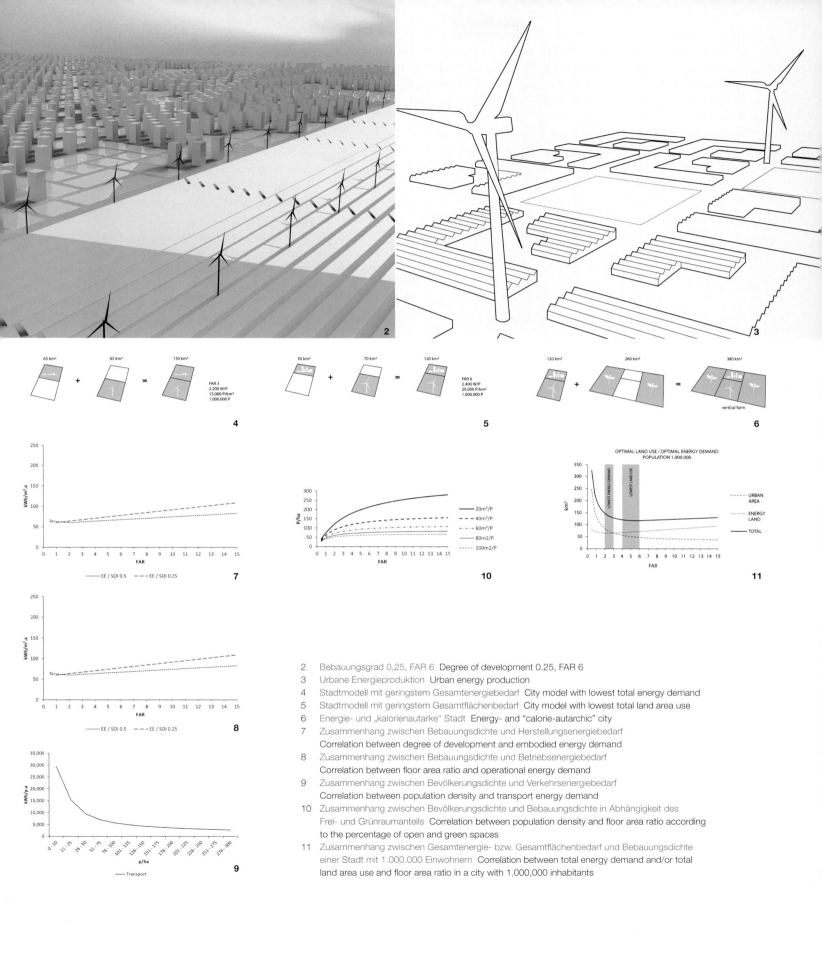

2

3

65 km³ + 65 km³ = 130 km³
FAR 3
2.200 W/P
15.000 P/km³
1.000.000 P

4

50 km³ + 70 km³ = 120 km³
FAR 6
2.400 W/P
20.000 P/km³
1.000.000 P

5

120 km³ + 260 km³ = 380 km³
vertical farm

6

kWh/m².a — FAR
------- EE / SOI 0.5   ---- EE / SOI 0.25

7

P/ha — FAR
— 20m²/P
--- 40m²/P
-·- 60m²/P
-··- 80m2/P
···· 100m2/P

10

OPTIMAL LAND USE / OPTIMAL ENERGY DEMAND
POPULATION 1.000.000
km² — FAR
LOWEST ENERGY DEMAND   LOWEST LAND USE
--- URBAN AREA
···· ENERGY LAND
— TOTAL

11

kWh/m².a — FAR
------- EE / SOI 0.5   ---- EE / SOI 0.25

8

kWh/p.a — p/ha
— Transport

9

2   Bebauungsgrad 0,25, FAR 6 Degree of development 0.25, FAR 6
3   Urbane Energieproduktion Urban energy production
4   Stadtmodell mit geringstem Gesamtenergiebedarf City model with lowest total energy demand
5   Stadtmodell mit geringstem Gesamtflächenbedarf City model with lowest total land area use
6   Energie- und „kalorienautarke" Stadt Energy- and "calorie-autarchic" city
7   Zusammenhang zwischen Bebauungsdichte und Herstellungsenergiebedarf
     Correlation between degree of development and embodied energy demand
8   Zusammenhang zwischen Bebauungsdichte und Betriebsenergiebedarf
     Correlation between floor area ratio and operational energy demand
9   Zusammenhang zwischen Bevölkerungsdichte und Verkehrsenergiebedarf
     Correlation between population density and transport energy demand
10   Zusammenhang zwischen Bevölkerungsdichte und Bebauungsdichte in Abhängigkeit des
     Frei- und Grünraumanteils Correlation between population density and floor area ratio according
     to the percentage of open and green spaces
11   Zusammenhang zwischen Gesamtenergie- bzw. Gesamtflächenbedarf und Bebauungsdichte
     einer Stadt mit 1.000.000 Einwohnern Correlation between total energy demand and/or total
     land area use and floor area ratio in a city with 1,000,000 inhabitants

darf für Energieproduktion zur vollständigen Bedarfsabdeckung mittels regenerativer Energiequellen – so liegen die Optima in einem wesentlich höheren Bebauungsdichtebereich von FAR 4 bis 6. Dies entspricht einer durchschnittlichen Anzahl von acht Geschossen bei einem Bebauungsgrad von 0,5 bis hin zu 24 Geschossen bei einem Bebauungsgrad von 0,25 (Abb. 11).

Abbildung 10 veranschaulicht schließlich die den Ergebnissen zugrundeliegenden Zusammenhänge zwischen Bevölkerungsdichte – ausgedrückt in Personen pro Hektar – und Bebauungsdichte. Generell können Aussagen hinsichtlich der Gesamtenergieeffizienz eines Stadtmodells nur durch eine Kombination der beiden Parameter getroffen werden, da als Extrembeispiel eine Bebauungsdichte mit FAR 10 – in Abhängigkeit der Dimension der öffentlichen Freiräume zwischen 20 m²/P und 100 m²/P – sowohl ca. 65 P/ha als auch 250 P/ha bedeuten kann. Dies wiederum hat einen wesentlichen Einfluss auf die flächige Ausbreitung einer Stadt und somit auf den Energiebedarf durch den Verkehrssektor.

Energieoptimierung versus Flächenoptimierung. Es zeigt sich, dass die untersuchten Stadtmodelle mit dem geringsten Gesamtenergiebedarf unter Berücksichtigung der regenerativen Energieproduktionsflächen nicht den geringsten Gesamtflächenbedarf aufweisen. Grund dafür ist, dass Städte mittlerer Bebauungsdichte zwar einen geringeren Energiebedarf als hoch verdichtete Städte aufweisen und daher auch geringere Energielandflächen benötigen (Abb. 4), allerdings die Landflächeneinsparung der urbanisierten Stadtfläche bei höheren Bebauungsdichten größer ist als die Einsparung im Bereich des Energielandes bei geringerer Bebauungsdichte. Somit ist die Gesamtstadtfläche bei hohen

> Unter den angenommenen Bedingungen bedeutet dies, dass das energetische Optimum im Bereich einer Bevölkerungsdichte von ca. 15.000 Personen pro km² erreicht ist.

Bebauungsdichten (FAR 4–6) geringer als bei niedrigen (FAR 0,5–1,5), mittleren (FAR 2–3) und extremen (FAR > 6) (Abb. 5).

Unter den angenommenen Bedingungen bedeutet dies, dass das energetische Optimum im Bereich einer Bevölkerungsdichte von ca. 15.000 Personen pro km² erreicht ist. Aufgrund der Notwendigkeit, dass Städte zukünftig ihren erforderlichen Energiebedarf selbst zu decken haben, werden die dafür notwendigen regenerativen Energielandflächen zu einem integralen Bestandteil von urbanen Systemen. Ein Ziel zukunftsfähiger Stadtplanung besteht daher in einer flächenbezogenen Optimierung, wodurch es durchaus zu einer Verschiebung zu höheren Bevölkerungsdichten bis ca. 20.000 Personen pro km² kommen kann. Bezieht man zusätzlich zur Energieproduktion auch eine Abdeckung des notwendigen Lebensmittelbedarfs der städtischen Bevölkerung in die Betrachtungen mit ein, so ergibt sich eine Flächenverteilung von ca. 65% für Nahrungsmittelproduktion, 20% für Energiebereitstellung und 15% für urbanisierte Flächen. Diese Verteilung erfordert einen Gesamtflächenzuwachs der Stadt von über 200% (Abb. 6).

sults of these explorations demonstrate how the lowest total energy demand—irrespective of the percentage of a city's open and green spaces—lies in the floor area ratio range of FAR 2 to 3. This equates to an average number of four to twelve stories, depending upon the respective degree of development. If we consider the energy-related absolute values, it becomes apparent that the total energy demand rises less strongly with a higher degree of development characterized by growing density than in the opposite case with a lower development degree. This fact is explainable through the smaller number of stories found in higher development scenarios at a constant level of floor area ratio (fig. 11).

If we consider the total land area use of the city models investigated—comprised of an urbanized city district, which equates to the sum of building plots and areas dedicated to open land and transport, as well as of land area use for energy production with demands completely met by renewable energy sources—the optima lie in a considerably higher floor area ratio range of FAR 4 to 6. This reflects results spanning from an average number of eight stories at a degree of development of 0.5 all the way to twenty-four stories at a development degree of 0.25 (fig. 11).

Finally, figure 10 illustrates the results of underlying associations between population density (expressed as person per hectare) and floor area ratio. Generally speaking, assertions can only be made about the total energy efficiency of a city model by combining these two parameters, since, to cite an extreme example, a floor area ratio of FAR 10—depending on the dimensions of public open spaces ranging between 20 m²/P and 100 m²/P—can mean either 65 P/ha or 250 P/ha. This, in turn, exerts substantial influence on the planar expansion of a city and thus on the energy demand engendered in the transportation sector.

Energy Optimization versus Land Optimization. As it turns out, the city models examined that demonstrated the lowest total energy demand, while taking renewable energy production spaces into account, do not count among those with the lowest total land area use. The reason for this is that medium density cities have lower energy demand than high density cities and therefore require less land for energy production (fig. 4), however, the reduction of urbanized land area achieved in high density structures is larger than the savings in the area of land for energy production at lower densities. Thus, the entire city area proves to be lower when floor area ratios are high (FAR 4–6) than when they are low (FAR 0.5–1.5), mid-range (FAR 2–3), or extreme (FAR > 6) (fig. 5).

Under the factors adopted here, this means that the energy-related optimum has been attained for the range of population density of ca. 15,000 people per km². Because of the necessity in future for cities to meet their own required energy

demands, the related renewable energy-producing land areas will eventually become an integral component of urban systems. A goal of sustainable urban planning therefore lies in the optimization of specific stretches of land, whereby this could potentially amount to a shift to even higher population densities of up to ca. 20,000 people per km². If, in addition to energy production, we also factor into our considerations the coverage of food demand necessary for an urban population, then a distribution of space of ca. 65 percent for food production, 20 percent for energy supply, and 15 percent for urbanized spaces results. This distribution would necessitate a total land area growth for cities of over 200 percent (fig. 6). Critical, therefore, is an integrated approach at a regional planning level as the fundamental requirement for a functional metabolism of a "Post-Oil City,"[12] an approach that goes hand in hand with urban planning ensuring that the systemic boundaries of the city do not end along the actual political borders. Despite possible vagueness in hypothetical city models, the results of this study clearly show that sustainable city planning that takes energy-related factors into consideration displays a tendency toward highly densified urban structures. However, extreme density from the perspective of space efficiency at today's energy standards does not appear sensible, for economization in the areas of transportation and urbanized city space are relativized by additional expenditures in the building sector.

In fact, a further reduction in total land area use of a city could ensue through the integration of necessary energy-production elements on a district level, whereby this would be accompanied by additional synergetic effects, ranging from the reduction of distribution losses to the substitution of structural components in the building sector. Such a vantage point on energy supply within an integral urban system thus fosters a completely new role for the individual structure as part of a whole within this architectural scale: the building becomes a power plant.

Translation Dawn Michelle d'Atri

Es bedarf somit eines ganzheitlichen Ansatzes auf der Ebene der Regionalplanung als grundlegende Voraussetzung für einen funktionsfähigen Metabolismus einer „Post Oil City"[12] und damit einer Stadtplanung, die die Systemgrenzen der Stadt nicht an ihren durch Ortstafeln manifestierten politischen Grenzen enden lässt. Trotz möglicher Unschärfen hypothetischer Stadtmodelle zeigen die Ergebnisse dieser Studie eindeutig, dass zukunftsfähiger Städtebau unter Berücksichtigung der energetischen Faktoren in Richtung hochverdichteter Stadtstrukturen tendiert. Allerdings erscheint eine extreme Verdichtung aus Sicht der Flächeneffizienz bei heutigen Energiestandards nicht sinnvoll, da die Einsparungen in den Bereichen Verkehr und urbanisierte Stadtfläche durch die Mehraufwendungen im Bereich des Gebäudesektors relativiert werden.

Vielmehr könnte eine weitere Reduktion des Gesamtflächenbedarfs einer Stadt durch Integration der notwendigen Energieproduktionselemente auf Quartiersebene erfolgen, wodurch es zu zusätzlichen Synergieeffekten wie der Verringerung von Leitungsverlusten bis hin zur Substitution von Bauteilen im Gebäudebereich kommt. Eine derartige Betrachtung der Energiebereitstellung innerhalb eines urbanen Gesamtsystems gibt somit dem Einzelobjekt als Teil des Ganzen eine völlig neue Rolle auf dieser architektonischen Maßstabsebene: das Gebäude wird zum Kraftwerk.

1 Samariterviertel im Bezirk Friedrichshain-Kreuzberg von Berlin, Überfliegung vom 24.Juli 2001 Samariterviertel in the district Friedrichshain-Kreuzberg of Berlin, overflight on July 24, 2001
Fotograf **photographer**: Sven Treder © STATTBAU Stadtentwicklungsgesellschaft mbH Berlin

Wann führt Dichte zu Beengung?

Eine empirische Studie zu Wahrnehmung und Bewertung von Bebauungsdichte

Der Begriff *Dichte* ist sowohl im architekturhistorischen Rückblick auf städtebauliche Typologien als auch aus umweltpsychologischer Perspektive betrachtet ambivalent besetzt. Eine große Zahl von Verhaltensoptionen für Stadtnutzer und die sich daraus ergebende lebensräumliche Vielfalt sind positive Konnotationen von baulicher Dichte. Räumliche Beschränkung und daraus resultierende Beengung stehen dem hingegen als negative Assoziationen von Bebauungsdichte gegenüber (Abb. 1).

When Does Density Lead to Crowding? An Empirical Study on the Perception and Judgment of Building Density.
The term *density* carries ambivalent connotations, both in retrospectively considering urban-development typologies from an architectural, historical perspective and in the context of environmental psychology. Positive significations of structural density include the large number of behavioral options for city users and the resulting diversity in living environments. Spatial restrictions and the crowding that ensues count among the contrasting negative associations of building density (fig. 1).

MARTIN BRUCKS

Bauliche Verdichtungsprozesse, die infolge der industriellen Revolution im ausgehenden 19. Jahrhundert eine rasante Dynamik entwickelten, hatten zugleich viele negative Konsequenzen. Die Lebensbedingungen in den Mietshäusern der Berliner Arbeiterbezirke waren durch Überbelegung der Wohneinheiten und schlechte hygienische Bedingungen geprägt. Die „Mietskaserne" wurde zu einem weit über die Stadtgrenzen hinaus bekannten Begriff. Durch Anpassung der Baugesetzgebung wurde versucht, den Verdichtungsprozess zu regulieren – insbesondere durch die Festlegung von Obergrenzen der baulichen Nutzung. Mit der Bauordnung von 1925 wurde in Berlin schließlich der Bau von Hinterwohngebäuden gänzlich verboten. Eine Reaktion darauf war die mit geringerer baulicher Ausnutzung verbundene städtebauliche Typologie der Zeilenbebauung.[1]

Im gegenwärtigen architektonischen und städtebaulichen Diskurs hingegen ist Dichte ein höchst positiv besetzter Begriff. Eingeleitet durch Konzepte der behutsamen Stadterneuerung[2] sowie der Kritischen Rekonstruktion[3] in den 1980er Jahren gewann die kompakte europäische Stadt wieder städtebaulichen Leitbildcharakter. Wichtige Merkmale dieses Leitbildes sind die funktionale Mischung, kurze Wege, Stärkung des öffentlichen Nahverkehrs bei gleichzeitiger Reduzierung des motorisierten Individualverkehrs sowie eine Erhöhung von Bebauungs- und Einwohnerdichte.[4] Der vielerorts durch Konzepte funktionaler Trennung der 1950er und 1960er Jahre bedingte Mangel an Urbanität soll damit überwunden werden. Die zu Beginn des 20. Jahrhunderts in Misskredit geratene Bautypologie des Berliner Mietshauses ist im ehemaligen Berliner Arbeiterbezirk Prenzlauer Berg heute essenzieller Bestandteil der Lebenskultur wohlsituierter Großstadtbürger.

Daraus wird ersichtlich, dass bei der Bewertung von baulicher Dichte die Reduktion auf eine Bautypologie sowie auf quantitative räumliche Faktoren unzulässige Verkürzungen darstellen würden. In Übereinstimmung damit steht, dass umweltpsychologische Studien einerseits negative Einflüsse von räumlicher Begrenztheit auf Wohnzufriedenheit und Gesundheit von Stadtnutzern nachweisen konnten.[5] Andererseits wird der baulich verdichtete Lebensraum „Stadt" aufgrund seiner zahlreichen Handlungsmöglichkeiten und Verhaltensoptionen für dessen Bewohner positiv bewertet.[6] Deshalb müssen die Bedingungen näher spezifiziert werden, unter denen bauliche *Dichte* zu *Beengung* führen kann.

Umweltpsychologische Crowding-Forschung. Das Forschungsfeld innerhalb der Psychologie, welches die Wirkung hoher sozialer und räumlicher Dichte auf menschliches Erleben und Verhalten thematisiert, wird

Architectural processes of densification, which developed a rapid dynamic owing to the Industrial Revolution toward the close of the nineteenth century, were simultaneously accompanied by various negative consequences. The living conditions in the tenement buildings of Berlin labor districts, for instance, were characterized by overcrowding within the housing units and by poor hygiene. *Mietskaserne*, or "tenement barracks," came to be a commonly known expression far beyond Berlin's city limits. Attempts were made at regulating the process of densification through adjustments to building legislation—especially through the stipulation of ceilings for building use. With the building regulations of 1925, the erection of backyard housing units was ultimately completely prohibited in Berlin. One reaction to this was the urban-development typology of terraced housing, which entailed a lower ratio of building use.[1]

In present-day architectural and urban-development discourse, in contrast, density is a term with strong positive connotations. Introduced in the 1980s through concepts of cautious urban renewal[2] as well as through critical reconstruction,[3] the compact European city once again acquired model character in terms of urban development. Important features of this paradigm include short distances, a blend of functionality, strengthening of local public transport accompanied by a concurrent reduction of individual motor-vehicle traffic, as well as an increase in building and population density.[4] This was meant to overcome the dearth of urbanity, caused by the conception of functional separation, as seen during the 1950s and 1960s in many locations. The building typology of the Berlin tenement building, which in the early twentieth century had fallen into disrepute, is today an essential part of the lifestyle culture of well-to-do metropolitan residents in Prenzlauer Berg, a onetime workers' district.

This goes to show that if we were to reduce our assessment of structural density to one single building typology or to quantitative spatial factors, then unreliable gaps would result. Correlating with this is the fact that studies on environmental psychology have demonstrated, on the one hand, a negative impact on living contentment and health in urban

1   Vgl. Hans Förster: „Die Entwicklung des Baurechts in Berlin seit der Jahrhundertwende", in: *Berlin und seine Bauten*, Teil II, Berlin 1964, S. 1–9.

2   Vgl. Hardt-Waltherr Hämer/Karl Ganser u.a. (Hg.): *Internationale Bauausstellung Berlin und behutsame Stadterneuerung. Hilfe für Menschen und Stadtteile im Wandel*. Dortmund 1995.

3   Vgl. Heidede Becker/Johann Jessen/Robert Sander (Hg.): *Ohne Leitbild? Städtebau in Deutschland und Europa*. Stuttgart/Zürich 1998.

4   Vgl. Dieter Apel/Michael Lehmbrock u.a.: *Kompakt, mobil, urban. Stadtentwicklungskonzepte zur Verkehrsvermeidung im internationalen Vergleich*, Berlin 1997.

5   Vgl. Paul A. Bell/Thomas C. Greene u.a.: *Environmental Psychology* (5. Aufl.), Fort Worth 2001; Lenelis Kruse/Carl-Friedrich Graumann/Ernst-Dieter Lantermann (Hg.): *Ökologische Psychologie. Ein Handbuch in Schlüsselbegriffen*, Weinheim 1996.

6   Vgl. Maria Amérigo/Juan Ignacio Aragonés: „A Theoretical and Methodological Approach to the Study of Residential Satisfaction", in: *Journal of Environmental Psychology*, 17, 1 (1997), S. 47–57.

1   See Hans Förster, "Die Entwicklung des Baurechts in Berlin seit der Jahrhundertwende," in *Berlin und seine Bauten*, Part II (Berlin, 1964), pp. 1–9.

2   See Hardt-Waltherr Hämer and Karl Ganser et al. (eds.), *Internationale Bauausstellung Berlin und behutsame Stadterneuerung: Hilfe für Menschen und Stadtteile im Wandel* (Dortmund, 1995).

3   See Heidede Becker, Johann Jessen, and Robert Sander (eds.), *Ohne Leitbild? Städtebau in Deutschland und Europa* (Stuttgart and Zurich, 1998).

4   See Dieter Apel and Michael Lehmbrock et al., *Kompakt, mobil, urban: Stadtentwicklungskonzepte zur Verkehrsvermeidung im internationalen Vergleich* (Berlin, 1997).

residents as stemming from limited space.[5] On the other hand, the structurally densified living space of "the city" has been positively noted by city residents due to its many opportunities for engaging in activities and for behavioral options.[6] Therefore, the conditions under which structural *density* could potentially foster *crowding* need to be explored in more detail.

Research on Crowding in Environmental Psychology.
The research field within psychology that thematizes the effects of heightened social and spatial density on human experience and behavior is summarized under the umbrella term "crowding." Here crowding is defined as the subjective experience of confinement as a result of a discrepancy between available and desired space.[7] Differentiated from this is perceived density as a value-neutral estimation of density conditions that objectively exist within the environment.[8] The experience of crowding involves an emotional and thus evaluative assessment of the situation. From an application-oriented vantage point, the *evaluative perspective* on the experience of crowding, as applied to the construct of building density so important for planning, is of particular relevance.

Crowding research counts among the most comprehensive research fields at the junction between environmental and social psychology.[9] And the English root word "crowd" references the sociopsychological origins of this line of research. Yet crowding research goes beyond a focus on social processes. Equally explored are the identification of spatial influencing factors and the description of *antecedent conditions* for facilitating the human experience of crowding. However, precisely those spatial influencing factors relevant to the creation of a crowding experience in outdoor space have not yet been adequately analyzed.[10]

City planning that is oriented to resident needs indeed must pose the question: How can urban-development densification measures be configured in a way that allows residents to feel comfortable despite high structural density? This is a question that must be collaboratively answered by architects,

unter dem Sammelbegriff *crowding* zusammengefasst. Dabei ist *crowding* als subjektives Erleben von Beengung infolge einer Diskrepanz zwischen verfügbarem und erwünschtem Raum definiert.[7] Davon unterschieden wird die wahrgenommene Dichte (*perceived density*) als wertfreie Einschätzung der objektiv in der Umwelt gegebenen Dichtebedingungen.[8] Beim Beengungserleben handelt es sich um ein emotionales und damit wertendes Urteil. Aus anwendungsbezogener Sicht ist die auf das planungsrelevante Konstrukt Bebauungsdichte bezogene *evaluative Perspektive* des Beengungsurteils von ganz besonderem Interesse.

Die *Crowding*-Forschung gehört zu den umfangreichsten Forschungsgebieten im Schnittbereich von Umwelt- und Sozialpsychologie.[9] Die Ableitung vom englischen Begriff *crowd* für Menschenmenge verweist dabei auf den sozialpsychologischen Ursprung dieser Forschungsrichtung. Jedoch werden in der *Crowding*-Forschung nicht nur soziale Prozesse fokussiert. Gleichermaßen sind auch die Identifizierung von *räumlichen* Einflussfaktoren sowie die Beschreibung von *Antezedenzbedingungen* für die Entstehung menschlichen Beengungserlebens eingeschlossen. Doch gerade die für das Entstehen von Beengungserleben im Außenraum maßgeblichen räumlichen Einflussfaktoren sind bisher nur unzureichend untersucht.[10]

Eine an Nutzerbedürfnissen orientierte Stadtplanung muss jedoch die Frage stellen: Wie können städtebauliche Verdichtungsmaßnahmen gestaltet sein, so dass sich Nutzer trotz hoher baulicher Dichte dort wohl fühlen? Eine Frage, die Architekten, Stadtplaner und Umweltpsychologen gemeinsam zu beantworten haben. Zunächst soll hier daher betrachtet werden, wie Bebauungsdichte in der städtebaulichen Planungspraxis reguliert wird.

Ausgangspunkte und Ziele der empirischen Untersuchung. Ein erster wichtiger Ausgangspunkt für die in der empirischen Studie zu fokussierenden Einflussfaktoren ist eine Betrachtung der Parameter, die der Bebauungs-

> Aus anwendungsbezogener Sicht ist die auf das planungsrelevante Konstrukt Bebauungsdichte bezogene *evaluative Perspektive* des Beengungsurteils von ganz besonderem Interesse.

dichteregulation in der gegenwärtigen städtebaulichen Planungspraxis zugrunde liegen. In städtischen Quartieren sind dabei bauliche Ausnutzungsmaße sowie Regelungen über einzuhaltende Abstandsflächen von unmittelbarer Bedeutung. Ausnutzungsmaße sind als Verhältniszahl definiert, bei der jeweils die Ausprägung eines baulichen Parameters (z.B. gebaute Fläche, gebautes Volumen) ins Verhältnis zu einer flächenräumlichen Bezugs-

5   See Paul A. Bell and Thomas C. Greene et al., *Environmental Psychology*, 5th ed. (Fort Worth, 2001); Lenelis Kruse, Carl-Friedrich Graumann, and Ernst-Dieter Lantermann (eds.), *Ökologische Psychologie: Ein Handbuch in Schlüsselbegriffen* (Weinheim, 1996).

6   See Maria Amérigo and Juan Ignacio Aragonés, "A Theoretical and Methodological Approach to the Study of Residential Satisfaction," *Journal of Environmental Psychology* 17, no. 1 (1997), pp. 47–57.

7   See Robert Gifford, *Environmental Psychology: Principles and Practice*, 3rd ed. (1987; repr., Colville, WA, 2002).

8   See Amos Rapoport, "Toward a Redefinition of Density," *Environment and Behavior* 7, no. 2 (1975), pp. 133–58.

9   See Jürgen Schultz-Gambard, "Dichte und Enge," in Kruse, Graumann, and Lantermann, *Ökologische Psychologie* (note 5), pp. 339–46.

10 See Anna Husemann, *Die Wahrnehmung und Bewertung von verdichteten Stadtquartieren* (Berlin, 2005).

7   Vgl. Robert Gifford: *Environmental Psychology. Principles and Practice* (3. Aufl.). Colville 2002.

8   Vgl. Amos Rapoport: „Toward a Redefinition of Density", in: *Environment and Behavior* 7, 2 (1975), S. 133–158.

9   Vgl. Jürgen Schultz-Gambard: „Dichte und Enge", in: Lenelis Kruse/Carl-Friedrich Graumann/Ernst-Dieter Lantermann (Hg.): *Ökologische Psychologie. Ein Handbuch in Schlüsselbegriffen*. Weinheim 1996, S. 339–346.

10 Vgl. Anna Husemann: *Die Wahrnehmung und Bewertung von verdichteten Stadtquartieren*, Berlin 2005.

Die rein quantitative Natur
der Regulierungsparameter hat
jedoch notwendigerweise zur Folge,
dass mögliche *qualitative* räumliche
Einflussfaktoren durch diese Parameter
prinzipiell nicht erfasst werden.

city planners, and environmental psychologists. So to start off with, we will explore how building density is regulated in the practice of urban-development planning.

Points of Departure and Objectives of the Empirical Study. A first important point of departure for the influencing factors targeted by this empirical study is an overview of the parameters upon which building density regulation is based in the practice of today's urban-development planning. Of immediate importance in city districts are structural utilization levels as well as regulations on the space to be maintained between buildings. Utilization levels are defined as ratios, whereby the manifestation of an architectural parameter (e.g. area or volume of a structure) is set into relation to a spatial reference unit.[11] In the case of particular zoning areas, respective upper limits are defined for maximal allowed structural utilization based upon these ratios, while the parameter of space between buildings ensures that a minimum of interstitial space is maintained.

It is important to note that all of these dimensional determinations follow a purely *quantitative* understanding of space. The influence of these quantitative spatial dimensions has already been documented in empirical studies—for both inside space[12] and outside space.[13] However, the purely quantitative nature of these regulative parameters inevitably results in certain possible *qualitative* spatial influencing factors not being principally covered by the parameters.

In the case of indoor space, the impact of *qualitative* spatial factors on the experience of crowding has already been proven in empirical studies. Spaces with real or even just visual means of escape in the form of doors or windows are considered less confining.[14] Also, distances of interaction between individuals shift depending on the layout of a space as well as on the position of activity within this space: observable in square rooms are greater distances than in rectangular rooms of the same floor area. And during activities in room corners, larger distances are maintained than during those in the middle of a

einheit gesetzt wird.[11] Für bestimmte Baugebiete werden anhand dieser Größen dann entsprechende Obergrenzen der maximal zulässigen baulichen Ausnutzung festgelegt. Der Parameter der Abstandsfläche regelt die Einhaltung von Mindestabständen zwischen Gebäuden.

Festzuhalten ist, dass all diese Größen einem rein *quantitativen* räumlichen Verständnis folgen. Der Einfluss dieser quantitativen räumlichen Dimension ist bereits durch empirische Studien belegt – sowohl für den innenräumlichen Bereich[12] als auch für den Außenraum.[13] Die rein quantitative Natur der Regulierungsparameter hat jedoch notwendigerweise zur Folge, dass mögliche *qualitative* räumliche Einflussfaktoren durch diese Parameter prinzipiell nicht erfasst werden.

Für den Innenraumbereich konnte der Einfluss *qualitativer* Raummerkmale auf Beengungserleben bereits in empirischen Studien nachgewiesen werden. Räume mit realen oder auch visuellen Fluchtmöglichkeiten in Form von Türen oder Fenstern werden als weniger beengend empfunden.[14] Auch Interaktionsdistanzen von Personen verändern sich in Abhängigkeit vom Grundriss des Raumes sowie der Position der Aktivität innerhalb des Raumes: In quadratischen Räumen sind größere Distanzen beobachtbar als in rechteckigen Räumen gleicher Grundfläche. Bei Aktivitäten in Raumecken werden größere Distanzen eingehalten als in der Raummitte.[15] All diese Effekte werden interpretiert als Folge eines permanent bestehenden Bedürfnisses, sich Ausweich- und Fluchtmöglichkeiten freizuhalten. Es ist davon auszugehen, dass phylogenetische Determinierungen dafür ursächlich sind.[16]

Von großem Interesse ist nun die Frage, ob auch für den außenräumlichen Bereich vergleichbare Einflussfaktoren auszumachen sind. Ziel der Untersuchung war es deshalb, empirische Evidenz für den Einfluss des qualitativen räumlichen Faktors *Verfügbarkeit von Ausweich- und Fluchtmöglichkeiten* auf Beengungserleben im Außenraum zu finden. Bisher liegen dazu keine empirischen Befunde vor.

Darüber hinaus interessierte, ob es Differenzen zwischen Planern und Nutzern in der Bewertung von architektonischen bzw. städtebaulichen Teilmerkmalen hinsichtlich Beengung gibt, da solche Unterschiede unmittelbar planungsrelevant wären.

Bezug auf psychologische Konzepte und Modellvorstellungen. Modelltheoretisch wird zunächst auf die integrativen *Crowding*-Ansätze von

11   For example, site occupancy index (SOI), floor area ratio (FAR), or cubic index. See Elisabeth Lichtenberger, *Stadtgeographie: Begriffe, Konzepte, Modelle, Prozesse*, vol. 1 (Stuttgart and Leipzig, 1998), p. 97.

12   See Eric Sundstrom, "Crowding as a Sequential Process: Review of Research on the Effects of Population Density on Humans," in Andrew Baum and Yakov M. Epstein (eds.), *Human Response to Crowding* (Hillsdale, 1978), pp. 13–116.

13   See Husemann, *Wahrnehmung und Bewertung von verdichteten Stadtquartieren* (note 10); Elke van der Meer and Martin Brucks et al., "Human perception of urban environment and consequences for its design," in Wilfried Endlicher and Patrick Hostert et al. (eds.) *Perspectives in Urban Ecology: Ecosystems and Interactions between Humans and Nature in the Metropolis of Berlin* (Berlin, Heidelberg, and New York, 2011), pp. 305–32.

14   See Lou McClelland and Nathan Auslander, "Perceptions of Crowding and Pleasantness in Public Settings," *Environment and Behavior* 10, no. 4 (1978), pp. 535–53.

11   Z.B. Grundflächenzahl (GRZ), Geschossflächenzahl (GFZ) oder Baumassenzahl (BMZ), vgl. Elisabeth Lichtenberger: *Stadtgeographie. Begriffe, Konzepte, Modelle, Prozesse*, Bd. 1, Stuttgart/Leipzig 1998, S. 97.

12   Vgl. Eric Sundstrom: „Crowding as a Sequential Process: Review of Research on the Effects of Population Density on Humans", in: Andrew Baum/Yakov M. Epstein (Hg.): *Human Response to Crowding*, Hillsdale 1978, S. 13–116.

13   Vgl. Husemann: *Wahrnehmung und Bewertung von verdichteten Stadtquartieren* (wie Anm. 10); Elke van der Meer/Martin Brucks u.a.: „Human Perception of Urban Environment and Consequences for its Design", in: Wilfried Endlicher/Patrick Hostert u.a. (Hg.): *Perspectives in Urban Ecology – Ecosystems and Interactions between Humans and Nature in the Metropolis of Berlin*, Berlin/Heidelberg/New York 2011, S. 305–332.

14   Vgl. Lou McClelland/Nathan Auslander: „Perceptions of Crowding and Pleasantness in Public Settings", in: *Environment and Behavior* 10, 4 (1978), S. 535–553.

15   Vgl. Gay H. Tennis/James M. Dabbs: „Sex, Setting and Personal Space: First Grade Through College", in: *Sociometry* 38, 3 (1975), S. 385–394.

16   Vgl. Irenäus Eibl-Eibesfeldt/Hans Hass: „Sozialer Wohnbau und Umstrukturierung der Städte aus biologischer Sicht", in: Irenäus Eibl-Eibesfeldt (Hg.): *Stadt und Lebensqualität: Neue Konzepte im Wohnbau auf dem Prüfstand der Humanethologie und der Bewohnerurteile*, Stuttgart 1985, S. 49–84.

Gifford[17] und Bell u.a.[18] Bezug genommen, welche viele zuvor entwickelte Theorien zur Erklärung von Beengungserleben in sich zu vereinen versuchen.

Als Einflusskategorien werden von Gifford physikalische Umweltfaktoren, soziale Faktoren und Persönlichkeitsfaktoren beschrieben. Innerhalb der physikalischen Umweltfaktoren benennt er als Einflussfaktoren neben der Quantität verfügbaren Raumes auch *qualitative* räumliche Faktoren („*arrangement of space*"[19]) sowie weitere physikalische Umweltfaktoren wie Klima und Lärm. Für den vorliegenden empirischen Ansatz ist dabei wesentlich, dass in Giffords Modell *qualitativen* räumlichen Faktoren *überhaupt* eine Bedeutung bei der Entstehung von Beengungserleben zuerkannt wird.

Bell u.a. ergänzen die Giffordschen Modellvorstellungen um ein wichtiges Element. Über die Benennung von Einflussfaktoren hinausgehend, spezifizieren sie explizit eine psychologische Antezedenzbedingung für die Entstehung von Beengungserleben. Sie gehen davon aus, dass wahrgenommener *Kontrollverlust* zu Beengung führt. Fischer und Stephan verstehen unter Kontrolle ein „dem menschlichen Individuum innewohnendes Bestreben, Ereignisse und Zustände seiner Umwelt beeinflussen, vorhersehen oder zumindest erklären zu können".[20] Es wird *Kontrollverlust* erlebt, wenn Umweltereignisse und -zustände *nicht* in erwünschtem Maße beeinflusst, vorhergesehen oder erklärt werden können. Dies schließt auch das *Nichtvorhandensein* erwünschter Verhaltensoptionen mit ein.

Diese kontrolltheoretische Modellvorstellung wird nun auf eine evolutionspsychologische Perspektive bezogen: Geht man danach von einem grundsätzlich bestehenden menschlichen Bedürfnis aus, sich Ausweich- und Fluchtmöglichkeiten freizuhalten, so kann deren Nichtvorhandensein im Sinne eines wahrgenommenen Kontrollverlusts als Auslöser für Beengungserleben verstanden werden. Auf entsprechende empirische Befunde aus dem Innenraumbereich wurde bereits verwiesen (Anm. 14 und 15).

Die dargestellte Ableitung wird gestützt durch weitere evolutionspsychologische Theorievorstellungen und empirische Befunde: Appleton geht z.B. davon aus, dass sich in frühen Phasen der phylogenetischen Entwicklung des Menschen dessen Überlebenswahrscheinlichkeit erhöhte, wenn dieser Orte aufsuchte, die zugleich Ausblick (*prospect*) und Schutz (*refuge*) boten.[21] Er postuliert in seiner *Prospect-Refuge*-Theorie, dass die menschliche Verhaltensregulation noch heute von derartigen phylogenetischen Determinanten beeinflusst ist. In einer aufwändigen Feldstudie konnten Atzwanger u.a. zeigen, dass Orte mit stärkerer *Prospect-Refuge*-Qualität im öffentlichen Raum in der Tat häufiger frequentiert werden und dass der Aufenthalt dort mit größerem Wohlbefinden verbunden ist.[22] In eine ver-

room.[15] All of these effects are interpreted as resulting from a permanently existing need to make sure that options for evasion and escape remain open. It can be assumed that phylogenetic determinations are at the root of this behavior.[16]

Consequently, of great interest now is the question as to whether comparable influencing factors apply to exterior settings. The objective of the study was therefore to collect empirical evidence about the influence of the qualitative spatial factor *availability of evasion and escape options* on the experience of crowding in outdoor space. To date, no conclusive empirical findings have been gathered.

Furthermore, an interest was expressed in finding out whether differences exist between planners and users in their assessment of architectural or urban-development partial factors as related to crowding, for such discrepancies would have direct relevance to planning.

Reference to Psychological Concepts and Conceptual Models. In terms of theoretical models, reference was first made to the integrative crowding approaches taken by Gifford[17] and by Paul A. Bell et al.[18] Both approaches attempt to compile various earlier theories on the experience of crowding into one work.

The influencing categories named by Gifford are physical factors, social factors, and personal factors. Among the physical factors cited are various influencing factors, such as—next to the quantity of available space—*qualitative* spatial factors ("arrangement of space"[19]) as well as other physical factors like temperature and noise. Important for the empirical approach outlined in this essay is the fact that in Gifford's model *qualitative* spatial factors play a role *at all* in the fostering of an experience of crowding.

Bell and his coauthors augment the Giffordian conceptual models with an important element. Going beyond a naming of influencing factors, they explicitly specify a psychological antecedent condition for the creation of an experience of crowding, presupposing that a perceived *loss of control* leads to crowding. Manfred Fischer and Egon Stephan define control as an "endeavor, inherent to the human individual, to influence, predict, or at least explain events and conditions within his environment."[20]

17 Vgl. Gifford: *Environmental Psychology* (wie Anm. 7).

18 Vgl. Bell u.a.: *Environmental Psychology* (wie Anm. 5).

19 Gifford: *Environmental Psychology*, S. 195 (wie Anm. 7).

20 Manfred Fischer/Egon Stephan: „Kontrolle und Kontrollverlust", in: Lenelis Kruse/Carl-Friedrich Graumann/Ernst-Dieter Lantermann (Hg.): *Ökologische Psychologie. Ein Handbuch in Schlüsselbegriffen*, Weinheim 1996, S. 166.

21 Vgl. Jay Appleton: *The Experience of Landscape*, London 1975; Ders.: „Prospect and Refuge Re-visited", in: *Landscape Journal* 3 (1984), S. 91–103.

22 Vgl. Klaus Atzwanger/Katrin Schäfer u.a.: „Wohlbefinden und Kooperation im öffentlichen Raum. Eine humanethologische Feldstudie", in: *Report Psychologie* 23, 5–6 (1998), S. 450–455.

15 See Gay H. Tennis and James M. Dabbs, "Sex, Setting and Personal Space: First Grade Through College," *Sociometry* 38, no. 3 (1975), pp. 385–94.

16 See Irenäus Eibl-Eibesfeldt and Hans Hass, "Sozialer Wohnbau und Umstrukturierung der Städte aus biologischer Sicht," in Irenäus Eibl-Eibesfeldt (ed.) *Stadt und Lebensqualität: Neue Konzepte im Wohnbau auf dem Prüfstand der Humanethologie und der Bewohnerurteile* (Stuttgart, 1985), pp. 49–84.

17 See Gifford, *Environmental Psychology* (note 7).

18 See Bell et al., *Environmental Psychology* (note 5).

19 Gifford, *Environmental Psychology* (note 7), p. 195.

20 Manfred Fischer and Egon Stephan, "Kontrolle und Kontrollverlust," in Kruse, Graumann, and Lantermann, *Ökologische Psychologie* (note 5), p. 166.

Potentials

Städtische Dichte in Zürich: Drei Gespräche

mit Fabian Hörmann und Frank Zierau, mit Kaschka Knapkiewicz und Axel Fickert, sowie mit Patrick Gmür, von Hans Gangoly und Markus Bogensberger.

Urban Density in Zurich: Three Talks with Fabian Hörmann and Frank Zierau, with Kaschka Knapkiewicz and Axel Fickert, and with Patrick Gmür, by Hans Gangoly und Markus Bogensberger.

Fabian Hörmann (FH) und Frank Zierau (FZ) sind Mitglieder der Architektengruppe Krokodil (EM2N, pool, Roger Boltshauser, Frank Zierau, Schweingruber Zulauf), die seit dem Jahr 2008 in Eigeninitiative eine raumplanerische Studie über den Großraum Zürich und die Entwicklung einer verdichteten Stadt im Glattal erarbeitet.

GAM: Ihr seid beide Architekten; wie hat sich Euer starkes Interesse an städtebaulichen Fragestellungen entwickelt?

FH: Das war eigentlich immer schon vorhanden. Wir sind es gewohnt, uns den gestellten Aufgaben anzunähern, bezogen auf die Parameter, die vorgegeben sind, alle Rahmenbedingungen abzuklopfen, aber auch das Städtische miteinzubeziehen, gerade wenn es eine Aufgabenstellung mit städtebaulicher Relevanz ist. Wir haben auch begonnen, uns mit dem Glattal zu beschäftigen, da wir oft mit Bauaufgaben konfrontiert waren, die

Fabian Hörmann (FH) and Frank Zierau (FZ) are members of the architects collective Krokodil (EM2N, pool, Roger Boltshauser, Frank Zierau, Schweingruber Zulauf), which has been conducting a self-initiated, spatial-planning study since 2008 on the Zurich metropolitan area and the development of a densified city in the Glattal Valley.

GAM: You are both architects. How did your strong interest in explorative urban-development questions come about?

FH: It has actually always been there. We are accustomed to approaching the problems we're presented with by considering the given parameters and sounding out all related framework conditions, but also by involving the municipal offices, especially when the task at hand is of urban-planning relevance.

We have also started to explore the Glattal Valley context since we have frequently been confronted with building assignments that play out beyond the city context. In this agglomeration area we are faced with situations that we don't want to go along with, that we would rather not reconstruct. So we instead seek counterpoints with the aim of integrating other qualities into these districts as well. Such interventions usually have a programmatic character, but very often relate to density — in the sense of built density, but also of experience density at central locations, such as at a train station within a village. So here we are dealing with spatial appearance and programmatic interventions that can then be based at such a location, thus creating a public sphere.

GAM: Yet the Krokodil collective does not settle for small-scale interventions (figs. 1–4).

FZ: For a long time we were missing the idea of a future urban-development plan for Zurich. We considered the City of Zurich's strategies as bowing to investors and therefore as some sort of Swiss compromise. For this reason, almost everyone was pretty much holding back until several young architectural firms finally got together and came to recognize that we all shared a similar view on the situation. Thus, our motivation was based less on the idea of intervening into urban planning as architects and more on the fact that those whose job it really is to attend to city development have not actually been doing so. The spatial planners are not doing spatial planning. We have no idea what they are planning, but it definitely is not space. Sure, this assertion is probably strongly made from the perspective of an architect, but it is precisely this vantage point that we wish to maintain. A personal motive is also that I spent time during my studies searching for quality in so-called peri-urban space. I reached a point where terms like *Zwischenstadt* didn't bring me any further, so I was forced to conclude that the supposed qualities simply do not exist.

GAM: How has this realization influenced the development of a densified city in Glattal Valley?

sich außerhalb des städtischen Kontexts befanden. In diesem Agglomerationsraum ist man mit Situationen konfrontiert, die man gar nicht nachvollziehen will, an denen man nicht weiterstricken möchte. So sucht man Kontrapunkte, um auch in solche Gegenden andere Qualitäten hineinzubringen. Diese Interventionen sind meist programmatischer Art, beziehen sich aber oft auf Dichte – im Sinne von gebauter Dichte, aber auch von Erlebnisdichte an zentralen Standorten, wie etwa an einem Bahnhof in einem Dorf. Es geht also um räumliche Erscheinung und programmatische Interventionen, die dann an einem solchen Ort angelagert sein können und Öffentlichkeit schaffen.

GAM: Die Krokodilgruppe begnügt sich aber nicht mit kleinmaßstäblichen Interventionen (Abb. 1–4).

FZ: Wir haben lange Zeit die Idee einer zukünftigen Stadtraumplanung für Zürich vermisst. Die Strategien der Stadt Zürich sahen wir als Verbeugung vor Investoren und eine Art schweizerischen Kompromiss. Deshalb war jeder eigentlich mit der Faust im Sack unterwegs, bis sich einige junge Büros einmal zusammengesetzt und erkannt haben, dass wir die Situation ähnlich beurteilen. Die Motivation war daher weniger als Architekt in den Städtebau einzudringen sondern vielmehr, dass jene, deren Aufgabe es eigentlich wäre, sich mit der Entwicklung der Stadt zu beschäftigen, diese nicht wahrnehmen. Die Raumplaner machen keine Raumplanung. Keine Ahnung, was die planen, aber den Raum definitiv nicht. Das mag vielleicht sehr aus der Perspektive eines Architekten behauptet sein, aber diese Sichtweise wollen wir uns auch bewahren. Ein persönliches Motiv ist auch, dass ich während des Studiums mit der Suche nach Qualität in dem sogenannten periurbanen Raum aufgewachsen bin. Irgendwann haben mir aber auch Begriffe wie Zwischenstadt nicht mehr weitergeholfen und ich musste feststellen, dass es die vermeintlichen Qualitäten schlicht und einfach nicht gibt.

GAM: Wie ist diese Erkenntnis in die Entwicklung einer verdichteten Stadt im Glattal eingeflossen?

FZ: Das Spezielle am Glattalprojekt ist vielleicht, dass es etwas macht, was man eigentlich vermeidet, wenn man sich mit Zersiedelung oder Flächenreform beschäftigt. Nämlich unbebaute Flächen zu gebrauchen. Aber die Idee ist zu sagen: gut, wir machen es nur dort, aber sonst nirgends. Das ist ja eigentlich der politische Knackpunkt im Städtebau. Das setzt eine neue Art der alten Planungshoheit voraus, die festlegt, wo etwas passieren darf,

und wo nicht. Das ist natürlich in der Schweiz – wie sonst wo in Europa – relativ brisant.

GAM: In eurer losen Architektengruppe ist die Verständigung untereinander vermutlich ein Schlüssel zum Projekt?

FH: Wir haben am Anfang wirklich viel diskutiert, sind nur gesessen und haben geredet. Und dann haben wir irgendwann gesagt, es ist Zeit, den Bleistift in die Hand zu nehmen, es soll etwas passieren. Aber damit etwas passieren konnte, mussten wir erst einmal vieles verstehen lernen. Wir haben uns die Situation des Großraums Zürich intensiv angesehen, wie funktioniert was, warum ist das jetzt so? In der Folge haben wir daraus unsere Schlüsse gezogen und uns auf die Bearbeitung des Glattals konzentriert, weil es sich um den dynamischsten Raum in der Schweiz handelt, der bereits jetzt gut erschlossen ist und über den Hub des Flughafens verfügt. Im Prinzip haben wir uns mit Themen beschäftigt, die sich durch die Arbeiten der Büros ziehen. Es geht um die Schaffung von übergeordneten Qualitäten, Freiräumen und Vernetzungen.

> **Die Motivation war daher weniger als Architekt in den Städtebau einzudringen sondern vielmehr, dass jene, deren Aufgabe es eigentlich wäre, sich mit der Entwicklung der Stadt zu beschäftigen, diese nicht wahrnehmen.**

GAM: Die traditionelle Maßstabsdifferenz zwischen Städtebau und Architektur besitzt für GAM.08 Dense Cities keine wirkliche Relevanz mehr, vielmehr fragen wir uns, auf welchen Maßstabsebenen architektonische Qualitäten festgelegt werden und wie sie sich messen lassen.

FZ: Wir betreiben ein Projekt, das rein von der Sparte her zur Raumplanung und zum Städtebau gehört. Wir haben am Anfang während der Untersuchung zum Großraum Zürich Gespräche mit dem Amt für Städtebau der Stadt Zürich geführt, die uns diese Frage gestellt haben: Ab wann wird aus Raumplanung Städtebau? Ich persönlich habe sowieso Probleme mit der Unterscheidung zwischen Städtebau und Architektur. Im Prinzip machen wir alle Städtebau, weil die Städtebauer es nicht machen. Michael Alder hat gesagt, er hätte nichts dagegen, in einer vermeintlich schlechten Wohnung zu leben, wenn die Umgebung gut ist. Vieles, was die Wohnung nicht hat, kompensiert ihr Umfeld.

FH: Also ich möchte jetzt nicht sagen, dass man schlechte Wohnungen machen soll, weil es draußen schön ist. Wir sehen es eher als Aufgabe, hybride Strukturen und neue Typologien zu entwickeln, um unseren Vorstellungen von Dichte gerecht zu werden.

GAM: Zum Thema Dichte sagt Dietmar Eberle, vereinfacht dargestellt: Wenn gewisse Kennzahlen festgelegt sind, die Höhe, Dichte und öffentliche Bereiche betreffend, dann ist eigentlich die stadträumliche Entwicklung determiniert. Kann man das wirklich so sehen?

FZ: Perhaps the special thing about the Glattal project is how it accomplishes something that we usually try to avoid when dealing with urban sprawl or zoning reform: this would be using unbuilt areas. But the idea is to say: okay, we'll do it here, but nowhere else. This really is the political crux of the matter in urban planning. It presumes a new form of the old sovereignty of planning, one that defines where what is allowed to happen and where not. In Switzerland—as in other parts of Europe—this is of course relatively volatile.

GAM: So communication among members of your loosely formed architect group is presumably a key component of the project?

FH: In the beginning we actually spent considerable time discussing, just sitting around and talking. And then we reached the point where it was time to pick up the pencil and start getting things done. But before we could accomplish anything, we first had to learn to understand many things. We intently scrutinized the situation within the Zurich metropolitan area, examining how different things work, why things are done the way they are. As a result, we came to our conclusions and started concentrating on Glattal Valley, for it is the most dynamic space within Switzerland that already has a good infrastructure and also possesses the airport hub. Basically, we were concentrating on topics that extend to the work areas of architectural firms. We are dealing with the creation of superordinate qualities, open spaces, and networks.

GAM: The traditional difference in scale between urban planning and architecture no longer carries any real relevance for GAM.08 Dense Cities. Instead we are wondering which scale levels are used for determining architectural qualities and how the latter can be measured.

FZ: We are running a project that in terms of sector clearly belongs to spatial planning and urban development. In the early stages, during our investigation of the Zurich metro area, we carried on conversations with members of the City of Zurich's Department of Urban Planning, who asked us the following question: At what point does spatial planning become urban planning? I myself happen to have problems with differentiations being made between urban planning and architecture. When it comes down to it, we are all doing urban planning because the urban planners are not doing it. Michael Alder has said that he wouldn't mind living in what is considered a poor apartment if the surroundings were good. Much of what is missing in an apartment can be compensated through its surrounding environment.

FH: Now I wouldn't want to say that we should make poor apartments because it's so lovely outside. We see it more as a calling to develop hybrid structures and new typologies in order to do justice to our conceptions of density.

1   Übergeordnete Identitätsträger (Flughafen, Hardwald, Drehscheibe ehem. Flugplatz, Greifensee) und Ausbau des öffentlichen Nahverkehrs (neuer Mittelverteiler von Uster via Leutschenbach zum Flughafen, S-Bahn Kurzschlüsse für direkte Verbindung von Uster zum Flughafen, Neue Tram/ Buslinien zur internen Feinverteilung). Superordinate identifying symbols (airport, Hardwald, hub former airport, Greifensee) and expansion of public transport system (new transport interchange nodes from Uster via Leutschenbach to the airport, urban rail short-circuits that enable a direct connection from Uster to the airport, new bus and streetcar lines for local distribution).

2   Die Stadt Glatt im Jahr 2060: Blick von Wallisellen Richtung Greifensee. Glatt city in 2060: Aerial view from Wallisellen towards Greifensee.

3   Die Stadt Glatt im Jahre 2060: Übergeordnete Grünraumfigur mit Boulevards, Alleen, Parks und Freiräumen vom Greifensee bis zum Flughafen zur Vernetzung der Nachbarschaften aus bestehenden Quartieren und Urbanisierungsclustern. Glatt city in 2060: Superordinate green space including boulevards, avenues, parks and open spaces from Greifensee to the airport to enable networking of the neighborhoods and urban clusters.

4   Blick vom Hochhaus der größten Shopping-Mall Richtung Greifensee: Eine Stadt im Werden! The view towards Greifensee from the high-rise of the largest shopping-mall: A city in the making!

© Gruppe Krokodil

5

5 Wohnbebauung Klee in Affoltern
Klee housing complex in Affoltern
© Christoph Schmäh, www.air-image.ch

GAM: On the topic of density, Dietmar Eberle has said (and I'm paraphrasing here): When certain parameters have been defined in terms of height, density, and public areas, then urban-spatial development is more or less predetermined. Can we really take this approach?

FH: To answer that we would first of all have to be more familiar with his soon-to-be-published study on density. But at first glance it seems that the direction he's going is not off base. It's fundamentally clear that a blended city district with public zones and properties along with a certain density will be conducive to an intensity of life. The question is whether this is the desired character of every district in the end, or whether it might also be possible to have more peaceful islands which simply embody a different density and nevertheless still possess sought qualities and are thus able to attract people into the city.

Kaschka Knapkiewicz (KK) and Axel Fickert (AF) are architects and run an architectural firm in Zurich.

GAM: Recently you finished building the Klee housing complex in Affoltern (fig. 5), a suburb of Zurich, and thus realized an interesting alternative model to classic housing development.

AF: We are primarily concerned not with density or retrospective densification, but rather with building a city. The building site was basically a no-man's-land. A few other architectural firms had already erected housing structures prior to us, which—though nice buildings—didn't bring any new dimensions into the area. They mainly just repeated what was already there. Our goal was to transfer themes from the core city into the agglomeration. Early on in this competition we asked ourselves what could inspire us city dwellers to move into the outskirts. We wanted to create an identifiable spatial figure and ended up being the only ones to propose something like that on a larger scale. In competitions we are meanwhile seeing entries with closed courtyards for similar situations.

KK: Aside from buildings by the firms Baumschlager Eberle and pool, nothing was there yet, but we already had an idea of what would be coming. Which is why we had the feeling that it would be a good idea to move a piece of city into this wilderness.

GAM: The topic of perimeter-block housing actually has come more strongly to the fore in very recent times.

KK: We are very appreciative of perimeter-block housing and still consider this form of building attractive. Especially important with form is outdoor space. We are therefore very concerned with the interstices. It's the greatest when we come upon quality outdoor space and can create a fitting world of housing to accompany it.

FH: Ich denke, dass man dazu seine demnächst erscheinende Studie zu Dichte genauer kennen müsste. Auf den ersten Blick hat man aber das Gefühl, dass die Richtung, die er nennt, stimmen könnte. Grundsätzlich ist klar, dass ein durchmischter Stadtteil mit öffentlichen Zonen und Liegenschaften und einer gewissen Dichte eine Lebensintensität verursacht. Die Frage ist, ob das am Ende der Charakter jedes Quartiers sein muss, oder ob es auch ruhigere Inseln geben kann, die einfach eine andere Dichte haben und trotzdem über gesuchte Qualitäten verfügen und somit Menschen in die Stadt holen.

Kaschka Knapkiewicz (KK) und Axel Fickert (AF) sind Architekten und betreiben ein Büro in Zürich.

GAM: Sie haben vor kurzem die Wohnbebauung Klee in Affoltern (Abb. 5), einem Vorort von Zürich, fertiggestellt und damit ein interessantes Gegenmodell zum klassischen Siedlungsbau realisiert.

AF: Uns geht es in erster Linie nicht um Dichte oder Nachverdichtung, sondern uns geht es ums Stadtmachen. Der Bauplatz war eigentlich Niemandsland. Vor uns haben bereits einige andere Büros Wohnbauten errichtet, die zwar ordentliche Bauten, aber keine neue Dimension in dieses Gebiet gebracht haben. Im Prinzip haben sie nur wiederholt, was bereits da war.

Unser Ziel war es, Themen aus der Kernstadt in die Agglomeration zu übertragen. Wir haben uns früh in diesem Wettbewerb gefragt, was uns als Stadtbewohner denn bewegen könnte, dort hinaus zu ziehen. Wir wollten eine identifizierbare räumliche Figur schaffen und waren dann die Einzigen, die so etwas wie eine Großform vorgeschlagen hatten. Mittlerweile gibt es bei Wettbewerben in vergleichbaren Situationen immer wieder Beiträge mit geschlossenen Höfen.

KK: Außer den Bauten von Baumschlager Eberle und pool stand nichts, wir wussten aber in etwa, was kommen wird. Darum hatten wir das Gefühl, es wäre gut, ein Stück Stadt in diese Wüste zu bauen.

GAM: Das Thema Blockrandbebauung ist tatsächlich in jüngster Zeit stärker in den Vordergrund getreten.

KK: Wir schätzen bestehende Blockrandbebauungen sehr und finden diese Form des Bauens auch immer noch schön. Besonders wichtig ist dabei der Außenraum. Wir beschäftigen uns daher sehr mit dem Dazwischen. Das Größte ist eigentlich, einen guten Außenraum zu finden und dazu eine geeignete Wohnwelt zu schaffen.

GAM: Also könnte man sagen, dass das Thema Außenraum die Ausgangsbasis für den Entwurf in Affoltern war?

AF: Ja, aber es kommt noch etwas hinzu, nämlich die Gliederungsfrage. In Affoltern war das ja ein siebengeschossiges Haus, wir wollten den Baukörper gliedern und haben dann eine Art Kolossalordnung entwickelt. Zwei Pakete mit zusammengefassten Geschossen und darauf dann eine Attika. Zusätzlich wird mit dem Tausch der Figur/Grundfarben der Charakter des Innenhofes von der Außenansicht unterschieden. Weiters haben wir außen einen hohen und innen einen niedrigen Sockel eingeführt. Als alles fertig war und die Anlage eröffnet wurde, liefen Leute und Bekannte, die nicht

Architekturprofis sind, durch die Siedlung, waren sichtbar erregt, hoch erfreut und sagten, die Stimmung erinnere sie an alte europäische Städte außerhalb der Schweiz; Bukarest, Wien – das hätte für sie einen gewaltig städtischen Ausdruck.

KK: Dahinter steht eine klassische Ordnung, die verfremdet wurde: Palladio, die Griechen, Attika, Piano Nobile – das kann man ja nicht neu erfinden.

GAM: Das heißt aber auch, dass man, wenn man von Dichte spricht, sowohl über städtische Formen nachdenkt, wie auch die konkrete Gestaltung nicht ignoriert werden kann.

KK: Ja, es darf auch keine Konkurrenz zwischen den Gebäuden geben. Statt einem „Ich bin der Größte" muss der Wille zu einer gemeinsamen Ordnung vorherrschend sein. Und das Bekenntnis zu einem gemeinsamen Ausdruck.

AF: Als Nachmoderne müssen wir uns fragen: Was ist es denn, was urbanen Ausdruck ausmacht oder urbane Sehnsucht verkörpert? Ist es die Struktur des Materials selber oder sind es Fassadenordnungen? Wir sollten nicht nur einfach historische Vorbilder nachbauen, sondern wir müssen uns klar darüber werden, welches heute die Merkmale sind, die für uns das „Flair der Stadt" ausmachen, das ja immer auch eine gewisse Monumentalität in sich trägt. Das Pathos der Stadt, die Großartigkeit der Erwartungen – das hat uns die Moderne ja leider verboten. Und jetzt müssen wir uns überlegen, wie es weitergehen soll.

GAM: Interessant an der Wohnbebauung Klee ist, dass die Öffnung zwischen innen und außen genau an den Innenecken passiert und nicht an der Frontseite in der Mitte. So ergibt sich eine spannende Erschließung des Hofs, die zu einer gewissen atmosphärischen Verdichtung führt und mit aufwändigen Details im Eingangsbereich unterstrichen wird.

KK: Wir haben in diesem Bereich sehr viele Stützen platziert. Damit nicht U-Bahn-ähnliche, zugige Durchgänge entstehen, sondern eher räumlich definierte Bereiche. Das ist viel spannender, man muss sich ein bisschen durchkämpfen durch die Eingänge.

GAM: Würden Sie auch sagen, dass es wichtig ist, eine maximale Gebäudehöhe einzuhalten?

KK: Ja, das kommt natürlich auf die Größe an. Bei diesem Hof hätte man mit dem sogenannten „Zürcher Untergeschoss" noch ein Geschoss gewinnen können. Dies tritt dann ein, wenn man mit dem Erdgeschossboden mindestens zehn Zentimeter unter dem Terrain bleibt. Das heißt, wir hätten mit einem zusätzlich noch möglichen, zurückspringenden Attikageschoss insgesamt sogar 9 anstatt 7 Geschosse erreichen können. Das wollten aber auch die Genossenschaften schon im Wettbewerb nicht. Das wären dann nochmal 40 bis 50 Wohnungen mehr gewesen, also eindeutig zu dicht.

AF: Während der Bauphase, als wir die erste Musterwohnung anschauen wollten, haben wir uns selbst verlaufen. Es gab zwei Musterwohnungen, und ich musste mich wirklich sehr konzentrieren, um zu wissen, ob ich jetzt rechts oder links gehen muss – es war also schwierig, sich zu orientieren. Erst als die Gerüste weg waren und die monumentale Fassadengliederung wirklich zum Tragen kam, hat sich das geändert.

GAM: So we could say that the topic of outdoor space was the point of departure for the Affoltern design?

AF: Yes, but there was something else as well, which was the issue of articulation. In Affoltern we were working with a seven-story building and wanted to lend articulation to the structure, so we developed a sort of colossal order. Two sections with consolidated stories and then topped with an attic level. Then, by interchanging the figuring/basic coloring, the character of the interior courtyard was distinguished from the exterior view. Furthermore, we introduced a high ground story to the inside and a low one to the outside. When everything was finished and the complex was opened, all kinds of people and acquaintances who are not architecture professionals were walking around the development—were visibly excited, delighted, and said that the atmosphere reminded them of old European cities outside of Switzerland. Bucharest, Vienna—to them, it had a strong city feel.

KK: This was all based on classical order in altered guise: Palladio, the Greeks, attika, piano nobile—these of course cannot be reinvented.

GAM: But this then means that—when speaking about density—it is important that urban forms be considered but, at the same time, that concrete design not be ignored.

KK: That's right. There shouldn't be any competition between the buildings. Instead of an "I am the greatest," it is the willingness to be part of a joint order that must prevail. And the decision for this to be mutually expressed.

AF: As postmodernists we have to ask ourselves: What is it that actually constitutes the expression of the urban or embodies yearning for the urban? Is it the structure of material itself or is it the façade structures? The point is not to just recreate historical models; instead, we must figure out which features are those that, in our view, represent the "city flair," which always bears the imprint of a certain monumentality. The pathos of the city, the magnificence of expectations—this was sadly forbidden us by modernism. And now we have to ponder where we are going to go from here.

GAM: What is interesting about the Klee housing development is that the openings between inside and outside are situated precisely at the inner corners instead in the middle of the front side. This creates an exciting access situation for the courtyard and leads to a certain atmospheric densification, which is underlined by elaborate details in the entry area.

KK: Here we placed quite a few supports, so that spatially defined areas come to life in lieu of subway-like, drafty passages. This is much more fascinating since people have to kind of navigate their way through the entryways.

GAM: Would you also say that it is important to adhere to a maximum building height?

KK: Well, that of course depends upon size. In the case of this development, we could have gained an extra story by creating a so-called "Zürcher Untergeschoss." This is the case when the ground-level is placed at a minimum of ten centimeters below ground. Here this would have meant that we could have even created nine instead of seven stories, granted we had also constructed a slightly retreating attic story as well. But the housing cooperatives were against this from the very beginning, even during the competition. Such a strategy would have created forty to fifty more apartments, thus clearly overdoing it on the density end.

AF: During the building phase when it came time to view the first sample apartments, we actually got ourselves lost. There were two sample apartments and I really had to concentrate in order to remember whether I needed to walk right or left—so it was difficult to keep our bearings. It wasn't until the scaffolding was removed and the monumental façade structure was brought to bear that this disorienting effect went away.

GAM: *Since your considerations are also directed at the urban-development scale, it seems to be inevitable that this scale will be adjusted.*

AF: Yes, the Krokodil collective, which dreams of a future city by the name of "Glattstadt," is for instance a phenomenon that points in this direction. In this context it is interesting to note that landscape architects are also starting to take action. They're saying: it really doesn't make sense that we come in at the end and only get to plant trees; it should be the other way around, that we influence the streets before the lots are parceled and the buildings erected. I find this an interesting idea. Even in the case of this collective, which is presently exploring how an agglomeration could be turned into a city, the urban-development quality of a representative boulevard is becoming a hot topic. Anyhow, they're exploring the matter. It's not enough, in their opinion, to relocate a central utilization form like a canton hospital out there; they apparently want to develop all urban spaces.

GAM: *Yes, for years people were fighting the use of classical elements.*

AF: We reached a point where postmodernism was deemed unworthy of discussion, and today it has become completely obsolete, strangely enough. This is quite unfair, for Krier and his colleagues had a lot of interesting things to say.

KK: The translation of our ideas into built form was the most difficult thing—how do we build today with such elements without it emerging in the end like a Mussolini redevelopment. This has always been a balancing act.

GAM: *Who can force quality within an urban development situation? Once the classic parameters have been defined, like*

GAM: *Da auch Sie mit Ihren Überlegungen in den städtebaulichen Maßstab gehen, scheint es irgendwie in der Luft zu liegen, dass man den Maßstab etwas ändert.*

AF: Ja, die Gruppe Krokodil, die von einer zukünftigen Stadt namens „Glattstadt" träumt, ist zum Beispiel ein Phänomen, das in diese Richtung weist. In diesem Zusammenhang ist interessant, dass die Landschaftsarchitekten langsam ebenfalls aktiv werden. Sie sagen: eigentlich dürften wir nicht am Schluss kommen und nur noch Bäume setzen, sondern umgekehrt, wir müssten die Straßen prägen, und erst dann soll parzelliert und gebaut werden. Das finde ich eine interessante Idee. Selbst bei der Gruppe Krokodil, die sich jetzt überlegt, wie sie aus der Agglomeration eine Stadt machen soll, ist sogar die städtebauliche Qualität einer Avenida wieder ein Thema. Die beschäftigen sich immerhin damit. Es genügt ihnen nicht, eine Zentrumsnutzung wie ein Kantonsspital dort hinaus zu verlegen, sondern sie wollen offenbar auch Stadträume ausstatten.

GAM: *Man hat sich ja jahrzehntelang dagegen gewehrt, klassische Elemente zu verwenden.*

AF: Die Postmoderne war irgendwann indiskutabel und ist heute seltsamerweise völlig vergessen. Das ist eigentlich ungerecht, denn Krier und seine Kollegen hatten viel Interessantes zu sagen.

KK: Die Übersetzung unserer Ideen ins Gebaute, das war das Schwierige – wie baut man heute mit solchen Elementen, ohne dass es am Schluss wie eine Mussolini-Sanierung herauskommt – es war immer eine Gratwanderung.

GAM: *Wer kann Qualitäten in einer Stadtentwicklung forcieren? Wenn man jetzt einmal die klassischen Parameter wie Bebauungsdichte und Höhe gegeben hat, wo wäre dann der nächste Schritt zu tun, um wirkliche Qualität zu erreichen?*

KK: Nur durch Wettbewerbe. Grundsätzlich läuft dies sehr gut hier in Zürich – der Standard ist hoch, es gibt viele Wettbewerbe.

AF: Aber man tritt dennoch auf der Stelle. Es ist immer wieder das Gleiche, man versandet in einer Art „Mainstream".

GAM: *Vielleicht ist wieder Zeit für große Ausstellungen zu städtischer Architektur. Mit Mailänder Beispielen oder Le Havre von Auguste Perret etwa.*

KK: Also Le Havre sofort!

AF: Wichtig ist die Frage, welche Struktur braucht der städtische Ausdruck? Und wenn man die Fassadenprospekte von Le Havre mit der Rue de Rivoli in Paris vergleicht, dann sind diese fast identisch – genau die gleiche Hierarchie. Da ist der erste Balkon auf der Höhe des Piano Nobile – dann

> Wir schätzen bestehende Blockrandbebauungen sehr und finden diese Form des Bauens auch immer noch schön. Besonders wichtig ist dabei der Außenraum. Wir beschäftigen uns daher sehr mit dem Dazwischen.

6 Stiftung „Wohnungen für kinderreiche Familien in Zürich",
Brunnenhof, Gigon/Guyer Architekten, Zürich Foundation
"Housing for large families in Zurich," Brunnenhof,
Gigon/Guyer Architekten, Zurich © Axel Fickert

7 Stiftung „Wohnungen für kinderreiche Familien", Brunnenhof,
Altbestand Foundation "Housing for large families in Zurich,"
Brunnenhof, existing structures

8 Quadro CS (Mitte rechts); Leutschentower Wohnhochhaus (links),
Leutschenbach Quadro CS (center-right); Leutschentower
high-rise apartment building (left); Leutschenbach

9 Hardbrücke (rechts); Steinfels-Areal (Mitte); Kehrricht-
verbrennung (rechts); Zürich-West Hardbrücke (right);
Steinfels-area (center); waste-to-energy plant (right); Zurich-West

floor area ratio and height, what would be the next step to be accomplished in attaining true quality?

KK: Only through competitions, which fundamentally works very well here in Zurich—the standard is high and there are many competitions.

AF: But all the same, we're not making enough progress. It's always the same story—we're bogged down in a kind of "mainstream."

GAM: Maybe it's once again time for large exhibitions on urban architecture, like with examples from Milan or Le Havre by Auguste Perret.

KK: Sure, Le Havre anytime!

AF: What's important is the question as to which structure urban expression needs. And if we compare the façade projects of Le Havre with the Rue de Rivoli in Paris, then we'll see that they are almost identical—the exact same hierarchy. There's the first balcony at the height of the piano nobile, then a pair of stories is seen, above that the second balcony, and then the attic story set slightly back. The entire city is conceived this way. Perret didn't even once wonder whether it was contemporary or not.

Patrick Gmür (PG) is an architect and has served as Director of the City of Zurich's Department of Urban Planning since 2009.

GAM: European discourse on architecture of recent years has been intensively focused on landscapes, slums, urban farming, and green buildings. The concrete city has been treated in a more cursory way. We are wondering about the ways in which architects are able to positively influence the development of cities?

PG: I, too, have noticed that the issue of the city from the perspective of the architect has seemed somewhat monotonous of late, in Switzerland and in Zurich as well. This is also my criticism of architects: they navigate a field where architecture and issues of space are contemplated at a high level, yet the context tends to be somewhat lost in the process. I have the nerve to say so, because up to almost two years ago I was likewise running an architectural firm and regularly involved in building in Zurich. And recently I've served on various juries where I've seen how context is frequently neglected. This is an area that architects and planners need to take into stronger consideration once more. In Zurich we face challenges that especially involve social-urban-planning problems. It is worthwhile to work through these cases with architects and planners instead of turning them over to developers. We must consider the direction in which Zurich should be moving: What is the vision? Where will we be fifty years from now? Will we be a

kommt eine Zweiergruppe, darüber der zweite Balkon; und danach die zurückgestufte Attika. Die ganze Stadt ist identisch aufgebaut. Perret hat nicht einmal die Frage gestellt, ob das zeitgemäß ist oder nicht.

Patrick Gmür (PG) ist Architekt und seit 2009 Leiter des Amtes für Städtebau der Stadt Zürich.

GAM: Der europäische Architekturdiskurs hat sich in den letzten Jahren intensiv mit Landscapes, Slums, Urban Farming und Green Buildings beschäftigt. Die konkrete Stadt wurde eher nebensächlich behandelt. Wir fragen uns, wie Architekturschaffende die Entwicklung von Städten positiv beeinflussen können?

PG: Ich stelle ebenfalls fest, dass das Thema der Stadt aus der Sicht des Architekten auch in der Schweiz und in Zürich momentan etwas eintönig ist. Das ist auch meine Kritik an den Architekten: sie bewegen sich auf einem Feld, wo auf einem hohen Niveau über Fragen des Raumes und über Architektur nachgedacht wird, dabei geht jedoch der Kontext ein bisschen verloren. Ich traue mich das zu sagen, denn ich habe bis vor nicht ganz zwei Jahren ein Architekturbüro geführt und viel in Zürich gebaut. In bin auch jetzt in vielen Jurys, wo ich feststelle, dass der Kontext oft vernachlässigt wird. Hier ist ein Feld, das die Architekten und Planer wieder verstärkt bearbeiten müssen. In Zürich sind wir vor allem bezüglich der sozialstädtebaulichen Fragen gefordert. Es lohnt sich, diesen Bereich durch die Architekten und Planer zu bearbeiten und nicht den Entwicklern zu überlassen.

> Es lohnt sich, diesen Bereich durch die Architekten und Planer zu bearbeiten und nicht den Entwicklern zu überlassen. Wir müssen uns überlegen, wohin sich Zürich bewegen soll, was ist die Vision, wo sind wir in 50 Jahren?

Wir müssen uns überlegen, wohin sich Zürich bewegen soll, was ist die Vision, wo sind wir in 50 Jahren? Sind wir eine Stadt, die so reich ist wie Monaco, die ein Museum besitzt wie Venedig, messen wir uns mit Singapur oder mit der Kreativwirtschaft von Berlin? Ich möchte damit sagen, dass Städtebau gut möglich ist, wenn man politischen Rückhalt hat und eine politische Vision hinter allem steht. Zürich hat eine gewisse politische Kontinuität. Das erlaubt der Stadtregierung, Zielvorstellungen zu erarbeiten. Sie hat das 2007 mit einem Blick auf die Zukunft im Jahr 2025 gemacht. Es wurden drei Fragen gestellt: wie leben wir, wovon leben wir und wie organisieren wir uns? Anhand dieser drei Fragen wurden Antworten in Form von politischen Statements formuliert. Diese Vorgaben können wir planerisch umsetzen.

GAM: Werden diese Vorgaben kontinuierlich reflektiert und wie wird deren Umsetzung evaluiert?

Es zeigt sich übrigens oft: das Blockrandprinzip funktioniert doch am besten. Allgemein wird das Thema des Wohnens heute nicht mehr so verkrampft betrachtet, es ist plötzlich vieles möglich geworden. Man baut nicht mehr eine Wohnung, in der man lange wohnt, sondern man baut Wohnungen, die sich am Bedarf orientieren. Das wird in Zürich auch unterstützt. Wir haben hier eine Leerquote von 0,02.

Über das architektonische Potenzial urbaner Dichte

„Auf den Punkt […] kommt der Städtebau dort,
wo er einen Ort mit *einem* Haus in Ordnung bringt."[1]

On the Architectural Potential of Urban Density
"Town planning attains its essence in those situations
when it can bring a place into order with one house."[1]

CHRISTIAN MUELLER INDERBITZIN

Über die Notwendigkeit baulicher Verdichtung von Städten – oder allgemeiner: der Bedeutung von Dichte für das Urbane – besteht mittlerweile weitum Einigkeit. Doch was meint eine solche Verdichtung? Lassen sich städtebauliche Qualitäten alleine an einem Mehr an baulicher Substanz festmachen? Wohl kaum. Als Gradmesser für städtebauliche Qualität muss vielmehr die bauliche Dichte um zusätzliche Dimensionen erweitert werden. Die Schwierigkeiten eines solchen Versuchs zeigen sich bereits in der begrifflichen Vielschichtigkeit von Dichte: man spricht nicht nur von Bebauungsdichte, sondern auch von Bevölkerungsdichte, Nutzungsdichte, atmosphärischer Dichte usw. Dementsprechend vielgestaltig und unscharf sind denn auch die Definitionen zur Dichte.

Man könnte sogar soweit gehen, Dichte überhaupt als Kriterium für städtebauliche Qualität infrage zu stellen, denn die *richtige* Dichte gibt es nicht. Es handelt sich vielmehr um eine relative Bezugsgröße, die ihren Wert aus dem jeweiligen Kontext einer Kultur, einer Stadt und letztlich sogar dem Quartier bezieht. In letzter Konsequenz legt das den Schluss nahe, dass andere Kriterien – beispielsweise morphologische, typologische, funktionale oder atmosphärische – vorrangig von Bedeutung sind und die bauliche Dichte – von hohem oder niedrigem Maß – lediglich das Resultat eines städtebaulichen Konzeptes ist.[2]

> Man könnte sogar soweit gehen, Dichte überhaupt als Kriterium für städtebauliche Qualität infrage zu stellen, denn die *richtige* Dichte gibt es nicht. Es handelt sich vielmehr um eine relative Bezugsgröße, die ihren Wert aus dem jeweiligen Kontext einer Kultur, einer Stadt und letztlich sogar dem Quartier bezieht.

Urbane Dichte. Dieser Essay plädiert für den synthetisierenden Begriff der *urbanen Dichte*. Mit urbaner Dichte ist eine Dichte an Netzwerken und Interaktionen zwischen einer möglichst hohen Zahl verschiedener Akteure gemeint. So können zwar zwischen verschiedenen Dichteformen Korrelationen bestehen – müssen aber nicht; eine hohe Bebauungsdichte erzeugt nicht zwingend eine hohe urbane Dichte. Entscheidend für die urbane Dichte ist der Begriff der *produktiven Differenzen*: „Urbane Kulturen unterscheiden sich von Dörfern dadurch, dass sie nicht um eine beherrschende *Eigenheit* herum gebaut sind, sondern um ein Geflecht von inneren Differenzen. Der städtische Raum ist damit genuin heterotopisch und asynchron. Die Schichtung der Stadt in unterschiedliche Zonen, Kulturen und Handlungszusammenhänge allein beschreibt noch keine urbane Qualität. Stadt entsteht gewissermassen in den Wirkungen des Fel-

Regarding the necessity of structural densification within cities—or, in more general terms, the meaning of density for the urban setting—consensus has meanwhile been reached all around. But what is meant by such densification? May urban-development qualities be defined merely by a higher quantity of structural substance? Hardly. In gauging urban-development quality, structural density must instead be expanded to encompass further dimensions. The difficulties encountered during such an attempt already become apparent in the terminological complexity of density: we not only speak of building density, but also of population density, utilization density, atmospheric density, and so forth. And the definitions of density are accordingly protean and vague.

We might even go so far as to question density's aptness as a criterion for urban-development quality, for there is no such thing as the *right* density. Instead, density is a relative reference value that draws its merit from the respective context of a culture, a city, or even a city district. Ultimately, this suggests that other criteria—for instance morphological, typological, functional, or atmospheric ones—are of primary importance and that structural density—of either high or low magnitude—is simply the offspring of an urban-development concept.[2]

Urban Density. This essay proposes that the synthetic term of *urban density* be used. Urban density connotes a density of networks and interactions between as many different players as possible. While correlations may arise between various forms of density, this must not necessarily be the case; a high level of building density does not inevitably engender high urban density. Decisive for urban density is the concept of *productive differences*: "Urban cultures differ from village cultures in that they are not built around a dominant 'distinctive character' but around a plexus of internal differences. Urban space is thus genuinely heterotopic and asynchronous. The stratification of the city into different zones, cultures, and contexts of action is not sufficient to describe an urban quality. In a sense, cities emerge as a consequence of what happens in the fields between the differences. In this interstice it is likely that the interplay of different cultures, groups, and forms of production will spark an unexpected and multilayered urban dynamic … The dynamic of urban differences is never aimed at homogeneity and synchronization but only at the productivity of diversity and the sum of the possibilities that lie hidden in interferences. Because the development of these energies can

1   Zitat Roger Diener, aus: Roger Diener/Martin Steinmann: *Das Haus und die Stadt. Diener & Diener – Städtebauliche Arbeiten*, Basel 1995, S. 11.

2   Vgl. Robert Kaltenbrunner: „Urbane Kondensation. Ein Streiflicht zur Frage der Dichte im jüngeren Städtebau", in: *Archithese* 3 (2011), S. 33 f.

1   Citation by Roger Diener from Roger Diener and Martin Steinmann, *Das Haus und die Stadt – The House and the City: Diener & Diener – Städtebauliche Arbeiten* (Basel, 1995), p. 11.

2   See Robert Kaltenbrunner, "Urbane Kondensation: Ein Streiflicht zur Frage der Dichte im jüngeren Städtebau," *Archithese* 3 (2011), pp. 33–34.

neither be entirely planned nor fully controlled, cities constantly reinvent themselves within this play of forces."[3]

So here we are talking about a qualitative understanding of density, one that synthesizes the factors responsible for urban qualities: in terms of a city's quality, only its *urban density* is of importance. Of course, this understanding of density describes a *field of potentiality* liberated from ideology; it also implies other facets, ones that are contradictory, fragmentary, and so forth (fig. 1) and shows no initial preference for a particular urban-development form. Martin Steinmann, in referencing the architecture of Diener & Diener and the Berlin context of the 1990s, writes that the block represents but one possibility: "The ville verte, in addition to the gray city, is also a part of the urban models at the end of the twentieth century."[4] And: "This is a town planning that refuses to participate in a large or total order. Such an order has become problematic; circumstances are, as a rule, too fragmented, economically as well as socially."[5]

Architectural Potentials. Even though a city's degree of urban density is ultimately determined by the interactions of its players, it is actually architecture that lays the foundation—or, figuratively speaking, sets the stage—and also integrates the responsible factors. Here, city and architecture practically become interchangeable concepts, as Rossi points out.[6] Also evident is how such architecture is not only expressed through its area-related parameters. Indeed, it must create spatial requisites so that precisely this interaction may take place: communication, commerce, play, contemplation, et cetera. This claim is not new and has often led to a *functionalist* design conception that is basically founded upon the objectives sketched here and that attempts to effectuate these through urban-development and architectural measures; in this scenario, urban quality is considered *producible*, which undeniably represents a fallacy.

This essay therefore fields the question as to whether one might encounter this situation with an opposite approach: Is it conceivable that urban density could be considered a respectively given, imagined quality—let's say, a design-related prerequisite—with urban-development and architectural design thus developed against this backdrop? Or, in other words: What are the architectural potentials of urban density? Such a design process can originate either with an already existing site or in one's imagination as an idealized context—in any case, it in-

des zwischen den Differenzen. In diesem Zwischenraum ist die Wahrscheinlichkeit angesiedelt, dass das Zusammenspiel von unterschiedlichen Kulturen, Gruppen und Produktionsformen eine unerwartete und vielschichtige Dynamik entfacht. […] Die Dynamik urbaner Differenzen ist nie auf Homogenität und Synchronisierung ausgerichtet, sondern allein auf Produktivität von Verschiedenem und auf die Summe der Möglichkeiten, welche sich in Interferenzen verbergen. Da die Entfachung dieser Energien weder vollständig geplant noch umfassend beherrscht werden kann, erfindet sich die Stadt in diesem Kräftespiel dauernd neu."[3]

Es geht also um eine qualitative Auffassung von Dichte, welche die für urbane Qualitäten verantwortlichen Faktoren synthetisiert: für die Qualität einer Stadt ist einzig deren *urbane Dichte* von Bedeutung. Selbstredend beschreibt diese Auffassung von Dichte ein von Ideologie befreites *Möglichkeitsfeld*, das auch Widersprüchliches, Fragmentarisches usw. miteinschließt (Abb. 1) und zunächst keine bestimmte städtebauliche Form präferiert. Martin Steinmann schreibt bezogen auf die Architektur von Diener & Diener und den Berliner Kontext der 1990er Jahre denn auch, dass der Block lediglich eine Möglichkeit darstellt: „[N]eben der grauen Stadt gehört auch die *ville verte* zum Bestand von Stadt-Modellen am Ende des 20. Jahrhunderts."[4] Und: „Es handelt sich um einen Städtebau, der sich der großen bzw. totalen Ordnung verweigert. Eine solche Ordnung ist schwierig geworden; die Verhältnisse sind in der Regel zu stark fragmentiert, wirtschaftlich wie auch gesellschaftlich."[5]

Architektonische Potenziale. Auch wenn letztlich die Interaktionen der Akteure einer Stadt den Grad an urbaner Dichte bestimmen, so ist es doch die Architektur, welche dafür den Rahmen – oder bildhaft gesprochen, die Bühne – setzt und die verantwortlichen Faktoren zu integrieren vermag. Stadt und Architektur werden dabei im Sinne Rossis zu praktisch austauschbaren Begriffen.[6] Es wird dabei auch evident, dass sich eine solche Architektur nicht einzig über ihre Flächenkennwerte ausdrückt. Sie muss vielmehr die räumlichen Voraussetzungen schaffen, damit eben diese Interaktion stattfinden kann: die Kommunikation, der Handel, das Spiel, die Kontemplation usw. Diese Forderung ist nicht neu und hat häufig zu einem *funktionalistischen* Entwurfsverständnis geführt, das quasi von den hier umrissenen Zielvorgaben ausgeht und versucht, diese städtebaulich und architektonisch umzusetzen; urbane Qualität wird dabei als *herstellbar* verstanden, was zweifellos einen Trugschluss darstellt.

Es wird hier deshalb die Frage aufgeworfen, ob nicht auch anders herum verfahren werden könnte: ist es denkbar, urbane Dichte hypothetisch als gegebene respektive imaginierte Qualität – sozusagen als entwerferische Voraussetzung – anzunehmen und vor diesem Hintergrund den städtebaulichen und architektonischen Entwurf zu entwickeln? Oder anders ausgedrückt: was sind die architektonischen Potenziale urbaner Dichte? Ein solches Entwurfs-

3   Roger Diener, Jacques Herzog, Marcel Meili, and Pierre de Meuron et al. (eds.), *Switzerland – An Urban Portrait* (Basel, 2005), p. 116.

4   Diener and Steinmann, *Das Haus und die Stadt* (note 1), p. 8.

5   Ibid., p. 14.

6   See Ueli Zbinden and Aldo Rossi (eds.), *Die Architektur der Stadt: Skizze zu einer grundlegenden Theorie des Urbanen* (Munich, 1998).

3   Roger Diener/Jacques Herzog/Marcel Meili/Pierre de Meuron u.a. (Hg.): *Die Schweiz. Ein städtebauliches Portrait*, Basel 2005, S. 116.

4   Diener/Steinmann: *Das Haus und die Stadt*, S. 9 (wie Anm. 1).

5   Ebd., S. 15.

6   Vgl. Ueli Zbinden/Aldo Rossi (Hg.): *Die Architektur der Stadt. Skizze zu einer grundlegenden Theorie des Urbanen*, München 1998.

verfahren kann sowohl vom vorgefundenen Ort als auch der Imagination eines idealisierten Kontextes ausgehen – in jedem Fall geht es um eine Transformation, um ein Überführen oder Freilegen einer spezifischen, städtischen Qualität durch Architektur.

Katalytische Architektur. Eine solche Architektur allgemein zu beschreiben ist unmöglich, da der hier umrissene Ansatz von den spezifischen Gegebenheiten einer Situation ausgehen muss und eine Durchdringung von Stadt, Haus und Grundriss sowohl inhaltlich als auch atmosphärisch voraussetzt. Zur Illustration der formulierten Thesen werden deshalb nachfolgend zwei Projekte aus der eigenen Praxis vorgestellt. Die Projekte besitzen beide den Anspruch, in der Kohärenz von Städtebau, Architektur und Wohnform urbane Dichte nicht *herstellen* zu wollen, sondern lediglich *freizulegen*.

Die Voraussetzung bei einem solchen Verfahren ist zunächst eine strukturelle Denkweise. In der Praxis unseres Büros versuchen wir deshalb beim Entwurf, ausgehend vom Kontext und dem gestellten Programm, jeweils ein gedankliches Modell zu entwickeln, das schrittweise und iterativ dazu in eine städtebauliche und architektonische Form übersetzt wird. Bei diesen Modellen handelt es sich wissenschaftstheoretisch um fiktive Modelle, da sie nicht ein Abbild der Wirklichkeit darstellen, nach dem etwas realisiert wird (deskriptiv), sondern in der Imagination entstehen und erst so Erkenntnisse für den Entwurf generieren (präskriptiv). Die Modellbildung ist deshalb vor allem eine heuristische Herausforderung: Welches sind die richtigen Strukturen, Analogien und gegebenenfalls Bilder bezogen auf das Programm und den Kontext? Welche Wesensmerkmale des Kontextes schlummern am Ort, die es mit dem Projekt freizulegen gilt?

Der Kontextbezug ist dabei selten ein typologischer oder morphologischer, sondern wird allgemeiner, umfassender und abstrakter verstanden – gewissermaßen als ein Feld von Suggestionen. In den meisten Fällen wird der *Kontext* sogar wie erwähnt imaginiert und idealisiert und so die Konstruktion desselben zu einem bestimmenden Teil des Modells.[7] Ein ähnliches Verfahren kann man bei Projekten von Alison und Peter Smithson beobachten, wo der Kontext zwar die ersten Anhaltspunkte bietet, diese allerdings weniger auf eine unmittelbare städtebauliche und architektonische Form als vielmehr auf eine modell- oder bildhafte Vorstellung über eben diesen Kontext abzielen: Damit wird dem realen, *äußeren* Kontext ein imaginärer, *innerer Kontext* (eine Idee vom Ort) überblendet. Der reale Kontext erhält erst über die Architektur seine eigentliche Prägung: „It would seem as if a building today is only interesting if it is more than itself; if it charges the space around it with connective possibilities."[8] Der umgebende Raum wird mit *verbindenden Möglichkeiten aufgeladen*, die Imagination formt den realen Kontext (Abb. 2–4).[9]

Der Charakter und die Beschaffenheit eines solchen Modells sind in unserer Arbeit jeweils von Projekt zu Projekt verschieden. Einmal ist eine

volves a transformation meant to convey or expose a specific urban quality by means of architecture.

Catalytic Architecture. It is impossible to describe such an architecture in general terms, for the approach outlined here must start with a situation's specific circumstances, and the penetration of city, building, and floor plan is required, both in respect to content and to ambience. Thus, in illustrating the formulated theses, two projects from my own practice will be presented in the following. Both projects aspire not to *produce* urban density but only to *expose* it through a coherence of urban development, architecture, and living style.

The first requirement in pursuing such a process is a structural mindset. Our architectural firm's practice, therefore, is focused on developing a respective conceptual model for each design, based upon context and the given objectives; this is then iteratively translated, step by step, into an urban-development and architectural form. Here we are dealing with fictitious models, epistemologically speaking, for they do not reflect a likeness of reality whence something is then created (descriptive); instead, they take form within the imagination and thereby generate insight for the design (prescriptive). This kind of model building therefore first and foremost represents a heuristic challenge: What are the right structures, analogies, and maybe even images as befits the objectives and the context? Which essential features within the context are slumbering on site, which this project intends to expose and liberate?

The contextual reference in such cases is seldom a typological or morphological one, but is instead conceived in a more general, comprehensive, and abstract way—in a sense, as a field of suggestions. Usually the *context* itself, as noted above, is even imaginary and idealized, and thus the construction of the same becomes a defining part of the model.[7] A similar procedure can be observed in projects by Alison and Peter Smithson, where the context may offer initial points of reference, yet these points are geared less toward an immediate urban-development and architectural form and more toward an exemplary or eidetic conception about these specific contexts: this allows the real, *outer context* to be superimposed with an imaginary, *inner context* (a conception of the place). The real context first attains its true character via the architecture: "It would seem as if a building today is only interesting if it is more than itself; if it charges the space around it with connective possibilities."[8] So the surrounding space is *charged*

---

7   Vgl. „Die Rationalisierung des Bestehenden. Oswald Mathias Ungers im Gespräch mit Rem Koolhaas und Hans Ulrich Obrist", in: *Arch+* 179 (2006), S. 6–11.

8   Alison Smithson/Peter Smithson: *Without Rhetoric. An Architectural Aesthetic 1955–1972*, Cambridge 1974, S. 36.

9   Vgl. Elli Mosayebi/Christian Mueller Inderbitzin: *Picturesque – Synthese im Bildhaften*, Zürich 2008, S. 38–47.

7   See "Die Rationalisierung des Bestehenden: Oswald Mathias Ungers im Gespräch mit Rem Koolhaas und Hans Ulrich Obrist," *Arch+* 179 (2006), pp. 6–11.

8   Alison Smithson and Peter Smithson, *Without Rhetoric: An Architectural Aesthetic 1955–1972* (Cambridge, MA, 1974), p. 36.

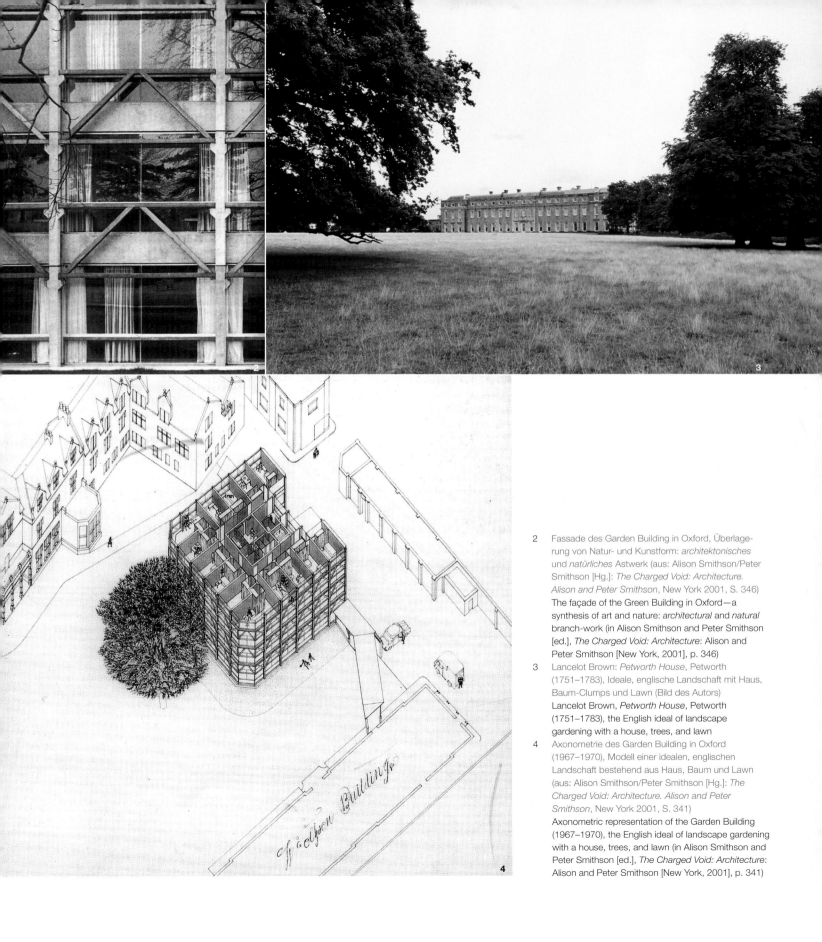

2 Fassade des Garden Building in Oxford, Überlagerung von Natur- und Kunstform: *architektonisches* und *natürliches* Astwerk (aus: Alison Smithson/Peter Smithson [Hg.]: *The Charged Void: Architecture. Alison and Peter Smithson*, New York 2001, S. 346)

The façade of the Green Building in Oxford—a synthesis of art and nature: *architectural* and *natural* branch-work (in Alison Smithson and Peter Smithson [ed.], *The Charged Void: Architecture*: Alison and Peter Smithson [New York, 2001], p. 346)

3 Lancelot Brown: *Petworth House*, Petworth (1751–1783), Ideale, englische Landschaft mit Haus, Baum-Clumps und Lawn (Bild des Autors)

Lancelot Brown, *Petworth House*, Petworth (1751–1783), the English ideal of landscape gardening with a house, trees, and lawn

4 Axonometrie des Garden Building in Oxford (1967–1970), Modell einer idealen, englischen Landschaft bestehend aus Haus, Baum und Lawn (aus: Alison Smithson/Peter Smithson [Hg.]: *The Charged Void: Architecture. Alison and Peter Smithson*, New York 2001, S. 341)

Axonometric representation of the Garden Building (1967–1970), the English ideal of landscape gardening with a house, trees, and lawn (in Alison Smithson and Peter Smithson [ed.], *The Charged Void: Architecture*: Alison and Peter Smithson [New York, 2001], p. 341)

5 Platzspitz Park in Zürich © Christian Mueller Inderbitzin

with connective possibilities, with imagination forming the real context (figs. 2–4).[9]

The character and nature of this kind of model in our work differ from project to project. Sometimes a single idea plays the key role, while other times several topics are consolidated and asserted with equal strength. Decisive for the success of a model composition is the language used, which functions, on the one hand, as operator or catalyst, but also simultaneously as control instrument. The linguistic phrasing or definition of a model gives an indication of its nature, conclusiveness, vagueness, and meaning. The form taken by this linguistic phrasing often takes the form of a (cognitive) metaphor, whereby model and metaphor become virtually equipollent. For metaphors are what lend the model vividness: they derive their catalytic agency from "an implicit comparison between two entities which are not alike but can be compared in an imaginative way. The comparison is mostly done through a creative leap that ties different objects together, producing a new entity in which the characteristics of both take part.[10]

Example 1: Speich-Areal Residential and Office Building, Zurich-Wipkingen. Our first example entails a project involving a residential and office building by the name of Speich-Areal in the western part Zurich. It is located between a perimeter-block district, a heterogeneous structure bordering on Wipkingerplatz, the Hardbrücke (Zurich's only municipal autobahn), and the Limmat river basin (figs. 6 and 8). The area belongs to a district conservation zone, which was established through the perimeter-block district up the hill and which sets essential federal building parameters for the project. Today the area is occupied by small, individual buildings and not widely used (fig. 7).

The idea for the design targeted a city-owned building that meets the demands of the district conservation zone while at the same time able to enhance the various different facets of the city with new character through an expressive, Janus-faced solution (fig. 15). The project accommodates these conditions with a voluminous structure which establishes—through its expressive form and two uniquely articulated sides—a powerful presence as well as individuality while simultaneously fulfilling a mediating function. Particularly referenced here is the prominent architectural formation on the Wipkingerplatz side, which possesses the power to give this locale a new identity (fig. 13). On the Hönggerstrasse side, the expression of this new structure ties into the perimeter-block buildings typical for this district, which are equipped with a classical arrange-

einzige Idee bestimmend, ein anderes Mal verdichten sich mehrere Themen und treten gleichwertig nebeneinander. Entscheidend für das Gelingen der Modellbildung ist die Sprache. Sie funktioniert einerseits als Operator oder Katalysator, gleichzeitig aber auch als Kontrollinstrument. Die sprachliche Fassung respektive Benennbarkeit eines Modells gibt Aufschluss über dessen Beschaffenheit, Schlüssigkeit, Unschärfe und Bedeutung. Die Form dieser sprachlichen Fassung besitzt dabei vielfach den Charakter einer (kognitiven) Metapher, wobei Modell und Metapher praktisch gleichbedeutend werden. Denn Metaphern machen das Modell erst anschaulich: Ihre katalytische Wirkung beziehen sie aus einem „Vergleich zwischen zwei Ereignissen, welche nicht gleich sind, aber in einer anschaulichen Art miteinander verglichen werden können. Der Vergleich wird meist durch einen schöpferischen Gedanken gefunden, der unterschiedliche Objekte miteinander verbindet und ein neues Bild erfindet, in welches die Charakteristiken beider einfließen."[10]

Beispiel 1: Wohn- und Gewerbehaus Speich-Areal, Zürich-Wipkingen. Das erste Beispiel zeigt das Projekt für ein Wohn- und Gewerbehaus in Zürich West. Das Speich-Areal befindet sich zwischen einem Blockrandquartier, einer heterogenen Bebauung um den Wipkingerplatz, der Hardbrücke – der einzigen Stadtautobahn in Zürich – und dem Flussraum der Limmat (Abb. 6 und 8). Das Areal ist einer Quartiererhaltungszone zugeordnet, welche im hangaufwärts gelegenen Blockrandquartier begründet liegt und wesentliche baugesetzliche Vorgaben für das Projekt setzt. Heute ist das Areal mit einzelnen, kleinen Gebäuden besetzt und wenig genutzt (Abb. 7).

Die Vorstellung des Entwurfs zielte auf ein städtisches Gebäude, das den Anforderungen der Quartiererhaltungszone gerecht wird und gleichzeitig über eine ausdrucksstarke, janusköpfige Lösung den jeweils anders

> Die sprachliche Fassung respektive Benennbarkeit eines Modells gibt Aufschluss über dessen Beschaffenheit, Schlüssigkeit, Unschärfe und Bedeutung.

gearteten Stadtseiten ein neues Gepräge geben kann (Abb. 15). Das Projekt trägt diesen Bedingungen mit einem Volumen Rechnung, das in seiner expressiven Gestalt und mittels zweier unterschiedlich formulierter Seiten eine hohe Präsenz und Eigenständigkeit aufbaut, dabei aber gleichzeitig eine vermittelnde Funktion erfüllt. Damit ist insbesondere die Kopfausbildung zum Wipkingerplatz gemeint, welche die Kraft besitzt, diesem Ort eine neue Identität zu geben (Abb. 13). Auf der Seite der Hönggerstrasse knüpft der Neubau in seinem Ausdruck an die quartiertypischen Blockrandbauten an, die über eine klassische Gliederung in Sockel, Regelgeschosse und Attika sowie architektonische Elemente wie Erker und Dachterrassen verfügen.

9   See Elli Mosayebi and Christian Mueller Inderbitzin, *Picturesque – Synthese im Bildhaften* (Zurich, 2008), pp. 38–47.

10   Oswald Mathias Ungers, *Morphologie: City Metaphors* (Cologne, 2011), p. 10.

10   Oswald Mathias Ungers: *Morphologie. City Metaphors*, Köln 2011, S. 10.

Sie wird mit einer plastischen Verwischung oder Verschmelzung der drei Bereiche überformt, die wesentlich zur Expressivität und der am Ort geforderten Ausdruckskraft beiträgt. Auch die Befensterung sucht eine Nähe zum Bestand. Gleichzeitig überführen die liegenden Lochöffnungen, welche zum Platz hin zu bandartigen Fenstern wechseln (Büronutzung), den Ausdruck in eine zeitgemäße Architektursprache. Auch die äußere Materialisierung mit leicht glänzender Keramik – in seiner Farbe an die typischen, ockerfarbenen Backsteine erinnernd – folgt dieser Absicht, kontrapunktiert respektive entmaterialisiert aber durch je nach Tageszeit unterschiedliche Lichtreflexionen die relative Massigkeit und Schwere des Körpers.

Auf der Flussseite wird durch eine feine Terrassierung des Gartens, die Ausbildung der *Hofgebäude* als Gebäudesockel sowie Balkone und Dachterrassen ein wiederum eigener Charakter erzeugt, der als vertikaler oder hängender Garten gelesen werden kann. Diese Idee wird mit der Vorstellung eines Grünraums überlagert, der sich sukzessive mit der Höhe kultiviert, das heißt von der *wilden* Natur des Flussraumes in einen immer *künstlicheren* Aggregatzustand übergeht. Mit dieser Entwicklung geht eine zunehmende Privatisierung der Grünräume einher: auf die untersten Bereiche am flussbegleitenden Weg, die im Zusammenspiel mit einer Lokalnutzung im Hofgebäude und der Wegverbindung ins Quartier durchaus öffentlich zugänglich sein können, folgen gemeinschaftliche Bereiche für das gesamte Haus (Abb. 12).

> Auf der Flussseite wird durch eine feine Terrassierung des Gartens, die Ausbildung der *Hofgebäude* als Gebäudesockel sowie Balkone und Dachterrassen ein wiederum eigener Charakter erzeugt, der als vertikaler oder hängender Garten gelesen werden kann.

Städtische Mischnutzung. Das Erdgeschoss vermittelt zwischen Straßen- und Flussseite: die hier angeordneten *Offenen Räume* verfügen zur Straße hin über *öffentliche* Raumbereiche mit Schaufenstern, die sich zum Garten und Fluss in einer Zweigeschossigkeit öffnen und sukzessive privatisieren lassen. Damit lassen sich diese Räume sowohl als Läden wie auch als Ateliers mit Wohnnutzung einrichten (Abb. 10 und 11). Im bestehenden Hofgebäude, das am öffentlichen Durchgang respektive der Wegverbindung zum Fluss liegt, wird ein Atelier sowie flussseitig ein kleines Lokal mit Terrasse – beispielsweise eine Gelateria für die sommerlichen Nutzer des Flussraumes – vorgeschlagen. Das Atelier könnte periodisch an einen Artist in Residence vergeben werden, um dem Ort eine Magnetkraft zu geben.

Über dem Erdgeschoss folgen drei identische Regelgeschosse, mit jeweils angemessen großen und von der Zimmeranzahl unterschiedlichen Wohnungen sowie einer gut unterteilbaren Gewerbefläche im Gebäudekopf. Die Wohnungsgrundrisse bieten einen großen, räumlichen Reichtum und verschiedene Nutzungsmöglichkeiten. Die Layouts reagieren zudem

ment of plinths, upper stories, and attics as well as architectural elements like oriels and roof terraces. The Speich-Areal building is transformed through a sculptural coalescing or amalgamating of the three areas, which strongly contributes to its own personal expressiveness and to that demanded by its situational context. The window design likewise seeks to approximate the given surroundings. At the same time, the recumbent openings that flow into ribbon-like windows on the plaza size (office space) imbue the building with contemporary architectural language. The outer materialization, too, with its slightly glossy ceramic veneer—in a color tone reminiscent of typical, ocher-colored bricks—is in line with this pursuit, with various reflections of light, depending on time of day, contrasting or dematerializing the relative massiveness or bulkiness of the structural shell.

On the river side, a personal character is in turn engendered—with the yard subtly terraced, the *courtyard structure* developed as plinth, plus balconies and roof terraces—that can be read as a vertical or hanging garden. This idea is superimposed by the conception of a section of greenery that becomes successively cultivated the higher it rises, meaning that it shifts from a state of *wild* nature at the riverbank to one of increasingly more artificial aggregation. Accompanying this development is the heightened privatization of the greenery spaces: in the lower sections along the river path, which could easily be made publicly accessible in accord with a local utilization of the courtyard building and the connecting path into the district, common areas for the entire building take form (fig. 12).

Urban Mixed Use. The ground floor mediates between the street and river ends of the building: the *open spaces* arranged here make available, on the street side, *public* spatial zones with display windows which, on the reverse side, open to the yard and river through a two-story design and can also be successively privatized. This allows these rooms to be used either as shops or as studios with integrated living space (figs. 10 and 11). The existing courtyard building, which lies along the public passage or pathway toward the river, has been designed to house a studio as well as a small riverfront restaurant with terrace, such as a gelateria for passersby enjoying the riverside area in summer. The studio could be periodically rented to an artist-in-residence, thus imbuing the site with magnetic attraction, so to speak.

Above ground level there are three identical upper stories, each with appropriately large apartments that possess a varied number of rooms as well as easily partitionable commercial space to the front of the building. The apartment ground plans offer an abundance of space and various utilization possibilities. Moreover, the layouts react to the difficult conditions for noise protection: an open room at the river end of the building, which is multipurpose in use and can be added to the apartment,

strongly privatized, with fruit trees arousing associations of former times.

Varying Density Forms. Both projects structurally densify the respective situation *to the inside*. In one case, a hardly used, practically deserted, inner-city area is filled with a large new structure of urban mixed zoning. In the second example, an unoccupied garden lot behind former farm areas is graced with a rather small residential structure. Despite awareness that such densification would make sense thanks to familiar reasoning, the driving force of the design concepts lay elsewhere: with the development of an idea that translates the factors specific to each respective situation into equally tailored architecture, or that engenders an architecture which makes the qualities of these factors visible and experienceable in an Ovidian sense.[14] Included among these factors is the person who would live, work, or stroll along there in future. And this person should encounter a different urban *density* in Zurich-Schwamendingen than in Zurich-West.

Translation Dawn Michelle d'Atri

tes, praktisch brachliegendes, innerstädtisches Areal mit einem großen Neubau und einer städtischen Mischnutzung besetzt. Im anderen Beispiel wird ein bisher nicht bebautes Gartengrundstück im Rücken von ehemaligen Bauernhöfen mit einem kleineren Wohnhaus bebaut. Trotz der Einsicht, dass eine solche Verdichtung aus bekannten Gründen sinnvoll ist, lag die treibende Kraft der Entwürfe woanders: nämlich bei der Entwicklung einer Vorstellung, welche die spezifischen Merkmale der jeweiligen Situation in eine ebenso spezifische Architektur überführt respektive eine Architektur erzeugt, welche die Qualitäten dieser Merkmale in Ovidschem Sinn sicht- und erlebbar macht.[14] Zu diesen „Merkmalen" gehört ganz wesentlich der Mensch, der in Zukunft dort wohnt, arbeitet oder flaniert. Und dieser Mensch soll in Zürich-Schwamendingen eine andere *urbane Dichte* vorfinden als in Zürich West.

14 In Ovid's *Metamorphoses* the act of metamorphosis reveals the essence of character, the actual being: "The fundamental also lives on in the new guise, and is determinative thereof. In its new guise, the essence is much more prominent and usually makes more sense than the previous form." Cited from Heinrich Dörrie, "Wandlung und Dauer: Ovids Metamorphosen und Poseidonios' Lehre von der Substanz," *Der altsprachliche Unterricht* 4, no. 2 (1959), pp. 95–116, esp. p. 97.

14 In den *Metamorphosen* von Ovid legt die Verwandlung stets den Kern des Charakters, das eigentliche Wesen frei: „Das Fundamentale lebt auch in der neuen Erscheinung fort und bestimmt sie. In der neuen Erscheinung tritt das Eigentliche viel stärker hervor und ist meist sinnvoller als das bisherige." Heinrich Dörrie: „Wandlung und Dauer. Ovids Metamorphosen und Poseidonios' Lehre von der Substanz", in: *Der altsprachliche Unterricht*, 4,2 (1959), S. 95–116, hier S. 97.

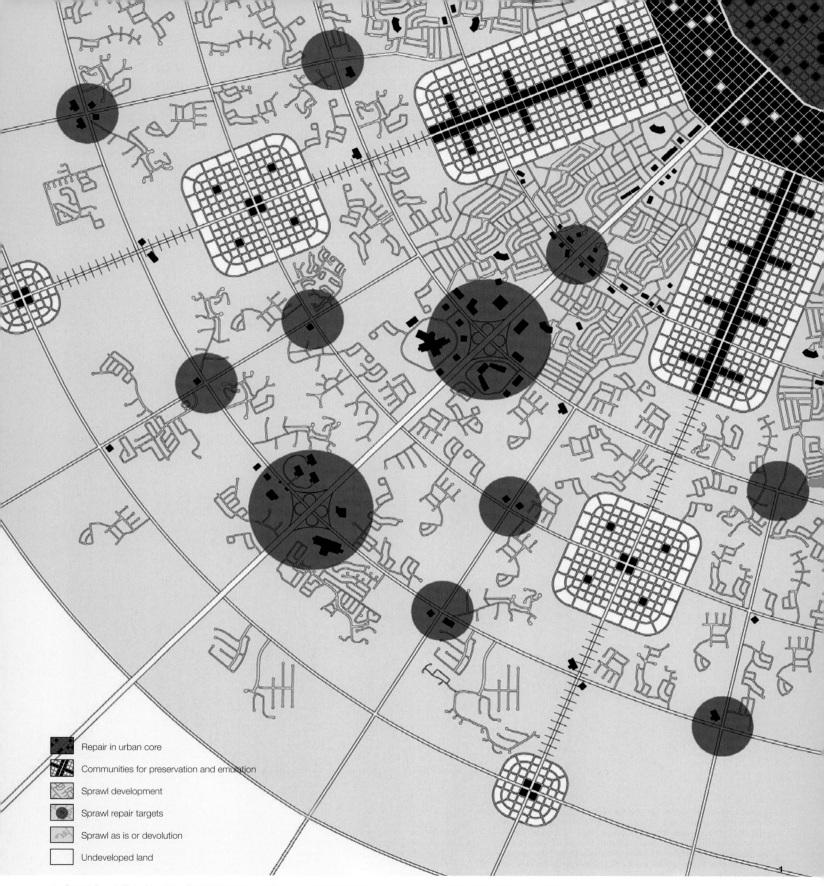

Repair in urban core

Communities for preservation and emulation

Sprawl development

Sprawl repair targets

Sprawl as is or devolution

Undeveloped land

1   Sprawl Repair-Ziele: Handels-, Beschäftigungs- und Transportknotenpunkte weisen ein großes Potenzial für die Sanierung auf.   Sprawl repair targets: commercial, employment, and transportation nodes showing great potential for redevelopment.   © Duany Plater-Zyberk & Company (DPZ)

The Sprawl Repair Method

How to Transform Sprawl into Complete,
Balanced Communities[1]

In 1963 Greek architect and town planner Constantinos Doxiadis published the book *Architecture in Transition*[2]. No mere contemplation on architecture, the book boldly called for a transition from traditional urbanism to new settlement patterns that would accommodate the car, its movement, and its speed. Doxiadis recognized the contrast between human-scaled and automobile-scaled development.

Die *Sprawl Repair*-Methode – wie man Zersiedelungsgebiete in umfassende, ausgewogene Gemeinschaften umgestaltet.[1] Im Jahr 1963 veröffentlichte der griechische Architekt und Stadtplaner Constantinos Doxiadis das Buch *Architecture in Transition*.[2] Statt eines bloßen Nachdenkens über Architektur fordert das Buch entschieden einen Wechsel von traditioneller Stadtplanung hin zu neuen Siedlungsstrukturen, die das Auto, seine Bewegung und sein Tempo berücksichtigten.

GALINA TACHIEVA

Doxiadis recognized the contrast between human-scaled and automobile-scaled development. He observed that cars change our perception of the built environment because they move faster than people and that they influence the city and its physical structure. Residences, shops, offices, schools, and other institutions of daily life do not need to be in close vicinity to each other when people move around in cars.

Today we have achieved most of Doxiadis' aspirations (and those of other utopian planners such as Le Corbusier) in the transition from pedestrian urbanism to car-oriented urbanism, from small blocks, narrow streets, and organic urban fabric designed for people to wide streets, big parking facilities, and highway interchanges designed for cars. This transition created a landscape dominated by suburban sprawl and has brought with it a gamut of unexpected negative consequences. It is evident that the transition was a mistake. The *Sprawl Repair Manual*[3] proposes another transition: the shift from auto-dependent, single-use, mega-block monocultures to complete and walkable human-scale communities.

The history and consequences of suburban development, specifically sprawl, are well documented. Numerous books articulate the trajectory of sprawl within its historical context—from the Federal Housing Administration's mortgages for new construction, the subsidies of the interstate highway system, and the tax laws allowing accelerated depreciation of commercial development, to the evolution of Euclidean zoning's separation of uses and the cultural mandate for separation by race. Recent publications put forward the need to redevelop sprawl and what specifically should be repaired; among them are *Greyfields into Goldfields*[4] and *Malls into Main Streets*,[5] as well as reports by the Congress for the New Urbanism. *Retrofitting Suburbia: Urban Design Solutions for Redesigning Suburbs*[6] by Ellen Dunham-Jones and June Williamson explains why we need to retrofit sprawl and, through illuminating and comprehensive analysis, documents successful examples of retrofits.

The *Sprawl Repair Manual* seeks to expand the literature as a guide that illustrates how to repair the full range of suburban conditions, demonstrating a step-by-step design process for the creation of more sustainable communities from those unsustainable places we have already created. This is a framework for designing the interventions, incorporating them into the regulatory system, and implementing them with permitting strategies and financial incentives.

Sprawl is predominantly considered an American phenomenon, but its precursors can be traced to Europe with the first suburbs and the Garden City

Doxiadis nahm damit Bezug auf den Gegensatz zwischen einer an einem menschlichen Maßstab orientierten Raumplanung und einer autobezogenen Entwicklung. Er merkte an, dass Autos unsere Wahrnehmung der gebauten Umwelt verändern, da sie sich schneller als Menschen fortbewegen und so die Stadt und ihre sichtbare Struktur beeinflussen. Wohnorte, Geschäfte, Büros, Schulen und andere Institutionen des täglichen Lebens müssen nicht in unmittelbarer Nähe zueinander sein, wenn Menschen mit dem Auto fahren.

Heute haben wir die meisten von Doxiadis' Forderungen (und die anderer utopischer Planer wie Le Corbusier) im Wandel von einem Städtebau für Fußgänger hin zu einem am Auto orientierten Urbanismus erreicht, von kleinen Blocks, engen Straßen und einem organischen Stadtgefüge, das für Menschen entworfen ist, hin zu breiten Straßen, umfangreichen Parkmöglichkeiten und Autobahnkreuzungen, die für Autos geplant sind. Diese Veränderung schuf eine von vorstädtischer Zersiedelung geprägte Landschaft und brachte ein Bündel unerwarteter negativer Folgen mit sich. Es wurde rasch klar, dass der Wechsel ein Fehler war. Das *Sprawl Repair Manual*[3] schlägt eine andere Veränderung vor: eine Umgestaltung der vom Auto abhängigen, auf eine Funktion ausgerichteten Megablock-Monokulturen in umfassende, fußläufige Gemeinschaften nach menschlichem Maßstab.

Die Geschichte und die Konsequenzen vorstädtischer Entwicklung – im Besonderen die Zersiedelung – sind gut dokumentiert. Zahlreiche Bücher fassen den Entwicklungsgang im historischen Kontext zusammen, von den Darlehen der staatlichen Wohnbauförderung für Neubauten, den Subventionen für das Autobahnsystem und den Steuergesetzen, die eine schnellere Abschreibung für gewerbliche Erweiterungen ermöglichen, bis hin zur Entstehung einer Euklidischen Zonentrennung nach Funktionen und dem kulturellen Mandat zur Rassentrennung. Aktuelle Veröffentlichungen betonen die Notwendigkeit, die Zersiedelungsgebiete neu zu erschließen und erörtern, was konkret verbessert werden sollte, wie beispielsweise *Greyfields into Goldfields*[4] und *Malls into Main Streets*,[5] sowie Berichte vom Kongress über den New Urbanism. *Retrofitting Suburbia:*

1 This article was adapted with permission from July/August 2011 DesignIntelligence, (di.net), Copyright Greenway Communications. Excerpted from the Sprawl Repair Manual, published by Island Press (islandpress.org) in 2010.

2 Constantinos A. Doxiadis, *Architecture in Transition* (London, 1963).

3 Galina Tachieva: *Sprawl Repair Manual* (Washington, DC, 2010).

4 Lee S. Sobel and Steven Bodzin, *Greyfields into Goldfields: Dead Malls become Living Neighborhoods* (Chicago, 2002).

5 Congress for the New Urbanism, *Malls into Mainstreets: An In-Depth Guide to Transforming Dead Malls into Communities* (Chicago, 2006).

6 Ellen Dunham-Jones and June Williamson, *Retrofitting Suburbia: Urban Design Solutions for Redesigning Suburbs* (Hoboken, NJ, 2008).

1 Dieser Text wurde mit freundlicher Genehmigung in veränderter Form aus DesignIntelligence Juli/August 2011, (di.net), Copyright Greenway Communications, übernommen. Der Auszug aus dem Sprawl Repair Manual wurde von Island Press (islandpress.org) im Jahr 2010 veröffentlicht.

2 Constantinos A. Doxiadis: *Architecture in Transition*, London 1963.

3 Galina Tachieva: *Sprawl Repair Manual*, Washington, DC 2010.

4 Lee S. Sobel/Steven Bodzin: *Greyfields into Goldfields. Dead Malls Become Living Neighborhoods*, Chicago 2002.

5 Congress for the New Urbanism. *Malls into Mainstreets. An In-Depth Guide to Transforming Dead Malls into Communities*, Chicago 2006.

Urban Design Solutions for Redesigning Suburbs[6] von Ellen Dunham-Jones und June Williamson erörtert, weshalb es nötig ist, die Zersiedelungsgebiete zu sanieren und erfolgreiche Beispiele der Sanierungen durch anschauliche und umfassende Analyse zu dokumentieren.

Das *Sprawl Repair Manual* versucht, die Literatur durch eine Anleitung zu erweitern, wie man die gesamte Bandbreite vorstädtischer Bedingungen verbessert, indem ein schrittweiser Entwurfsprozess zur Schaffung von nachhaltigeren Gemeinschaften ausgehend von den nicht nachhaltigen Orten aufgezeigt wird, die wir bereits geschaffen haben. Es ist eine Anweisung, um Maßnahmen zu entwickeln, diese in das baurechtliche System einzubeziehen und sie mit Strategien, die eine Genehmigung ermöglichen und finanziellen Anreizen umzusetzen.

Die Zersiedelung wird vor allem als amerikanisches Phänomen betrachtet, doch ihre Vorstufen können bis nach Europa mit den ersten Vorstädten und der Gartenstadt-Bewegung zurückverfolgt werden. Mit einer bedeutenden Städtebautradition hat sich Europa nicht bis zu den schlimmsten Extremen der Zersiedelung gesteigert, solange sie nicht in verschiedenen Erscheinungsformen importiert wurde, sodass in den Peripherien der meisten Großstädte die gleichen Mängel wie in ihren amerikanischen Gegenstücken diagnostiziert werden können. Die europäische Art der Zersiedelung ist unterschiedlich in Bezug auf ihren historischen Kontext und die Morphologie. Die europäische Zersiedelung tauchte später als die amerikanische in einer höheren Bebauungsdichte und in einer weniger „erfolgreichen" Weise auf. Doch erleben die Stadtränder von Rom, Paris, London und vielen anderen europäischen Hauptstädten eine ähnliche, für das Auto geschaffene Trennung von Funktionen, eine Fragmentierung und einen Verlust von fußläufiger Erschließung. Die Zersiedelungsflächen setzen sich aus Ansiedelungen zusammen, in denen soziale Wohnbauten mit privaten, spekulativen Wohngebieten in einer planlosen, unstrukturierten Weise gemischt werden. Diese äußeren Zonen sind durch einen Mangel an Verbindungswegen, öffentlichen Räumen und Betrieben geprägt. Diese Sektoren, wie sie sich heute darstellen, miteinander zu verbinden, ist eine Herausforderung, da sie unabhängige, monofunktionale Enklaven mit geringer Dichte sind. Was wir brauchen, ist ein System einer gezielten Verdichtung und Verknüpfung zwischen wichtigen Verkehrsadern und kommerziellen Knotenpunkten. In diesem Sinne kann die *Sprawl Repair*-Methode auch im europäischen Kontext nach einigen Anpassungen an örtliche Gegebenheiten sinnvoll sein.

6   Ellen Dunham-Jones/June Williamson, *Retrofitting Suburbia*, Hoboken, NJ 2008.

Movement. Europe, having a significant tradition in its town building, did not escalate into the worst extremes of sprawl until it was imported in various incarnations where the peripheries of most of the largest cities can be diagnosed with the deficiencies of their American counterparts. The European type of sprawl is different in terms of historic context and morphology. The European sprawl appeared later than the one in the U.S., in higher-density built form and in a less "booming" manner. However, the outskirts of Rome, Paris, London and many other European capitals suffer from similar car-oriented separation of uses, fragmentation and the lack of walkability. The sprawling pattern is made up of settlements, in which public housing is mixed with private speculative residential areas in a confused, unstructured manner. These outer zones are characterized by a lack of connectivity, public spaces, and services. Connecting these sectors as they stand today is a challenge, as these are independent, low-density, single-use enclaves. What is needed is a system of targeted intensification and connectivity between important transportation and commercial nodes. In this sense, the sprawl repair method can—after some adjustments to the local conditions—be useful also in the European context.

The Need to Repair Sprawl. Sprawl is an outdated and dysfunctional form of development. Its gargantuan problems have been pointed out over the past few decades, but the recent economic and real estate calamities—with shopping centers, office parks, and entire subdivisions failing economically and socially—demonstrate the urgent need to address these problems. The responsible and sustainable way to deal with sprawl is neither to abandon it nor to continue building in the same pattern but to repair and reorganize as much of it as possible into complete, livable, and robust communities. Sprawl is inflexible in its physical form and will not naturally mature into walkable environments. Without precise interventions, sprawl might morph to some degree but it is unlikely that this development will result in a diverse, sustainable urbanism. It is imperative that we repair sprawl consciously and methodically through design, policy, and incentives. In spite of the endless challenges posed by sprawl, many opportunities exist, and this is the right time to tackle them. Rising energy costs will make long commutes unaffordable. A changing climate compels us to pollute less. We need to increase physical activity to overcome the epidemic of obesity and chronic diseases. Some arguments for sprawl repair are of economic nature. In the U.S., baby boomers and millennials are emerging as a new class of buyers and are creating a major shift in the housing market. Together they represent more than 135 million people, many of them oriented towards a diverse, compact ur-

> What is needed is a system of targeted intensification and connectivity between important transportation and commercial nodes. In this sense, the sprawl repair method can—after some adjustments to the local conditions—be useful also in the European context.

banism. According to AARP's report "Home and Community Preferences of the 45+ Population," aging baby boomers will prefer to retire in their suburban homes, which are their largest personal investments. If we provide nearby amenities, senior residents can potentially age in their familiar place and invest in existing neighborhoods instead of moving. We need to "amenitize" sprawling single-use developments to accommodate these growing needs. Employment decentralization is a fact, and most businesses are located outside city limits. Existing single-use, auto-oriented workplaces and commercial hubs can be redeveloped into complete communities with balanced uses and transportation options. Existing jobs can be saved, and new jobs, many of them green, can be created in the process of—and as a result of—transforming sprawl. The sprawl repair method offers a comprehensive strategy to accomplish these imperatives. Based on knowledge gained from built projects,[7] the method incorporates the repair of the full range of suburban development types. It demonstrates a step-by-step process for the creation of more sustainable human settlements out of our wasteful sprawling landscape. The method provides a framework for designing the interventions, incorporating them into the regulatory system, and implementing them with permitting strategies and financial incentives. The approach addresses a range of scales from the region down to the community, street, block, and building. The method identifies deficiencies in typical elements of sprawl and determines the best remedial techniques for those deficiencies. Recommendations for regulatory and economic incentives are also addressed.

To identify the proper targets for repair, it is essential to understand the form and structure of sprawl in the American built environment. Sprawl and suburbia are not synonymous.

Sprawl Repair Defined. Sprawl repair transforms failing or potentially failing single-use and car-dominated developments into complete communities that have a better economic, social, and environmental performance. The objective of the sprawl repair strategy is to build communities based on the neighborhood unit, similar to the traditional fabric that was established in cities and suburbs prior to World War II. The primary tactic of sprawl repair is to insert the missing elements of functioning community fabric—buildings, density, public space, additional connections—to complete and diversify the mono-cultural agglomerations of sprawl: residential subdivisions, strip shopping centers, office parks, suburban campuses, malls, and edge cities. By systematically modifying the reparable areas (turning subdivisions into pedestrian-friendly neighborhoods and shopping centers and malls into town centers) and leaving to devolution those areas that are irreparable (aban-

---

7   Built or under construction sprawl repair projects include Mashpee Commons, arguably the first greyfield development in the U.S.; Downtown Kendall, Florida, an edge city repair; Legacy Town Center, Texas, a corporate office mixed-use infill, among many others.

212

Die Notwendigkeit zur Umgestaltung der Zersiedelung.

Die Zersiedelung ist eine veraltete und dysfunktionale Form der Raumerschließung. Auf ihre gewaltigen Probleme wurde in den vergangenen Jahrzehnten hingewiesen, doch die jüngsten Wirtschafts- und Immobilienkrisen – mit Einkaufszentren, Bürokomplexen und ganzen Wohnsiedlungen, die wirtschaftlich und sozial verfehlt sind – zeigen die dringende Notwendigkeit auf, diese Probleme aufzugreifen. Eine verantwortungsvolle und nachhaltige Art, mit der Zersiedelung umzugehen, besteht darin, weder die Bauten aufzugeben, noch sie im gleichen Muster weiterzubauen, sondern so viel wie möglich davon zu verbessern und zu komplettieren, um lebenswerte und starke Gemeinschaften neu zu organisieren. Die Zersiedelung ist in ihrer physischen Form unflexibel und wird sich nicht von selbst zu einer fußläufigen Umgebung weiterentwickeln. Ohne bestimmte Eingriffe könnte sich die Zersiedelung bis zu einem gewissen Grad verändern, doch ist es unwahrscheinlich, dass diese Entwicklung zu einem vielfältigen, nachhaltigen Urbanismus führt. Es ist dringend erforderlich, dass wir die Zersiedelung bewusst und methodisch durch Entwurf, politisches Handeln und Anregungen reparieren. Trotz der endlosen durch die Zersiedelung entstandenen Herausforderungen gibt es viele Möglichkeiten und nun ist der richtige Zeitpunkt, um dies anzugehen. Steigende Energiekosten machen lange Pendelfahrten unwirtschaftlich. Die Klimaveränderungen zwingen uns, die Umwelt weniger zu belasten. Wir müssen die körperliche Aktivität erhöhen, um die Epidemie der Übergewichtigkeit und chronische Krankheiten zu überwinden. Einige Begründungen für die Umgestaltung der Zersiedelung sind wirtschaftlicher Natur. In den USA haben sich die „Babyboomer" und die „Millenium-Generation" als neue Klasse von Käufern gebildet und erzeugen einen wichtigen Wandel auf dem Wohnungsmarkt. Zusammen repräsentieren sie mehr als 135 Millionen Menschen, von denen sich viele an einer abwechslungsreichen, dichten Stadtstruktur orientieren. Laut dem AARP-Bericht „Home and Community Preferences of the 45+ Population" werden es die alternden „Babyboomer" bevorzugen, sich in ihren Häusern in der Vorstadt, die ihre größten persönlichen Investitionen darstellen, zur Ruhe zu setzen. Wenn wir nahe gelegene Annehmlichkeiten bieten, können ältere Einwohner möglichst in ihrer gewohnten Umgebung alt werden und in bestehende Viertel investieren anstatt umzuziehen. Wir müssen die monofunktionalen Planungen der Zersiedelungsgebiete „attraktiver" machen, um sie den wachsenden Anforderungen anzupassen. Die Dezentralisierung der Beschäftigung ist eine Tatsache und die meisten Betriebe befinden sich außerhalb der Stadtgrenzen. Bestehende monofunktionale, für den Autogebrauch angelegte Arbeitsplätze und kommerzielle Knotenpunkte können zu umfassenden Gemeinschaften mit ausgewogenen Nutzungen und Transportmöglichkeiten neu gestaltet werden. Bestehende Arbeitsplätze können erhalten

und neue Arbeitsplätze – viele von ihnen „grün" – können im Prozess und als Folge der Umwandlung der Zersiedelungsgebiete geschaffen werden. Die *Sprawl Repair*-Methode bietet eine umfassende Strategie, um diese Ansprüche zu erreichen. Die Methode beruht auf Kenntnissen, die aus gebauten Projekten gewonnen wurden,[7] und beinhaltet die gesamte Bandbreite von vorstädtischen Entwicklungstypen. Sie zeigt ein schrittweises Verfahren, bei dem aus unserer ausufernd zersiedelten Landschaft nachhaltigere, menschenwürdige Siedlungen geschaffen werden. Die Methode legt allgemeine Regeln für die Gestaltung von Eingriffen vor, die in das baurechtliche System einbezogen und mit Strategien zur Genehmigung und finanziellen Anreizen umgesetzt werden. Der Ansatz richtet sich an mehrere Maßstabsebenen von der Region hin zur Gemeinde, der Straße, dem Block und dem Gebäude. Die Methode erfasst Defizite in typischen Elementen der Zersiedelungsgebiete und bestimmt die beste Technik zur Abhilfe für diese Mängel. Empfehlungen für rechtliche und wirtschaftliche Anreize werden ebenfalls angesprochen.

Der Begriff *Sprawl Repair*. *Sprawl Repair* wandelt fehlgeschlagene oder möglicherweise verfehlte monofunktionale und vom Auto dominierte Entwicklungsregionen in umfassende Gemeinschaften mit einer verbesserten wirtschaftlichen, sozialen und ökologischen Leistung um. Das Ziel der *Sprawl Repair*-Strategie besteht im Aufbau von Nachbarschaften, die auf Vierteln ähnlich dem traditionellen Gefüge beruhen, das in den Städten und Vororten vor dem Zweiten Weltkrieg errichtet wurde. Die hauptsächliche Methode von *Sprawl Repair* ist, die fehlenden Elemente für eine funktionierende Gemeinschaft einzufügen – Gebäude, Dichte, öffentlichen Raum, zusätzliche Verbindungen – um die monokulturellen Ansammlungen der Zersiedelung zu ergänzen und vielfältiger zu gestalten: Wohnsiedlungen, langgestreckte Supermärkte, Bürokomplexe, vorstädtische Universitätscampus-Gebiete, Einkaufszentren und Außenstadtzentren. Durch die systematische Umgestaltung der reparablen Gebiete (indem die Siedlungen in fußgängerfreundliche Nachbarschaften sowie Einkaufszentren und Geschäftshäuser in städtische Zentren umgeformt werden) und dem Rückgang jener Bereiche, die irreparabel sind (indem sie aufgelassen oder in Parks, landwirtschaftliche Flächen oder Naturraum umgewandelt werden), können Teile der Vorstadt als lebenswertere nachhaltige Gegenden neu organisiert werden. Um die geeigneten Zielgebiete für die Reparatur zu definieren, ist es wesentlich, Form und Struktur der Zersiedelung im amerika-

donment or conversion to park, agricultural, or natural land), portions of suburbia can be reorganized into more livable and sustainable communities. To identify the proper targets for repair, it is essential to understand the form and structure of sprawl in the American built environment. Sprawl and suburbia are not synonymous. There are three generations of suburbia that need to be differentiated in terms of their walkability: pre-war suburbs, post-war suburbs, and late twentieth century exurbs. Pre-war suburbs developed along railroad and streetcar corridors and, therefore, have always been quite compact and walkable. In contrast, the latter two types abandoned the pedestrian-centered neighborhood structure in favor of auto-centric dispersion and can be considered sprawl. Sprawl repair concentrates on these two tiers of suburbs.

The Method. Sprawl repair begins with an analysis of the regional scale (fig. 1). While complete communities—cities, towns, and villages—are identified for preservation and emulation, unsustainable but salvageable sprawl elements are identified for repair. For sprawl elements that are beyond repair, the decision must be made whether to leave them as they are, convert them to farmland, or let them devolve into open space.

The sprawl repair method comprises urban design as well as techniques of regulation and implementation. The final products of sprawl repair are communities in which people are provided with better living conditions that do not require the use of the automobile and, as a result save energy and resources, ultimately contributing to a healthier environment. The process leading from the state of sprawl to the state of more effective, sustainable urbanism is dependent on the specific target site, including physical boundaries, regional context and connectivity, ownership pattern, demographics, politics, and economic potential, as well as different construction methods and available technology, materials, and work force. As a result, sprawl repair strategies take a variety of paths, some direct and expeditious, others gradual and sequential. Figure 2 shows the transformation of a sprawl repair target into a complete community. The change of quality of life is represented along the horizontal axis, while the vertical axis shows the quantitative change in the reduction of energy, resources, and infrastructure use per capita after the transformation. The process of transformation is shown in multiple paths: direct (straight line), phased (stepped line) and indirect (circuitous line). The direct path represents a case in which economics and timing support one big-effort, single-phase, radical repair. The phased path includes several steps, with portions of the project developed at different times. The indirect path represents a sequence of changes that bring the project closer to the final repaired state but in a longer, incremental progression of trial and adjustment.

Figure 3 compares the selected urban indicators before and after sprawl repair of a single-family subdivision. It illustrates the redevelopment potential of sprawl as expressed by changes of urban indicators. The density increases substantially—sufficient to support transit. It should be emphasized that transit works at a larger, regional scale, coordinated between retrofitted nodes. For example, a minimum density of 15 units to the acre can support a frequent local bus service. The case shown analyzes occupant density rather than resident or employee density because the sprawl elements have single uses that are re-balanced in the process of sprawl repair. The occupant den-

---

7   Zu den gebauten oder im Bau befindlichen *Sprawl Repair*-Projekten gehören Mashpee Commons, das wohl erste Sanierungsprojekt in den USA; Downtown Kendall Florida, die Erneuerung einer Edge City; Legacy Town Center, Texas, eine Unternehmenszentrale mit gemischt genutzten Teilen, und viele mehr.

The process leading from the state
of sprawl to the state of more effective,
sustainable urbanism is dependent
on the specific target site, including
physical boundaries, regional context
and connectivity, ownership pattern,
demographics, politics, and economic
potential, as well as different
construction methods and available
technology, materials, and work force.

nischen gebauten Umfeld zu verstehen. Zersiedelung und Vorstadt sind nicht synonym. Es gibt drei Generationen von Vorstädten, die in Bezug auf ihre Fußläufigkeit unterschieden werden müssen: Vororte der Vorkriegszeit, Vororte der Nachkriegszeit und den Speckgürtel am Ende des 20. Jahrhunderts. Vororte der Vorkriegszeit entstanden entlang von Eisenbahn- und Straßenbahnkorridoren und waren daher immer ziemlich dicht und fußläufig begehbar. Im Gegensatz dazu gaben die beiden späteren Vorstadttypen die nach den Fußgängern orientierte Struktur der Viertel zugunsten einer auf das Auto hin gerichteten Zersplitterung auf, die man als Zersiedelung bezeichnen kann. *Sprawl Repair* konzentriert sich auf diese beiden Arten von Vorstädten.

Die Methode. *Sprawl Repair* beginnt mit einer Analyse des örtlichen Maßstabs (Abb. 1). Während gewachsene Gemeinschaften – Großstädte, Städte und Dörfer – durch Bestand und Erneuerung definiert werden, werden in Zersiedelungsgebieten die nicht nachhaltigen, aber verbesserbaren Elemente ermittelt, um sie brauchbar zu machen. Für jene Teile der Zersiedelung, die nicht mehr zu beheben sind, muss eine Entscheidung gefällt werden, ob man sie so belässt, wie sie sind, in Ackerland umwandelt oder als Naturraum sich rückbilden lässt.

Die *Sprawl Repair*-Methode umfasst städtebauliche Entwürfe sowie Techniken für die Regulierung und Umsetzung. Das Endprodukt von *Sprawl Repair* sind Gemeinschaften, in denen Menschen mehr Lebensqualität vorfinden, ohne auf den Gebrauch des Autos angewiesen zu sein und in der Folge Energie und Ressourcen sparen, um letztlich zu einer gesünderen Umwelt beizutragen. Der Prozess, der vom Zustand der Zersiedelung zu einer effektiveren, nachhaltigeren Stadtplanung führt, ist vom individuellen Zielgebiet abhängig und umfasst dessen physische Grenzen, den regionalen Kontext und die Verbindungswege, die Eigentumsverhältnisse, die Demografie, die Politik und die wirtschaftliche Leistungsfähigkeit ebenso wie verschiedene Bauweisen und die Verfügbarkeit von Technologie, Material und Arbeitskräften. Daher schlagen *Sprawl Repair*-Strategien eine Vielzahl von Wegen ein, einige davon direkt und rasch, andere stufenweise und aufeinander aufbauend. Die Abbildung 2 zeigt die Umwandlung eines *Sprawl Repair*-Zielgebiets in eine umfassende Gemeinschaft. Die Veränderung in der Lebensqualität ist auf der horizontalen Achse dargestellt, während die vertikale Achse die quantitativen Abweichungen bei der Reduktion von Energie, Ressourcen und der Nutzung der Infrastruktur pro Kopf nach der Umgestaltung anzeigt. Der Prozess der Veränderung wird auf mehreren Wegen dargestellt: direkt (gerade Linie), in Phasen (abgestufte Linie) und indirekt (gekrümmte Linie). Der direkte Pfad stellt den Fall dar, bei dem Ökonomie und zeitliche Koordinierung eine mit großem Aufwand betriebene, einphasige, radikale

CSD Zone	Acres by Zone
CSD 1 Single-family	131
CSD 2 Multi-family	0
CSD 3 Commercial Strip	0
CSD 4 Business Park	0
CSD 5 Shopping Mall	0

Total Emissions	6,345.7 mT CO_2/yr
Emissions per Person	**10.94 mT CO_2/yr**

COMPLETE COMMUNITY COMPOSITION

Transect Zone	Acres by Zone	Mixed Use and Housing Type
T1	0	
T2	0	
T3	40	
T4	20.5	
		40% Single-family Housing 60% Multi-family Housing
		9% Retail, Office and Lodging
T5	40.5	
		0% Single-family Housing 100% Multi-family Housing
		12% Retail, Office and Lodging
T6	0	
		0% Multi-family Housing
		0% Retail, Office and Lodging
CIVIC		
	29.8	Civic Space
	0.2	Civic Buildings

Total Emissions	15,056 mT CO_2/yr
Emissions per Person	**6.74 mT CO_2/yr**

CO_2 EMISSIONS PER PERSON

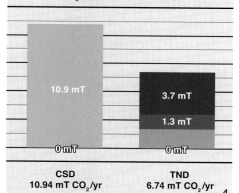

CSD 10.94 mT CO_2/yr	TND 6.74 mT CO_2/yr
10.9 mT	3.7 mT / 1.3 mT
0 mT	0 mT

4

Transformation	Categories	Before	After	Improvement of Urban Indicators
	Site acreage, acres	131	131	1.0
	Total built area,[1] sq. ft.	2,305,196	3,218,863	1.4
	Total building footprint,[2] sq. ft.	432,768	807,382	1.9
	Total building area,[3] sq. ft.	548,688	1,248,841	2.3
	Total occupant load, occupants	2,098	7,169	3.4
	Occupant density, occupants per acre	16	55	3.4
	Parking area per capita, sq. ft. per occupant	64	66	1.0
	Thoroughfare area per capita, sq. ft. per occupant	773	216	0.3
	Thoroughfare length per capita, ft. per occupant	6	2.2	0.4

1 Total built area comprises all construction, including buildings, parking, and thoroughfares.
2 Total building footprint comprises all building footprints, regardless of use.
3 Total building area comprises all building square footage. Garages of single-family residences are included.

2

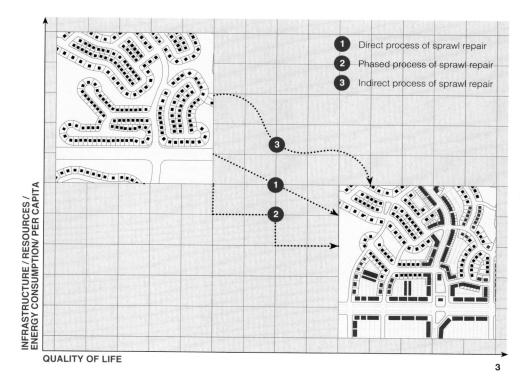

INFRASTRUCTURE / RESOURCES / ENERGY CONSUMPTION/ PER CAPITA

1 Direct process of sprawl repair
2 Phased process of sprawl repair
3 Indirect process of sprawl repair

QUALITY OF LIFE

3

2 Quantitativer Vergleich urbaner Indikatoren in einer Einfamilienhaussiedlung. Quantitative comparison of urban indicators in a single-family subdivision.

3 Konzeptionelle Darstellung der möglichen Wege einer Sprawl Repair und ihre Auswirkung auf den Ressourcenverbrauch pro Kopf sowie die Lebensqualität. Conceptual representation of possible paths of sprawl repair and their effects on resource use per capita and quality of life.

4 CO_2-Fußabdruck pro Siedlungsmodell – ein Vergleich zwischen der Zersiedelung und ihrer Umwandlung in eine vollständige Gemeinschaft. Carbon footprint per settlement pattern - a comparison between sprawl and its repair into a complete community.

© Duany Plater-Zyberk & Company (DPZ)

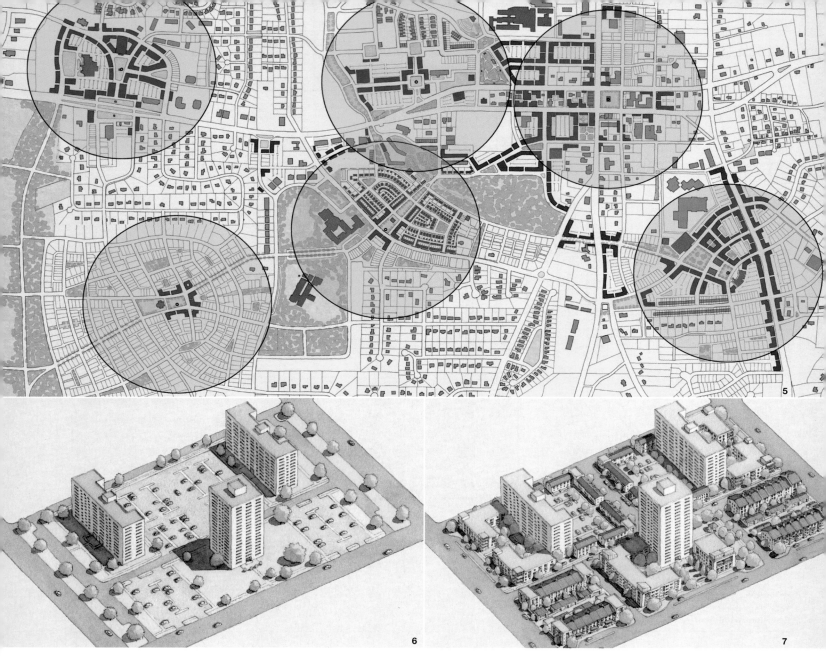

5 Die *Sprawl Repair*-Methode nutzt den Aktionsradius von Fußgängern, um Viertel
und Stadtzentren, die an den Transit angebunden werden sollten, darzustellen.
The sprawl repair method uses pedestrian sheds to delineate neighborhoods
and town centers which should be connected by transit.

6–7 Ein herkömmlicher Stützen-Platten-Bau, der in Blockbebauungen nach menschlichem Maßstab mit Reihenhäusern, gemischt genutzten Gebäuden und fußgänger-
freundlicheren Straßen umgestaltet wird. A standard slab and tower block repaired
into more human-scale blocks complete with townhouses, mixed-use buildings and
more walkable streets.

© Duany Plater-Zyberk & Company (DPZ)

Verbesserung ermöglichen. Der in Phasen verlaufende Weg plant mehrere Schritte ein, wobei die Projektteile zu unterschiedlichen Zeiten erstellt werden. Der indirekte Pfad zeigt eine Abfolge von Änderungen auf, die das Projekt immer näher an die endgültige verbesserte Situation heranführen – jedoch in einer längeren, schrittweisen Entwicklung von Erprobung und Anpassung.

Die Abbildung 3 stellt ausgewählte städtische Indikatoren vor und nach der *Sprawl Repair* einer Siedlung mit Einfamilienhäusern gegenüber. Sie veranschaulicht das Sanierungspotenzial der Zersiedelungsgebiete, das durch den Wandel der städtischen Indikatoren zum Ausdruck gebracht wird. Die Dichte wird deutlich angehoben – ausreichend um den Transit zu fördern. Es sollte betont werden, dass der Transit in einem größeren, regionalen Maßstab zwischen zwei aufeinander abgestimmten, sanierten Knotenpunkten funktioniert. Beispielsweise kann durch eine Mindestdichte von 15 Einheiten pro Acre eine regelmäßige lokale Busverbindung geschaffen werden. Der dargestellte Fall analysiert die Einwohnerdichte anstatt der Wohnsitz- oder Beschäftigungsdichte, da die Elemente der Zersiedelung Einzelnutzungen aufweisen, die im Verlauf der *Sprawl Repair* wieder ausbalanciert werden. Die Einwohnerdichte (die Anzahl der Menschen, die in einem Gebiet von einem Acre wohnen und arbeiten) erhöht sich nachdrücklich und zeigt so das Sanierungspotenzial des Erneuerungsgebietes.

Zwei kritische, in der Abbildung dargestellte Parameter sind die Länge und Oberfläche von Verkehrsflächen pro Einwohner vor und nach der *Sprawl Repair*. Die Verringerung dieser Messwerte ist wesentlich. Ähnliche Reduktionen können für andere Infrastrukturelemente angenommen werden, sodass weniger Einrichtungen pro Bewohner benötigt werden, wenn ein Teil der Zersiedelung mit der aufgezeigten Methode verbessert worden ist. Auf lange Sicht ist eine solche Erneuerung kostengünstiger und effizienter, als neue Stadterweiterungen in weit entfernten Orten zu errichten. Darüber hinaus wird eine Reihe von Leistungskriterien benutzt, um Parameter für die Vorteile der Verbesserung von Zersiedelungsgebieten aufzustellen. Die Zahlen der CO_2-Fußabdrücke pro Person werden drastisch verringert, wenn die zersiedelten Elemente in fußgängerfreundliche Modelle mit gemischter Nutzung umgewandelt werden, die die Grundlage für eine kohlenstofffreie Niedrigenergie-Zukunft bereiten. Gemeinsam mit den qualitativen Entwurfswerkzeugen liefern diese quantitativen Methoden Argumente für politische Veränderungen, um so Anreize für *Sprawl Repair* zu schaffen (Abb. 4).

Bei der Durchführung von *Sprawl Repair* sollte eine umfassende Methode angewendet werden, die aus Stadtplanung, Richtlinien und Strategien für die Finanzierung und wirtschaftlichen Anreizen besteht – den gleichen Mitteln, die die Zersiedelung zum führenden Modell der Raumentwicklung gemacht haben. Wenn man diese Werkzeuge in der Sanierung und Neu-

sity (number of people residing and working in an area per acre) increases dramatically, showing the redevelopment potential of this repair site.

Two critical metrics shown in the figure are the length and surface of thoroughfares per capita before and after sprawl repair. The reduction of these measurements is substantial. Similar reductions can be expected for other infrastructure, meaning less infrastructure is required per capita when a sprawl element is repaired with the demonstrated techniques. In the long run, such repair is less expensive and more efficient than building new sprawl in far-flung locations. In addition, a series of performance criteria are used to provide metrics of the benefits of repairing sprawl. Carbon footprints per person are dramatically reduced when sprawl elements are transformed into mixed-use, pedestrian-friendly patterns that are the basis for a post-carbon, low-energy future. Together with the qualitative urban design tools, these quantitative tools make a case for policy changes to incentivize sprawl repair (fig. 4).

Sprawl repair should be pursued using a comprehensive method based on urban design, regulation, and strategies for funding and incentives—the same instruments that made sprawl the prevalent form of development. When focused on retrofit and redevelopment, these tools transform the existing physical environment from sprawl to complete communities.

Urban Design Techniques. Sprawl repair should be applied to all urban scales, including the repair of a regional domain, the transformation of sprawl elements at the community scale, the re-configuration of conventional suburban blocks as well as the reuse, expansion, and adaptation of single structures. The urban design method at the regional scale includes several steps that produce a document mapping the structure of sprawl repair. The steps determine the physical boundaries of the regional domain, delineate the areas to be preserved and reserved, prioritize the salvageable commercial and employment nodes, determine the potential transit and infrastructure networks, identify the sprawl repair targets, and

> Carbon footprints per person are dramatically reduced when sprawl elements are transformed into mixed-use, pedestrian-friendly patterns that are the basis for a post-carbon, low-energy future.

(after the transfer of development rights) assemble the final sector map. Urban design at the community scale concentrates on restructuring sprawl into neighborhoods, transit corridors, and well-balanced districts that have short walking distances to daily needs and provide healthier environments to a multigenerational population. It has long been established that most people will choose not to walk if a destination is more than five minutes away (roughly a quarter-mile). The distance covered in this five-minute walk is commonly called a pedestrian shed and is usually represented in planning documents by a circle with a quarter-mile radius (fig. 5). Larger circles of a half-mile radius are used when the pedestrian sheds are centered on a transit stop, as people are willing to walk longer to such destinations. The delineation of

These emblematic structures, via modest urban design interventions, have the potential to contribute to a more diverse, harmonious, and walkable urban fabric. Rather than being demolished, existing suburban buildings are repurposed or lined with new structures, often taking advantage of suburbia's typically excessive setbacks and parking lots.

gestaltung anwendet, bilden sie die bestehende physische Umgebung von Zersiedelungsgebieten in vollständige Gemeinschaften um.

Urbane Entwurfstechniken. *Sprawl Repair* sollte auf allen städtebaulichen Maßstäben angewendet werden, was die Erneuerung auf regionaler Ebene, die Umformung zersiedelter Elemente auf kommunaler Stufe, die Umgestaltung herkömmlicher vorstädtischer Wohnblöcke ebenso wie die Wiederverwertung, den Ausbau und die Adaptierung einzelner Gebäude einschließt. Die urbane Entwurfsmethode im regionalen Maßstab umfasst mehrere Schritte, bei denen dokumentiert wird, wie die Struktur der *Sprawl Repair* ausgearbeitet wird. Die Abschnitte legen die physischen Grenzen auf gebietsmäßiger Ebene fest, bezeichnen, welche Bereiche erhalten und welche verwendet werden, bestimmen, wo der Schwerpunkt der Wirtschafts- und Beschäftigungsknotenpunkte liegt, die zu sanieren sind, ermitteln die möglichen Transit- und Infrastrukturnetze, erfassen die *Sprawl Repair*-Zielsetzungen und fügen (nach Anpassung an die Raumordnungsbestimmungen) den endgültigen Plan der Sektoren zusammen. Städtebauliche Entwürfe auf kommunaler Ebene konzentrieren sich auf die Umstrukturierung der Zersiedelungsgebiete in Viertel, Transitverbindungen und ausgewogene Distrikte, in denen man auf fußläufig kurzem Weg den täglichen Bedarf decken kann und bieten so eine gesündere Umgebung für eine Bevölkerung aus unterschiedlichen Generationen. Es ist seit langem bekannt, dass die meisten Menschen sich entschließen, nicht zu Fuß zu gehen, wenn der Zielort mehr als fünf Minuten entfernt ist (ungefähr eine Viertelmeile). Die Entfernung, die in diesem fünfminütigen Spaziergang zurückgelegt wird, ist allgemein als Reichweite einer fußläufigen Erschließung bekannt und wird meistens in Planungsunterlagen als Kreis mit einem Radius von einer Viertelmeile dargestellt (Abb. 5). Größere Kreise mit einem Radius von einer halben Meile werden verwendet, wenn der Aktionsradius der Fußgänger auf einer Transitanbindung beruht, da die Bewohner bereit sind, längere Distanzen zu diesen Punkten zurückzulegen. Das Konzept der fußläufigen Reichweite wird im regionalen Maßstab durchgeführt, doch wird der städtebauliche Entwurf auf kommunaler Ebene abgehandelt. Der Aktionsradius von Fußgängern stellt ein einfaches aber wesentliches Instrument dar, um die Größenordnung und Fußläufigkeit in vom Auto dominierten, vorstädtischen Gegenden zu untersuchen.

Nachdem die fußläufigen Reichweiten bestimmt sind, werden die Viertel und Stadtzentren gestaltet, indem eine Reihe von urbanen Entwurfstechniken angewendet wird. Dazu gehört die Einführung von neuen Gebäudetypen, die eine größere Heterogenität in Bezug auf Nutzungen ermöglichen (Wohnen, Büros, Geschäfte, Hotels, Verwaltung), indem sie Verkehrswege miteinander verbinden und verbessern, um ein fußgänger-

freundliches Stadtgefüge zu schaffen und die Parkmöglichkeiten effizienter zu machen, um zukünftige Städtebauentwicklungen zu ermöglichen und nicht ausgelastete Parkflächen zu beseitigen. Offen zugänglichen, öffentlichen Raum zu definieren, ist eine wichtige städtebauliche Entwurfstechnik, sodass eine Hierarchie von klar abgegrenzten Bereichen für die gemeinsame Nutzung geschaffen wird. Die Einbindung von Nahrungserzeugungen vor Ort wird zu einem führenden Trend und kann für alle Erneuerungsbereiche empfohlen werden, da sie auf einfache Weise Gärten und bepflanzte Parzellen vorsieht, auch wenn die Stadtgestaltung insgesamt erst neu strukturiert wird. Urbane Entwürfe im Maßstabe von Gebäudeblöcken beschäftigen sich mit Methoden, wie diese Gebiete in kleineren städtischen Ausbauschritten verändert und ausgeführt werden, um Teil von einem zukünftigen fußgängerfreundlichen Stadtgefüge zu werden. Großflächige vorstädtische Mega-Blöcke werden in kleinteiligere Volumen zerlegt, indem neue Straßen und Passagen angelegt und so zusammenhängende Muster für weitere Sanierungen aufgebaut werden (Abb. 6–7).

Die Erneuerung im Maßstab von Gebäuden ergänzt die kommunale Ebene und den Blockbereich, da sie sich mit den hauptsächlichen Gebäudetypen beschäftigt, die für die Zersiedelung verantwortlich sind: Ranch-Häuser, „McMansions", Drive in-Restaurants, Tankstellen, Geschäftszeilen, und andere mehr. Diese zeichenhaften Bauten haben durch einfache urbane Gestaltungseingriffe das Potenzial, zu einem vielfältigeren, harmonischeren und fußläufigen Stadtgefüge beizutragen. Anstatt sie abzureißen, werden die bestehenden vorstädtischen Gebäude mit einer neuen Nutzung belegt oder mit neuen Bauten ergänzt, die oft die typischen Rücksetzungen der Gebäude in den Vororten und die Parkflächen ausnutzen.

Rechtliche Bestimmungen. Obwohl es sich gezeigt hat, dass durchgängig begehbare, vielfältige Planungen mit gemischten Nutzungen besser funktionieren als zersiedelte Gebiete, ist es noch immer schwierig, sie baurechtlich genehmigen zu lassen und zu finanzieren. Darüber hinaus ist es nicht möglich, die Zersiedelung innerhalb der bestehenden Praxis und Politik der Flächenwidmungsplanung zu verbessern, die die Zersiedelung begünstigen. Für ein wirksames Eingreifen in den Vororten ist eine vollständige Überarbeitung der aktuellen Flächenwidmungsnutzung erforderlich. Da es nicht möglich ist, dies in einer einzigen umfassenden Neuregelung durchzuführen, müssen von den Gemeinden neue Richtlinien erlassen werden, entweder jeweils nacheinander als gebietsmäßige Auflage parallel zu oder anstelle von bestehenden Bestimmungen. In allen Fällen müssen diese Vorschriften wirkungsvolle Anreize für ein gesundes Wachstum anstelle von Zersiedelung schaffen. Um die Schwierigkeiten im Zusammenhang mit der Errichtung und Erhaltung von zersiedelten Stadtgebieten zu überwinden, wurde ein schrittweiser Prozess in der Einführung von Gestaltungs-

pedestrian sheds is accomplished at the regional scale but urban design is negotiated at the community scale. The pedestrian shed is a simple but essential tool in the pursuit of order and walkability in auto-oriented suburban environments.

After the pedestrian sheds are determined, the neighborhoods and town centers are shaped using a range of urban design techniques. They include the introduction of new building types that allow a greater heterogeneity in terms of uses (residential, office, retail, lodging, civic), connecting and improving thoroughfares to create a pedestrian-friendly urban fabric, and rationalizing parking to accommodate future urbanization and eliminate underutilized parking. Defining open and civic space is an essential urban design technique that involves the creation of a hierarchy of well-defined spaces for common use. The integration of local food production is becoming a predominant trend and is recommended for all repair sites, as they can easily accommodate gardens and allotments, even while their urbanism is being redesigned. Urban design at the block scale deals with techniques for transforming blocks into smaller urban increments and preparing them to become part of a future pedestrian-friendly urban fabric. Large suburban mega-blocks are broken down into a finer grain of smaller blocks by introducing new streets and passages, thereby establishing a coherent pattern for further redevelopment (figs. 6–7).

Repair at the building scale complements the community and block scales as it deals with the main building stereotypes that define sprawl: ranch houses, McMansions, drive-through gates/restaurants, gas stations, and strip centers, among others. These emblematic structures, via modest urban design interventions, have the potential to contribute to a more diverse, harmonious, and walkable urban fabric. Rather than being demolished, existing suburban buildings are repurposed or lined with new structures, often taking advantage of suburbia's typically excessive setbacks and parking lots.

Regulatory Techniques. Even though mixed-use, walkable, and diverse projects have proven to perform better than environments affected by sprawl, it is still difficult to approve and finance them. Furthermore, it is impossible to repair sprawl using most existing zoning practices and policies, which encourage the creation of sprawl. A total overhaul of current zoning practices is required for an effective intervention in suburbia. As this is impossible to do in a single, sweeping motion, new codes must be adopted by municipalities, one at a time, as overlay districts, in parallel, or in place of existing codes. In all cases, these codes must powerfully incentivize smart growth rather than sprawl. To overcome the difficulties related to building and maintaining sprawl, a gradual process of adopting form-based codes has been started by some municipalities and cities. Form-based codes regulate the form of the built environment, allowing and encouraging pedestrian-friendly urbanism. A model form-based code is the SmartCode,[8] a comprehensive ordinance that enables smart growth community patterns and the transformation of portions of sprawl into walkable

---

8   See Duany Plater-Zyberk & Company, *SmartCode v9.2..* (Miami, 2010), accessible online at: http://www.smartcodecentral.org (accessed December 19, 2011).

urbanism. The code includes a special sector (Sprawl Repair Sector G-5)[9] that is assigned to areas that are currently single-use and have disconnected conventional development patterns but have the potential to be completed or redeveloped into neighborhoods and urban centers. Some of the sprawl areas will be up-zoned to accommodate higher but well-designed density and allow the introduction of mixed uses and transit. This creates the regulatory basis for successional growth and the transformation of sprawl elements into viable neighborhoods with more transportation and housing choices. Conventional suburban blocks may be reconfigured to receive higher densities and additional uses. At the scale of the building, one of the most important issues will be to allow flexible uses within existing structures (houses becoming live-work units, big-box retail becoming office space or civic buildings) and increased density within existing parcels and lots (mansions turned into multifamily housing or assisted living facilities, or the addition of accessory units). Another important task is to create standards to calm and repair dangerous thoroughfares and make them safe for walking and bicycling while creating connections between residential areas, shops, workplaces, schools, civic buildings, and recreation. The SmartCode operates according to the rural-to-urban transect, an organizational framework and planning methodology that enables the comprehensive and effective redevelopment of sprawling communities into more sustainable patterns. The transect is not a mandatory tool to be imposed on planners and local governments. A transect is a concept originally used by ecologists to describe distinct natural habitats but has been extended to cover the human habitat. The transect as it relates to the built environment organizes structural elements

> The lack of rural-to-urban logic in sprawl is one of the fundamental differences from traditional urbanism. The transect is broken into zones, each representing a complex habitat of different building types, streetscapes, and public spaces.

according to an increasing density and complexity, from the countryside to the urban core. The lack of rural-to-urban logic in sprawl is one of the fundamental differences from traditional urbanism. The transect is broken into zones, each representing a complex habitat of different building types, streetscapes, and public spaces. This is in contrast to sprawl, in which each element is a single-use agglomeration, usually a monoculture of a single building type (fig. 8). The transect zones represent zoning conditions that are similar to the ones administered by conventional zoning codes, except they include not only the building use, density, height, and setback requirements but also how buildings relate to each other and how together they shape the public realm.

richtlinien von einigen Gemeinden und Städten begonnen. Vorschriften über die Ausgestaltung bestimmen die Form der gebauten Umgebung, indem sie fußgängerfreundliche Städtebauplanungen ermöglichen und fördern. Ein Modell einer Gestaltungsrichtlinie ist der *SmartCode*,[8] der als umfassende Verordnung ein intelligentes Wachstum für Gemeinschaftsflächen und die Umwandlung von zersiedelten Teilen in fußläufige Stadtteile vorsieht. Die Vorschrift berücksichtigt ein besonderes Gebiet (*Sprawl Repair Sector* G-5),[9] in dem zurzeit eine Einzelnutzung mit separaten, herkömmlichen Bebauungsformen vorherrscht, das jedoch über das Potenzial verfügt, ergänzt und als Viertel und Stadtzentren erneuert zu werden. Einige der Zersiedelungsbereiche sollen aufgestockt werden, um eine höhere, doch besser geplante Dichte zu erreichen und gemischte Nutzungen und Verkehrsanbindungen zu ermöglichen. Dies schafft die rechtliche Grundlage für künftiges Wachstum und die Umgestaltung der zersiedelten Bereiche in lebensfähige Viertel mit mehr Auswahl an Verkehrsverbindungen und Wohnmöglichkeiten. Herkömmliche vorstädtische Blockbebauungen können neu gestaltet werden, um eine höhere Dichte und zusätzliche Nutzungen zuzulassen. Im Maßstab von Gebäuden ist eines der wichtigsten Themen die flexible Verwendung innerhalb bestehender Bauten (Häuser, die Wohn- und Arbeitseinheiten werden, Einkaufsmärkte, die Raum für Büros und öffentliche Einrichtungen bieten) und die Anhebung der Dichte bei vorhandenen Liegenschaften und Gebäuden (Villen, die in Mehrfamilienwohnhäuser oder Einrichtungen für betreutes Wohnen umfunktioniert werden, oder an die Teile angebaut werden). Eine weitere wichtige Aufgabe besteht in der Bildung von Regeln, um gefährliche Durchgangsstraßen zu beruhigen und zu verbessern und sie so für Fußgänger und Radfahrer sicher zu gestalten, sowie Verbindungen zwischen Wohngebieten, Geschäften, Betrieben, Schulen, öffentlichen Bauten und Erholungseinrichtungen herzustellen. Der *SmartCode* funktioniert nach dem *rural-to-urban-transect*, einem Stadtplanungsmodell und organisatorischen Rahmen, der eine umfassende und wirksame Sanierung von zersiedelten Gemeinschaften in nachhaltigere Gebiete ermöglicht. Dieser Transekt ist kein verbindliches Instrument für Planer und Behörden vor Ort. Es ist ursprünglich ein Konzept von Ökologen zur Beschreibung unterschiedlicher natürlicher Lebensräume, doch wurde es auch zur Erfassung des menschlichen Habitats herangezogen. Der Verlauf der Beobachtungspunkte in Bezug auf die gebaute Umwelt ordnet die Gebäudekörper nach einer ansteigenden Dichte und

8   Duany Plater-Zyberk & Company. *SmartCode v9.2.*, Miami 2010, online unter: http://www.smartcodecentral.org (Stand: 19.12.2011).

9   Galina Tachieva: *Sprawl Repair Module to the SmartCode*, Miami 2009, online unter: http://transect.org/docs/sprawl_pdfs.zip (Stand: 13.12.2011).

9   See Galina Tachieva, *Sprawl Repair Module to the SmartCode* (Miami, 2009), accessible online at: http://transect.org/docs/sprawl_pdfs.zip (accessed December 13, 2011).

(see fig. 5), then no more than a minimum value for spatial development of public and private open spaces has been reached. And public space, in spite of comparatively low building height, can actually still be perceived as being clearly defined. Now doubts may certainly arise about the validity of defining of urban qualities through simple compliance with density values, but within the explorative question at hand these number games verify that which is obvious: a lack of liveliness. An elevation of population numbers through an expansion of housing supply represents an effective means of improving this situation. Due to building-policy-related limitations, previous attempts at affecting an increase in living space have been concentrated on spatially exhausting existing structures, meaning the expansion of basement apartments and the enlargement of attics, which tends to impair protected roofscapes. These approaches go hand in hand with familiar spatial and structural weaknesses. If we disregard the current policy situation, then quantitatively noteworthy spaces for retrospective densification can certainly be found in the well-preserved Gründerzeit districts: for one, the mostly empty yard areas, and also the space above the eaves. However, erecting structures within the courtyards where greenery is cultivated would not only destroy the special quality of Graz perimeter-block developments and also foster an air of confinement within the yards; it would also entail large, concentrated construction mass. For an average block, while assuming the smallest amount of distance between the buildings, such horizontal densification would call for a height of ten stories[18] in order to attain the increase in area necessary for a two-story addition of highest living quality (see fig. 5).[19] From a qualitative perspective, the preference clearly lies in favor of vertical densification, for the encroachment of the surroundings that would be induced by developing the yards in a way that inevitably generates a sense of confinement cannot be deemed acceptable. By contrast, the annexing of a circumferential addition—as a rim that surrounds the entire perimeter block as a unique architectural structure—harbors, next to several basic prerequisites, a variety of advantages as compared to the parceled attic extensions practiced up to now.

Construction in existing contexts as a strategy for promoting sustainability can only ever be successful when it takes existing factors into consideration, yet without favoring traditional design or romanticisms over conventional lifestyles and societal forms. Therefore, considering this prerequisite, the ad-

tes Geschäfts- und Gassenleben mit vielfältigen Nahversorgungs- und Gastronomiefunktionen konzentriert sich an wenigen Punkten. Belebte Erdgeschosszonen fördern das urbane Leben und umgekehrt, lassen sich aber nicht erzwingen, sondern können erst mit dem Erreichen bestimmter Dichteparameter existieren, die in den Grazer Quartieren nicht gegeben scheinen. Bevölkerungsdichte, Beschäftigtendichte und deren Ausgewogenheit spielen hierbei sicher eine gewichtigere Rolle als die bauliche Dichte,[15] die in erster Linie auf quantitative räumliche Ausnutzung zielt, jedoch per se noch keinen Aufschluss über die Anwesenheit von agierenden Personen zu Tage und in der Nacht gibt. Dennoch gibt Dietmar Eberle nach eingehenden Vergleichen städtischer Quartiere als bauliche Minimaldichte für funktionierende Durchmischung und Fußläufigkeit einen Kennwert von 1,5 bis 1,6 an.[16] Erst von da an könne Urbanität entstehen. Mit dem im exemplarischen Grazer Stadtausschnitt ermittelten Wert von 1,3 (siehe Abb. 5) erreicht man gerade die genannten Mindestwerte für die räumliche Ausbildung der öffentlichen und privaten Freibereiche. Und tatsächlich kann der öffentliche Raum trotz vergleichsweise niedriger Bebauung als klar definiert wahrgenommen werden. Nun mag durchaus Zweifel an einer Definition urbaner Qualitäten durch bloße Erfüllung von Dichtekennzahlen bestehen, dennoch bestätigen diese Zahlenspiele in der gegenständlichen Fragestellung das Offensichtliche, nämlich den Mangel an Belebtheit. Die Anhebung der Bevölkerungszahlen durch Ausweitung des Wohnungsangebotes stellt ein probates Mittel zur Verbesserung dieser Situation dar. Bisherige Versuche, einen Zuwachs an Wohnflächen zu erlangen, konzentrierten sich aufgrund gesetzlicher Einschränkungen auf die räumliche Ausreizung der vorhandenen Volumina, also die Erweiterung in Kellerwohnungen und die geschützte Dachlandschaft beeinträchtigende Einzelausbauten der Dachböden mit den bekannten räumlichen und bauphysikalischen Schwachstellen. Klammert man die derzeitige Gesetzeslage aus, so sind in den gut erhaltenen Gründerzeitquartieren durchaus quantitativ nennenswertere Flächen zur Nachverdichtung vorhanden: Zum einen die weitgehend leeren Höfe, zum anderen der Raum oberhalb der Trauflinien. Jedoch würde eine Verbauung der Innenhöfe mit dem privaten Grün nicht nur die spezielle Qualität der Grazer Blockrandbebauungen zerstören und hofseitig Enge erzeugen, sondern auch große konzentrierte Baumassen erfordern. Eine derartige horizontale Verdichtung verlangt bei minimalstem Gebäudeabstand in einem durchschnitt-

Nur die grundstücksübergreifende Betrachtung des Blocks lässt eine Loslösung von den Zwängen der kleinteiligen Strukturiertheit der Einzelbauten zu.

---

18 The ground area of the courtyard in a typical Graz perimeter block is ca. 83 × 36 m, the floor area of the building ca. 60 × 13 m, and space between the buildings ca. 11.5 m.

19 As calculated by the Design 5 course in the Institute of Architectural Typologies at Graz University of Technology, 2008.

15 Vgl. Häussermann: *Phänomenologie und Struktur städtischer Dichte*, S. 25 (wie Anm. 2).

16 Dietmar Eberle: „Dichte", Vortrag Dense Cities Conference, Graz 2011, online unter: http://www.densecities.org (Stand 12.8.2011).

lichen Block eine Höhe von 10 Geschossen,[17] um den Flächengewinn einer zweigeschossigen Aufstockung höchster Wohnqualität zu erzielen (siehe Abb. 5).[18] Nach qualitativen Gesichtspunkten fällt die Präferenz zugunsten der vertikalen Verdichtung hier eindeutig aus, denn die Beeinträchtigung des Umfeldes durch die Enge generierende Verbauung der Höfe kann nicht zumutbar sein. Dagegen birgt eine umlaufende, den gesamten Blockrand als singuläres Bauwerk umschließende Aufstockung auch gegenüber den bisher praktizierten parzellenweisen Dachbodenausbauten neben einigen Grundbedingungen auch eine Vielfalt an Vorzügen:

Bauen im Bestand als Nachhaltigkeitsstrategie kann immer nur unter Rücksichtnahme auf das Vorhandene, aber ohne Anbiederung an tradierte Bauformen oder Romantizismen gegenüber überkommenen Lebensweisen und Gesellschaftsformen erfolgreich sein. Die den gesamten Block als Ganzes umfassende Aufstockung von Blockrandbebauungen bedeutet unter dieser Voraussetzung also keinesfalls die Zerstörung des Vorhandenen, sondern eine effizientere Nutzung der vorhandenen Ressourcen sowie die respektvolle Sicherstellung des Weiterbestandes. Die vorhandene Bausubstanz wird konserviert, indem sie den beständigen Sockel für Neues bildet. Die Monumentalität des bestehenden Ensembles wird durch einen einheitlichen Aufbau noch zusätzlich unterstrichen, wohingegen einzelne Dachgeschossausbauten oder parzellenweise Aufstockungen Inhomogenität erzeugen.

Nur die grundstücksübergreifende Betrachtung des Blocks lässt eine Loslösung von den Zwängen der kleinteiligen Strukturiertheit der Einzelbauten zu. Dies schafft planerische und gestalterische Freiheiten, gleichzeitig aber auch vielfältige ökonomische und ökologische Synergien, die bei einer parzellengebundenen Betrachtungsweise nicht gegeben sind. Aus kleinen Einzelbaulosen mit einigen wenigen Wohnungen werden Bauvorhaben in wirtschaftlich und siedlungsräumlich interessanten Größenordnungen. Die gut ausgebaute öffentliche Infrastruktur wird intensiver genutzt, ein weiterer flächiger Ausbau in das Umland überflüssig, Wartung und Reparatur wirtschaftlicher. Gebäudeintern bietet sich als Synergie die Möglichkeit, haustechnischen Investitionsrückstand großflächig zu beseitigen und die Bauten ökologisch auf den neuesten Stand zu bringen, was ein wertvoller Beitrag zur Luftverbesserung der ganzen Stadt wäre. Durch Anwendung höchster ökologischer und energetischer Standards im Neubau bietet die vertikale Nachverdichtung zudem die Chance zur Verbesserung der Gesamtenergiebilanz der Gebäude auch ohne thermische Sanierung der historischen Fassaden.

Die Befreiung aus dem engen baulichen Korsett zwischen Brandmauern und Stiegenhäusern ermöglicht eine echte Vielfalt an Wohnungstypen in der jetzigen Dachzone und damit eine sinnvolle Antwort auf die Frage nach einem diversifizierten innerstädtischen Wohnungsangebot bis hin zum Einfamilienhausersatz mit privatem Freibereich. Dadurch, dass nicht jedes bestehende Stiegenhaus zur Erschließung der Aufstockung hoch gezogen und mit einem Aufzug nachgerüstet werden muss, sondern erst die feuerpolizei-

dition of stories to perimeter-block developments where the entire block as a whole is encompassed by no means implies the destruction of the buildings at hand. Instead, this reflects the more efficient utilization of existing resources as well as a respectful guarantee that the structure will stay standing. The existent building will be preserved in that it forms an abiding plinth for something new. The monumentality of the established ensemble is then further underlined by a uniform construction, whereas individual attic enlargements or parceled additions instead engender inhomogeneity.

Only reflection on the perimeter block that takes the lot situation as a whole into account allows for a disengagement from the constraints imposed by the compartmentalized nature of the individual buildings. This approach generates a freedom of planning and design but also, at the same time, manifold economic and ecological synergies that are not present when taking a parcel-bound vantage point. Individual structural sections with just a few apartments turn into building projects of interesting economic and spatial-development scope. The well-established public infrastructure is more intensively used, making additional planar expansion into surrounding regions unnecessary as well as maintenance and repair more economical. To the inside of the building, there is the synergetic possibility of a large-scale elimination of investment gaps and of bringing the buildings up to date ecologically, which would represent a valuable contribution to cleaner air for the whole city. By integrating the highest ecological and energy-related standards in the new structural section, the act of retrospective vertical densification moreover offers an opportunity to improve the buildings' total energy balance even without a thermal rehabilitation of the historical façades.

Liberation from the right structural corset between fire walls and stairwells facilitates a true richness of apartment types in the new attic zone and thereby a sensible answer to the issue of needing alternatives ranging from a diversified inner-city residential living situation to a replacement for the one-family house surrounded by private open space. The fact that not every existing stairwell must be continued on up to access the upper addition or retrofitted with an elevator—instead, fire regulations specify the maximum clearance for vertical access—makes this flexibility in designing layout attainable while also yielding much higher floor space.

The gardens located in the inner yards would then be united and opened for all residents of adjacent buildings to use, for higher levels of density necessitate more open space,[20] not

---

17 Die Hofgrundfläche im exemplarischen Grazer Block beträgt rd. 83 × 36 m, die Gebäudegrundfläche rd. 60 × 13 m, der Gebäudeabstand rd. 11,5 m.

18 So die Ergebnisse der Lehrveranstaltung Entwerfen 5 am Institut für Gebäudelehre der TU Graz, 2008.

20 See Thomas K. Keller, "Das Kriterium der Dichte im Städtebau," in Lampugnani, Keller, and Buser, *Städtische Dichte* (note 1), pp. 39–48, esp. p. 44.

Berlin

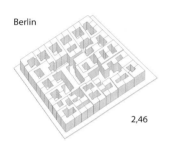

2,46

Prenzlauer Berg
Quartiersdichte: 2,46
Bebauungsgrad: 0,48
Geschossanzahl: 5-7
Traufhöhe: 22m

Wien

2,58

Josefstadt
Quartiersdichte: 2,58
Bebauungsgrad: 0,59
Geschossanzahl: 2-7
Traufhöhe: 6,5-23m

Graz

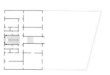

1,30

Sankt Leonhard
Quartiersdichte: 1,3
Bebauungsgrad: 0,41
Geschossanzahl: 1-5
Traufhöhe: 6-18,5m

Graz 2.1

Formen der
Nachverdichtung

horizontal 2,1

vertikal 2,1

5

3   Bestandsanalyse: Nutzungsdurchmischung und
    ruhender Verkehr Status analysis: Mixed use and
    stationary traffic © Institut für Gebäudelehre, TU-Graz
    (Masterstudio Nachverdichtung WS 2010/11).

4   Neue Dachlandschaften New roofscapes © Institut
    für Gebäudelehre, TU-Graz/Stephan Brugger.

5   Typologischer Vergleich Comparison of typologies
    © Institut für Gebäudelehre, TU-Graz (3D-Karten-
    grundlage: Berlin: © GeoBasis-DE/SenStadt III [2011];
    Wien: Stadt Wien, MA 41 – Stadtvermessungsamt,
    Magistrat Graz, Stadtvermessungsamt).

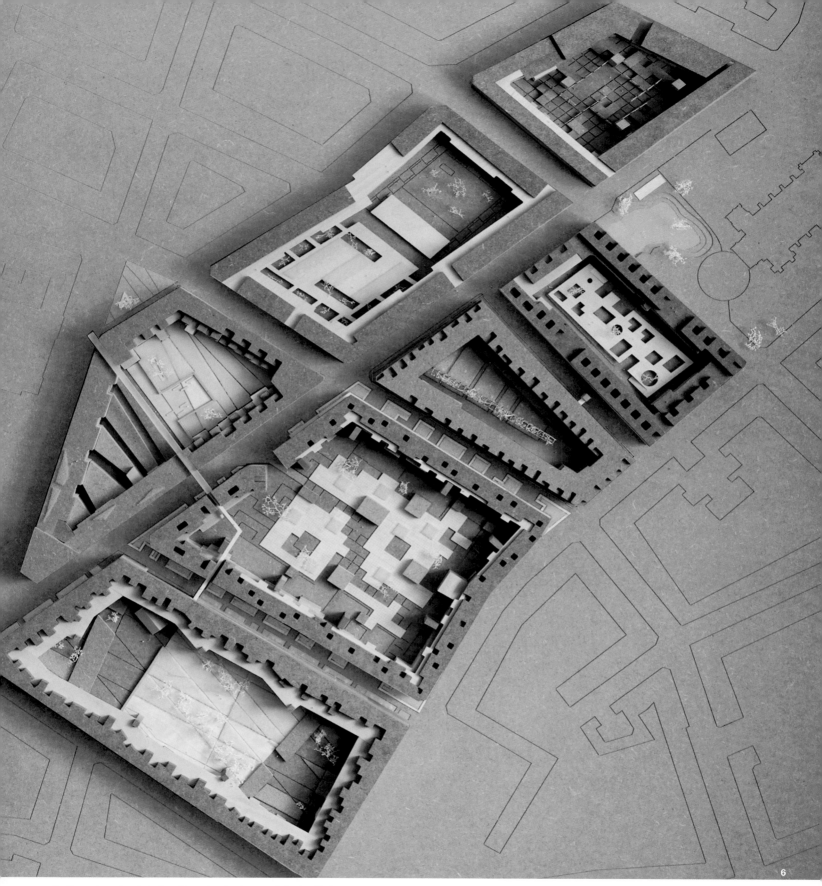

6   Neue urbane Landschaften **New urban landscapes** © Institut für Gebäudelehre, TU-Graz (Masterstudio Nachverdichtung WS 2010/2011).

short period of time.[5] In Europe and the USA, this initially led, in the first half of the twentieth century, to an adaptation of already existent housing typologies in order to meet the need for living space, but also to guarantee a maximized utilization of existing sites. The projects thus called to life, such as the housing developments by Henri Sauvage in Paris but also the settlements by Bruno Taut in Berlin,[6] count among the ideational precursors to large-scale housing structures and already exhibited fundamental characteristics to be found in later buildings: densification of housing capacity which still operated within the existing city layout, but simultaneously also the integration of functional areas for public use within a building, which accommodated urban elements of public space as an essential building feature.

Influenced by the life ideals of modernity and by Le Corbusier's urban-development concepts, large-scale housing structures facilitated extremely dense living.[7] At the same time, large public spaces were generated as an extension of the existing urban context; their novel, never-before-seen dimensions were difficult for most residents to grasp being that fundamentally new spatial qualities and atmospheres were featured.[8]

Most of the housing conceptions in which these projects are rooted, having found expression through layout design, are oriented to ideas of modernity; here, the concept of functional separation and rationalization was not only established for the development of urban space, but also applied to the design of the specific living situation. Ground plans were drafted with kitchen, bath, living rooms, and bedrooms, and while individual room size and orientation were adapted to the intended functions, they accordingly lacked flexibility. And they seemed completely unsuitable for accommodating shifting needs. Due to an increase in urban population and the resulting shortage of housing in the 1960s and 1970s, the social housing market boomed. During this period the majority of the large-scale housing projects in Europe, but also in the USA, Asia, Africa, North America, and South American, were built. Corviale, a project by architect Mario Fiorentino located near Rome that was planned and built between 1974 and 1982, represents one of the superlative projects realized within this epoch at 37 meters in height and 23.5 meters in depth. The dimensions of this architectural structure mirror the modern nation's still visibly invincible trust in the potentials of constructing spaces for society.

Like many other projects realized during this time period, La Corviale was originally constructed as part of an even larger

lungen von Bruno Taut in Berlin gehören,[6] zählen zu den ideellen Vorläufern der Großwohnungsbauten und weisen schon grundlegende Charakteristika der späteren Bauten auf: die Verdichtung der Wohnfunktion, die noch im bestehenden Stadtgrundriss funktioniert, und gleichzeitig die Integration von Funktionsflächen für öffentliche Nutzungen innerhalb des Gebäudes, die das städtische Element des öffentlichen Raums als wesentlichen Bestandteil mit ins Gebäude holen.

Beeinflusst von den Idealen der Moderne zum Leben und Le Corbusiers Ideen für den Städtebau ermöglichten Großwohnungsbauten ein extrem verdichtetes Wohnen.[7] Gleichzeitig wurden große öffentliche Räume als Erweiterung des bestehenden urbanen Kontextes erzeugt, deren neue, noch nicht dagewesene Dimensionen für die meisten Bewohner schwer zu fassende, weil fundamental neue räumliche Qualitäten und Atmosphären aufwiesen.[8]

Die den Projekten zugrundeliegenden Vorstellungen zum Wohnen, die in der Grundrissgestaltung ihren Ausdruck fanden, orientierten sich mehrheitlich an den Ideen der Moderne, welche die Idee der Funktionstrennung und Rationalisierung nicht nur für die Entwicklung des Stadtraums entwickelte, sondern diese auch auf die Gestaltung der Wohnung übertrug. Es entstanden Grundrisse mit Küche, Bad, Wohn- und Schlafzimmern, deren einzelne Raumgrößen und Orientierung zwar an die dafür vorgesehene Funktion angepasst, aber in Folge wenig flexibel waren. Für eine Anpassung an wechselnde Bedürfnisse erschienen sie gänzlich ungeeignet. Durch den Anstieg der Stadtbevölkerung und die Wohnungsknappheit in den 1960er und 1970er Jahren boomte der soziale Wohnungsbau. In diesem Zeitraum entstand die Mehrzahl der großmaßstäblichen Wohnungsbauprojekte in Europa aber auch in den USA, Asien, Afrika, Nord- und Südamerika. Corviale, ein vor Rom gelegenes Projekt des Architekten Mario Fiorentino, das zwischen 1974 und 1982 geplant und fertiggestellt wurde, stellt mit knapp einem Kilometer Länge, 37 Metern Höhe und einer Tiefe von 23,5 Metern eines der Superlativprojekte dar, die innerhalb dieser Epoche realisiert wurden. In den Dimension dieses Bauwerks spiegelt sich das noch sichtbar unerschütterliche Vertrauen des modernen Staates in die Möglichkeiten, für eine Gesellschaft Räume zu konstruieren.

Wie viele andere Projekte, die in diesem Zeitraum entstanden, war auch La Corviale ursprünglich als Teil eines größeren Plans realisiert worden, um die Städte, die unter dem rasanten Anstieg der Bevölkerung und den daraus resultierenden Folgen litten, zu entlasten und neu zu strukturieren. In vielen größeren europäischen Städten führte die Umsetzung der Pläne zum Bruch

Durch den Anstieg der Stadtbevölkerung und die Wohnungsknappheit in den 1960er und 1970er Jahren boomte der soziale Wohnungsbau.

5   See Silvio Macetti, *Großwohneinheiten* (Berlin, 1968); Philippe Panerai, Jean Castex, Jean-Charles Depaule, *Vom Block zur Zeile: Wandlungen der Stadtstruktur*, Bauwelt-Fundamente (Wiesbaden, 1985).

6   See Wüstenrot Stiftung, ed., *Geschichte des Wohnens*, vol. 3 (Stuttgart, 1997).

7   See Nasrine Seraji, *Logement Matière de nos Villes, Chronique Européenne 1900–2007* (Paris, 2007).

8   Ibid.

6   Vgl. Wüstenrot Stiftung (Hg.): *Geschichte des Wohnens*, Band 3, Stuttgart 1997.

7   Vgl. Nasrine Seraji: *Logement Matière de nos Villes, Chronique Européenne 1900–2007*, Paris 2007.

8   Vgl. ebd.

der bis dahin zusammenhängenden Stadtstruktur, da sie große Infrastrukturen vor allem für den Automobilverkehr in den bestehenden Stadtgrundriss implantierten: Neue Stadtteile, deren Gestaltung auf der Idee der Funktionstrennung basierten und die auf den Automobilverkehr ausgerichtet waren, wurden dadurch nicht nur als Erweiterungen gebaut, sondern auch in die bestehende Stadtstruktur implantiert. In den Plänen konkretisierte sich, wie die Städte der Zukunft organisiert werden und wie sich neues städtisches Leben in ihnen generieren könnte.[9] Gedanken zum Einsatz neuer Techniken, neuer Kommunikationsformen, neuer Formen der Bewegung und neue Ideen zum kommunalen Leben bestimmten aber nicht nur die großen Pläne, sondern fanden sich vor allem auch in der Organisation der Großwohnungsbauprojekte wieder, die im Zuge der Umsetzung der Pläne realisiert wurden.

Beispielsweise sollten Le Corbusiers „Rue Interieure" oder in den Projekten der Smithsons die „Streets in the Sky" im Gebäude die Straßen ersetzen. Das „Plateau", wie es in den Projekten Ekbathan in Teheran[10] und Les Olympiades oder Le Front de Seine in Paris vorkommt, verbannte die Autos ins Erdgeschoss und bot den Bewohnern einen neuen Stadtraum, der meist oberhalb und abgetrennt von der normalen Straßenebene der umgebenden Stadt positioniert und nur der Nutzung von Fußgängern vorbehalten war.[11] Auch die Wohnungen veränderten sich durch die Neuerungen der Technik. Wo es ein Badezimmer in jeder Wohnung gab, Warmwasser und Zentralheizung, isolierte sich die Wohnung immer mehr im Gebäude und wurde zur Zelle, die zwar dem Bewohner Komfort bot, aber nicht flexibel genug war, um sich den wechselnden Bedürfnissen der Bewohner anzupassen.[12]

Die daraus resultierenden neuen Organisationsformen der Gebäude führten zusammen mit ihrer Größe oftmals zum direkten räumlichen Bruch mit den bestehenden Typologien der Städte.

Die daraus resultierenden neuen Organisationsformen der Gebäude führten zusammen mit ihrer Größe oftmals zum direkten räumlichen Bruch mit den bestehenden Typologien der Städte. Diese Entwicklung wurde durch den politischen Umstand verstärkt, dass die Projekte oft als Teil größerer Pläne gedacht worden waren, die nicht oder nur teilweise ausgeführt wurden. Verbindende Elemente zur umgebenden Stadt fehlten oft und wurden nicht oder nur teilweise realisiert. Folglich lagen die Großwohnungsbauprojekte oft schon kurz nach ihrer Entstehung wie isolierte Inseln im unmit-

plan aimed at disencumbering and restructuring cities that were suffering from a rapid surge of population growth and the inevitable consequences. In many larger European cities the realization of plans led to fractures within what had previously been a cohesive city fabric, for these projects implanted large infrastructures, especially for motor traffic, into the existing city layout: new city districts, the design of which was based upon the idea of functional separation and which were devised to cater to motor traffic, were thus not only constructed as extensions but also simply implanted into the existing urban structure. These plans came to specify how cities of the future were to be organized and how new urban life could be generated there.[9] Yet thoughts on the implementation of new technologies, new forms of communication, new avenues for movement, and new ideas about communal life influenced not only the larger plans but could especially be found in the organizational planning of large-scale housing projects that were realized as part of such larger plans.

For example, Le Corbusier's "Rue Interieure" was meant to replace streets, as were the "streets in the sky" within buildings in the Smithsons' projects. The "Plateau," as is seen in the Ekbathan projects in Teheran[10] and Les Olympiades or Le Front de Seine in Paris, relegated cars to the ground floor and offered residents a new urban space which was usually positioned above and separated from the regular street level of the surrounding city and thus reserved for use by pedestrians.[11] Living quarters also changed thanks to the innovations of new technology. With each apartment now possessing its own bathroom, warm water, and central heating system, the apartment unit became increasingly isolated within the building and turned into a cell which, though offering its inhabitants modern conveniences, was nevertheless not flexible enough to adapt to the changing needs of residents.[12]

The resultant new ways of organizing the buildings, along with their massive size, often led to a direct spatial disruption of existing city typologies. Such developments were reinforced by the political factor of projects frequently being conceptualized as part of even larger plans that were either never or only partly carried out. Moreover, elements connecting such developments to the surrounding city were often lacking or were likewise never or only partly realized. As a consequence, large-scale housing projects tended to be positioned, after

9   Vgl. Benevolo Leonardo: *Die Geschichte der Stadt*, Frankfurt am Main 2000.

10   Das Projekt Ekbathan, gelegen im Westen der Stadt Teheran, ist in Europa weitgehend unbekannt, verdient in diesem Kontext aber einen besonderen Hinweis, da es zur Zeit seiner Entstehung mit über 70.000 Wohnungen das größte bis dahin errichtete Wohnungsbauprojekt Asiens war und ebenfalls den Vorgaben der modernen Stadtplanung folgte. Es gilt als wichtige Referenz für den islamischen und vorderasiatischen Raum.

11   Vgl. Seraji: *Logement Matière* (wie Anm. 7).

12   Vgl. *Arch+*, Wohnen, Edition 176/177, Aachen 2006.

9   See Benevolo Leonardo, *Die Geschichte der Stadt* (Frankfurt am Main, 2000).

10   The Ekbathan project, located in the west section of Teheran, is mostly unknown in Europe yet in this context deserves a special reference. At the time of its construction, accommodating over 70,000 apartment units, it was the largest housing project in Asia of the time and also adhered to modern urban-planning standards. Ekbathan is considered an important referential example within Islamic and Near Eastern territory.

11   See Seraji, *Logement Matière* (note 7).

12   See *Arch+*, Wohnen, Edition 176/177 (Aachen, 2006).

Ab 1750
Starting 1750

Europa, USA
Beginn der industriellen Revolution, Bevölkerungswachstum durch Landflucht und Immigration in den Städten führt zu hoher Wohnraumnachfrage die nicht bewältigt wird
Beginning of the industrial revolution; population growth through rural exodus and immigration to cities results in a higher demand for living space that cannot be met

England
Beginn Übergang von Agrar- zu Industriegesellschaft
Beginning of the shift from an agrarian to an industrial society

Um 1800
Ca. 1800

Europa, USA
Handwerksfamilien wohnen unter einem Dach, teilweise mit bis zu 12 Personen in einem Zimmer
Craftsmen families living under one roof, up to 12 people per room

Paris
Erste *Maison mixte* in der Innenstadt, verschiedene soziale Schichten in einem Haus
First *Maison mixte* in the city center, with individuals from various social strata residing in one house

1811

Deutschland
Germany
Gründung der Krupp-Werke von Friedrich Krupp mit erstem Gussstahlwerk in Essen
Founding of the Krupp works by Friedrich Krupp with the first cast-steel foundry in Essen

1750   1760   1770   1780   1790   1800   1810   1820

Illustration zu Charles Fouriers sozialer Utopie „Blick auf eine Phalenstère" (Modellarchitektur für eine Gemeinschaft). Illustration of Charles Fourier's social utopia, "View of a Phalenstère" (Model Architecture for a Community).
Von by Daubigny Charles-Francois, Cabinet des Estampes, Bibliothèque Nationale de France.

1809

Frankreich France
Charles Fourier
Utopie einer Lebensgemeinschaft, sog. Phalanstères, Gebäude mit gemeinschaftlichen Aktivitäts- und Kochmöglichkeiten für ca. 1.600 Personen
Utopia of communal living, the so-called "Phalanstère," a building offering opportunities for collective activities and cooking, designed for ca. 1,600 people

1824

Blick auf eine Gemeinschaft nach dem Vorschlag Robert Owens. View of a community designed according to Robert Owen's proposal.
Von by F. Bate, in „The Association of all Classes of all Nations", 69, Great Queen Street, Lincoln's Inn Fields, London, 1838.

1851

England
Gründung der Muster-siedlung Saltaire bei Bradford durch Titus Salt, neben Arbeiterwohnhäusern entstanden zahlreiche Gemeinschaftseinrichtungen
Titus Salt founds the model settlement Saltaire near Bradford, which offers various different communal amenities alongside housing for workers

Saltaire, Gesamtplanung von Lockwood and Mawson. Saltaire, overall plan by Lockwood and Mawson.

1851

1824

USA
Robert Owen
Gründung New Harmony, Indiana USA, Utopie von einer genossenschaftlich konzipierten Kolonie, in der alle arbeiten und alle alles gemeinsam besitzen
Establishment of New Harmony, Indiana, USA, a utopia taking the form of a jointly designed colony where everyone works and everything is owned collectively

England
Joseph Aspdin erfindet den Portlandzement
Joseph Aspdin invents Portland cement

Ab 1844
Starting 1844

Deutschland
Germany
Industrialisierung führt, bedingt durch Massenzustrom in den Städten, zu akutem Wohnungsmangel, Überbelegung von vorhandenem Wohnraum
Industrialization leads to an acute shortage of housing, caused by the mass influx into cities, as well as to an overoccupancy of existing living space

1853

USA
Erfindung des Sicherheitsaufzugs von Elisha Graves Otis
Elisha Graves Otis invents a safety elevator

1848

England
Verabschiedung des ersten Gesundheitsgesetzes, Kanalisation, fließendes Wasser, Verbot von Kellerwohnungen
The first health-care legislation is passed; also new is canalization, running water, and a ban on basement apartments

Um 1850–1869
Ca. 1850–69

Paris
Erstes Entstehen von Kollektivwohnstätten für Arbeiter am Ortsrand. Die sogenannten *Cités*, sind abgetrennte Gebiete für kasernenartige Wohnkomplexe.
First appearance of collective residences for workers in the city outskirts, called *Cités*, which are fenced in areas for housing complexes, similar to barracks

1892

Frankreich France
Erfindung des Platte balken von Francois Hennebique
Francois Hennebiqu invents the T-beam

1894–1902

Deutschland
Germany
Karl Benz stellt das erste Automobil in Serie her, das Automobil wird als Fortbewegungsmittel allen sozialen Schichten zugänglich
Karl Benz produces the first series of aut mobiles, making the motor vehicle availal to all social classes a means of transporta

320 — 1830 — 1840 — 1850 — 1860 — 1870 — 1880 — 1890

1833

England
Erfindung des Fließbands
The conveyor belt is invented

1841–1856

USA
Charles Sears und and **Nathan Sparks** setzen Fouriers Utopien in die Realität um, Gründung North American Phalanx (NAP), New Jersey, USA, der zentrale Part mit Esszimmer, Gemeinschaftsraum, Bibliotheken etc. ein Flügel für ruhige Aktivitäten, ein Flügel für lautere Aktivitäten z. B. spielende Kinder, Musik, ein Flügel für zahlende Gäste
convert Fourier's utopias to reality by founding North American Phalanx (NAP), New Jersey, USA. The community is comprised of a central section with a dining area, a common room, libraries, and so forth, as well as a wing for low-key activities, a wing for louder activities such as playing children, music, and a wing for paying guests

Die North American Phalanx um 1850. The North American Phalanx community.

1850

The Tree Magnets, Town, County, and Town-Country.

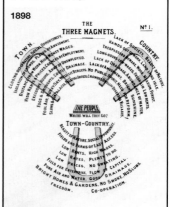

1898

1898

England
Ebenezer Howard publiziert *Tomorrow. A Peaceful Path to Social Reform* das die Grundlage der Gartenstadtbewegung darstellt, Gründung der Garden City Association ein Jahr später
publishes *Tomorrow A Peaceful Path to Social Reform*, which forms the basis of th Garden City Moveme with the Garden City Association founded one year later

completion, like islands within neighboring urban space.[13] Due to a difference in scale from the developmental setting, to the building size and unfinished elements, these structures were inclined to remain isolated from the rest of the urban environment; yet they offered residents an opportunity to individually interpret and appropriate existing open spaces, such as proved to be the case at Ekbathan in Teheran, at Corviale in Rome, and at Neuen Zentrum am Kottbusser-Tor in Berlin Kreuzberg.[14]

However, shortly after these buildings were erected, not only did the political landscape shift, so did socioeconomic conditions. The first oil crisis of 1974 put an end to the economic boom and sent the social state into a position of crisis that would last for decades, with the end of the crisis simultaneously signifying the social state's slow decline, which in turn led to the termination of state-financed housing projects.

Under these conditions, the further implementation of such grand plans was often aborted. Modern society—as was still being imagined at the beginning of the twentieth century and during the economic upswing following the Second World War—was no longer the goal that was being politically and socially pursued. As such, the realized housing projects remained behind as fragments, both in the real urban context and in its social embeddedness within theoretical discourse.[15]

With the disintegration of the social state at the end of the twentieth century, social housing in Europe likewise disappeared and, along the way, so did its iconic figurehead: large-scale housing. Once vaunted for its spatial and social achievements, after 1980 it was rejected by multiple fronts for precisely the same reasons. Large-scale housing, which goes by a range of different names including "the projects," was written off as an inhumane living environment.[16] Apartment layouts tailored to life's basic needs as well as the outside separation from pedestrians and vehicles—labeled as "terrible spatial" conditions or "dreary" and "anonymous"—were made responsible for the social difficulties arising within many of these new buildings. Furthermore, the sheer size of the structures emphasized the aspect of responsibility, as expressed by these developments, that had been assumed for their residents. Consequently, in many places the public authorities step by step relinquished

telbaren Stadtraum.[13] Durch den maßstäblichen Bruch mit ihrer Umgebung, ihre Größe und unvollendete Elemente waren sie zwar oft vom übrigen Stadtraum isoliert, boten ihren Bewohnern aber die Möglichkeit, bestehende Freiräume für sich zu interpretieren und anzueignen, wie dies z.B. in Ekbathan in Teheran, bei Corviale in Rom und beim Neuen Zentrum am Kottbusser-Tor in Berlin Kreuzberg der Fall war.[14]

Doch kurz nachdem die Bauten realisiert worden waren, änderten sich nicht nur die politischen Verhältnisse, sondern auch die sozio-ökonomischen Bedingungen. Die erste Ölkrise 1974 beendete den wirtschaftlichen Boom und beförderte den Sozialstaat auf Jahrzehnte in eine Krise, deren Ende gleichzeitig seinen langsamen Abbau bedeutete, was in der Folge wiederum zum Ende der staatlich finanzierten Wohnprojekte führte.

Unter diesen Umständen wurde die weitere Umsetzung der großen Pläne oft fallen gelassen. Die moderne Gesellschaft, so wie man sie sich noch zu Beginn des 20. Jahrhunderts und durch den wirtschaftlichen Aufschwung nach Ende des zweiten Weltkriegs erträumt hatte, war nicht mehr das Ziel, das politisch und sozial verfolgt wurde – die realisierten Wohnungsbauprojekte blieben dadurch Fragmente, nicht nur im realurbanen Kontext, sondern auch in ihrer sozialen Einbettung und im theoretischen Diskurs.[15]

Mit dem Zusammenbruch des Sozialstaates zum Ende des 20. Jahrhunderts verschwand auch der soziale Wohnungsbau in Europa und mit ihm seine Ikone, der Großwohnungsbau. Zuvor für seine räumlichen und sozialen Errungenschaften gerühmt, wurde er mehrheitlich nach 1980 aus denselben Gründen abgelehnt. Der großmaßstäbliche Wohnungsbau, auch bekannt als „Großwohneinheit", Großwohnsiedlung, Plattenbau, Projects (USA) etc. wurde als unmenschliche Wohnform abgehakt.[16] Die auf die genauen Anforderungen des Lebens bemessenen Wohnungsgrundrisse und die im Außenraum vollzogene Trennung von Fußgängern und Autos wurden als „schlimme räumliche Zustände", „trist" und „anonym" mit für die sozialen Schwierigkeiten verantwortlich gemacht, die in vielen der neuen Bauten auftraten. Zudem trat in der Größe der Gebäude der Aspekt der Verantwortung hervor, die sich in diesen Gebäuden ausdrückte und die man gegenüber den Bewohnern übernommen hatte. Als Folge zog sich vielerorts die öffentliche Hand nach und nach aus dem Bau zurück, und es wurde nach 20 Jahren Jubel auf einmal über Verkauf und Sprengung von Gebäuden nachgedacht, die in der Regel kaum 20 Jahre alt waren. Die Idee des Großwohnungsbaus galt als gescheitert, war sie doch sozial und räumlich mit der neuen Ära unverträglich.

Die Sprengung von Pruitt-Igoe 1966 in New York und die Erfahrungen der sozialen Segregation aus der Banlieue von Paris wurden zu Symbolen des Verfalls des Sozialstaates. Mit dem Scheitern des modernen Städtebaus,

---

13 Here Les Olympiades in Paris and the Neue Zentrum Kreuzberg in Berlin have been cited as examples since both were erected in the context of larger infrastructural projects that never ended up being realized.

14 The free planes in Corviale were gradually turned into apartments by the residents themselves. The city withdrew its support from the project, and only several of the originally planned buildings were realized. At the Pallasseum in Berlin Schöneberg, the freely accessible areas were mostly used by teenagers, for the open areas and playgrounds designated by the project plan were never realized. In Ekbathan, many areas, especially the roofs, were likewise reconfigured by teenagers as meeting points while the complex's former pools were turned into skating rinks.

15 See Kenneth Kolson, *Big Plans: The Allure and Folly of Urban Design* (Baltimore and London, 2001).

16 See Liselotte Ungers, *Die Suche nach einer neuen Wohnform: Siedlungen der zwanziger Jahre damals und heute* (Stuttgart, 1983).

13 Als Beispiele seien hier Les Olympiades in Paris und das Neue Zentrum Kreuzberg in Berlin genannt, die beide im Kontext größerer Infrastrukturprojekte errichtet wurden, die dann nicht realisiert wurden.

14 Die freie Ebene in Corviale wurde nach und nach von den Einwohnern selbst mit Wohnungen ausgebaut. Die Stadt zog sich aus dem Projekt zurück und von den ursprünglich geplanten weiteren Bauten wurden die wenigsten realisiert. Im Pallasseum in Berlin Schöneberg wurden die freien Erschließungsflächen vor allem durch Jugendliche genutzt, denn die zum Projekt gehörenden Freiflächen und Spielplätze wurden nicht realisiert. In Ekbathan wurden viele Flächen vor allem auf den Dächern ebenfalls von Jugendlichen als Treffpunkte umgestaltet und auch die ehemaligen Pools der Anlage wurden als Skatebahnen genutzt.

15 Vgl. Kenneth Kolson: *Big Plans. The Allure and Folly of Urban Design*, Baltimore/London 2001.

16 Vgl. Liselotte Ungers: *Die Suche nach einer neuen Wohnform. Siedlungen der zwanziger Jahre damals und heute*, Stuttgart 1983.

dessen Kernelement die Großwohnungsbauten waren, scheiterte vor allem die Grundannahme, dass der Staat die Planung für die Gesellschaft und damit die Verantwortung übernehmen könne.[17]

Doch alleine in Europa lebt ein Großteil der Bevölkerung in Großwohnungsbauten und in manchen Stadtteilen, wie z.B. im Berliner Stadtteil Süd-Schöneberg, wohnen 2.500 von 19.000 Einwohnern in einem Gebäudekomplex, dem „Pallasseum", einem neungeschossigen Komplex, der aus vier Gebäudeteilen besteht, dessen Dachflächen als öffentliche Räume konzipiert wurden.[18] Das „Pallasseum" gehört zu jenen Gebäuden, die während der 1980er und 1990er Jahre vom Abriss bedroht waren. Doch die ökologischen und ökonomischen Bedingungen zu Beginn des 21. Jahrhunderts ermöglichen es nun, einen neuen Blick auf diese Bauten zu werfen und damit eine heterogene Stadtgesellschaft zu generieren. Denn die hohe Dichte und die mögliche Integration von freien Flächen im Gebäude bieten konkrete Ansätze für die Ausbildung einer ökologisch nachhaltigen und für Beteiligung offenen Stadtgesellschaft.

Vom städtischen Problemfall zum urbanen Potenzial – ökologische und ökonomische Bedingungen für die Wiederentdeckung der Großwohnungsbauprojekte als Typologie für eine nachhaltige Stadtgesellschaft. Obwohl sich die meisten Kommunen heute aufgrund finanzieller Schwierigkeiten aus dem öffentlichen Wohnungsbau zurückgezogen haben, spricht man zumindest in Europa zu Beginn des 21. Jahrhunderts wieder über die Relevanz von dichten Wohnungsbauten.[19]

Ökologische wie ökonomische Bedingungen haben sich verschärft und bezahlbarer Wohnraum in Innenstädten in Europas Metropolen wird knapp.[20]

> Ökologische wie ökonomische Bedingungen haben sich verschärft und bezahlbarer Wohnraum in Innenstädten in Europas Metropolen wird knapp.

Das, was den Großwohnungsbauprojekten als revolutionärer Ansatz innewohnt und was als Beispiel für die Planung der Post-Kyoto-Metropole einer erneuten Betrachtung wert ist, sind vor allem zwei Aspekte der Großwohnungsbauten der 1960er und 1980er Jahre: die hohe Dichte an Wohnflächen und die öffentlichen Funktionsflächen im Gebäude. Dies macht es nötig, die Bauten nicht einfach nur zu verdammen, sondern sie erneut einer Analyse zu unterziehen. Diese würde nicht nur ermöglichen, die bestehenden Bauten um- und weiterzubauen, sondern auch neue Ansätze für die Entwicklung

responsibility for the structures, so that after twenty years of jubilation people were all of a sudden considering selling or demolishing the buildings, most of which had barely even seen the passing of two decades. The concept of large-scale housing was said to have failed and to be both socially and spatially irreconcilable with the new times.

The 1966 demolition of Pruitt-Igoe in New York and the social segregation experienced in the banlieues in Paris came to be symbolic for the decline of the social state. With the floundering of modern urban development, whose core element was large-scale housing, above all came the collapse of the fundamental assumption that government could take on the planning of society and, in turn, the concomitant responsibility.[17]

But in Europe alone, a large segment of the population resides in large-scale housing. In some districts, here by example of the Berlin district of Süd-Schöneberg, 2,500 of 19,000 people live in a building complex, in this case the "Pallasseum," a nine-story development that is comprised of four separate buildings, with roof areas conceptualized as collective space.[18] The "Pallasseum" counts among those buildings that were threatened by demolition in the 1990s. However, the ecological and economic conditions prevalent at the beginning of the twenty-first century have now made it possible to take a new look at such structures and to use them to generate a more heterogeneous urban society. This is because high density along with the possible integration of open areas within a building offer concrete starting points for the formation of an ecologically sustainable and participative urban society.

From Urban Problem to Urban Potential: Ecological and Economic Conditions for the Rediscovery of Large-Scale Housing Projects as a Typology for Sustainable Urban Society. Although most municipalities have long since stopped investing in public housing due to financial difficulties, the topic of dense housing structures has now, in the early twentieth-century, once again gained in relevance, at least in Europe.[19]

Conditions have become exacerbated on both the ecological and the economic fronts, making affordable living space scarce in the downtown areas of European metropolises.[20] That which can be considered an inherently revolutionary approach

17 Vgl. Wouter Vanstiphout: „Design is Politics", Antrittsrede gehalten am 9. Juni 2010 an der Delft University of Technology.

18 Das Projekt „Pallasseum" wird auch als Sozialpalast oder „Sozialpallast" nach der Pallasstraße benannt, die es überspannt. Der Bau steht in Berlin Schöneberg auf der ehemaligen Stelle des Berliner Sportpalastes.

19 Vgl. Aurora Fernández Per/Javier Mozas/Javier Arpa (Hg.): *HoCo. Density Housing Construction & Costs*, Vitoria-Gasteiz 2009; Javier Mozas/Aurora Fernández Per (Hg.): *Density: New Collective Housing*, Vitoria-Gasteiz 2006; Aurora Fernández Per/Javier Arpa (Hg.): *Density Projects*, Vitoria-Gasteiz 2007; Rudy Uytenhaak: *Cities Full of Space. Qualities of Density*, Rotterdam 2008.

20 Vgl. Martin van Schaik/Otakar Mácel (Hg.): *Exit Utopia. Architectural Provocations 1956–76*, München 2005.

17 See Wouter Vanstiphout, "Design is Politics," inauguration speech held on June 9, 2010 at the Delft University of Technology.

18 The "Pallasseum" project is also called "Social Palast" or "Sozialpallast" after the street Pallasstraße which it straddles. The building is located in the Schöneberg district of Berlin at the site of the former Berlin Sportpalast.

19 See Aurora Fernández Per, Javier Mozas, and Javier Arpa (eds.), HoCo: Density Housing Construction & Costs (Vitoria-Gasteiz, 2009); Javier Mozas and Aurora Fernández Per (eds.), *Density: New Collective Housing* (Vitoria-Gasteiz, 2006); Aurora Fernández Per and Javier Arpa (eds.), *Density Projects* (Vitoria-Gasteiz, 2007); Rudy Uytenhaak, *Cities Full of Space: Qualities of Density* (Rotterdam, 2008).

20 See Martin van Schaik and Otakar Mácel (eds.), *Exit Utopia: Architectural Provocations 1956–76* (Munich, 2005).

1906

Dänemark Denmark
Kopenhagener Einküchenhaus als Vorreiter des sog. Einküchenhauses in Deutschland, charakteristisch für diesen Wohntyp ist die Zentralisierung der Hauswirtschaft
The Copenhagen Einküchenhaus (one-kitchen house) is created and serves as trailblazer for the Einküchenhaus in Germany. Characteristic for this housing type is centralized house-keeping

Einküchenhaus, Kopenhagen Copenhagen:
(1) Zentralküche central kitchen
(2) Speiseaufzug dumbwaiter
1907
1 2

1902–1920

Stahlbeton als Baumaterial gewinnt in der modernen Architektur an Bedeutung und wird in den folgenden Jahren auch im Wohnungsbau eingesetzt.
Reinforced concrete takes on stronger significance in modern architecture and starts being implemented in housing construction.

1908

England
Gründung Homesgarth, Letchworth Gardencity, gemeinsamer Einkauf von Lebensmitteln und Brennmaterialien, sowie gleichmäßige Verteilung der Kosten für Küchen- und Dienstpersonal an die Bewohner
Founding of Homesgarth, Letchworth Garden City, where food and fuel are jointly purchased and costs for kitchen and service personnel shared among the residents

Grundriss floor plan Homesgarth, Architekt architect Clapham Lander.
1908

1909

Deutschland Germany
Einküchenhaus in Berlin-Friedenau, von Albert Gessner
Einküchenhaus in the Friedenau district of Berlin, by Albert Gessner

Model model of an Einküchenhaus, Architekt architect Albert Gessner.
1909

Deutschland Germany
Einküchenhaus, Berlin-Friedenau
mit zentraler Zubereitungsküche, kein gemeinschaftlicher Speiseraum, stattdessen Essensaufzüge für einzelne Wohnungen
with a central prep kitchen and dumbwaiters for the individual apartments in lieu of a joint dining area

1914–1918

Erster Weltkrieg
First World War
anschließend in den meisten europäischen Ländern einsetzende Wohnungsnot und Landflucht
which resulted in housing shortages and rural exodus in most European countries

1922

Frankreich France
Le Corbusier
Immeuble Villas
um einen großen gemeinschaftlichen Hof sind kleine Villen auf der Etage angeordnet, jeweils an den Ecken zusätzliche gemeinschaftliche Räume, wie Party-räume mit Küchen etc.
where small villas are arranged around a large common yard with each corner housing further common rooms like party rooms with kitchens, etc.

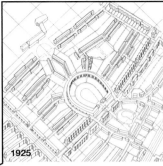
1922
Le Immeuble Villas, Le Corbusier.
1922

1925

UDSSR USSR
Durch politische Veränderungen initiiert, entstanden erste Neubauten von Wohnungs- und Baugenossenschaften mit gemeinschaftlichen Einrichtungen
Political change spawns the first new structures built by housing and building cooperatives with joint facilities

Deutschland Germany
Bau der Hufeisensiedlung in Britz, Berlin von Bruno Taut, Wohnbebauung mit gemeinschaftlichen Außenbereichen
The Hufeisensiedlung (horseshoe settlement) by Bruno Taut, a housing complex with common outside areas, is erected in the Britz district of Berlin

Hufeisensiedlung, Bruno Taut.
1925

1926

Deutschland Germany
Entwicklung Frankfurter Küche von Magarete Schütte-Lihotzky
The Frankfurter Küche (Frankfurt Kitchen) is developed by Margarete Schütte-Lihotzky

Frankfurter Küche, Magarete Schütte-Lihotzky.

1826

1927–1930

Österreich Austria
Bau Karl-Marx Hof von Karl Ehn, als autonome Gemeinschaft, die „Stadt in der Stadt" geplant, um einen großen Hof herum sind Wohnungen und gemeinschaftliche Folgeeinrichtungen angeordnet
The Karl-Marx-Hof by Karl Ehn is conceptualized and built as an autonomous community that offers a „city within the city." Arranged around a large courtyard are apartments and common facilities

1910   1920   1930

1929

Deutschland
Germany
CIAM II Kongress
Wohnung für das Existenzminimum, zum Wohnen gehört mehr als nur die Wohnung selbst. Es beinhaltet ebenso Folge- wie Gemeinschafts-einrichtungen.
Apartment for those living on a minimum subsistence income. Here housing encompasses more than just the apartment itself; it likewise includes common rooms and facilities.

1930

UDSSR USSR
Erste Kommunehäuser, Aufhebung der bürger-lichen Familie, hin zur neuen sozialistisch kom-munistischen Familie, Befreiung der Frau von Hausarbeit durch Ver-gesellschaftung des Haushalts, Verpflegung, Kinderbetreuung, u. a. Kollektivgedanke des Kommunismus soll sich auch baulich zeigen.
First communal houses are built signaling the end of the bourgeois family and fostering the new socialist-communist family, freeing women from housework by integrating shared housekeeping, meal preparation, childcare, etc. The collective idea of communism is purposefully translated into architectural form.

1945

Zweiter Weltkrieg
The Second
World War
Der Zweite Weltkrieg endet, zerstörte Städte in Europa, einsetzende Wohnungsnot
The Second World War ends, leaving Europe with destroyed cities and fostering housing shortages

1945–1952

Frankreich France
Unité, d'Habitation,
Marseille, Le Corbusier
Leitbild der vertikalen Stadt im Gebäude, 337 Wohneinheiten, Wohnfunktionen und an-dere Funktionen werden gestapelt, in der Unité in Marseille befinden sich ein kleines Hotel, eine Wäscherei, Kindergarten Freilufttheater und Sporthalle
A model of the vertical city in building form with 337 housing units, whereby housing and other functions are stacked. The Unité in Marseille houses a small hotel, laundry facilities, daycare, an open-air theater, and a gymnasium

1945–1950

Babyboom
Babyboom-Jahre in Europa, Wiederaufbau der zerstörten Städte setzt ein
The baby boom years in Europe and the start of reconstruction efforts within the leveled cities

Unité d'Habitation, Le Corbusier.

1952

1930   **1940**   **1950**   **1960**

1933

Frankreich/
Griechenland
France/Greece
CIAM IV Kongress, Charta von Athen,: Ideal der funktional gegliederten Stadt
CIAM IV Congress, Athens Charter, the ideal of a functionally arranged city

Niederlande
Netherlands
Bergpolder Gebäude von Brinkmann, Leendert van de Vlugt in Rotterdam
Bergpolder apartment building by Johannes Brinkman and Leendert van den Vlugt in Rotterdam

1948

Brasilien Brazil
Wohngebäude Pedregulho von Affonso Eduardo Reidy in Rio de Janeiro, Freigeschoss für andere Nutzungen, öffentlicher Weg durch das Gebäude mit Blick über die Landschaft
Pedregulho apartment building by Affonso Eduardo Reidy in Rio de Janeiro, with an open floor for other utilizations as well as a public avenue through the building and landscape views

1949

Schweiz
Switzerland
CIAM VII Kongress, die Charta of Athen wird angenommen
CIAM VII Congress, the Athens Charter is adopted

1951

England
„Golden Lane" Wettbe-werbsbeitrag von Alison und Peter Smithson, Netzwerk aus Gebäuden wird in bestehende Stadt-struktur integriert, offene Straßendecks „Street in the Air", Grünzonen und Läden erschließen die Wohnungen und bilden zugleich soziale Räume
Golden Lane competi-tion submission by Alison and Peter Smithson, whereby a network of buildings is integrated into the existing urban fabric. Open road sur-faces become "streets in the air," and green areas and stores are accessible to the apart-ments while simulta-neously fostering space for social life.

Golden Lane, Alison und and Peter Smithon.

1951

within large-scale housing projects, and which is worth reconsidering as an example in planning the post-Kyoto metropolis, involves two aspects found in large-scale housing structures of the 1960s and 1980s: the high density of living space and the public functional spaces within the building. It follows that, instead of being simply condemned, these buildings need to be subjected to renewed analysis. This would not only make it possible to renovate and continue building the existing structures, but also to come upon new approaches for the development of more dense typologies. For if the twenty-first-century city is to be saved from disintegration into many small private parcels, it is crucial that we deliberate on collective space, especially in areas of high density, where urban society can meet and where issues affecting the public can be negotiated on a daily basis.

The principles of modern urban planning—with its functional separation—offer a great challenge for the conversion of urban areas created under the influence of modernism, which includes large-scale housing structures, all the way to the post-Kyoto city. Considering the need for dense urban structures on the one hand and green spaces on the other, the post-Kyoto city opens up new possibilities for large-scale housing projects. Densification, municipal facilities, public participative areas, and easy access to local public transport appear to be aspects that are just as pertinent today as they were fifty years ago.

Yet before these structures continue to be demolished, it is important that they be reevaluated with a view to this new context. The buildings represent genuine referential projects when it comes to exploring new dense typologies. More than just the question of density in general is touched on here, for in this context it is also possible to discuss the connection between social and spatial issues as well as the question of sharing and negotiation as is so critical within urban society.

It is worth our while to reflect on two particular strategies here: for one, on the renovation or continued building of existing projects in order to make them more flexible, but also in order to completely exhaust their potential for existing urban environments. Taking priority here—in lieu of such considerations as demolition, partial demolition, or privatization—should be an investigation of the outdated concepts so as to discover new approaches and to sensibly build upon these established structures in further planning. Also, these buildings should be precisely analyzed so that fitting inferences can be made for new large-scale housing projects.

The large-scale housing structures that were erected between the 1960s and 1980s are generally well connected with local public transport. Also, they feature areas that would be available for targeted retrospective densification. Large stretches of greenery or paved areas are available for use as vehicle-free vegetation zones. What is more, these available areas also harbor potential for resident involvement, as is found in German

dichter Typologien zu finden. Denn wenn die Stadt des 21. Jahrhunderts nicht in viele kleine Privaträume zerfallen soll, muss vor allem in den dichten Gebieten über den kollektiven Raum nachgedacht werden, in dem sich die Stadtgesellschaft treffen kann und in dem täglich öffentliche Fragen verhandelt werden können.

Die Prinzipien der modernen Stadtplanung – mit ihrer Teilung der Funktionen – eröffnen eine große Herausforderung für den Umbau der unter dem Einfluss der Moderne entstandenen Stadtflächen, zu denen die Großwohnungsbauten gehören, hin zur Post-Kyoto-Stadt. Mit der Notwendigkeit von dichten urbanen Strukturen einerseits und grünen Räumen andererseits eröffnet die Post-Kyoto-Stadt wieder neue Möglichkeiten für Großwohnungsprojekte. Verdichtung, kommunale Einrichtungen, öffentliche Flächen zur Partizipation und eine gute Erschließung an den öffentlichen Nahverkehr scheinen Aspekte zu sein, die heute ebenso aktuell sind wie vor 50 Jahren.

Bevor die erwähnten Bauten weiter abgerissen werden, sollten sie in diesem Kontext eine neue Bewertung erfahren. Die Bauten sind ernsthafte Referenzprojekte, wenn es um die Zukunft der neuen dichten Typologien geht. Hier wird nicht nur die Frage der Dichte im Allgemeinen berührt, sondern in diesem Zusammenhang kann auch wieder über die Verbindung von sozialen und räumlichen Fragen und die für eine urbane Gesellschaft wichtige Frage von Teilen und Verhandeln diskutiert werden.

Es lohnt sich, hier über zwei Strategien nachzudenken, zum einen über den Um- und Weiterbau der bestehenden Projekte, um sie flexibler zu machen, aber auch um ihre Potenziale für die vorhandenen urbanen Räume voll auszuschöpfen. Dabei sollten im Vordergrund weniger die Überlegungen über Abriss, Teilabriss oder Privatisierung stehen, sondern vielmehr die älteren Konzepte untersucht werden, um neue Ansätze zu finden und die hier angelegten Strukturen weiter auszubauen und sie sinnvoll weiter zu planen. Zum anderen sollten die Gebäude genau analysiert werden, um aus ihnen für neue Großwohnungsbauprojekte die richtigen Schlussfolgerungen zu ziehen.

> Bevor die erwähnten Bauten weiter abgerissen werden, sollten sie in diesem Kontext eine neue Bewertung erfahren. Die Bauten sind ernsthafte Referenzprojekte, wenn es um die Zukunft der neuen dichten Typologien geht.

Die Großwohnungsbauten, die in den 1960er bis 1980er Jahren entstanden, sind meist gut an den öffentlichen Nahverkehr angeschlossen; sie weisen zudem Flächen auf, die für Nachverdichtung mit Programmen zur Verfügung stehen. Große Grünflächen oder versiegelte Flächen stehen zur Benutzung für autofreie Grünräume zur Verfügung. Daneben stellen diese Flächen auch ein Potenzial für die Partizipation der Anwohner zur Verfügung, wie wir es in deutschen Städten in Form von Jugendprojekten finden, die unnachahmlich zur lokalen Identifikation mit einem Ort in der Stadt beitragen. Dies sind Orte in der Stadt, an denen neue Formen der Mikro-Mobilität zur Anwendung kommen können, neue Typologien eingeführt werden

oder auch neue Formen der sozialen Zusammenarbeit entstehen können. Ähnlich dem Konzept der Stadt in der Stadt, das schon 1927 im Karl-Marx-Hof in Wien und später als Konzept für eine Stadt von Ungers[21] auftaucht, bieten diese Beispiele mit ihrer Größe und ihrer meist von der direkten Umgebung klar unterscheidbaren Gestalt die Möglichkeit zur Identifikation für einzelne Gruppen innerhalb der Gesellschaft. Die meist für unterschiedliche Nutzungen offenen Freiflächen, die zu den großen Gebäuden gehören, bieten Möglichkeiten zur temporären Aneignung und tragen so zur Bildung einer ausdifferenzierten Stadtgesellschaft bei.

Zum einen ist es die Idee des Freiraums, der eine Form von Öffentlichkeit und damit verhandelbarem Raum sowohl ins Gebäude bringt und mit den riesigen öffentlichen Flächen in den dichten Stadtstrukturen heute ein großes Potenzial für weitere Entwicklungen hat. Die in vielen Gebäuden angelegten Sonderfunktionen folgen der Idee der Nutzungsteilung, da die Wohnungen oft knapp gehalten sind und es notwenig erscheint, Funktionen auszulagern. In der Unité oder im Einküchenhaus finden wir Nutzungen, die aus den einzelnen Wohnungen ausgelagert werden und sich in offenstehenden Räumen Waschküchen, Küchen oder größere Flächen für Sondernutzungen teilen. Dieser Ansatz zur Teilung von Flächen ist besonders interessant, wenn man über die Realisierung von billigem Wohnraum nachdenkt. Minimaleinheiten können geschaffen werden; andere Nutzungen können geteilt werden. Der Wettbewerbsbeitrag „Boba Fett", der 2002 für den Projektwettbewerb Bernerstraße vorgelegt wurde, kann als neuer Ansatz im Großwohnungsbau gesehen werden, der die Idee der Trennung und Sonderräume wieder aufgreift.[22] In dem dichten Gebäude finden sich neben den Wohnflächen auch wieder großzügige Flächen für gemeinschaftliche Nutzungen. Interessant sind in diesem Beispiel auch die Sonderräume, die den einzelnen Wohnungen zuzuordnen sind und die einen neuen Grad an Flexibilität in die Benutzung der Wohnung einführen. Ähnliche Ansätze sind seit 2002 wieder vermehrt gerade in dichten Bauten zu finden,[23] sie lassen sich mit den Kellerräumen vergleichen, die auf den selben Ebenen wie Wohnungen liegen und geteilt werden können, wie im Gebäude in der Rue des Amiraux in Paris oder im Komplex der Autobahnüberbauung Schlangenbaderstraße in Berlin. Auch sie erlauben einen schnelleren Wohnungswechsel und ein schnelles Umräumen innerhalb der Wohnungen und bieten den Bewohnern ein gewisses Maß an Flexibilität.

Zudem sind die meisten dieser Bauten, obwohl sie im Zuge der autogerechten Stadt entstanden sind, im Grunde innerhalb des Stadtgefüges besser ohne Auto zu erschließen als alle anderen Wohntypologien, die eine ähnliche Dichte aufweisen, da sie oft sehr gut an den öffentlichen Verkehr angebunden sind und die vorhandenen Freiflächen sowie im Gebäude befindlichen Erschließungsstrukturen gut für neue Mikro-Mobilitätssysteme genutzt werden können. Dies ist in dem Beispiel „Park Hill Housing" in

cities in the form of youth projects that inimitably contribute to local identification with one place within a city. These are urban loci where new forms of micro-mobility can find application, where new typologies can be introduced, or where new forms of social collaboration can also develop. Similar to the concept of a city within a city, which first emerged in 1927 at the Karl-Marx-Hof in Vienna and later as a concept for a city designed by Ungers,[21] these examples—considering their size and distinct form, which is easy to tell apart from neighboring buildings—offer individual groups within society a chance to stand out. Open stretches, as belong to the larger buildings, are usually available for different utilization purposes and offer opportunities for temporary appropriation, thus contributing to the establishment of a differentiated urban society.

On the one hand, it is the idea of free space that brings a form of publicness, and therefore also negotiable space, into buildings and thus today shows great potential for further development through such large public areas within the dense urban fabric. The special functions assigned to many buildings are pursuant to the idea of shared usage, for apartments are generally less elaborate, which apparently makes it necessary to outsource functionality. In the Unité or in the Einküchenhaus we find utilizations that have been moved out of the apartment space itself and are instead shared in unlocked areas like laundry rooms, kitchens, or larger spaces for special use. This approach to sharing areas is of particular interest when we contemplate the realization of inexpensive living space. Minimal units could be created and other usage areas shared. The competition entry Boba Fett, which was submitted in 2002 for the Bernerstraße project competition, can be considered a new approach to large-scale housing that once again takes up the idea of sharing and special-use rooms.[22] This dense building again allocates ample space for collective utilization next to the regular living quarters. Of particular interest in this example are the special-use rooms assigned to individual apartments, which introduce a new degree of flexibility into the use of the apartment. Similar approaches have been increasingly seen since 2002, especially in dense buildings;[23] they are comparable to basement rooms but are situated on the same story as the apartments and can be shared among residents, such as in buildings along the Rue des Amiraux in Paris or in the Schlangenbader Straße complex built as an autobahn terrace in Berlin. They, too, allow for an

21 Vgl. O. M. Ungers: „Die Stadt in der Stadt", in: Erika Mühlthaler (Hg.): *Lernen von O. M. Ungers, Arch+* 181/182, Aachen 2006.

22 Vgl. Wettbewerbsbeitrag Boba Fett von John Bosch, Andreas Kittinger, Ünal Karamuk, Jens Richter, Urs Primas für den Projektwettbewerb Bernerstrasse, Zürich-Altstetten, 2001/02 veranstaltet durch das Hochbaudepartement der Stadt Zürich, Auftraggeber: Liegenschaftenverwaltung der Stadt Zürich.

23 Vgl. Aurora Fernández Per/Javier Mozas/Javier Arpa (Hg.): *DBOOK. Density, Data, Diagrams, Dwellings*, Vitoria-Gasteiz 2007.

21 See O. M. Ungers, "Die Stadt in der Stadt," in Erika Mühlthaler (ed.), *Lernen von O. M. Ungers, Arch+* 181/182 (Aachen, 2006).

22 See the Boba Fett competition entry by John Bosch, Andreas Kittinger, Ünal Karamuk, Jens Richter, Urs Primas for the project competition Bernerstrasse, Zurich-Altstetten, 2001/02 organized by the City of Zurich's public buildings department, commissioned by the City of Zurich's property administration office.

23 See Aurora Fernández Per, Javier Mozas, and Javier Arpa (eds.), *DBOOK: Density, Data, Diagrams, Dwellings* (Vitoria-Gasteiz, 2007).

1955–1960

Frankreich France
Wohngebäude Les
Courtilliéres in der
Banlieue von Paris von
Émile Aillaud, großer
Wohnkomplex mit
offenem Grundgeschoss
für andere Nutzungen
und großem freiem
Gemeinschaftshof
Les Courtilliéres
apartment building
by Émile Aillaud in a
banlieue of Paris, a large
housing complex with
a ground floor open to
other utilizations and a
large, open common
courtyard

Les Courtilliers, Emile Aillaud
1960

1966

Publikation von O. M.
Ungers, *Die Großform
im Wohnungsbau*
Publication by O. M.
Ungers by the name
of *Die Großform im
Wohnungsbau*

1971

USA
Buckminster Fuller
Old Man River Projekt
project, Saint Louis
Gigantischer Wohnkomplex mit 1,5 km Durchmesser, für 125.000 Bewohner geplant, Runder
in der Mitte offener Bau,
mit gemeinschaftlichen
Flächen im gesamten
Gebäude
A gigantic housing complex at 1.5 kilometers in
diameter, planned to
house 125,000 residents.
As a round structure
with an open courtyard,
the common areas are
spread throughout the
entire building

1977

Schnittdiagram Autobahnüberbauung sectional diagram of the autobahn superstructure Schlangenbaderstraße, Georg Heinrichs.

1973–1985

Österreich Austria
Wohnpark Alt Erlaa
in Wien von Glück,
Requart & Reinthaller,
Großwohnbauten mit
Schwimmbädern in
den Dachflächen und
Gemeinschaftseinrichtungen
Alt Erlaa housing park
by Glück, Requart &
Reinthaller in Vienna,
involving large-scale
housing structures with
swimming pools set into
the roof surfaces and
common facilities

1977

Deutschland
Germany
Autobahnüberbauung
Schlangenbaderstraße
in Berlin von Georg
Heinrichs und Wolf
Bertelsmann, 600 m
langer Wohnungsbau
mit 1064 Wohneinheiten, öffentlichem
Geschoss und großen
öffentlichen Terrassen
The Schlangenbaderstraße autobahn superstructure by Georg
Heinrichs and Wolf
Bertelsmann is built in
Berlin. The structure
is a 600-meter-long
housing complex with
1,064 apartment units,
a public level, and large
public terraces

953

ting 1953

kreich France
1 IX Kongress,
hr von der Charta
Athen
1 IX Congress,
nciation of the
ns Charter

1956

Niederlande
Netherlands
CIAM X Kongress,
Habitat organisiert von
Team X
CIAM X Congress,
habitat organized by
Team X

1960

UDSSR USSR
Kommunehaus von
N. Ostermann, pro Geschoss gibt es einen kollektiven Speisesaal mit
Zubereitungsküche, Gemeinschafts- und Folgeeinrichtungen befinden
sich im Mittelgebäude
Communal building by
N. Ostermann. Each
story has its own collective dining hall with a
prep kitchen, with common rooms and facilities
located in a central
building

1966–1972

England
Alison und and
Peter Smithson
Robin Hood Gardes
Gemeinschaftlicher Hof,
breite offene Gänge als
Gemeinschaftsfläche
im Haus
With a common courtyard and broad, open
passageways serving
as common space
within the building

Robin Hood Gardens,
Alison und and
Peter Smithon.
1972

1960

1970

1980

1961–1977

Frankreich France
Georges Candillis,
Alexis Josic,
Shadrach Woods
New Town Toulose
le Mirail
Großmaßstäbliche Wohnungsbauten die durch
gemeinsame Treppentürme und Freigeschosse verbunden sind
Large-scale housing
structures that are
connected through
common stair towers
and open floors

1962–1967

Deutschland
Germany
Bau Märkisches Viertel
in Berlin unter Mitwirkung von O. M. Ungers
The Märkisches Viertel
in Berlin is built with the
support of O. M. Ungers

1968–1973

Italien Italy
Wohnkomplex
Gallatherese in Mailand
von Aldo Rossi, Wohnbebauung mit riesigen
Gemeinschaftsflächen
und Gemeinschaftseinrichtungen
Gallatherese housing
complex by Aldo Rossi
in Milan, a residential
development with vast
common areas and
joint facilities

1972–1982

Italien Italy
Bau La Corviale in der
Banlieue von Rom von
Mario Fiorentino, 958 m
lang, in der 4. und 5. Etage befindet sich Freigeschosse, die sich wie
eine 1 km lange Straße
durch das Gebäude
zieht das für gemeinsame Einrichtungen gedacht war. Heute leben
8.000 Menschen in La
Corviale.
La Corviale by Mario
Fiorentino is built in a
suburb of Rome. The
structure is 958 meters
long with an open level
stretching along the 4th
and 5th stories which
resembles a one-kilometer-long street spanning the length of the
building and which was
originally conceptualized
for common facilities.
Today 8,000 people
reside at La Corviale.

La Corviale,
Mario Fiorentno,
Schnitt section.
1982

Sheffield und in Toulouse Le Mirail sogar schon in der Planung intendiert gewesen. In der Siedlung „Park Hill" sollten die offenen Korridore mit einem kleinen Auto abgefahren, und Milch, Zeitungen und Brötchen an die Bewohner verteilt werden. Als Konzept für Lieferservices und für altengerechte Wohnungen ist dies interessant, wenn man über die Realisierung von großen Flächen nachdenkt. Ein Beispiel, wo die Idee der Mikro-Mobilität innerhalb eines Gebäudes aufgegriffen wurde, ist das Projekt „Office Urbanism" von Hitochi Abe, das einen extrem verdichteten Bürokomplex vorschlägt, in dem sich die einzelnen Mitarbeiter mit verschiedenen Mikro-Mobilitätssystemen, wie dem Roller oder dem Mini-Schlepper im Gebäude bewegen. Diese Räume sind in den Großwohnungsbauten vor allem die ins Gebäude verlegten „Straßen", die zum Teil über eine Breite von vier Metern verfügen und teilweise außen oder innen liegen. In vielen Beispielen wurden sie als problematisch angesehen, weil sie anonym waren und nicht durch die Bewohner benutzt wurden. Durch neue Regelwerke und zusätzliche Einbauten könnten diese Räume aber zu wichtigen Orten in den Städten werden: Sie sind privater als die tatsächlichen Straßen und bieten – durch die vorhandenen breiten Flure – zudem Raum für Nachverdichtung. Ihnen wohnt die Idee des Teilens von Raum inne und sie haben den Ausdruck eines öffentlichen Raums innerhalb oder in Verbindung mit den Bauten. Hier ließe sich auch ansetzen, wenn man versucht, im Inneren Umbaumaßnahmen vorzunehmen oder durch Bauten zu ergänzen, sowie wenn man verhandelbaren öffentlichen Raum anbieten möchte, der sowohl den Bewohnern als auch den Menschen aus den umliegenden Wohnvierteln offensteht. Somit könnten diese Projekte auch als Vorbild dienen, wenn es darum geht, autofreie oder zumindest teilweise autofreie urbane Räume zu gestalten.

Die Projekte sind oftmals sehr gut an den öffentlichen Nahverkehr angeschlossen. Bestehende Parkflächen können umgewidmet werden und statt Autos können die Distanzen mit Mikro-Mobilitätssystemen ausgestattet werden, die an ein Gebäude angegliedert sind und für die Strecken im und ums Gebäude oder aber für eine Vernetzung eines Gebäudes mit einem umliegenden Viertel und zur Anbindung an das öffentliche Nahverkehrssystem genutzt werden können. Für größere Entfernungen können Sharing- oder Shuttle-Systeme eingerichtet werden. In diesem Zusammenhang ist über die Umwidmung von Parkflächen in neue Freiräume oder als Bauflächen für ergänzende Typologien nachzudenken. Grünräume können entweder teilprivatisiert oder zur Pacht ausgeschrieben werden (Dauer der Miete); es könnten aber auch gemeinschaftliche Nutzflächen entstehen.

Neue Formen von Grünflächen können auf den Gemeinschaftsflächen angelegt werden, die neben der Nutzung als reine Aufenthaltsflächen (Erschließungsflächen) auch wieder temporäre Nutzungen aufnehmen können. Ökologisch sind diese Projekte Vorreiter, denn sie benötigen für die Erschließung im urbanen Raum im Grunde keine Autos und haben bei einer hohen Wohndichte relativ kleine versiegelte Flächen in den Stadträumen.

Im Großraum Paris, wo in den nächsten Jahren neue Wohnungen für 1,5 Millionen Menschen realisiert werden sollen, ist die Diskussion um Großwohnungsbauprojekte wieder aktuell. Aber auch in Berlin, wo im Sommer 2011 der Wahlkampf um den Berliner Senat stattfand, war das Thema Wohnen – erstmals wieder seit 1978 – an oberster Stelle in den Parteiprogrammen zu finden und es wird wieder nach staatlich finanzierten Wohnungen gefragt. Noch geht es in Berlin nicht um die Frage nach dich-

easy changing of apartments or for rearranging within the same apartment, thus enhancing flexibility for the residents.

Moreover, most of these buildings are essentially more accessible within the city limits without a vehicle—even though they were designed as part of a car-friendly city—than all other housing typologies of similar density. This is because they are usually very well positioned within the public transportation system and because the existing open spaces as well as the in-building infrastructure can be easily used for new micro-mobility systems. This was even purposefully taken into consideration during the planning process in the case of Park Hill Housing in Sheffield and Le Mirail in Toulouse. In Sheffield's Park Hill, for example, the open corridors were designed to accommodate a small car delivering milk, newspapers, and pastries to the residents. This holds interest as a concept for delivery services and for elderly-friendly apartments, especially when we ponder constructions that span large areas. One example showing how the idea of micro-mobility within a building has been thematized is the Office Urbanism project by Hitochi Abe, which proposes the development of an extremely dense office complex where individual employees move about the building using different micro-mobility systems, such as a scooter or a mini-tractor. In such large-scale housing structures, these spaces predominately serve as "streets" that have been relocated into the building area, as it were; they sometimes have a width of up to four meters and are positioned either indoors or outdoors. In many cases, these spaces have been considered problematic since they are anonymous and not used by the residents. Yet thanks to new policies and additional installations, the spaces have become important sites within cities: they are more private than the real streets and also offer—through the wide existing corridors—space for retrospective densification. Inherent to these particular areas is the idea of sharing space, and they manifest as public space within or in connection to the buildings. This would also be a good place to start when thinking to initiate interior conversions or supplementing space with new structures as well as when wanting to offer negotiable public space that is open both to the building residents and to those from neighboring residential districts. In this way, such projects can also serve as models when it comes time to design urban spaces that are intended to be completely or at least partially vehicle-free.

Such projects are frequently very well positioned for accessing local public transport. Existing parking lots can be rededicated and, in lieu of cars, distances might be equipped with micro-mobility systems that are integrated into the building structure. These systems may be used for traveling within and around a building or else for networking a building with a neighboring district and connecting it to the local public transport system. For larger stretches, sharing or shuttle solutions

might be established. In this context, it makes sense to consider redesignating parking lots as new open spaces or as development zones for complementary typologies. Greenery areas may either be partially privatized or leased out (for the length of the rental agreement), and collective useable areas could also be created.

New types of green spaces could be landscaped in the collective areas, which in addition to utilization as pure leisure areas (open-access areas) might also be once again appropriated for temporary usage. Ecologically speaking, these projects have a pioneering function, for they basically do not require any vehicles for accessing urban space and, at a high level of housing density, represent relatively small, paved areas within urban space.

In the Paris metropolitan area, where new apartments for 1.5 million residents will have been realized in coming years, the discussion on large-scale housing projects has once again become topical. But in Berlin, too, where the summer of 2011 saw elections for the Berlin senate, the topic of housing moved to the very top of party platforms—for the first time since 1978—and people are once again demanding publicly subsidized apartments. While Berlin is not yet concerned with the issue of dense topologies, this can be expected to change very soon due to the rapidly escalating rent situation. If this is indeed the case, then it would be desirable, considering sustainable planning needs, for discourse on dense typologies to also include the topic of the sustainable city as a planning parameter. The decisions made here will surely prove decisive not only for future large-scale housing structures within European cities, but also for the direction in which cities will develop, both socially and ecologically.

This work is based on a research project analyzing large-scale housing projects and dense typologies as a reference for the post-Kyoto metropolis. It was conducted at the Laboratory of Integrative Architecture (LIA) at the Technical University Berlin by Vesta Nele Zareh and LIA students in Berlin between 2008 and 2010. For more information, see: www.zazazaza.eu and www.lia.tu-berlin.de

Participating students between 2008 and 2010: Andrea Alessio, Sandra Bienek, Bruno Cruz, Marie-Charlotte Dalin, Veronica Fandl, Yoann Fiévet, Judith Haas, Nina Hosni, Eva Kanagasabai, Sebastian Kloos, Paul Lambeck, Hannah Logan, Halit Oener, Camille Patenotre, Lorenz Pressler, Philipp Rudzinski, Maria Scheicher, Manuela Thomas, Stefan Tietke, Tatjana Trindade.

Translation Dawn Michelle d'Atri

ten Typologien, aber es ist abzusehen, dass diese Diskussion aufgrund der rasant steigenden Mieten auch hier wieder zum Thema wird. Wenn dem so ist, wäre es im Sinne einer nachhaltigen Planung wünschenswert, wenn die Diskussion über dichte Typologien auch das Thema der nachhaltigen Stadt als Planungsparameter miteinbeziehen würde. Die Entscheidungen, die hier getroffen werden, bestimmen wohl nicht nur darüber, wie die zukünftigen großen Wohnungsbauten in den europäischen Städten aussehen werden, sondern auch in welche Richtung sich die Städte sozial und ökologisch entwickeln werden.

Der Text basiert auf einem Forschungsprojekt, das zwischen 2008 und 2010 von Vesta Nele Zareh zusammen mit Studenten der Technischen Universität Berlin bei LIA dem Labor für Integrative Methoden der Architektur zu Großmaßstäblichen Wohnungsbauprojekten und ihrer Rolle für die Post-Kyoto-Metropole durchgeführt wurde. Weitere Informationen unter: www.zazazaza.eu und www.lia.tu-berlin.de

Am Projekt beteiligte Studenten zwischen 2008 und 2010: Andrea Alessio, Sandra Bienek, Bruno Cruz, Marie-Charlotte Dalin, Veronica Fandl, Yoann Fiévet, Judith Haas, Nina Hosni, Eva Kanagasabai, Sebastian Kloos, Paul Lambeck, Hannah Logan, Halit Oener, Camille Patenotre, Lorenz Pressler, Philipp Rudzinski, Maria Scheicher, Manuela Thomas, Stefan Tietke, Tatjana Trindade.

1　Innenhof *Central courtyard* © Terreform

New York City (Steady) State: A Figure-Ground Switch[1]

As part of a larger project to investigate the potential for the transition of New York to a condition of complete self-sufficiency, Terreform Inc. and Sorkin Studio have been looking at a number of enabling morphological transformations. One of these is the "figure-ground switch," in which nineteenth century blocks see their built mass migrate into the space of the street, freeing the block interiors for the inscription of agriculture and other public uses.

New York City (Steady) State. Eine Änderung der Figur-Grund-Wahrnehmung[1]. Als Teil eines größeren Projekts zur Untersuchung der Möglichkeit, New York vollständig selbstversorgend zu organisieren, hat sich Terreform Inc. und Sorkin Studio eine Anzahl von morphologischen Transformationen angesehen, die solch einen Zustand ermöglichen könnten. Eine dieser Transformationen ist eine andere „Figur-Grund-Wahrnehmung", im Zuge derer die Blockrandbebauungen des 19. Jahrhunderts in ihrer Bausubstanz dem Straßenraum zugehörig erscheinen, während der innere Raum dieser Blöcke zur Einschreibung mit landwirtschaftlichen und anderen öffentlichen Nutzungen frei wird.

MICHAEL SORKIN • MAKOTO OKAZAKI • YING LIU

SUNNYSIDE QUEENS, New York City, NY

	EXISTING SITUATION	Scenario 1	Scenario 2	Scenario 3
POPULATION		2,210		
HOUSEHOLDS		850		
BUILDING AREA	195,643 SQFT	185,377 SQFT	163,728 SQFT	142,079 SQFT
TOTAL FLOOR AREA	1,173,858 SQFT	3,168,576 SQFT	2,403,328 SQFT	1,173,858 SQFT
FLOOR LEVELS (RESIDENTIAL)	6	25	25	25
FOOD DEMAND		3,788,625 LBS/yr*		
FOOD PRODUCTION AREA	0	2,276,401SQFT	1,531,053 SQFT	381,248 SQFT
TRADITIONAL FARMING	0	212,743 SQFT	234,382 SQFT	256,041 SQFT
FOOD GROWING CELLS	0	5,957 UNITS	5,957 UNITS	5,957 UNITS
VERTICAL FARM TOWER (25 LEVELS)	0	2 TOWERS	2 TOWERS	0
VERTICAL FARM TOWER (50 LEVELS)	0	16 TOWERS	8 TOWERS	0
FOOD OUTPUT	0	4,122,327 LBS/yr	2,573,716 LBS/yr	830,927 LBS/yr
SUFFICIENCY RATIO	0%	108.8%*	67.9%*	2.2%*

*Calculated on a daily diet of 2000 kcal per person.

2   Änderung der Figur-Grund-Wahrnehmung (100 Prozent Selbstversorgung mit Nahrungsmitteln)
      Figure-ground switch (100 percent food supply schema)

3   Bestehende Blockstruktur in Sunnyside Existing Sunnyside neighborhood grid

4   Änderung der Figur-Grund-Wahrnehmung Figure-ground switch

5   Grunddaten für diese Untersuchung Basic numbers for this speculation

6   Straßenansicht Street view

© Terreform

Als wir damit begannen, dieses formale Manöver zu untersuchen, war unsere Sichtweise zu einfach. Dennoch stand und steht die Idee, dass es möglich ist, den Traum der Moderne von einem Leben im Grünen mit einer traditionelleren Vorstellung von der Zentralität der Straße zu kombinieren, weiterhin im Zentrum des Vorhabens. Die Art von Stadt, in der dies möglich sein könnte, wurde als eine verstanden, in der das Wesen der städtischen Zirkulation radikal verändert worden war, indem Straßen größtenteils vom Autoverkehr entlastet und von Fußgängern, Fahrrädern, Bussen und relativ wenigen kleinen, langsamen, nicht-emissionsbelasteten Fahrzeugen bevölkert wurden. Den Charakter dieser Straßen stellten wir uns als eindeutig vormodern vor und eine spezielle Inspirationsquelle bildeten diesbezüglich die mittelalterliche und die islamische Stadt.

Auch wenn diese Transformation offensichtlich reizvoll und vorstellbar ist, wurde sie hauptsächlich in Hinsicht auf die Bewegung und den öffentlichen Bereich und auf Strategien zur Umgestaltung des Verhältnisses von öffentlichen zu privaten Räumen in der Stadt hinterfragt. In der Konzeptionsphase widmeten wir der Analyse der tatsächlich hinreichenden Kenngrößen und der Beziehung zwischen der neuen Morphologie und den Bedürfnissen und Größenverhältnissen der bestehenden Stadtbevölkerungen nur wenig Zeit. Mit der Vertiefung unserer Forschung in Hinsicht auf die Produktion von Nahrungsmitteln erkannten wir aber beispielsweise, dass auch wenn wir alle neuen Dachterrassen und die Innenhöfe für die Landwirtschaft nutzen würden, deren Ertrag trotzdem nicht mehr als etwa zwei Prozent der Bevölkerung eines Standortes ernähren könnte.

Die konzeptionelle Aussage von New York City (Steady) State ist somit eine Erprobung der vollständigen Selbstversorgung, die auf der Vorstellung von einer Stadt basiert, deren ökologischer Fußabdruck und politische Grenzen parallel verlaufen. Mit diesem maximalen Szenario schufen wir uns selbst eine Basis, um nicht nur die Möglichkeit völliger urbaner Autarkie beurteilen, sondern auch ihre Erwünschtheit hinsichtlich Form und Praxis überprüfen zu können. Ihre Attraktivität wurde ebenfalls in Bezug auf ihre Umsetzbarkeit getestet und obwohl wir nun genügend Ergebnisse gesammelt haben, um zu zeigen, dass es möglich ist, die derzeitige Bevölkerung der Stadt New York mit Nahrungsmitteln zu versorgen, die ausschließlich innerhalb der Stadtgrenzen erzeugt werden, sind die wirtschaftlichen, politischen, kulturellen, kulinarischen und morphologischen Argumente dafür, dies auch zu tun, kompliziert, insbesondere für den Randbereich.

When we first began to investigate this formal maneuver, we looked at it too simply. To be sure, the idea that it was possible to combine the modernist fantasy of living in greenery with a more traditional idea of the centrality of the street was and remains at the center of the proposition. The kind of city in which this might be possible was understood to be one in which the nature of urban circulation had been radically transformed with streets largely removed from the automobile system and inhabited by pedestrians, bikes, busses and relatively few small, slow, non-emitting vehicles. The character of these streets was imagined as decidedly pre-modern and a particular inspiration was the medieval and Islamic city.

While there's an obvious appeal and viability to this transformation, it was largely directed to questions of movement and of the public realm, to strategies for reconfiguring the ratio of public to private space in the city. At the conceptual outset, we devoted little time to analyzing the actual metrics of sufficiency, the relationship of the new morphology to the needs and numbers of existing populations. As we deepened our research into the production of food, for example, we realized that even if we devoted all of the new terraced roof-tops and interior courts to agriculture, the harvest was insufficient to feed more than around two percent of the population of the site.

The conceptual predicate of New York City (Steady) State is the test of complete self-sufficiency, imagining a city with an ecological footprint coterminus with its political boundaries. By pushing to the maximum, we gave ourselves a basis for judging not simply the possibility of complete urban autarky but for looking at its desirability as both form and practice. Desire is also subject to tests of practicality and although

> The character of these streets was imagined as decidedly pre-modern and a particular inspiration was the medieval and Islamic city.

we have now completed enough work to demonstrate that it's possible to feed the current population of the City of New York with food grown entirely within its boundaries, the economic, political, cultural, culinary, and morphological arguments for doing this are complex, particularly at the margin.

Vertical farms—the sine qua non of self-sufficient urban agriculture—require enormous investment, recast the skyline, are incapable of producing certain foods in appropriate quantities, and reinvent the city's planetary position in ways that some will not find completely positive. Indeed, one of the primary impediments to a "self-sufficient" system of vertical urban agriculture is the very high energy input required for both illumination and heating as well as for the massive construction. Although enough thirty

1   Eine Version dieses Textes erschien bereits in *SLUM LAB Magazine: Last Round Ecology*, hg. von Alfredo Brillembourg und Denise Hoffman Brandt, New York, 2011, und eine gekürzte Version wurde unter dem Titel „The Figure/Ground Switch" in: *Terreform Inc.*, New York 2011 veröffentlicht, online unter: http://terreform.info/ (Stand: 21.11.2011).

1   A version of this article also appears in Alfredo Brillembourg and Denise Hoffman Brandt (eds.), *SLUM LAB Magazine: Last Round Ecology* (New York, 2011) and an abbreviated version was published as "The Figure/Ground Switch" in *Terreform Inc.* (New York, 2011), accessible online at: http://terreform.info/ (accessed November 21, 2011).

Consideration of these possibilities
leads to the kind of synergistic
speculations that are the core of the
of New York City (Steady) State.
Adding residential units to the site
means that housing can be subtracted
elsewhere in the city. This is useful
in any reconsideration of those parts
of New York that are built at suburban
densities and heavily dependent
on automobiles.

Vertikale Farmen – die unerlässliche Voraussetzung für selbstversorgende urbane Landwirtschaft – erfordern enorme Investitionen, gestalten die Skyline um, können bestimmte Nahrungsmittel nicht in ausreichender Menge erzeugen und erfinden die globale Position der Stadt in einer Weise neu, die einige nicht nur ausschließlich positiv auffassen werden. Insbesondere der enorm hohe Energiebedarf für Beleuchtung und Beheizung sowie für die massiven Konstruktionen ist gewiss eines der entscheidendsten Gegenargumente für ein „selbstversorgendes" System vertikaler urbaner Landwirtschaft. Obwohl genügend 30-stöckige landwirtschaftliche Türme (unter Verwendung hochentwickelter hydroponischer Techniken) gebaut werden könnten, um die Stadt auf zwei Prozent ihrer totalen Grundfläche mit Nahrungsmitteln zu versorgen, würde die fotovoltaische Anlage zur Energieversorgung eine Fläche benötigen, die fast dreieinhalbmal so groß wie die gesamte Stadt wäre – etwa 750.000 Acres. Alternativ könnten auch 28 Atomkraftwerke diese Aufgabe übernehmen, doch das ist, um es zurückhaltend auszudrücken, wohl kaum der Sinn der Sache.

Das hier dargestellte Projekt in Sunnyside, Queens, verdeutlicht dieses Dilemma. Es geht von der grundlegenden Annahme aus, dass die Bevölkerung der untersuchten Blöcke konstant bleibt und das zu versorgende Gebiet die Dimensionen der betrachteten Straßen und Blöcke nicht überschreitet. Die Fragestellung richtet sich dann auf die praktische Anwendbarkeit der Lösung des Problems der Nahrungsversorgung auf unterschiedlichen Maßstabsebenen. In der vagen Skizze einer anderen Figur-Grund-Wahrnehmung erscheint die Morphologie durchaus attraktiv, doch ihr wahres Potenzial für eine ernsthafte intensive Nahrungsmittelerzeugung bleibt sehr gering.

Interessanter ist für uns das 100-Prozent-Schema, denn es besitzt einen stilvollen, Kowloon-artigen urbanen Geschmack. Die Dichten und die architektonischen Beziehungen sind ansprechend und der Kontrast zwischen den engen Straßen und den ausgedehnten Innenbereichen ist reizvoll. Allerdings haben die vertikalen Farmen, auf denen das Schema beruht, durchaus ihre Probleme. Das hinderlichste davon ist die Tatsache, dass die Dichte der Türme eine leistungsfähige Dämmung in den unteren Etagen gefährdet. Das schließt zwar die Nahrungsproduktion nicht aus, bedeutet aber, dass der Energiebedarf für die künstliche Beleuchtung ansteigt. Eine Lösung wäre die Nutzung der unteren Turmebenen für andere Zwecke – auch als Wohnraum. Eine andere Möglichkeit wäre einfach weniger Türme zu bauen. Beides verringert die Möglichkeiten, vor Ort Nahrungsmittel zu erzeugen.

Die Abwägung dieser Möglichkeiten führt zu jenen synergistischen Spekulationen, die den Kern von New York City (Steady) State bilden. Wohnraum an den Standorten zu planen, bedeutet, dass woanders in der Stadt Wohnraum abgezogen werden kann. Dies erweist sich bei der Planung im Bestand

7 Szenario 1 (100 Prozent Selbstversorgung mit Nahrungsmitteln)
  Scenario 1 (100 percent food supply)
8 Szenario 2 (68 Prozent Selbstversorgung mit Nahrungsmitteln)
  Scenario 2 (68 percent food supply)
9 Szenario 3 (2 Prozent Selbstversorgung mit Nahrungsmitteln)
  Scenario 3 (2 percent food supply)

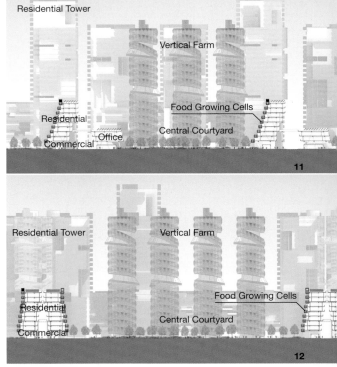

10   New York (Steady) State: Blick auf die Wohngegend von Sunnyside Yards
     New York (Steady) State, Sunnyside neighborhood view
11   Schnitt Nord-Süd   North-south section
12   Schnitt Ost-West   East-west section

Rezensionen

Neue Fließende Welt oder Architektur-Animé?

Kissing Architecture

Sylvia Lavin

Point: Essays on Architecture,

hg. von Sarah Whiting

Princeton/Oxford: Princeton University Press, 2011

Englisch, 136 Seiten, 33 Farbabbildungen,

5 SW-Abbildungen, Hardcover

ISBN 978-0-691-14923-3

EUR 12,99

In *Kissing Architecture* (1) zeichnet Sylvia Lavin eine Gegenbewegung zur Ideologie der modernen Architektur nach, die anstelle einer funktionalen und formalen Sichtweise vielmehr die affektiven Bedingungen zwischen den gebauten Objekten und den emotionalen Reaktionen der Benutzer erforscht. Sie verwendet das Bild des Küssens als Metapher für eine vorübergehende Verbindung von Oberflächen, wodurch sich die Grenzen der Identität dieser Körper erweitern und gar aufheben können und eine neue Form der Kommunikation entsteht.

Doch sieht Lavin diese Verständigung nicht im Sinn der Aussagen einer *architecture parlante*, wie sie sich häufig in postmodernen Entwürfen finden, denn: „No one can speak when kissing" (S. 14). Vielmehr wird der direkte Ausdruck des Gesichtes (*face*) und analog jener der Ansicht (*façade*) unterbrochen und verdeckt, um einen anderen, intensiv verschiedene Sinne miteinbeziehenden Austausch zu ermöglichen. Andy Warhols Anmerkung folgend, „Two people kissing always look like fish", ist für Lavin die Bedeutung dieser Erfahrung keineswegs a priori vorgegeben und eingrenzbar, sondern situativ und individuell – und kann auch wie bei den erwähnten Kaltblütern ganz ohne emotionale Reaktion sein (S. 1).

In ihrer Theorie einer *kissing architecture* geht es jedoch nicht nur um die vielfältigen Beziehungen der architektonischen Hüllen zueinander, die oft durch Einführung neuer Medien und multidisziplinärer Praktiken immer wieder neu definiert werden, sondern vor allem um die Intensivierung der erzielten Effekte. Als Beispiel führt sie die audiovisuelle Installation *Pour Your Body Out (7354 Cubic Meters)* (2008) der Schweizer Künstlerin Pipilotti Rist in dem von Yoshio Taniguchi geplanten Marron Atrium des Museum of Modern Art in New York an. Die riesigen weißen Wände, welche die runde, ebenfalls von Rist entworfene Sitzlandschaft in der Mitte umgeben, werden mit Videosequenzen von Tulpenbeeten, Fliegenpilzen und anderen paradiesisch anmutenden, rosafarbenen oder giftgrünen Traumsequenzen bespielt. Den Schlüssel für die psychodelische Wirkung der Installation sieht Lavin gerade in der architektonischen „Banalität" des MoMA mit seiner modernen, puristischen Formensprache, die nach Clement Greenberg wesentlich für die avantgardistische Kraft der modernen Kunst und ihrer Medien sei – während es dem Kitsch, ebenso wie der Kommerzialisierung und Massenkultur, allein um die Nachahmung affektiver Reaktionen ohne Bezugnahme auf die Natur des Kunstmediums gehe.[1]

Die Arbeiten des amerikanischen Künstlers Doug Aitken sind für Lavin ein anderes Beispiel für eine *kissing architecture*, wie sie im Außenraum und im großen Maßstab funktioniert. In der Filminstallation *Sleepwalkers* (2007) auf den An-

Reviews

New Floating World or Architectural Animé?

Kissing Architecture

Sylvia Lavin

Point: Essays on Architecture, Sarah Whiting (ed.)

Princeton/Oxford: Princeton University Press, 2011

English, 136 pages, 33 color illustrations,

5 b/w illustrations, hardcover

ISBN 978-0-691-14923-3

EUR 12.99

In *Kissing Architecture* (1), Sylvia Lavin traces a countermovement to the ideology of modern architecture, one that explores the affective conditions between the built object and the emotional reactions of the users instead of taking a functional and formal approach. The author uses the image of kissing as a metaphor for a transient connection between surfaces by which means the boundaries of the identity of these bodies may be expanded or even nullified so that a new form of communication can emerge.

Yet Lavin does not view this arrangement as asserting *architecture parlante*, as can frequently be found in postmodern designs, for: "No one can speak when kissing" (p. 14). Instead, the direct expression of the "face" and, at the same time, that of the "façade" are interrupted and concealed so as to facilitate different, intensely distinct signification with an inclusive exchange. Along the lines of Andy Warhol's remark that "Two people kissing always look like fish," Lavin by no means considers this experience to be a priori predefined and limitable, but instead to be situative and individual—and also to be, as in the case of the aforementioned cold-blooded creatures, completely devoid of emotional reaction (p. 1).

Yet her theory of *kissing architecture* involves not only the multifarious interrelationships between the architectural shells that are so often redefined again and again by the introduction of new media and multidisciplinary practices, but also more significantly the intensification of the achieved effects. She cites as an example the audiovisual installation *Pour Your Body Out (7354 Cubic Meters)* (2008) by Swiss artist Pipilotti Rist in the Marron Atrium (designed by Yoshio Taniguchi) of the Museum of Modern Art in New York. Projected onto the massive white walls—which surround a rounded, centrally positioned seatingscape also designed by Rist—are video sequences of tulip patches, fly agaric mushrooms, and other pinkish or bilious-green dream sequences of a paradisiacal air. In Lavin's view, the key to the psychedelic feel of the installation specifically rests with the architectonic "banality" found at the MoMA, with its modern, purist

sichten des MoMA zeigt Aitken fünf verschiedene Episoden von New Yorker Nachtschicht-Arbeitern, deren monumentale Gesichter in langsamen Bewegungen über die Außenhaut des Gebäudes ziehen. Durch den enormen Maßstab adressieren die Filminstallationen je nach Entfernung zur Oberfläche zwei verschiedene Arten von Zusehern: Während die nahe vorbeigehenden Flaneure in den Filmsequenzen den Gemütsbewegungen der Gesichter direkt folgen können, die Struktur des Gebäudes selbst jedoch kaum erfassen, wird den Beobachtern, die sich weiter weg im städtischen Umfeld befinden und die Bilder nur fragmentiert sehen können, vielmehr ein plastisch-räumlicher Eindruck der Architektur vermittelt – ohne jedoch detaillierte Informationen über den Film selbst zu bekommen.

Sylvia Lavin, die Autorin zahlreicher Publikationen und Professorin für Geschichte und Theorie der Architektur an der UCLA und weiters Gastprofessorin an Universitäten wie Princeton

und Harvard ist, hat sich mit dem Einfluss von neuen Technologien und visuellen Medien auf unsere Wahrnehmung von Architektur bereits in ihrem 2005 erschienenem Buch *Form Follows Libido: Architecture and Richard Neutra in a Psychoanalytic Culture* und weiteren Essays über Neutra, die diesem Buch vorangegangen waren, beschäftigt.[2] Auch die Projekte von Neutra funktionieren als eine Maschine oder Matrix, die ver-

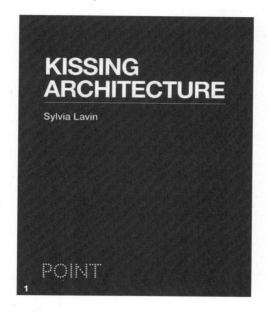

1   Clement Greenberg: „Avant-Garde and Kitsch", in: *Partisan Review* 6, 5 (1939), S. 34–49; ders.: *Art and Culture. Critical Essays*, Boston 1961.

2   Sylvia Lavin: *Form Follows Libido. Architecture and Richard Neutra in a Psychoanalytic Culture*, Cambridge, MA 2005.

formal vocabulary—which, according to Clement Greenberg, is essential for the avant-gardist power of modern art and its media, while kitsch itself is, like commercialization and mass culture, solely concerned with the imitation of affective reactions without making reference to the nature of the artistic medium.[1]

Lavin cites the work of American artist Doug Aitken as another example of *kissing architecture*, for the way it works on a large scale in outdoor space. In his film installation *Sleepwalkers* (2007), projected upon the façade of the MoMA, Aitken presents five different episodes in the lives of New York night-shift workers, their monumental visages moving along the building's outside skin in slow motion. Due to the enormous scale

involved, these film installations address two different kinds of viewers depending on their proximity to the projection surface. Those strolling close by are able to directly follow the emotions conveyed in the faces within the film sequences yet without really noticing the structure of the building itself. Yet the viewers who are located farther away within the urban surroundings can only see the images in a fragmented manner, so that a graphic-spatial impression of the architecture is conveyed, though without detailed information about the film itself.

Sylvia Lavin—author of numerous publications, professor of the history and theory of architecture at UCLA, and also guest professor at other universities, including Princeton and Harvard—was already exploring how new technologies and visual media influence our perception of architecture in her 2005 book *Form Follows Libido: Architecture and Richard Neutra in a Psychoanalytic Culture* and in other essays about Neutra preceding this book.[2] Neutra's proj-

1   Clement Greenberg, "Avant-Garde and Kitsch," *Partisan Review* 6, 5 (1939), pp. 34–49; Clement Greenberg, *Art and Culture: Critical Essays* (Boston, 1961).

2   Sylvia Lavin, *Form Follows Libido: Architecture and Richard Neutra in a Psychoanalytic Culture* (Cambridge, MA, 2005).

schiedene reale und virtuelle Blickwinkel und Bildausschnitte ineinander verweben, um traditionelle Sehgewohnheiten aufzuheben und den Betrachter intensiv in die Umgebung eintauchen zu lassen.[3] In der Analyse von Neutras Entwürfen der 1950er und 1960er Jahre ebenso wie in *Kissing Architecture* verwendet Lavin den von Kevin Lynch entwickelten Begriff der *imageability*, um mithilfe von bestimmten architektonischen Elementen und Mustern ein deutliches, starkes, lebendiges Bild der Atmosphäre an einem bestimmten Ort zu vermitteln.[4] Neutra selbst spricht von einem visuellem Oszillieren und simultaner Doppelerkenntnis, ähnlich wie Lavin bei der Wirkung von Aitkens Arbeiten.

Diese komplexen Beziehungen zwischen Ort, Außenhaut und Innenleben heben für Lavin die Distanz zum Objekt auf und schaffen eine „Intimität", die einen Gegenentwurf zur Theorie einer kritischen und autonomen Architekturpraxis darstellt, denn: „A critical kiss is a bite, not a kiss" (S. 14). In *Kissing Architecture* – ein Titel, der wie eine Provokation im gegenwärtigen Diskurs über immersive Räume klingt – nennt sie dieses Konzept *superarchitecture*, in Anlehnung an die von Archizoom und Superstudio gestaltete Ausstellung *Superarchitettura in Pistoia* im Jahr 1966,

in der Collagen und Installationen die rationalen, funktionalistischen Prinzipien der Moderne, wie undifferenzierten Raster und modulare Elemente, in utopischen, oft unrealisierbaren Metastrukturen hinterfragen. Diese teils absurden urbanen Landschaften werden mithilfe der Technologie (der 1960er Jahre) zu projektiven Containern, und versuchen so das Verständnis von Architektur als autonome Objekte zu destabilisieren und die Grenzen zwischen realen und imaginären Räumen zu verwischen. In ähnlicher Weise schlägt Lavin eine Erweiterung des Architekturmediums vor, eine hybridisierte Praxis, die sich auch in Arbeiten von UNStudio, Diller & Scofidio, Foreign Office Architects, Greg Lynn FORM, Herzog & de Meuron und OMA findet.

Sylvia Lavins Idee einer *kissing architecture* präsentiert eine originelle, provokative Darstellung eines erweiterten Architekturbegriffs, wie er auch im gegenwärtigen Architekturdiskurs durch eine Neubewertung des Umfangs und Geltungsbereiches von Architektur jenseits von Form und Typologie, Funktionalität und Determinismus, Ressourcenverbrauch und Klimaschutz gefordert wird. Beispielsweise wird in Philippe Rahms Arbeiten, die von einer *physiologischen* zu einer *meteorologischen* Dimension der Wahrnehmung

gelangen, Atmosphäre nicht, wie bei Lavin, als ästhetisches Kriterium, sondern wörtlich auf einer mikroskopischen Ebene aufgefasst.[5] Durch den stets schwankenden sensorischen, elektromagnetischen und chemischen Austausch zwischen Körper und Raum werden Veränderungen der physischen Elemente wie Temperatur-, Luftfeuchtigkeits-, Druck- und Belichtungsverhältnisse direkte, oft einzige Werkzeuge der architektonischen Gestaltung.

Auch Protagonisten anderer Fächer haben die Beziehung von Oberflächen für sich entdeckt, wie Peter Sloterdijk in seiner Trilogie *Sphären* – angeregt durch Buckminster Fullers geodätische Kuppeln, das Konzept der Tensigrität oder Archigram/ Ron Herrons *Air House Project* für Cardiff (1965), bei dem Luft, Leichtigkeit und Atmosphäre in

3 Sylvia Lavin: „Richard Neutra and the Psychology of the American Spectator", in: *Grey Room* 1 (2000), S. 42–63, hier S. 56.

4 Kevin Lynch: „On Imageability", in: ders.: *The Image of the City*, Cambridge, MA 1960.

5 Philippe Rahm: „Architecture of Meteorology and Atmosphere", in: *GAM.07*, 2011, S. 134–141.

6 Peter Sloterdijk: *Sphären*. Bd. 3, *Schäume*, Frankfurt am Main 2004, S. 27–28; Bettina Funcke: „Against Gravity. Bettina Funcke talks with Peter Sloterdijk", (2005), online unter: http://www.bookforum.com/archive/feb_05/ funcke.html (Stand: 21.3.2009).

ects also function like a machine or a matrix that intertwines various real and virtual perspectives and image details, with an aim to counteract traditional viewing habits and to intensively immerse the viewer in the surroundings.[3] Both in *Kissing Architecture* and in analyzing Neutra's designs from the 1950s and 1960s, Lavin invokes the term "imageability" coined by Kevin Lynch so as to convey (while also aided by certain architectural elements and patterns) a clear, sharp, vivid image of the atmosphere enveloping a certain location.[4] Neutra himself speaks of a visual oscillation and a simultaneous double cognition, similar to Lavin's approach to the effect of Aitken's works.

The complex relations between place, outer skin, and inner life offset, in Lavin's opinion, the distance to the object and create an "intimacy" that represents a counterdraft to the theory of a critical and autonomous architectural practice, for: "A critical kiss is a bite, not a kiss" (p. 14). In *Kissing Architecture*—a title that sounds like

a provocation in current discourse on immersive spaces—she calls this concept *superarchitecture*, making reference to the exhibition *Superarchitettura* put on by Archizoom and Superstudio in Pistoia from 1966. This exhibition presented collages and installations that were challenging the rational, functionalist principles of modernism, like undifferentiated grids and modular elements, found in utopian, often unrealizable metastructures. Such (sometimes absurd) urban landscapes were turned into projective containers with the help of (1960s) technology and thus attempted to destabilize the conception of architecture as autonomous objects and to obliterate the boundaries between real and imaginary space. In a similar way, Lavin proposes an extention of the medium of architecture—a hybridized practice that can be likewise found in the works of UNStudio, Diller & Scofidio, Foreign Office Architects, Greg Lynn FORM, Herzog & de Meuron, and OMA.

Sylvia Lavin's idea of *kissing architecture* offers an original, provocative representation of

an expanded conception of architecture, as is being demanded in present-day architectural discourse through a reevaluation of architecture's scope and domain, beyond form and typology, functionality and determinism, resource consumption and climate protection. As an example, Philippe Rahm's work—which shifts from a *physiological* to a *meteorological* dimension of perception—atmosphere is not, as in the case of Lavin, considered an aesthetic criterion but is instead taken literally at a microscopic level.[5] Thanks to the continually fluctuating sensorial, electromagnetic, and

3 Sylvia Lavin, "Richard Neutra and the Psychology of the American Spectator," *Grey Room* 1 (2000), pp. 42–63, esp. p. 56.

4 Kevin Lynch, "On Imageability," in *The Image of the City* (Cambridge, MA, 1960).

5 Philippe Rahm, "Architecture of Meteorology and Atmosphere," *GAM.07* (2011), pp. 134–41.

6 Peter Sloterdijk, *Sphären*, vol. 3, *Schäume* (Frankfurt am Main, 2004), pp. 27–28; Bettina Funcke, "Against Gravity: Bettina Funcke Talks with Peter Sloterdijk" (February–March 2005). Accessible online at: http://www.bookforum.com/archive/feb_05/funcke.html (accessed March 21, 2009).

transparenten Membranhüllen eingefangen zum wichtigsten Teil des Entwurfs werden. Die Forderung eines „air-conditioning" Projekts im letzten Band *Schäume* schließlich kann als Umkehrung der traditionellen Auffassung von Substanz als das Solide und Schwere aufgefasst werden: Ist nun das Leichte, Mobile, auch Formlose – der Luftraum zwischen den Objekten – das wichtigste Medium um gesellschaftliche Veränderung und zukünftige Gestaltung anzuregen?[6] Oder wird Gebautes zur Hülle und Projektionsfläche für physiologische Wirkungen, jedoch ohne soziale Aspekte zu berücksichtigen – was eine völlig losgelöste Vorstellung von Autonomie der Architektur „frei" von einem Bezug zum Benutzer repräsentiert?

Ingrid Böck

Architektur und Experiment

Experiments. Architektur zwischen Wissenschaft und Kunst
Ákos Moravánszky/Albert Kirchengast (Hg.)

TheorieBau
Berlin: Jovis Verlag, 2011
Deutsch und Englisch, 272 Seiten, zahlreiche Abbildungen, kartoniert
ISBN 978-3-86859-040-1
EUR 32,90

Die neue, an der ETH Zürich herausgegebene Reihe *TheorieBau* widmet sich in interdisziplinären Essay-Sammlungen Begriffen, die für die Theorien von Kunst, Architektur und Wissenschaft relevant sind. Der nun vorliegende zweite Band vertieft sich in das Verhältnis von Architektur und Wissenschaft und basiert auf einem 2008 veranstalteten Nachwuchssymposium.

Untersuchungen zur Beziehung von Architektur und Wissenschaft haben zuweilen schon skurrile Ergebnisse gezeitigt. Man denke nur an *Architecture and the Sciences*, wo unter anderem die Zusammenhänge zwischen Anatomie und Viollet-le-Duc oder zwischen den Flächenbombardements des Zweiten Weltkriegs und postmoderner Dezentralisierung aufgezeigt wurden.[1] Im Gegensatz dazu fokussiert *Experiments* (2) grundsätzlichere weil methodologische Fragestellungen und spricht mit dem Experiment eine diffizile Querschnittsmaterie an – wird der Begriff doch

nicht nur in Kunst, Architektur und Wissenschaft unter ganz unterschiedlichen Prämissen in Anspruch genommen, sondern zieht zudem, schon innerhalb der „Wissenschaft", einen nicht gerade schlanken Methodendisput hinter sich her.

Unter diesen Vorzeichen wagt der Sammelband viel, insinuiert sein Titel doch, dass es hier weniger um „experimentelle Architektur" im landläufigen, alle unkonventionelle Baupraxis mit einschließenden Sinn, sondern eher um das architektonische Experiment in einem strengeren Wortgebrauch ginge: Um Architektur, die auf wissenschaftlich begreif- und beschreibbaren Experimenten basiert, oder zumindest auf irgendwie analogen Erkenntnismethoden. Solche Erwartungen erfüllt der Band allerdings nicht durchgehend.

Dem Thema am nächsten kommt der Beitrag „Das Experiment als Entwurfsmethode. Zur Möglichkeit der Integration naturwissenschaftlichen Arbeitens in die Architektur" von Toni Kotnik. Darin wird erläutert, in welcher Weise physikalische Experimente Architekten wie Antoni Gaudí, Heinz Isler oder Frei Otto bei der Formgenerierung unterstützten, wie sie den angesprochenen

1   Antoine Picon/Alessandra Ponte (Hg.): *Architecture and the Sciences. Exchanging Metaphors*, Princeton 2003.

chemical exchange between body and space, changes in physical elements like conditions of temperature, humidity, pressure, and light exposure become direct and often unique tools for architectural design.

Protagonists from other fields have likewise discovered the relationship between surfaces, such as Peter Sloterdijk in his trilogy *Sphären* (Spheres) — inspired by Buckminster Fuller's geodesic domes, by the concept of tensegrity, or by Archigram/Ron Herron's *Air House Project* for Cardiff (1965) in which the air, lightness, and atmosphere captured in transparent membrane envelopes became the most important aspect of the design. The claim made by an "air-conditioning" project in the final volume of *Schäume* (Bubbles) can ultimately be interpreted as the inversion of the conventional understanding of substance as being something solid and heavy: Are things that are light, mobile, and formless — the air between objects — now the most important medium for motivating societal change and future

design?[6] Or are built structures to become shell and projection surface for physiological effects, yet without taking social aspects into consideration — which would represent a completely detached conception of the autonomy of architecture that is "free" from any reference to the user?

Ingrid Böck (translation Dawn Michelle d'Atri)

Architecture and Experimentation

Experiments: Architecture between Sciences and the Arts
Ákos Moravánszky and Albert Kirchengast (eds.)
TheorieBau
Berlin: Jovis Verlag, 2011
German and English, 272 pages, numerous illustrations, paperback
ISBN 978-3-86859-040-1
EUR 32.90

The new series *TheorieBau*, published by the Swiss Federal Institute of Technology Zurich and comprising interdisciplinary collections of essays, is dedicated to concepts that hold relevance for theories of art, architecture, and science. The publication at hand, which is the second volume in the series and is based on a young-talent symposium held in 2008, delves into the relationship between architecture and the sciences.

Studies on correlations between architecture and the sciences have occasionally ended with rather absurd results. Let's take the case of *Architecture and the Sciences*, where associations between anatomy and Viollet-le-Duc were for instance recorded, or between World War II carpet bombing and postmodern decentralization.[1] In contrast, *Experiments* (2) fundamentally focuses on more fundamental (since methodological) explorative questions and, in highlighting the exper-

1   Antoine Picon and Alessandra Ponte (eds.), *Architecture and the Sciences: Exchanging Metaphors* (Princeton, 2003). **273**

EXPERIMENTS

ÁKOS MORAVÁNSZKY
ALBERT KIRCHENGAST
(HRSG./EDS.)

ARCHITEKTUR ZWISCHEN WISSENSCHAFT UND KUNST
ARCHITECTURE BETWEEN SCIENCES AND THE ARTS

jovis

---

und Bauingenieurwesen zueinander passen und wie ein digitales, algorithmisches Experimentieren den Entwurfsprozess begleiten kann. Leider wird letzteres nur kurz am für Istanbul entworfenen Masterplan von Zaha Hadid Architects expliziert. Die Schlussfolgerungen, dass das Resultat eines Experiments selbst noch keinen Entwurf darstellt, oder dass „die Auswahl wie auch die Durchführung und anschließende Interpretation von Experimenten subjektiv motivierte Handlungen" sind, „die keiner allgemein akzeptierten, wissenschaftlichen Konvention folgen können" (S. 48), überraschen kaum und ebnen den nachfolgenden Beiträgen den Weg zu einem weicheren Verständnis von „Experiment".

So analysiert Martino Stierli, welche Rolle der fotografisch unterstützten Feldforschung in der Architektur und Kunst der 1960er Jahre zukommt. Er liefert dabei einen Abriss über die dokumentarischen Standards verpflichtete und gleichzeitig anthropologisch motivierte Fotografie in Amerika, und zeigt auf, wie sie vor allem die Arbeit von Robert Venturi und Denise Scott Brown beeinflusst hat. Deren „Deadpan-Haltung" (ihr Anspruch, die „Außenwelt ‚objektiv' und von eigenen Vorurteilen unbelastet festzuhalten", S. 74) macht deutlich, wie weich der Begriff des

Experiments in seiner architekturtheoretischen Verwendung werden kann, apparatives Dispositiv zur Beobachtung hin oder her.

Lose sind die Fäden, die Amy Kulper in ihrem Beitrag „Experimental Divide. The Laboratory as Analog for Architectural Production" zwischen dem „Laboratorium" und den experimentellen Architekturen von Peter Eisenman oder Archigram spannt. Anhand ausgewählter Bildbeispiele skizziert sie, wie man sich das aufgeräumte Laboratorium der Aufklärung oder die chaotische Werkstatt des Alchemisten vorzustellen hat und welche Methodologien aus deren Verbildlichungen ablesbar sind. Die Analogien beider Tropen zu den nachfolgend beschriebenen Architekturexperimenten, die wiederum alle in die Zeit der 1960er Jahre fallen, sind freilich mehr rhetorisch als zwingend.

Auch die übrigen architekturhistorischen Beiträge greifen über die 1960er Jahre nicht hinaus: Marie Theres Stauffer findet in den katoptrischen Maschinen und theatralischen Spiegelexperimenten des 16. und 17. Jahrhunderts das Vorbild barocker Spiegelkabinette und -galerien. Am Beispiel der Organisationsberater Wolfgang und Eberhard Schnelle schildert Andreas Rumpfhuber, welchen Einfluss kybernetische Quantifizierungen und eth-

---

iment, addresses difficile interdisciplinary material—for not only is the term "experiment" used in the arts, architecture, and the sciences under completely different premises; it also has been the subject of a rather hefty dispute regarding methods, especially within the "sciences."

Under these auspices, the collection proves daring, for its title even insinuates that the volume pertains not to "experimental architecture" in generally accepted, unconventional building practice with all that it signifies, but rather to the architectural experiment in a more strict usage of the word: to architecture that is based upon scientifically comprehensible und describable experiments, or at least upon some manner of analog methods of recognition. However, such expectations are not consistently met by the book.

Most closely approximating this topic is the contribution "Experiment as Design Method: Integrating the Methodology of the Natural Sciences in Architecture" by Toni Kotnik. His essay details the ways in which physical experiments have sup-

ported architects like Antoni Gaudí, Heinz Isler, or Frei Otto in generating forms; and also how, for these architects, the experiments have served as a medium for integrating "nature's processes of self-formation" into design processes. This is accompanied by a stringent description of the methodological issues raised by the concept of the experiment within the sciences since Aristotle as well as by allusions to the ways in which mathematics, architecture, and civil engineering interrelate and how digital, algorithmic experimentation can enhance the design process. Unfortunately, the latter is only briefly explicated by example of the master plan for Istanbul developed by Zaha Hadid Architects. The conclusions reached—that the result of an experiment itself by no means constitutes a design, or that both "the selection and the implementation and subsequent interpretation of activities that are subjectively motivated by experiments are unable to follow any generally accepted scientific convention" (p. 49)—are hardly surprising and pave the way for the sub-

sequent contributions in asserting a softer understanding of the "experiment."

It follows that Martino Stierli analyzes the role played by photographically supported field research in the architecture and art of the 1960s. Here he provides an outline of photography in America, which is both anthropologically motivated and dedicated to documentary standards, and also shows how it has primarily influenced the work of Robert Venturi and Denise Scott Brown. The "deadpan attitude" of these two artists (their claim to "capture the exterior world 'objectively' and free from one's own prejudices," p. 75) illustrates how soft the term "experiment" can become in its architectural-theoretical application, all observance of the apparatus/dispositif aside.

Loose are the threads that Amy Kulper, in her essay "Experimental Divide: The Laboratory as Analog for Architectural Production," spans between the "laboratory" and the experimental architecture of Peter Eisenman or Archigram. Citing select illustrative examples, she sketches a picture

nografisch inspirierte Beobachtungen auf die Gestaltung des Großraumbüros „Buch und Ton" im Verlags- und Versandhaus Bertelsmann hatten. Sein kritischer Beitrag zeigt auf, wie genau Arbeitsabläufe analysiert wurden, um so den vermeintlich basisdemokratisch strukturierten Raum einer Bürolandschaft der 1960er Jahre nach kapitalistischen Grundsätzen zu optimieren. Georges Teyssots Beitrag schließlich wird im Versuch, Walter Benjamins verlorene Abhandlung über den Jugendstil zu rekonstruieren, selbst zum Experiment.

Zeitgenössische Architektur ist im Band zumindest durch ein Interview der Herausgeber mit dem Architekten Christian Kerez und dem Tragwerksexperten Joseph Schwartz vertreten. Freilich geht das Interview von einem sehr vagen Begriff des Experiments aus und führt auch zu eher unspektakulären Feststellungen, die ihrem Inhalt nach wohl auch zahlreichen anderen Architekten zu entlocken gewesen wären: Dass klare Zielsetzungen Experiment von Spielerei unterscheiden, dass ein Bau im Idealfall „so zwingend" ist, dass er nicht anders vorstellbar ist, oder dass Bildhaftigkeit idealerweise „nicht Ausgangspunkt sondern Endpunkt des Entwurfs" (S. 123) ist. Hier liest sich vieles wie ein Propädeutikum architektonischer Entwurfslehre. Insgesamt ist *Experi-*

ments. Architektur zwischen Wissenschaft und Kunst ein facettenreicher, wenig stringenter und also typischer Tagungsband. Eine grundsätzliche Reflexion über das Experiment in der Architektur kann er nicht bieten. Immerhin wirft er die richtigen Fragen auf: Ob es überhaupt ein genuin künstlerisches oder architektonisches „Experimentieren" gibt und, wenn ja, wie es sich vom naturwissenschaftlichen Experiment unterscheidet. Statt eine Architekturgeschichte oder -theorie des Experiments zu offerieren, zeigt der Band vielmehr die Grenzen auf, denen ein interdisziplinärer Rekurs auf den Begriff des Experiments notwendigerweise unterliegt.

Ulrich Tragatschnig

Ins Netz
gegangen?

Das Wissen der Architektur.
Vom geschlossenen Kreis zum offenen Netz
Gerd de Bruyn/Wolf Reuter
ArchitekturDenken 5
Bielefeld: transcript Verlag, 2011

Deutsch, 189 Seiten, zahlreiche SW-Abbildungen, broschiert
ISBN 978-3-8376-1553-1
EUR 19,80

Der fünfte Band der im transcript Verlag erscheinenden und von Jörg H. Gleiter herausgegebenen Reihe *ArchitekturDenken* widmet sich unter dem Titel *Das Wissen der Architektur* dem ehrgeizigen Projekt einer *wissens*theoretischen Reformulierung der Architektur als universeller Wissenschaft; eine Rolle, derer sich die Disziplin nämlich in der Moderne nicht mehr gewiss sein kann, so die beiden Autoren Gerd de Bruyn, Professor für Architekturtheorie an der Universität Stuttgart, und Wolf Reuter, Architekt und ehemals Professor für Theorien und Methoden des Planens an derselben Universität. Dieser Fortbestand als eigenständige „strenge" Wissenschaft – und nicht „nur" als angewandte – ist in Zeiten des verschärften Wettbewerbs um Forschungsmittel aber geradezu überlebenswichtig, wie mit dem Blick auf die derzeitige Hochschulpolitik in Deutschland betont wird, was aber wohl auch für Österreich Gültigkeit besitzt.

Zu Beginn folgt der Text Gedankengängen, die Gerd de Bruyn bereits im Sammelband *Die*

of how we might imagine the orderly laboratory of the Enlightenment or the chaotic workshop of an alchemist as well as which methodologies can be discerned from these depictions. The analogies of the two tropes on the subsequently described architectural experiments, all of which are positioned in the 1960s, are naturally more rhetorical than cogent.

The other architectural-historical contributions do not extend beyond the 1960s either. Marie Theres Stauffer identifies the precursor to the baroque house and gallery of mirrors in the catoptrical machines and theatrical mirror experiments of the sixteenth and seventeenth centuries. Citing the example of organizational consultants Wolfgang and Eberhard Schnelle, Andreas Rumpfhuber in turn describes the influence that cybernetic quantifications and ethnographically inspired observations had on the design of the large-scale office "Buch und Ton" in the Bertelsmann publishing house and mail-order business. His critical essay conveys how precisely working pro-

cesses were analyzed so as to optimize the supposed grass-roots-democratically arranged space of a 1960s office landscape according to capitalist fundaments. And finally, Georges Teyssot's contribution itself becomes an experiment when an attempt is made to reconstruct Walter Benjamin's lost treatise about Art Deco.

In this publication, contemporary architecture is represented, at any rate, by an interview conducted by one of the editors with architect Christian Kerez and structural expert Joseph Schwartz. The interview indeed follows the premise of a very vague conception of the experiment and leads to rather unspectacular statements which, in terms of content, likely could have been elicited from numerous other architects: that clear objectives are what differentiate the experiment from dalliance; that a building is, in an ideal case, "so compelling in itself that it cannot be imagined any other way," or that pictoriality is ideally "not the source but the end point of the concept" (p. 123). Much of what is written here

reads like a propaedeutic to architectural design theory. All in all, *Experiments: Architecture between Sciences and the Arts* is a multifaceted volume that is less stringent and thus less typical as far as conference publications go. Yet it fails to facilitate fundamental reflection on experimentation within architecture. All the same, it does field the right questions: Does genuine artistic or architectural "experimentation" even exist? And, if so, then how does it differ from a scientific experiment? Instead of offering an architectural history or theory of the experiment, the volume instead reveals the limitations that inevitably go hand in hand when taking interdisciplinary recourse to the concept of the experiment.

Ulrich Tragatschnig (translation Dawn Michelle d'Atri)

Enzyklopädische Architektur (ArchitekturDenken 2) dargelegt hat: Es wird ein „vormoderner" Zustand einer enzyklopädischen Verfasstheit der Architektur postuliert, die seit der Antike in der Lage gewesen sei, kosmische Ordnung und Harmonie in gebaute Artefakte zu übersetzen, wobei sich der Mikrokosmos Haus und der Makrokosmos Welt vollständig entsprachen. Seit der Aufklärung – die historische Einordnung bleibt generell sehr vage – und den beginnenden Differenzierungsprozessen der Moderne sei dieser der Architektur so wesentliche Charakter des Enzyklopädischen jedoch zusehends dem Verfall preisgegeben. Auch die historischen Avantgarden wären nicht in der Lage, dem entgegenzuwirken, da sie in ihrem Streben nach Komplexitätsreduktion gegen die sich faktisch vollziehende Moderne gerichtet seien.

In *Das Wissen der Architektur* (3) soll an diese Problematik durch den Wechsel von der historischen, avantgardistischen zur strukturalistischen, epistemologischen Perspektive neu herangegangen werden und die Frage nach der Möglichkeit des Fortbestehens des Enzyklopädischen der Architektur in der Moderne mit einem der Disziplin attestierten Paradigmenwechsel vom geschlossenen Kreis des Wissens zu einem offenen Netz beantwortet werden. Dieses Netz des Wissens zeich-

net sich durch sein permanentes und keinen allgemeingültigen Regeln folgendes Wachstum aus, wird aber in einem kurzen Exkurs klar von der ebenso populären wie problematischen Vorstellung eines wildwuchernden Rhizoms abgegrenzt. Das Wachstum des Netzes wird nämlich gesteuert durch den Akteur im Entwurfsprozess – zum Teil rational fundiert, zum Teil intuitiv. Das „Wissen der Architektur" ist demnach in erster Linie „Handlungswissen" und wird als solches in den folgenden zwei Hauptkapiteln durchdekliniert: Einmal als „Intervention im Kontext", einmal anhand des Diskurses „Architektur und Macht". Diese Themenbereiche knüpfen nun auch an Wolf Reuters Forschungsschwerpunkt, die Analyse von Diskurs und Machtstrukturen in Bezug zum architektonischen Entwurfsprozess, an.

„Kontext" und „Macht" werden in besagten beiden Abschnitten jeweils selbst als offene Netze verstanden, die zwar in ihrer Dynamik unvorhersehbar und unüberschaubar sind, jedoch aktiv gestaltet werden können und auch müssen. Die Autoren beschreiben hier sehr plastisch, wie Architektinnen und Architekten beispielsweise auf der einen Seite festlegen, ob der Einsatz eines Materials in den Zusammenhang globaler Wirtschafts- und Umweltpolitik gestellt werden soll,

Gerd de Bruyn, Wolf Reuter
Das Wissen der Architektur

[transcript]   Architektur**Denken** 5

3

und wie sie auf der anderen Seite rhetorischen Fähigkeiten oder gar ihr physisches Erscheinungsbild ausspielen, um soziales Kapital und damit „Macht" zu generieren. Zahlreiche Verweise auf

Caught in the Net?

Das Wissen der Architektur:
Vom geschlossenen Kreis zum offenen Netz
Gerd de Bruyn and Wolf Reuter
ArchitekturDenken 5
Bielefeld: transcript Verlag, 2011
German, 189 pages, copious b/w illustrations,
paperback
ISBN 978-3-8376-1553-1
EUR 19.80

Under the title *Das Wissen der Architektur*, the fifth volume in the series *ArchitekturDenken*, edited by Jörg H. Gleiter and published by transcript, attempts the ambitious epistemological project of reformulating architecture as a universal science, a role that the discipline in modernity has shied away from claiming, according to the two authors Gerd de Bruyn, professor of architectural theory at the University of Stuttgart, Wolf Reuter, architect and former professor of

theories and methods of planning at the same university. With regard to the current higher education policy in Germany, they insist that in times of increased competition for research funds the discipline can only survive if it manages to reassert its status as an independent rigorous science instead of a merely applied one—a claim that probably applies to Austria as well.

At the beginning the text follows the same train of thought that Gerd de Bruyn suggested already in the anthology *Die Enzyklopädische Architektur (ArchitekturDenken 2)*: he postulates a "pre-modern" condition of an encyclopedic architecture, which since ancient times translated cosmic order and harmony into built artifacts, with the microcosm of the house corresponding completely to the macrocosm of the universe. Even though the historical details of the argument remain very vague, it is suggested that the Enlightenment and the early differentiation processes of modernity led to the atrophy of this encyclopaedic aspiration that is so essential to

architecture. Neither were the historical avant-gardes able to counter the corrosive process, because their desire to reduce complexity contradicted the character of the emerging modernity.

In *Das Wissen der Architektur* (3) this problem is reformulated by changing the historical focus on the avantgarde to a structuralist and epistemological perspective so that the question of the persistence of encyclopedic architecture in the modern era can be answered by shifting the paradigm from the closed circle of knowledge to be an open network. While this network of knowledge is characterized by its permanent growth that obeys no general rules, the authors explain in a brief digression that it should not be confused with the popular and problematic notion of an uncontainably sprawling rhizome, as the growth of the network is subject to the partly rational and partly intuitive control of the actor in the design process. Describing architectural knowledge as primarily "practical knowledge," the authors analyze it in two chapters, in

das Baugeschehen und aktuelle Architekturprojekte spannen in diesem Teil des Buches das derart weitverzweigte architektonische Wissensnetz sehr anschaulich auf und entschädigen so für einige mühsame etymologische „Selbstvergewisserungen" (ἀρχιτέκτον etc.) und wenig produktive Exkurse (Alexander von Humboldt als Vordenker des Netzes etc.), die vor allem den ersten Teil des Buches mitunter etwas sperrig machen.

Am Ende dieser Auseinandersetzungen mit den Aspekten des „Handlungswissens" der Architektur steht schließlich die These von der Komplementarität von Diskurswissen, welches durch Intervention im Kontext generiert, und Macht, welche durch Interaktion in sozialen Netzwerken permanent neu verhandelt wird. Beides bestimmt den Charakter des enzyklopädischen Netzes, in dem der Diskurs fortwährend Machtstrukturen hinterfragt, Macht wiederum den Diskurs einschränkt und so weiter. Dieses differenzierte Konzept eines netzförmig strukturierten Wissens scheint damit tatsächlich geeignet, das Universelle, das „Enzyklopädische" der Architektur – freilich unter Aufgabe des *Zyklos* – auch in der Moderne fortbestehen zu lassen. Ist damit also das Versprechen des Buches eingelöst, die Architektur als universelle „Wissenschaft" zu rehabilitieren?

Aufschlüsse dazu gibt der letzte Abschnitt, der in Überlegungen zu einer netztheoretischen Architekturästhetik besteht. Hier müsste sich erweisen, ob sich aus dem bisher erarbeiteten Konzept des Netzes unmittelbar Kriterien zur Beurteilung von Gebautem ableiten lassen, die eine selbstständige Wissenschaft Architektur natürlich unbedingt benötigt. Gerd de Bruyn und Wolf Reuters schlagen hier vor, das „vormoderne" Begriffspaar Proportion (Maßstäblichkeit) und Dekorum (Mäßigkeit) durch die Kategorien Originalität und Kontextualität zu ersetzen. In der Moderne würden sich – so der Schlusssatz des Textes – ästhetische Qualitätsmaßstäbe danach ausbilden, „wie ein Gebäude einen gegebenen Kontext zu berücksichtigen weiß und einen neuen Kontext zu bilden vermag, sodann: wie originell und auratisch ein Bauwerk ist und *welche Spannung sich zwischen seiner Kontextualität und der Originalität des Entwurfs aufbaut*" (S. 182).

Diese letzte These wirft jedoch gerade hinsichtlich des Netzparadigmas einige Fragen auf: Wie soll Kontextualität beurteilt werden auf Basis eines höchst dynamischen Konzepts von Kontext, der sich diskursiv in einem offenen Netz möglicher Bezüge permanent rekonfiguriert, der also niemals einfach „gegeben" ist? Wie kann im end-

losen Wechselspiel zwischen Diskurs und Macht Originalität als intersubjektives Kriterium etabliert werden? Die Möglichkeiten einer reflexiven Auseinandersetzung mit Architektur, die wissenschaftlichen Ansprüchen genügt, werden also nur sehr vage skizziert. Die Frage, *wie* Forschung und Lehre mit dem attestierten Paradigmenwechsel hin zum offenen Netz produktiv umgehen können, wird nicht beantwortet. Generell wird der akademische Bereich, um den es ja in erster Linie gehen soll, in den analytischen Teilen des Buches seltsamerweise ausgeblendet.

Das *Wissen der Architektur* ist somit ein höchst lesenswerter und – in dieser Hinsicht auch erfolgreicher – Versuch, für die Architektur den Begriff eines netzförmigen Wissens, der ja für zahleiche Disziplinen sehr attraktiv und erklärungsmächtig erscheint, zu erschließen. Ob dies ausreicht, die Rolle einer universellen Wissenschaft abzusichern, ist jedoch zu bezweifeln, da die Diskussion eines netzförmig strukturierten Wissenschaftsbetriebs in der Architektur ausständig bleibt. Das Buch ist aber in jedem Fall ein faszinierendes und tragfähiges intellektuelles Netz, das offen für zahlreiche weitere Anknüpfungen ist.

Stefan Fink

---

terms of "contextual interventions" and within the discourse of "architecture and power." These issues relate in particular to one of Wolf Reuter's research foci, the analysis of discourse and power structures in relation to the architectural design process.

In the two chapters, context and power are understood as open networks, the dynamics of which are unpredictable and unmanageable, but which can and must be actively shaped nonetheless. The authors describe vividly how architects, on the one hand, determine, for example, whether the use of a material should be seen in the context of global economic and environmental politics, and, on the other hand, generate social capital and thus power by playing out their rhetorical skills or even physical appearance. In this part of the book, the extended network of architectural knowledge is clearly illustrated by numerous references to real construction processes and current architectural projects which make up for the tedious etymological "self-as-

surances" (on ἀρχιτέκτον etc.) and unproductive digressions (Alexander von Humboldt as the mastermind of the network etc.), which make the first part of the book occasionally a bit unwieldy.

This investigation of the practical knowledge of architecture concludes with the thesis that discursive knowledge, generated through contextual interventions, and power, constantly (re)negotiated through interaction in social networks, are complementary. Both determine the character of the encyclopedic network in which the discourse always questions power structures while power in turn puts restrictions to the discourse, and so on. This differentiated understanding of knowledge that is structured as a network seems well suited to describe the universal, the "encyclopedic" in architecture in such a (circular) way that it may persist even in modernity. Can we then agree that the book redeems its promise to reestablish architecture as a universal science?

Some clues may be derived from the final section which considers architectural aesthetics

from the network point of view. This section shall demonstrate that the concept of network directly entails the criteria for the evaluation of the built environment, as such criteria naturally are absolutely necessary for architecture as an independent science. Here, Gerd de Bruyn and Wolf Reuters propose to replace the "premodern" conceptual pair of proportion (scale) and decorum (appropriateness) by the categories of originality and contextuality. In modernity, then, or so the final sentence of the book argues, aesthetic criteria measure "how a building responds to a given context and construes a new one; and moreover, how original and auratic a building is and *what kind of tension it builds between its contextuality and its originality*" (p. 182).

This last point, however, raises some questions regarding the network paradigm: How can contextuality be judged with regard to a highly dynamic concept of context which is never simply given but always in the process of being discursively reconfigured in an open network of pos-

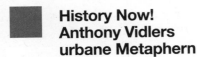

History Now!
Anthony Vidlers
urbane Metaphern

The Scenes of the Street and Other Essays

Anthony Vidler

New York: The Monacelli Press, 2011

Englisch, 368 Seiten, 341 Abbildungen, Hardcover

ISBN 978-1-58093-270-7

EUR 37,99

Erst Mitte des 20. Jahrhunderts nahm die historische Disziplin wieder die Rolle eines nützlichen und anerkannten Ansatzes auf dem Gebiet des Entwurfs und seiner architektonischen Theorie ein. Dieses späte Erkennen der Relevanz der Geschichte für die architektonische Praxis wird oft der Moderne und ihrer Abkehr von historischen Referenzen zugunsten des Neuen angelastet. Aber ist und war die moderne Architektur nicht immer schon von historischen Diskursen geprägt? So lautet das mit einem rhetorischen Fragezeichen versehene Argument Anthony Vidlers, der uns mit seiner neu erschienen Aufsatzsammlung daran erinnert, dass die Geschichte einen unerlässlichen Fundus bereitstellt, um aktuelle Phänomene der Gegenwartsarchitektur und Stadtplanung zu erforschen.

Es ist daher keineswegs überraschend, dass der das Buch eröffnende und namensgebende Aufsatz, der erstmals 1978 veröffentlicht wurde, eine umfangreiche historische Studie der europäischen Stadtlandschaften des 18. und 19. Jahrhunderts darstellt; insbesondere skizziert Vidler eine architektonische Entwicklungsgeschichte der Straße. In den acht Unterkapiteln bezieht sich der Autor auf verschiedene Denker der Aufklärung und resümiert deren Stadttheorien und (utopische) Architekturvisionen. So enthält der Essay Unterkapitel, wie zum Beispiel, „Ledoux and the Porticoes of Arcadia" oder „Haussmann and the Boulevards of Empire". Wie Vidler schon im Vorwort festhält, hat die rege Verwendung von historischen Referenzen zwei wichtige Funktionen: Einerseits artikulieren sie die „intellektuellen Antworten auf die sozialen und politischen Bedingungen der Nachkriegsmoderne" (S. 7) und andererseits tragen sie zu einem besseren Verständnis von Gegenwartsdiskursen im Bereich der Architektur und Stadtplanung bei.

Vidler beginnt seinen umfangreichen Essay mit der Interpretation des Renaissance-Architekten Sebastiano Serlio von Vitruvs drei Arten von Szenerien (die tragische, die komische, die satyrische), um so auf eine metaphorische Verbindung zwischen der Straße und der Bühne, oder anders gesagt zwischen sozialem Leben und szenischer Aufführung hinzuweisen. Serlios unterschiedliche Bühnenbilder, so argumentiert Vidler, hätten nicht nur die bloße Funktion von Szenografie, sondern dienten vielmehr auch als „Masken ... der Ideologie" (S. 17), welche die im Italien der Renaissance vorherrschende soziale Ordnung verdeckten. Sehr oft sind Vidlers historische Szenen – kurze Episoden zur Architektur und Stadtentwicklung von Paris, Manchester und London im 18. und 19. Jahrhundert – metaphorischer Natur: So beschreibt Vidler beispielsweise Laugiers Vorstellung der Stadt als Garten oder aber Pierre Patte's Darstellung von Paris als einem (kranken) menschlichen Körper.

Im Großen und Ganzen liefert der erste Aufsatz im Band eine sorgfältig ausgearbeitete Chronik der diversen Ansätze der Stadtforschung, die zwischen 1750 und 1871 in Europa entstanden sind. Manchmal hat es jedoch den Anschein, dass Vidlers eigene kritische Stimme in der Faktenflut verschwindet und der Text dadurch Gefahr läuft, als reine historische Materialsammlung gelesen und verstanden zu werden. Wenn Vidlers Methodik darauf abzielt, die Vergangenheit zu rekonstruieren, um die Gegenwart besser verstehen zu kön-

sible references? How can originality be established as an intersubjective criterion in the incessant interplay between discourse and power? The book outlines only very vaguely the conditions for an architectural reflexion that would satisfy scientific expectations. The question how research and teaching could deal productively with the alleged paradigm shift toward open networks is not answered. In general, although academic research into architecture is presumably the primary area of concern, it is strangely blanked out in the analytical parts of the book.

In sum, *Das Wissen der Architektur* is certainly worth reading—and in this respect also successful—as an attempt to apply to architecture the concept of networked knowledge that in many disciplines appears as a very attractive and powerful explanation. Whether this concept suffices to ground the claim for architecture as a universal science, however, remains to be doubted as there is no discussion of an architectural science organized as a network. Nonetheless, the book is always a fascinating and viable intellectual network in itself, ready to be further extended.

Stefan Fink (translation Grace Quiroga)

History Now!
Anthony Vidler's
Urban Metaphors

The Scenes of the Street and Other Essays

Anthony Vidler

New York: The Monacelli Press, 2011

English, 368 pages, 341 illustrations, hardcover

ISBN 978-1-58093-270-7

EUR 37.99

It was not until the mid-twentieth century, that the field of history was reintroduced as a valuable and accepted approach to the fields of architectural theory and design. This belated awareness of history's significance for architectural practice is often attributed to modernism's vigorous efforts to reject historical reference for the sake of the new. But: Modern architecture is, and has always been, the result of historical discourse. Hence the proposition of architectural historian Anthony Vidler, who, with his newly published collection of essays, reminds us that history is the essential tool with which to approach current phenomena in contemporary architecture and urban planning.

Therefore it comes with little surprise that the book's eponymous essay—first published in 1978—presents an extensive historical study about the urban landscape of eighteenth and nineteenth century Europe, particularly tracing the architectural and historical development of the street. In each of the eight subchapters, Vidler makes reference to important thinkers of the Enlightenment era, recapitulating their theories and (utopian) visions on urbanism. For example, the essay includes subchapters entitled "Ledoux and the Porticoes of Arcadia" or "Haussmann and the Boulevards of Empire." As Vidler makes clear in the book's

nen, so überlässt er doch die kritische Evaluation der historischen Episoden häufig dem Leser. Trotz dieser kleinen Schwachstelle beweist der Text immer wieder Vidlers Sattelfestigkeit in anderen Disziplinen (Literatur, Philosophie, Psychologie, Kulturwissenschaften), wodurch sein Hauptargument überzeugend gestützt wird: Historische Formen, ob sie nun wirklich oder imaginär sind, werden sich auch in Zukunft „als die Agenten der Reaktion, Reform und Revolution immer wieder reproduzieren, und zwar in unterschiedlichen Erscheinungsformen und in dialektischer Opposition" (S. 17).

Der zweite Teil des Buches ist im Umfang weniger homogen und besteht aus sechs einzelnen Aufsätzen, die einer strengen chronologischen Ordnung nach Themengebieten unterzogen sind. Besonders erwähnenswert ist sicherlich der Aufsatz „Transparency and Utopia: Constructing the Void from Pascal to Foucault", in dem Vidler die gängige Interpretationen des Raumes der Aufklärung („Enlightenment space") als streng rationalen, transparenten und panoptischen Raum kritisch infrage stellt. In theoretischer Bezugnahme auf zwei Architekten des 18. Jahrhunderts – Claude-Nicolas Ledoux und Étienne-Louis Boulée – arbeitet Vidler vielmehr Raumkonzepte heraus, die ihre Wirkungskraft nicht aus dem Rationalismus,

sondern aus der Obskurität und aus sublimen Effekten beziehen. Andere Beiträge des zweiten Teils setzen das Thema des architektonischen Symbolismus fort.

Der dritte und letzte Teil des Buches markiert den Übergang zu Vidlers Lesarten des Urbanismus im 20. Jahrhundert. In sieben Essays werden unterschiedliche Erscheinungsformen des Urbanen präsentiert: Französischer Utopismus, Tony Garniers *Cité Industrielle*, Le Corbusiers *Unités d'Habitation* oder die Praxis des Fotourbanismus zählen zu den Kernthemen, die in diesem Abschnitt besprochen werden. Während alle Texte dieses Teils durch die große Anzahl von historischen Details beeindrucken, die in angemessener Präzision geschildert werden, läuft der Leser manchmal Gefahr, sich in der Ansammlung von Titel, Namen und Zitaten zu verlieren – auch deshalb, weil die eigenen Thesen des Autors nicht immer klar durchscheinen. Das Buch endet schließlich mit „Books in Space", einem Essay über Dominique Perrault's *Bibliothèque Nationale*, die in einer selbstreferenziellen Art und Weise die Schlussmetapher der Stadt als Buch bildet, oder eher als „ein Buch, das aus einer unendlichen Anzahl von anderen Büchern besteht, fast so wie in den Regalen einer Stadtbibliothek" (S. 345).

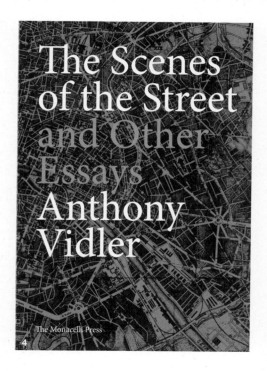

The Scenes of the Street and Other Essays
Anthony Vidler

The Monacelli Press
4

Die Gegenwart durch die Linse der Vergangenheit zu betrachten, war auch schon in früheren Werken Vidlers Grundpostulat, was in seinem Buch *Histories and the Immediate Present* (2008) wohl am stärksten zum Ausdruck kommt. Allerdings ist Vidlers historischer Architekturan-

preface, the heavy use of historical references has two crucial functions: On the one hand, it gives voice to "the intellectual responses to the social and political conditions of postwar modernity," (p. 7) and on the other, it enables a better understanding of contemporary debates in the fields of architecture and urbanism.

Vidler begins his extended essay with the Renaissance architect Sebastiano Serlio's interpretation of Vitruvius' three theatrical street scenes (tragic, comic, satyric), thus suggesting a metaphorical relationship between street and stage or respectively, social life and dramatic performance. Serlio's different stage sets, Vidler claims, do not only function as mere *mise en scènes* for dramatic action but also as "masks of … ideology" (p. 17) that conceal the predominant social order of Renaissance Italy. More often than not, Vidler's historical scenes—indeed brief historic episodes on architecture and urban development of eighteenth and nineteenth century Paris, Manchester, and London—are metaphorical in nature: According-

ly, Vidler discusses Laugier's conception of the city as a garden or Pierre Patte's reading of Paris as a (sick) body.

Overall, the opening essay of this collection provides an elaborate chronicle of the diverse positions on urbanism that developed in Europe between 1750 and 1871. At times, however, Vidler's text lacks a voice of its own, thus running the risk to be read and understood as historical paraphrase only. If Vidler's methodology aims at reconstructing the past for the sake of understanding the present, he often leaves the critical evaluation of the historical episodes to the reader. In spite of this minor weakness, however, the essay demonstrates Vidler's firm grasp of other disciplines (literature, philosophy, psychology, cultural studies) whereby his main argument is convincingly supported: Historical forms of urbanism, be they real or imagined, continue to "reproduce themselves again and again, in different guises and in dialectical opposition, as the agents of reaction, reform, or revolution" (p. 17).

The second part of the book is less homogenous in scope, as composed of six individual essays that follow a strict chronological order regarding their subject matter. Noteworthy are, for example, "Transparency and Utopia: Constructing the Void from Pascal to Foucault" in which Vidler questions dominant readings of "Enlightenment space" as strictly rational, transparent, or panoptic. Theoretically supported by two eighteenth century architects—Claude-Nicolas Ledoux and Étienne-Louis Boulée—Vidler argues in favor of spatial concepts that draw their power not from rationalism but from obscurity and sublime effects. Other essays of the second part continue the theme of architectural symbolism.

The third and final part of the book marks the transition to Vidler's readings of twentieth century urbanism. It features seven essays that concentrate on different manifestations of urban form: French utopianism, Tony Garnier's *Cité Industrielle*, Le Corbusier's *Unités d'Habitation* or the practice of Photourbanism are among the themes discussed. **279**

satz niemals starr oder eindimensional. Im Gegenteil lokalisieren seine Studien die Geschichte der Architektur in vielen anderen Disziplinen und führen sie neuen Kontexten zu, wodurch ein Bild der Stadt gezeichnet wird, das immer dynamisch und vielschichtig ist. Bester Nachweis dafür ist sein bekanntestes Buch *The Architectural Uncanny* (1994), in dem Architektur, Literaturwissenschaft und psychoanalytische Theorie ineinandergreifen und dadurch neue Zusammenhänge für das Schreiben von Architekturgeschichte generieren.

Aber auch im vorliegenden Band „motivieren historische Fragestellungen", wie Vidler selbst anmerkt, „die Transformationen der Geschichtsschreibung selbst" (S. 7). Vidler meint damit, dass die heutige Geschichtsschreibung Faktoren wie Multiplizität, Ambivalenz und Obskurität miteinbeziehen muss, da die Vergangenheit nicht mehr als streng archivierte, nur fernab unserer Lebenswelt existierende betrachtet werden kann. Vielmehr formt die Geschichte einen Teil dieser Lebenswelt. Wenn Vidler in seinem Einleitungsaufsatz die Pariser Straßen des 18. Jahrhunderts pessimistisch als hässlich, verwirrend, reform- und verschönerungsbedürftig beschreibt, stellt er eine „unheimliche" Analogie her zu unserem heutigen „Planeten der Slums und seinen zunehmenden

Umweltproblemen" (S. 7) und verweist genereller betrachtet auf den chaotischen Eklektizismus, der viele postmoderne Stadtkulturen definiert.

Insgesamt bietet *The Scenes of the Street and other Essays* (4) einen sehr guten Überblick über Vidlers vielschichtiges theoretisches Spektrum und liefert einen wertvollen Beitrag nicht nur für Architekturhistoriker sondern auch für all jene, die sich mit der Entwicklung der europäischen Stadt auseinandersetzen.

Petra Eckhard (Übersetzung Petra Eckhard)

Reloaded or Recoded?

Structuralism Reloaded.
Rule-Based Design in Architecture
and Urbanism
Tomás Valena/Tom Avermaete/
Georg Vrachliotis (Hg.)
Stuttgart/London: Edition Axel Menges, 2011
Englisch, 392 Seiten, Hardcover
ISBN 978-3936681475
EUR 86,00

Strukturalismus liegt derzeit im Trend. Der englischsprachige Sammelband *Structuralism Reloaded* (5) ist ein heterogener, aber genau deswegen auch äußerst wertvoller Beitrag zur aktuellen Diskussion. Das Buch enthält Texte von 47 Autoren. Es basiert auf einer Tagung, die im Jahr 2009 an der TU München stattgefunden hat. Der aus der Populärkultur entlehnte Begriff „Reloaded" (*Matrix Reloaded*, der zweite Teil der kultigen Matrix-Filmtrilogie, hat die Verwendung des Begriffs als quasi gleichbedeutend mit „the sequel" in den Sprachgebrauch eingeführt) wurde, sozusagen als „Branding", von der Tagung beibehalten. Damit bekommt das Buch eine leicht ironische Schlagseite, denn *Matrix Reloaded* war ja bekanntlich nicht unbedingt ein würdiger Nachfolger des ersten Teils, sondern eher ein lieblos (über-)produziertes Machwerk, das die Popularität des ersten Teils kommerziell ausweiden sollte. Wer das große und seitenstarke Buch aufschlägt, merkt aber sofort, dass den Herausgebern diese Ironie fern liegt, ja womöglich nicht einmal bewusst ist. Es ist ein breit angelegter Sammelband, der durchwegs nüchterne, seriös-wissenschaftliche Texte und Positionen versammelt.

Der Band ist in fünf Sektionen gegliedert. Die erste Sektion, „The Structuralist Activity and Ar-

While all of Vidler's essays in this section impress with a high amount of historical detail and appropriate accuracy, the reader might, at some points, get lost in the accumulation of titles, names, and quotes, also because it is not always discernible what the author's own thesis is. The book closes with "Books in Space," an essay about Dominique Perrault's *Bibliothèque Nationale* that—in a highly self-referential fashion—establishes the closing metaphor of the city as a book, or rather as "a book composed of an infinite number of other books as if on the shelves of a public library" (p. 345).

Reading the present through the lens of the past has also been Vidler's premise in his previous works, most notably in *Histories and the Immediate Present* (2008). Yet, his historical approach to architecture is never stable or one-dimensional, since his studies always transpose architectural history to other disciplinary contexts, thus painting a picture of the urban that is dynamic and multifaceted. Proof for that being his well-known book *The Architectural Uncanny* (1994) which brings

together architecture, literary studies, and psychoanalytic theory, thus forging new connections to the writing of architectural history. But also in the collection at hand, as Vidler himself notes, the "historical inquiries … engage the transformations in history writing itself" (ibid.). What Vidler implies here is that historiography in our day and age must allow for multiplicity, ambivalence, and obscurity since the past is no longer securely archived and absent from our lives but part of our present reality. When Vidler, in his opening essay, pessimistically depicts eighteenth century Paris and its streets in a state of ugly disarray, striving for cure, reform, and embellishment, he draws an uncanny analogy to our present-day "'planet of slums' and its deteriorating environments" (p. 7) and, more generally, to the chaotic eclecticism that marks postmodern urban culture as such.

Hence, *The Scenes of the Street and other Essays* (4) is a truly valuable collection of Vidler's multifaceted oeuvre and a must-have not only for scholars of architectural history but for any-

one interested in the development of the European city.

Petra Eckhard

Reloaded or Recoded?

Structuralism Reloaded:
Rule-Based Design in Architecture
and Urbanism
Tomás Valena, Tom Avermaete, and
Georg Vrachliotis (eds.)
Stuttgart/London: Edition Axel Menges, 2011
English, 392 pages, hardcover
ISBN 978-3936681475
EUR 86.00

Structuralism is trendy again. The anthology *Structuralism Reloaded* (5) is a heterogeneous but, precisely for this reason, valuable contribution to the current discussion. Based on a confer-

chitecture", beleuchtet die Ursprünge des Begriffes und seine Bedeutung für die Architektur. Er beginnt mit einem Text von Roland Barthes von 1964, in welchem dieser die auch damals schon nicht ganz klaren Charakteristiken der strukturalistischen Aktivität gegenüber anderen theoretischen Strömungen herauszuschälen versucht. Die mit „Heroic Structuralism" überschriebene zweite Sektion nimmt sich einiger Hauptprotagonisten, bzw. ihrer Bauten an: Team 10, John Habraken, viele holländische Beispiele von van Eyck bis Hertzberger. „Structuralist Trajectories" fasst den Begriff weiter und nimmt Architekturen, die auf strukturalistische Gedanken zurückgeführt werden können, ins Visier: Werke von Louis Kahn, Paul Rudolph, Jose Luis Coderch, Kenzo Tange oder Jørn Utzon sind Teil von dem, was Herausgeber Avermaete eine breitere Mentalität, eine Geisteslandschaft –„a broader mentality, a mindscape" (S. 188) – nennt. Das gilt ebenso für Modulbauweisen und Präfabrikationssysteme, insbesondere aber auch für viele Projekt gebliebene oder überhaupt als fantastische Architekturen angelegte Projekte wie die Arbeiten von Yona Friedman oder der Metabolisten. In „Neo-Structuralism and Digital Culture" schließlich wird die digitale Gegenwart ins Blickfeld genommen,

der eigentliche Grund warum die Strukturalismusdebatte derzeit wieder so aufgeflammt ist. In der abschließenden Sektion, „Case Studies", werden einige Beispiele aus dieser digitalen Architekturproduktion vorgestellt.

Es ist also ein breites, vielgestaltiges Panorama, das in dem Buch ausgebreitet wird. Tomas Valena schreibt im einleitenden Artikel, dass eine einheitliche Sichtweise auf das Phänomen Strukturalismus keineswegs das Ziel der Publikation war. Stattdessen soll die Summe der Beiträge ein authentisches Bild des gegenwärtigen Diskurses entstehen lassen – inklusive Redundanzen und Widersprüchlichkeiten. Diese Rezension versucht denn auch keine Zusammenfassung zu geben, sondern greift einzelne Beiträge heraus, ohne dass diese Auswahl wertend oder auch nur besonders repräsentativ sein will. Sie soll neugierig auf mehr machen, denn das Buch ist eine Fundgrube.

Jörg H. Gleiter's Text „Structural Thinking in Architecture" ist in der ersten Sektion eingeordnet, die sich um ein Gesamtbild des Phänomens bemüht. Statt die Geschichte anhand der üblichen Protagonisten nachzuerzählen, versucht er die Entstehung des Strukturalismus in der Architektur unabhängig vom Begriff zu erklären. Für Gleiter gibt es einen „Structuralism *avant la lettre*". Die

Ursprünge des strukturalistischen Denkens findet er im Barock, etwa in den französischen Gartenanlagen von Le Nôtre, denen er bereits eine duale Ordnung zuschreibt, auch wenn es noch nicht die Übertragung von linguistischen Strukturen auf kulturelle Phänomene ist, die später als Unterscheidung von *langue* und *parole* das duale System des Strukturalismus ausmachen. Wesentlich ist Gleiter, dass die strukturalistische Grundthese eine Dualität ohne Hierarchie ist. Er beschreibt mit Deleuze Struktur als etwas, das an sich keine Materialität besitzt und sich nur in dem zeigt, was eine Struktur aufweist. Als nach so einem dualen Prinzip strukturalistisch „*avant la lettre*" konzipiertes Gebäude führt Gleiter die Mole Antonelliana an, das zwischen 1863 und 1900 in Turin erbaute, eklektisch gestapelte Backsteingebäude, das bei gleicher Struktur mal wie ein klassischer Tempel, mal wie eine Moschee aussieht. Schließlich zeigt er mit Eisenman, dass strukturalistisches Denken Komplexität nicht reduziert, sondern eigentlich erst ermöglicht. Die Regeln – die Algorithmen – mit denen die dualen Ordnungen miteinander in Beziehung gesetzt werden, sind für Gleiter der eigentliche Entwurfsgegenstand des Strukturalismus.

Dirk van den Heuvel macht den Auftakt zur zweiten Sektion mit seinem Text unter dem Titel

ence held at TU München in 2009, the book contains texts by 47 authors. With its allusion to popular culture (*Matrix Reloaded*, second of an iconic trilogy, established the term "Reloaded" as synonymous with "the sequel"), the title gives the book ironic appeal (*Matrix Reloaded* was a less than worthy follow-up to the successful first movie), but a flip through its many pages is enough to realize that no irony was intended by the editors of this volume. The anthology brings together a broad spectrum of contributions to the subject of Structuralism and all positions are presented in an entirely serious and scholarly manner.

There are five sections; the first, "Structuralist Activity and Architecture," sheds light on the origins of the term and its relevance for architecture, opening with a 1964 text by Roland Barthes in which he tries to define the characteristics of Structuralism and distinguish it from other theoretical movements—not an easy task even then. The second section, "Heroic Structuralism," surveys some of the main protagonists and their build-

ings, citing Team 10, John Habraken, and many Dutch examples from van Eyck to Herzberger. "Structuralist Trajectories" widens the scope and discusses architectural projects derived from or strongly influenced by structuralist ways of thinking—the works of Louis Kahn, Paul Rudolph, Jose Luis Coderch, Kenzo Tange, and Jørn Utzon are part of what editor Tom Avermaete calls "a broader mentality, a mindscape" (p. 188) as are various modular and prefabrication systems. Many influential unbuilt or utopian projects by Yona Friedman or the Metabolists are also discussed in this section. In "Neo-Structuralism and Digital Culture," the digital present—the main reason why Structuralism is enjoying its current revival—comes into view. In the concluding "Case Studies," examples from contemporary digital architectural production are presented, often by the architects themselves.

Thus a broad and varied panorama of Structuralism is presented in this remarkable book. As editor Tomás Valena writes in the introductory

article, no unified view of the phenomenon of Structuralism is offered, instead, a broad array of positions portrays the current state of debate. Rather than attempt any kind of synopsis, this review goes on to discuss texts that caught the reviewer's interest (without suggesting that they are the best or representative of the entire volume) in the hope that they make the reader curious for more. This book is indeed a treasure trove.

Jörg H. Gleiter's text "Structural Thinking in Architecture" is part of the first section which tries to establish an overview of the phenomenon. Instead of narrating the history of its usual protagonists, Gleiter explains the development of Structuralism in architecture independently of the term. For Gleiter there is a "Structuralism *avant la lettre*." He finds the roots of structuralist thinking in architecture in baroque times, for example in the French gardens of Le Nôtre to which he attributes a dual order, albeit not one of *langue* and *parole*, which later became known as the dual system of Structuralism. To Gleiter it is essential that

„,A New and Shuffled Order': The Heroic Structuralism and Other Variants". In sehr anschaulicher Weise zeichnet er die verschiedenen Strömungen innerhalb des Strukturalismus der 1960er Jahre auf. Zwischen den holländischen Exponenten, welche auf formal elegante, aber deutungsoffene Strukturen Wert legten und den angelsächsischen Positionen, welche einen abstrakteren und technokratischeren Ansatz des Bauens für das „anonyme Kollektiv" verfolgten, gab es häufig Auseinandersetzungen, die sich auch in der Geschichtsschreibung niederschlugen, welche wahlweise die eine oder die andere Seite des Phänomens ausblendete. So etwa bei Banham, welcher Team 10 kaum erwähnt und das von Candilis, Josic, Woods erbaute Gebäude der FU Berlin – ein Paradebeispiel für den von Alison Smithson geprägten Begriff des *mat-building* – zwar als wichtigen Meilenstein anerkannte, gleichwohl aber dessen mangelnde Bildqualität kritisierte, indem er es „unsettlingly ineloquent" nannte. Auf das gegenwärtige Revival der strukturalistischen Tendenzen bezogen meint van den Heuvel, dass man diese zynisch als Beispiel für das zyklische Wiederkehren von Modeströmungen sehen könne, oder aber als Gelegenheit, an die von van Eyck beschworenen Eigenschaften wie Mehrdeutigkeit, poetische Vagheit und latente Rückbezüglichkeiten – „multi-meaning, poetic vagueness and dormant reciprocities" (S. 107) – wieder anzuknüpfen.

Georg Vrachliotis eröffnet den Teil über „Neo-Structuralism and Digital Culture". Schon auf dem Buchumschlag ist die These zu lesen, dass die Informationstechnologie für das neue Interesse am Strukturalismus verantwortlich ist, weil sie einen neuen Umgang mit Komplexität ermöglicht. In den 1970er Jahren ist der Strukturalismus an seiner eigenen Komplexität gescheitert, die mit damaligen Mitteln nicht bewältigt werden konnte. Durch die seither entwickelten digitalen Techniken besteht diese Beschränkung heute nicht mehr – der Komplexität sind scheinbar keine Grenzen mehr gesetzt. Vrachliotis versucht, diese optimistischen Erwartungen etwas differenzierter zu fassen. Er ortet Theorie-Defizite bei den digitalen Werkzeugbauern ebenso wie mangelnde Technik-Kenntnisse bei den Skeptikern dieser Entwicklungen, zitiert aber auch Antoine Picon, der vermutet, dass auf diesem Weg viele produktive Missverständnisse entstanden sind. Vrachliotis geht auf die Modebegriffe *pattern*, *complexity* und *code* genauer ein und zeigt ihre verschiedenen Bedeutungen im theoretischen Diskurs auf. Die Digitalisierung von Entwurfsverfahren führt, so Vrachliotis, zu einer zweifachen Entwertung: Einerseits werden Architekten, die sich solcher digitaler Entwurfsverfahren bedienen, nicht mehr in der Rolle des Demiurgen gesehen, andererseits wird der Entwurfsprozess zu einer digitalen Kulturtechnik verwässert (S. 265). Am Ende werden die neuartigen Entwurfsprozesse allerdings nicht an sol-

duality does not imply hierarchy. Citing Deleuze, he describes structure as something immaterial that becomes visible in that which possesses it. As a building that was conceived according to such a dual principle and is thus structuralist *avant la lettre*," he describes the Mole Antonelliana, the eclectic brick building built between 1863 and 1900 in Turin that mixes styles and formal vocabulary in a way that defies categorization. Gleiter writes of meanings in a state of flux, comparable to the "floating signifiers" of Structuralism (p. 84). Gleiter ends by examining Eisenman, showing that structuralist thinking does not reduce complexity, but enables it, arguing that the rules—the algorithms—by which the dual orders are set in relation to one another are the essence of structuralist design, challenging their author both analytically and synthetically and shifting the nature of the architecture "from an originally mainly iconic character to an indexical one" (p. 86).

Dirk van den Heuvel opens the second section with a text titled "'A New and Shuffled Order': The Heroic Structuralism and Other Variants" that vividly describes the different trends and disputes that took place in the 1960s between the Dutch, who sought formal elegance and openness for interpretation, and the Anglo-Saxons who pursued a more abstract and technocratic approach to building for the "anonymous collective" in which freedom of the individual was central. These disputes found their way into literature about structuralist architecture which tends to blank out one or the other side of the phenomenon. Reyner Banham, for example, hardly mentions Team 10 and, whilst he recognizes the FU Berlin building of Candilis, Josic, Woods—a prime example of what Alison Smithson termed a mat-building—as a milestone, he nevertheless criticizes its lack of "powerful imagery," calling it "unsettlingly ineloquent" (p. 101). With respect to the current revival of Structuralism, van den Heuvel states that it can be taken cynically as "evidence of the cycles of fashion to which architecture practice has fallen victim under this regime of neo-liberal ideology." On the other hand, the revival can be seen as a possibility to rediscover aspects of architecture that van Eyck treasured as "multi-meaning, poetic vagueness and dormant reciprocities" (p. 107) which, as van den Heuvel puts it, "may help us turn things around, once again" (ibid.).

Georg Vrachliotis opens the section entitled "Neo-Structuralism and Digital Culture." The idea that "information technology, which has opened up new possibilities for dealing with complexity" is responsible for the new interest in Structuralism is stated on the book's cover. If, in the 1970s structuralism failed because it encountered limits in complexity that were insurmountable at the time, the digital means of today could make them computable. Vrachliotis puts the high hopes many have with regard to this computability into perspective by identifying a theory-deficit on the part of those who create digital tools and a lack of technical understanding on the part of their detractors. Yet he also cites Antoine Picon in supposing that many productive misunderstandings have thus come

chen Einschätzungen, sondern an der Qualität ihrer gebauten Werke gemessen. Vrachliotis zitiert Teyssot und Jacques, die im Hinblick auf das Metropol Parasol Projekt von Jürgen Mayer H. den programmatischen Titel „Algorithms can talk" gewählt haben (S. 266) und die in der Verschmelzung von unterschiedlichsten Prozessen zu einer gebauten Form eine neue Legitimierung solcher Objekte sehen. Vrachliotis sieht das kritisch, dennoch: Wenn Algorithmen in Form von Gebäuden sprechen, dann werden sie offenbar interessant.

Lediglich die letzten vierzig Seiten des Buches sind schließlich den „Case Studies", einem Streifzug durch diese Welt der sprechenden Algorithmen gewidmet. Auch hier bleibt sich das Buch treu: die Beispiele sind bunt und uneinheitlich, auch in der Qualität. Man hätte sich etwas mehr Auswahl gewünscht, aber auch so geben die jeweils in kurzen Beiträgen vorgestellten Bauten und Projekte einen anregenden Einblick in die digital entwerfende Szene. Im Beitrag von Thomas Wortmann wird aus „Structuralism Reloaded" „Structuralism *Recoded*", was, wenn man mehr Beispiele gebracht hätte, vielleicht der bessere Buchtitel gewesen wäre. Auch so wird aber deutlich, dass die Algorithmen schon in erfreulich vielen Sprachen sprechen und strukturalistische

Ideen heute in vielerlei Interpretationen wieder fruchtbar werden können.

Urs Hirschberg

Architektur und Kapitalismus. Ein neues Kapitel einer langen Partnerschaft

Architecture, Crisis and Resuscitation. The Reproduction of Post-Fordism in Late-Twentieth-Century Architecture
Tahl Kaminer
Abington/New York: Routledge, 2011
Englisch, 201 Seiten, 14 SW-Abbildungen, Taschenbuch
ISBN 978-0-415-578240
EUR 37,99

Schon fast 40 Jahre sind seit der Erstausgabe von Manfredo Tafuris *Progetto e utopia* (auf Englisch *Architecture and Utopia*) vergangen. Unter den Schlüsselwerken der Architekturtheorie des 20. Jahrhunderts hat kein anderer Text die Beziehung zwischen Kapitalismus und Architektur so ausführlich und unerbittlich dargestellt. Obwohl Tafuris Werk einen starken Einfluss auf die nachfolgende Generation der Architekturtheoretiker hatte, lässt sich kaum einer der seither publizierten einschlägigen Texte als dessen Nachfolger bezeichnen. Dafür gibt es mehrere Gründe. Die poststrukturalistischen Tendenzen, welche die Architekturtheorie der nachfolgenden Jahre dominierten, standen den „großen" wirtschaftstheoretischen Konzepten (einschließlich des Begriffes *Kapitalismus* selbst), die den Ankerpunkt marxistischer Diskurse bildeten, kritisch gegenüber. In diesem Klima liefen Texte wie *Progetto e utopia* Gefahr als totalitäre Meistererzählungen empfunden zu werden. Dazu kommt, dass sich am Horizont des düsteren Tafurischen Bildes der architektonischen Praxis kein Weg für die Architekten abzeichnete, ihrer unbewussten bzw. ungewollten Komplizenschaft mit dem Kapitalismus zu entkommen. Während sich die einen daher dem herrschenden intellektuellen Klima der Zeit anschlossen und den Begriff *Kapitalismus* für totalitär, überholt und irrelevant für die architektonische Praxis hielten, entschieden sich die anderen dafür, jegliche kritische und „moralische" Ambitionen der Architektur zu verwerfen und mit kindlichem

---

about. He closely examines the popular terms "pattern," "complexity," and "code" to clarify their changing meanings in the theoretical discourse. The digitalization of design processes, according to Vrachliotis, leads to a twofold cultural devaluation; on the one hand, the architects that use such methods are no longer viewed as demiurges, on the other hand, the design process itself is seen as a "digitally watered-down cultural technique" (p. 265).

Nevertheless new design processes will be judged by the results they produce and Vrachliotis cites Teyssot and Jacques, who, with respect to the Metropol Parasol project of Jürgen Mayer H., use the programmatic title "Algorithms can talk." Vrachliotis is critical, but it's hard to deny: when algorithms talk in the form of buildings, they become interesting.

Only the last 40 pages of the book are devoted to "Case Studies," a foray through the world of speaking algorithms. The book stays true to itself, the examples are colorfully mixed and varied, as is their quality. A larger selection would have given greater insight, but as it is, this chapter gives an engaging glimpse into the digital design scene. In the contribution of Thomas Wortmann, "Structuralism Reloaded" becomes "Structuralism *Recoded*," which, with more case studies, might have been the better title for the book. Still, the selection makes it clear that algorithms can talk in a joyful variety of languages and that today's reinterpretations of structuralist ideas can indeed bear interesting fruits.

Urs Hirschberg (translation Urs Hirschberg)

Architecture and Capitalism: A New Chapter in a Long-Term Relationship

Architecture, Crisis and Resuscitation: The Reproduction of Post-Fordism in Late-Twentieth-Century Architecture
Tahl Kaminer
Abington/New York: Routledge, 2011
English, 202 pages, 14 b/w illustrations, paperback
ISBN 978-0-415-57823-3
EUR 37.99

Almost forty years have passed since Manfredo Tafuri's *Progetto e utopia* (*Architecture and Utopia*) was first published. No other work in twentieth century architectural theory scrutinizes the relationship between capitalism and architecture as comprehensively and relentlessly. Even though Tafuri's book exercised a strong influence on the following generation of theorists, there is hardly any relevant text that could be described as its successor. There are many reasons for this. The poststructuralist tendencies, which dominated architectural theory in subsequent years, criticized the "grand" economic concepts that formed the anchor point of Marxist discourse, including the concept of capitalism itself. In this climate texts such as *Progetto e utopia* stood the danger of being taken

Enthusiasmus auf den Wellen der turbulenten neoliberalen Globalisierung zu surfen.

Tahl Kaminers Buch *Architecture, Crisis and Resuscitation* (6) mit dem Untertitel *The Reproduction of Post-Fordism in Late-Twentieth-Century Architecture* markiert deshalb einen Wendepunkt. Freilich ist der an der TU Delft lehrende Architekturtheoretiker nicht der erste und einzige seit Tafuri, der es versuchte, die komplexen Beziehungen zwischen architektonischer Praxis und globaler Wirtschaftspolitik zu reflektieren. Unter den neueren Publikationen mit ähnlicher Thematik zeichnet sich Tahl Kaminers Arbeit aber durch eine besondere Qualität aus, die sie mit Tafuris Klassiker teilt: nicht nur die wirtschaftspolitische Gegenwart, sondern auch die architektonischen Tendenzen werden im Kontext ihrer geschichtlichen Entwicklung dargestellt. Dadurch gelingt es dem Autor eine Falle zu vermeiden, in die seit Frederic Jamesons *Postmodernism or, The Cultural Logic of Late Capitalism* viele Theoretiker getappt sind – nämlich eine einzelne Richtung der zeitgenössischen Architektur (oder sogar ein einzelnes Architekturbüro) als einzig relevante Repräsentation des gegenwärtigen Kapitalismus darzustellen, wodurch alle anderen „Wege" der Disziplin entweder ignoriert, als Sackgassen ab-

gewertet oder als kritische Gegenpole zur „dominanten" Tendenz emporgelobt werden. Demgegenüber erscheint bei Tahl Kaminer die Architektur als ein feines, heterogenes und durch hochkomplexe Beziehungen geflochtenes Gewebe, dessen interne Dynamik nichtsdestotrotz mit externen wirtschaftspolitischen Prozessen und Wandlungen zusammenhängt.

Die Hauptthese des Buches lautet, dass die vielfältigen und scheinbar disparaten Vektoren der architektonischen Praxis und Theorie seit der Krise der Moderne eines gemeinsam haben: Sie waren spezifische, aber miteinander verflochtene Reaktionen der Disziplin auf die Krise der industriellen Gesellschaft bzw. Anpassungsstrategien an die Bedingungen des Post-Fordismus. Aus diesen einzelnen Vektoren resultiert ein großes dreistufiges „Manöver" der architektonischen Disziplin: erstens die anfängliche Krise, die als interner Kollaps der architektonischen Moderne begriffen wurde, aber eigentlich eine Internalisierung der allgemeinen Krise des industriellen Kapitalismus darstellt; zweitens der Rückzug in die Autonomie der sogenannten „Papier-Architektur"; drittens der neue Aufschwung der Disziplin in den 1990er Jahren, der durch eine vollständige Anpassung an den post-fordistischen Kontext

und eine Internalisierung der neoliberalen Ideologie geleistet wird.

Der beschriebene Prozess wurde laut Tahl Kaminer durch einen spezifischen, die architektonische Disziplin überhaupt konstituierenden Umstand ermöglicht: nämlich durch die Kluft, welche die *architektonische Zeichnung* von dem *realisierten Gebäude* trennt. Daraus resultiere die grundlegende Vorliebe der Disziplin für das Ideelle gegenüber dem Realen. Während diese Vorliebe einerseits den Rückzug in die ideelle Welt der „Papierarchitektur" im Moment der Krise ermöglichte, verhalf sie andererseits der Disziplin zu ihrer Erholung in den 1990er Jahren. Damals verlangte das für den Post-Fordismus charakteristische fortgeschrittene Stadium des Warenfetischismus nach der „Autonomie" und der „künstlerischen Kreativität" der architektonischen Praxis, wobei dem „ideellen Gehalt" des architektonischen Produktes der Vorzug vor seinen funktionell-materiellen Qualitäten gegeben wurde.

Die in sich abgeschlossene und flüssige Argumentationslinie des Textes hat jedoch auch einige problematische Aspekte, von denen hier nur auf einen hingewiesen werden kann. Während das Hauptargument eigentlich eine medientechnische Verankerung hat – die architektonische *Zeichnung*

for totalitarian master narratives. Moreover, there was in Tafuri's gloomy vision no horizon of hope for architects to escape their unconscious or inadvertent complicity with capitalism. While some architects aligned themselves with the prevailing intellectual climate of the time, declaring the concept of capitalism too abstract, outdated, and irrelevant for the practice of architecture, others discarded any critical and "moral" aspirations of architecture and decided to surf the waves of turbulent neoliberal globalization with childlike enthusiasm.

Tahl Kaminer's book *Architecture, Crisis and Resuscitation* (6), subtitled *The Reproduction of Post-Fordism in Late-Twentieth-Century Architecture*, marks a turning point. An architectural theorist who teaches at Delft University of Technology, the author is certainly not the first or only thinker since Tafuri to reflect on the complex relationships between architectural practice and global economic policies. However, Tahl Kaminer's work stands out among recent publications on similar topics by virtue of a quality it shares with

Tafuri's classic: not only present economic policies, but also the architectural trends of today are analyzed in the context of their historical development. This allows the author to avoid a trap in which many theorists have fallen since Frederic Jameson's *Postmodernism or, The Cultural Logic of Late Capitalism* — namely, presenting a single tendency of contemporary architecture (or even a single architectural studio) as the only relevant representation of contemporary capitalism, so all other paths of the discipline are either ignored, dismissed as a dead end, or hailed as critical opposite poles to "dominant" tendencies. In contrast, in Tahl Kaminer's book architecture appears as a fine, heterogeneous, and complex weave of relationships whose internal dynamics nonetheless depend on external economic processes and transformations.

The main thesis of this book is that the diverse and seemingly disparate vectors of architectural practice and theory since the crisis of modernity actually have one thing in common: they rep-

resented different but interrelated reactions of the discipline to the crisis of industrial society, or strategies to adapt to the conditions of Post-Fordism. These individual vectors produced a grand, three-step "maneuver" of the architectural discipline: firstly, the initial crisis, mistaken for an internal collapse of modern architecture when it actually represented the internalization of the general crisis of industrial capitalism; secondly, the withdrawal into the autonomy of the so-called "paper architecture;" and thirdly, the resuscitation of the discipline in the 1990s, achieved through a complete adaptation to the post-Fordist context and the internalization of neoliberal ideology.

The process was premised on a circumstance that according to Tahl Kaminer is constitutive for the very discipline of architecture: namely, the fissure cleaving the *architectural drawing* from the *realized building*. This results in the basic preference of the discipline for the ideal over the real. While this preference on the one hand allowed the retreat in the ideal world of "paper architecture" in

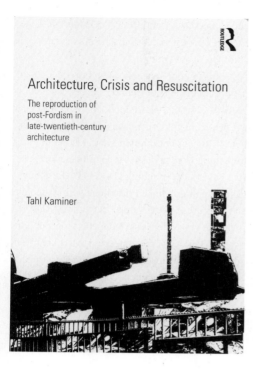

Architecture, Crisis and Resuscitation

The reproduction of post-Fordism in late-twentieth-century architecture

Tahl Kaminer

wird als konstitutive Eigenheit der Disziplin betrachtet — unterlässt der Autor eine genauere medienwissenschaftliche Ausarbeitung dieser These. Dadurch wird der Eindruck erweckt, dass sich die große historisierende Geste des Textes auf einen Punkt stützt (die medientechnische Konstitution der Disziplin), dessen Geschichte und Wandlungen selbst aber im Buch eher randständig bleiben.

Der Vergleich mit *Progetto e utopia* lässt aber auch eine andere Problematik der Tafurischen Kritik im Text Tahl Kaminers wiedererkennen — wie *Progetto e utopia* bleibt auch *Architecture, Crisis and Resuscitation* auf der rein analytischen Ebene und enthält dementsprechend keinen projektiven Ansatz für die Entwicklung von architektonischen Handlungsmöglichkeiten. Dabei ist der Analyse ein latenter Pessimismus immanent, denn wie unterschiedlich und eigenwillig die Wege auch immer sind, die seine Protagonisten gehen, scheinen all diese Wege (auf jeweils eigene Weise) die wirtschaftspolitischen Sachverhalte und die sie unterstützenden Ideologien zu reproduzieren. Anders gesagt, es zeichnet sich kein einziger Weg ab, auf dem es für ArchitektInnen möglich wäre, aktiv an der Veränderung der genannten Sachverhalte teilzunehmen.

Um die starke Kritik an den verdeckten ideologischen Inhalten zeitgenössischer Architektur, mit der uns Tahl Kaminer konfrontiert, nicht zum Auslöser einer resignierten Haltung werden zu lassen, könnte sie aber auch als ein erster notwendiger Schritt auf dem Weg zur Neudefinition und Ausweitung der architektonischen Handlungsmög-lichkeiten im post-fordistischen Zeitalter gelesen werden. Denn ohne die Schärfe und Klarheit derartiger Analysen können die sich als oppositionell und kapitalismuskritisch positionierenden architektonischen Projekte kaum mehr als trügerische Strategien zur Beseitigung des schlechten Gewissens sein. Die Lektüre von *Architecture, Crisis and Resuscitation* bietet die Gelegenheit, die vorherrschende Naivität solcher wohlmeinenden „sozial-engagierten" Projekte zu überwinden.

Ana Jeinić

Die Architektur der Zukunft lesen

Architektur zwischen Kunst und Wissenschaft. Texte der tschechischen Architektur-Avantgarde 1918–1938 (7)
Jeannette Fabian/Ulrich Winko (Hg.)
Berlin: Gebr. Mann Verlag, 2010
Deutsch, 396 Seiten, 115 SW-Abbildungen,
Klappenbroschur
ISBN 978-3-7861-2506-8
EUR 39,00

the moment of crisis, it also helped the discipline to recover in the 1990s. At that time the advanced stage of commodity fetishism, typical of Post-Fordism, desired the "autonomy" and the "artistic creativity" of architectural practice, whereby the "ideal content" of the architectural product was prioritized above functional and material qualities.

Tahl Kaminer's self-contained and fluid line of argumentation also has some weak points, only one of which can be discussed here. While the main argument stresses the medium—in that the architectural *drawing* is seen as the factor that constitutes the discipline—the author fails to elaborate this thesis from the perspective of media studies. This gives the impression that the great historicizing gesture of the text rests on a foundation (the media-technical constitution of the discipline) whose history and transformations itself remain astonishingly marginal in the book.

The comparison with Tafuri also reveals another problematic aspect that Tahl Kaminer shares with the classic text: both *Progetto e utopia* and *Architecture, Crisis and Resuscitation* remain on a purely analytical level without any projective guidelines that could help open up new possibilities of architectural agency. Thus, a certain latent pessimism is inherent to the text because as diverse and idiosyncratic the different tendencies of contemporary architecture may be, they all seem condemned to reproduce (each in its specific way) the existing economic structures and their supporting ideologies.

Tahl Kaminer's powerful critique of the hidden ideological contents of contemporary architecture need not, however, trigger an attitude of resignation, for it could also be read as the necessary first step towards a redefinition and expansion of architectural agency in the post-Fordist era. Such critical acuity and clarity are needed to prevent projects intended as oppositional to and critical of capitalism from degrading into deceptive strategies to suppress the architecture's bad conscience. The reading of *Architecture, Crisis and Resuscitation* could probably help to overcome the prevailing naivety of such well-meaning projects of social commitment.

Ana Jeinić (translation Grace Quiroga)

Reading the Architecture of the Future

Architektur zwischen Kunst und Wissenschaft: Texte der tschechischen Architektur-Avantgarde 1918–1938 (7)
Jeannette Fabian and Ulrich Winko (eds.)
Berlin: Gebr. Mann Verlag, 2010
German, 396 pages, 115 b/w illustrations,
softcover with flaps
ISBN 978-3-7861-2506-8
EUR 39.00

Anthologies, as we know, might codify the existing canon, contradict it along the lines of a contra-canon, or else enhance it with new perspectives.

Anthologien können bekanntlich den bestehenden Kanon festschreiben, im Sinne eines Gegen-Kanons konterkarieren oder aber um neue Perspektiven erweitern. Letzteres unternimmt eine von Ulrich Winko und Jeannette Fabian herausgegebene Textsammlung zur Theorie der Prager Architekturavantgarde. Das in den letzten zehn Jahren

boomende Medium architekturtheoretischer Anthologien erhält durch diesen Band Nachschub aus einem geografischen Raum, der aufgrund der bestehenden Sprachbarrieren der Mehrheit deutschsprachiger Wissenschaftler für viele immer noch schwer zugänglich ist. Der Band umfasst Manifeste, Programmschriften, Selbstdarstellungen und Analysen, die ursprünglich in Monografien und Zeitschriften – mehrheitlich in dem besonders fruchtbaren Zeitraum Mitte der 1920er Jahre – erschienen sind und von Fabian vom Tschechischen ins Deutsche übertragen wurden. Es handelt sich dabei um Texte von Josef Chochol, Karel Honzík, Jaromír Krejcar, Jiří Kroha, Vít Obrtel, Oldřich Starý, Karel Teige, Bedřich Václavek u.a., die im Original an zum Teil schwer erreichbaren Stellen publiziert sind.

Hervorgegangen ist das Buch aus einem Forschungsprojekt zur Prager Architekturavantgarde, über dessen Ziele und Vorgangsweise man leider nur wenig erfährt. Winko, der in München Architekturtheorie, Ästhetik und Philosophie der Kunst lehrt, hat bereits 2006 im selben Verlag gemeinsam mit Tomáš Valena einen Band mit (Sekundär-)Texten zur Prager Moderne herausgegeben.[1] Fabian, wissenschaftliche Mitarbeiterin am Institut für Slawistik der Humboldt-Universität, erar-

beitete ihre Dissertation zum Poetismus als ästhetische Theorie und künstlerische Praxis der tschechischen Avantgarde.[2]

Der Titel der Textsammlung bezieht sich auf die in zahlreichen der Beiträge aufgeworfene Frage, ob die Arbeit des Architekten denn in Bezug auf den Konstruktivismus als rein wissenschaftliche Tätigkeit interpretiert werden solle. In der Einleitung werden die 1920 gegründete, progressive Künstlervereinigung „Devětsil" (Pestwurz), die eine politisch linke Einstellung vertrat, und die eigens gegründete Architektensektion „ARDEV" sowie die von Karel Teige redigierte Monatsschrift *Stavba* (Bau) als Vernetzungspunkte des kreativen und intellektuellen Milieus im Prag der Zwischenkriegszeit hervorgehoben. Die Diskussionen der ersten Jahre nach der Republiksgründung kreisten um die Frage nach den Aufgaben der Kunst und Künstler in einer neuen revolutionären Gesellschaftsordnung. Ab 1922 bildeten die Architekten des Devětsils ein eigenes konstruktivistisches

1   Vgl. Tomáš Valena/Ulrich Winko (Hg.): *Prager Architektur und die europäische Moderne*, Berlin 2006 (hg. unter Mitarbeit von Jeannette Fabian).

2   Vgl. Jeannette Fabian: *Poetismus. Ästhetische Theorie und künstlerische Praxis der tschechischen Avantgarde. Ein Beitrag zur europäischen Avantgardeforschung*, Dissertation, München 2007.

The latter is the approach taken by the collection of texts compiled by Ulrich Winko and Jeannette Fabian on theory in the architectural avant-garde in Prague. The medium of the architectural-theoretical anthology, which has been booming during the past decade, is augmented by this volume from a geographical area that still remains somewhat difficult to access for the majority of German-speaking experts due to language barriers. The volume encompasses manifestos, programmatic writings, self-representations, and analyses that were originally published in monographs or newspapers—most during the especially productive mid-1920s time period—and now translated by Fabian from Czech into German. Included are texts by Josef Chochol, Karel Honzík, Jaromír Krejcar, Jiří Kroha, Vít Obrtel, Oldřich Starý, Karel Teige, Bedřich Václavek, and others, originally published in ways that now make them very difficult to obtain.

The book was developed as part of a research project on the architectural avant-garde in Prague.

Unfortunately, the reader learns very little about the project's goals and approaches. Winko, who teaches architectural theory, aesthetics, and art philosophy in Munich, had previously edited a volume with (secondary) texts on Prague modernism together with Tomáš Valena, which was published in 2006 by the same publishing house.[1] Fabian, who is a member of the academic faculty at the Institute for Slavic Studies, Humboldt University, Berlin, wrote her dissertation on Poetism as an aesthetic theory and artistic practice within the Czech avant-garde.[2]

The title of the text collection references a question fielded within numerous of the contributions: Should an architect's work really be interpreted as a purely scientific pursuit when related to Constructivism? In the book's introduction, the progressive artists' collective "Devětsil" (Butterbur), founded in 1920 and aligned to the political left, is highlighted, along with the architects group "ARDEV" as well as the monthly publication *Stavba* (Building), edited by Karel Teige, special-

ly founded as networking hubs for Prague's creative and intellectual set between the two world wars. Discussions during the initial years after the Republic's founding revolved around the question of the role of art and artists in a new, revolutionary societal order. Starting in 1922, the Devětsil architects developed their own Constructivist identity, which is considered the basis for the Poetism proclaimed by Teige in 1923. "In Teige's view, Constructivism represents the progressive, technical-scientific foundation of life—'the ratio, the construction, the order, the discipline,' whereas Poetism is 'the crown of life: pure poetry'" (p. 15).

The majority of the texts published here were written by Teige, the intellectual leader of the Czech architects of his generation. As of the 1980s,

1   See Tomáš Valena and Ulrich Winko (eds.), *Prager Architektur und die europäische Moderne* (Berlin, 2006), edited with the assistance of Jeannette Fabian.

2   See Jeannette Fabian, *Poetismus: Ästhetische Theorie und künstlerische Praxis der tschechischen Avantgarde. Ein Beitrag zur europäischen Avantgardeforschung*, dissertation (Munich, 2007).

Selbstverständnis aus, das als Basis für Teiges 1923 proklamierten Poetismus gesehen wird. „Der Konstruktivismus repräsentiert für Teige die fortschrittliche technisch-wissenschaftliche Grundlage des Lebens – ‚die Ratio, die Konstruktion, die Ordnung, die Disziplin' wohingegen der Poetismus ‚die Krone des Lebens: reine Poesie' ist" (S. 15).

Die Mehrzahl der hier publizierten Texte stammt von Teige, der geistigen Führungsfigur der tschechischen Architekten seiner Generation. Er ist seit den 1980er Jahren in internationalen Publikationen wiederentdeckt worden und gehört heute zu den bekanntesten Persönlichkeiten der tschechischen Avantgarde. Daneben erscheint im Besonderen auch Jaromír Krejcar als Autor theoretischer Schriften. Einen speziellen Fundort für die Anthologie stellt der von Bedřich Feuerstein, Jaromír Krejcar, Josef Šima und Karel Teige herausgegebene Almanach *Život II* (Leben II) von 1922 dar. Hier wurden erstmals in Prag die Anforderungen an die moderne Architektur formuliert und die tschechischen Bestrebungen der internationalen Architekturbewegung, v.a. den Arbeiten von Le Corbusier, gegenübergestellt.

Die dreißig in dem Band versammelten Texte sind in drei Abschnitten, denen jeweils Kommen-

tare zu den in der Folge abgedruckten Schriften vorangestellt sind, thematisch gebündelt. In einigen der Texte des ersten Abschnitts („Der Aufbruch zu einer neuen Architektur") wird Amerika als das internationale Zentrum einer modernen Zivilisation betrachtet. Vergleichbar mit Le Corbusiers puristischer Architekturtheorie gehören für Jaromír Krejcar Automobile, Flugzeuge und im Besonderen Transatlantikliner zu den neuen Leit- und Vorbildern einer von der Ästhetik der Maschine geprägten Architektur.

Der Band führt die Vernetztheit der internationalen Avantgarde vor Augen. Aufmerksam gelesen wurden in Prag nicht nur aktuelle Publikationen wie die Bauhaus-Schriften, sondern auch die Texte von Otto Wagner, den man als Pionier der vorhergehenden Architektengeneration schätzte. Eine besonders intensive Auseinandersetzung erfuhren die neuesten Tendenzen der sowjetrussischen Avantgarde, wovon man sich im zweiten Abschnitt („Der Konstruktivismus oder Architektur zwischen Kunst und Wissenschaft") überzeugen kann.

Die Herausgeber zeigen in ihren Kommentaren auch Widersprüche auf. So wird etwa darauf hingewiesen, dass Teige in seinem Text „Zur Theorie des Konstruktivismus" von einer neuen

konstruktivistischen Ästhetik spricht, obwohl der Konstruktivismus in Teiges Auslegung „weder einen individualästhetischen Standpunkt noch einen künstlerischen Ismus oder gar eine Modeerscheinung, sondern eine – vergleichbar mit dem universalen Charakter der Wissenschaft, Technik oder Hygiene – allgemeingültige, d.h. jenseits der individuellen künstlerischen Intentionen zu situierende und über die nationalen Grenzen hinausgehende Einstellung" repräsentiere (S. 135).

Eine besondere Rolle spielte der französische Purismus im Prager Milieu. Le Corbusiers außerordentliche Popularität unter den Architekten und Theoretikern ging zum Großteil auf Karel Teiges Vermittlungtätigkeit zurück. Eine aus Anlass von Le Corbusiers Entwurf für ein als „Stadt der Weltkultur" konzipiertes „Mundaneum" öffentlich geführte Auseinandersetzung, die man im dritten Abschnitt vollständig nachlesen kann, markiert den schließlich erfolgten Bruch zwischen Teige und Le Corbusier. Sie repräsentiert nach Meinung der Herausgeber „zweifelsohne einen der bedeutendsten, aber zugleich unbekanntesten architekturtheoretischen Diskurse der klassischen Moderne" (S. 230). Dabei ging es um einen Konflikt zwischen Teiges wissenschaftlichem und Le Corbusiers poetischem Funktionalismus. Die

he has been rediscovered within international publications and today counts among the most famous personalities of the Czech avant-garde. Another author of theoretical writings specifically presented here is Jaromír Krejcar. A distinctive facet of the anthology is the almanac *Život II* (Life II) of 1922, which was edited by Bedřich Feuerstein, Jaromír Krejcar, Josef Šima, and Karel Teige. Here, for the first time in Prague, demands made on modern architecture were defined and Czech efforts contrasted vis-à-vis those from the international architecture movement, especially with the works of Le Corbusier.

The thirty texts compiled within this volume are thematically arranged in three sections, with commentary on the respectively following writing preceding it. In some of the texts from the first section (entitled "Departure to a New Architecture"), America is positioned as the international center of a modern civilization. Comparable to Le Corbusier's purist architectural theory, Jaromír Krejcar considers automobiles, airplanes, and

most especially transatlantic liners to be among the new models and paragons of an architecture influenced by the aesthetics of the machine.

The volume makes plain the interconnectedness of the international avant-garde. Being read in Prague were not only current publications like the Bauhaus writings, but also texts by Otto Wagner, who had been an appreciated pioneer of the previous generation of architects. Granted especially intensive attention in Prague are what were the most recent trends of the Soviet avant-garde, which the reader can explore in the second section ("Constructivism or Architecture between Art and Science").

In their commentaries, the editors point out contradictions. For example, it is noted that Teige, in his text "On Constructivist Theory," is speaking of a new Constructivist aesthetics although Constructivism in Teige's interpretation is represented by "neither an individual-aesthetic standpoint, nor an artistic ism, nor even a fad. Rather, it is—as compared to the universal character of science, technology, or hygiene—a generally ac-

cepted mindset, one that is situated at the far side of individual artistic intentions and that extends beyond national borders" (p. 135).

French Purism played a special role in the Prague scene. Le Corbusier's exceptional popularity among these architects and theorists can be traced back to Karel Teige's mediating role. In the third section we can read about a discussion conducted publicly on the occasion of Le Corbusier's design for a "Mundaneum" conceived as a "city of global culture," which marked the breach that ultimately ensued between Teige and Le Corbusier. According to the volume's editors, it represents "without doubt one of the most important, but at the same time little-known, architectural-theoretical discourses of classical modernism" (p. 230). Of issue here was a conflict between Teige's scientific and Le Corbusier's poetical Functionalism. The quintessence of this conflict may be described as such "that Teige interpreted Le Corbusier's theory of the 'house as a machine for living in,' which was based upon the latter's Purist aesthetic

Quintessenz dieses Konfliktes lässt sich so beschreiben, „dass Teige die mit Anspielung auf Le Corbusiers puristische Architekturästhetik geäußerte These vom ‚Haus als einer Maschine zum Wohnen' in einem wörtlichen Sinne versteht, d.h. in einem wissenschaftlich-technischen und nicht – wie Le Corbusier – in einem ästhetischen Sinne" (S. 233). Die Replik Le Corbusiers auf Teige ist an sich schon bemerkenswert, da Le Corbusier sonst auf Kritik seiner Arbeiten nie öffentlich reagierte.

Der dritte Abschnitt („Die Verteidigung der Architektur und die Soziologie des Wohnens") schließt mit Karel Teiges Beitrag „Zur Soziologie der Architektur" und Jiří Krohas Text „Das soziologische Fragment des Wohnens", das dieser als ersten Schritt zur Etablierung einer „Wissenschaft des Wohnens" versteht.

Was der qualifiziert kommentierten Textsammlung fehlt, ist eine Erläuterung der Intentionen, des Auswahlprozesses und der Auswahlkriterien. So lässt sich nicht nachvollziehen, weshalb aus den rund fünfzig Publikationen Karel Teiges die abgedruckten ausgewählt worden sind, wie es zur Entscheidung für bestimmte Themenbereiche gekommen ist und ob es Texte und damit Inhalte gibt, die bewusst ausgeklammert worden sind.

Das tut jedoch der Tatsache keinen Abbruch, dass Prag, die Hauptstadt der jungen tschechoslowakischen Republik, durch diese Anthologie eindrucksvoll als eines der Zentren der europäischen Architekturavantgarde vorgeführt wird, ein Zentrum, das sich durch ein – etwa im Vergleich zum Wien der Zwischenkriegszeit – besonders hohes Niveau der geführten Diskurse auszeichnete. In diesem Sinn stellt der Band eine notwendige Kanonkorrektur dar.

Antje Senarclens de Grancy

 ## Bausteine für eine Bildtheorie der Architektur

The Embodied Image.
Imagination and Imagery in Architecture
Juhani Pallasmaa
Chichester: John Wiley & Sons Ltd, 2011
Englisch, 151 Seiten, 60 Abbildungen
(Farbe und SW), broschiert
ISBN 978-0-470-71191-0 (hb)
EUR 30,00

In unserem Zeitalter des Massenkonsums werden Bilder oft als rein visuelle Oberflächen gehandelt – gehaltlose materielle oder mentale Repräsentationen. Fiktive Bilderwelten verdrängen zusehends unsere Wirklichkeit. *The Embodied Image* (8) beschreibt die Stärkung unserer sinnlichen Erfahrung als zentrale Verpflichtung von Architektur und Kunst. Die menschliche Imagination wird als Fundament der Wirklichkeitsbildung interpretiert, wodurch eine *Re-Poetisierung* der Welt durch *verkörperte Bilder* künstlerischer Imagination möglich scheint.

Das Buch des bekannten finnischen Architekten, Universitätsprofessors und Autors Juhani Pallasmaa knüpft an seine langjährige Beschäftigung mit dem Thema Verkörperung und Imagination in Kunst und Architektur verbunden mit einer Kritik an der Vorherrschaft des Sehsinns an, und setzt Kernthemen von *The Eyes of the Skin – Architecture and the Senses* (1995) und *The Thinking Hand. Existential and Embodied Wisdom in Architecture* (2009) fort. Die Abhandlung verfolgt keine streng fortschreitende Argumentation, sondern beleuchtet das Thema Bild und Imagination von verschiedenen Perspektiven und verdichtet es zu einem ansehnlichen Thesenkomplex. Die zahlreichen nicht hierarchischen

---

of architecture, in a literal way, i.e., in a scientific-technical way and not—as Le Corbusier—in an aesthetic way" (p. 233). Le Corbusier's riposte to Teige's interpretation is notable in and of itself being that Le Corbusier almost never reacted publicly to critiques of his work.

The third section ("Defending Architecture and the Sociology of Housing") concludes with a contribution by Karel Teige by the name of "On the Sociology of Architecture" and Jiří Kroha's text "The Sociological Fragment of Housing," which is understood by the author to be a first step in the establishment of a "Science of Housing."

Missing from this competently commented compilation of texts is a statement on the intentions involved and on both the process and the criteria of selection. As such, we cannot quite understand why these particular texts by Karel Teige were chosen from his nearly fifty publications, how certain thematic areas came to be selected, and whether any texts and, in consequence, any content were purposefully excluded.

This, however, does not detract from the way that Prague, now the capital of the young Czech Republic, is strikingly presented in this anthology as one of the centers of the European architectural avant-garde—a center that was distinguished by especially high discursive standards as compared, let's say, to Vienna during the interwar period. On that note, let it be said that this volume offers a necessary canonical correction.

Antje Senarclens de Grancy
(translation Dawn Michelle d'Atri)

Building Blocks for an Image Theory of Architecture

The Embodied Image:
Imagination and Imagery in Architecture
Juhani Pallasmaa
Chichester: John Wiley & Sons Ltd, 2011
English, 151 pages,

60 illustrations (color and b/w), paperback
ISBN 978-0-470-71191-0 (hb)
EUR 30.00

In our age of mass consumption, images are often stressed as purely visual surfaces—as contentless material or mental representations. Fictitious pictorial worlds are increasingly suppressing our reality. *The Embodied Image* (8) describes the strengthening of our sensory experience as the central obligation of architecture and art. The human imagination is interpreted as the fundament of reality creation, whereby a "re-poeticizing" of the world through "embodied images" from an artistic imagination seems conceivable.

This book by Juhani Pallasmaa, a well-known Finnish architect, university professor, and author, draws on his long-standing preoccupation with the topic of embodiment and imagination in art and architecture, along with a critique of the dominance of the sense of vision. It carries on core themes from *The Eyes of the Skin: Architecture*

Unterkapitel spiegeln die parallele Führung mehrerer verschränkter und aufeinander aufbauender Diskurse. Fünf Hauptkapitel führen grundsätzlich von der vorherrschenden repräsentativen Rolle des Bildes über seine Grundlage in der Imagination zum künstlerischen Bild und schließlich speziell zum architektonischen Bild.

Wie stehen Wirklichkeit und das Imaginäre zueinander? Pallasmaa folgt einer phänomenologischen Sichtweise, die beide in einen untrennbaren Zusammenhang stellt. Während der Logozentrismus der traditionellen westlichen Philosophie zwischen materieller Welt und immateriellem Denken trennt, sieht Merleau-Ponty unser Denken maßgeblich durch mentale Bilder geprägt, die ihrerseits unmittelbarer Ausdruck unserer Körperlichkeit sind. Sprache entsteht nicht aus Wörtern, sondern ist der verkörperte Ausdruck neuronaler Energien. Imagination ist keine Fiktion, sondern, wie es Sartre formuliert, ein Orientierung des Bewusstseins zu den Dingen (S. 28 f., 34 f.). Pallasmaa beschreibt sie als den körperlich-bildhaften Ausdruck unseres Weltverständnisses.

Die biohistorische Exkurse der Abhandlung eröffnen neue Sichtweisen auf die Grundlage künstlerischer Bildlichkeit: Im Kontext des Überlebens war es für den Menschen wichtig, mitunter fragmentarische Sinneseindrücke augenblicklich zu einem bedeutungsvollen Gesamtbild zu verarbeiten. Noch heute interpretieren wir Bilder stets unbewusst, bevor wir sie intellektuell erfassen. Bilder öffnen einen direkten Kanal zu unseren Emotionen und zu unserem Selbst. Unsere Interpretation der Realität lässt sich nicht von der biologischen Geschichte unseres Bildvermögens abstrahieren.

Der Autor unterscheidet zwei Typen von Bildern in Bezug auf ihre Einwirkung auf das Subjekt: Da gibt es die manipulativen Bilder des Konsums, die die Fantasie konditionieren und das Subjekt verwirren. Auf der anderen Seite stehen die Bilder der Kunst, die unsere Selbstwahrnehmung, Emotionen und Imagination stärken. Letztere nennt Pallasmaa in Anlehnung an Bachelard die *poetischen Bilder*. Es handelt sich um bedeutungsvolle sinnliche Erfahrungen, die sowohl durch visionäre Architektur als auch durch Kunst oder Literatur vermittelt werden können. Das poetische Bild transzendiert seine materielle Essenz, indem es beim Betrachter einen Bewusstseinszustand schafft, der eine imaginative Welt evoziert; die kognitive und emotionale Singularität eines Kunstwerks, die körperlich und mental erfahren und verinnerlicht wird. Die Anatomie des poetischen

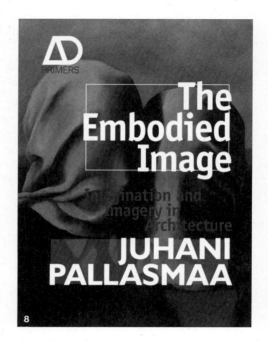

Bildes ist ein fundamentaler Dualismus von realer und imaginärer Existenz (S. 93).

Pallasmaa beschreibt die Funktion der Architektur als die Vermittlung zwischen Kosmos und menschlichem Maßstab. Architektur schafft keine externen Bilder, sondern solche, die unmittelbar in unsere raumzeitliche Lebenswelt integriert

and the Senses (1995) and *The Thinking Hand: Existential and Embodied Wisdom in Architecture* (2009). The treatise does not follow a strictly progressive line of argumentation but rather highlights the topic of imagery and imagination from various perspectives while densifying it to a handsome complex of theses. The numerous non-hierarchical subchapters mirror the parallel direction of various intervolved and reciprocally constructive discourses. Five main chapters fundamentally lead from the reigning representative role of the image, to the artistic image via its grounding within the imagination, and ultimately to the architectural image in particular.

How are reality and the imaginary interrelated? Pallasmaa takes a phenomenological approach that inextricably correlates both. While the logocentrism of traditional Western philosophy separates the material world and immaterial thought, Merleau-Ponty considers our thinking to be essentially influenced by mental images, which for their part represent an immediate expression of our corporeality. Language is accordingly not fostered by words but instead represents the embodied expression of neuronal energies. Finally, imagination is not fiction but rather, as Sartre has phrased it, an "orientation of consciousness towards things" (pp. 28 and 34). Pallasmaa describes it as the physical-pictorial expression of our understanding of the world.

The biohistorical digressions of the treatise open up new vantage points based upon artistic imagery: in the context of survival, it was crucial that people were able to instantaneously assimilate fragmentary sensory input into a meaningful overall picture. We still today invariably interpret images on an unconscious level, before they are apprehended by our intellect. Pictures open a direct channel to our emotions and to our self. Our interpretation of reality cannot be abstracted from the biological history of our pictorial capability.

The author differentiates between two types of images when it comes to how they impact the subject. First, there are the manipulative images of consumption that condition the imagination and confuse the subject. Second, there are art images that strengthen our self-perception, emotions, and imagination. Pallasmaa calls the latter "poetic images" with reference to Bachelard. Implied here are meaningful sensory experiences that may be conveyed both through visionary architecture and through art or literature. The poetic image transcends its material essence as it fosters a state of consciousness in the viewer that in turn evokes an imaginative world. The anatomy of the poetic image is a fundamental dualism of real and imaginary existence (p. 93).

Pallasmaa describes the function of architecture as that of mediating between the cosmos and the human scale. Architecture does not create external images but rather those that are intuitively integrated into our spatiotemporal lebenswelt. According to Bachelard, we are born in the context of architecture, and our empirical experience is structured through architecture (p. 119). Meaningful architecture houses us as sensory and conscious

sind. Nach Bachelard werden wir in den Kontext der Architektur geboren, und unsere empirische Erfahrung wird durch Architektur strukturiert (S. 119). Bedeutungsvolle Architektur behaust uns als sinnliche und bewusste Wesen, und ist eine Erweiterung von Körper und Geist. Heute sieht sich die Architektur zwei gegensätzlichen Drohungen ausgesetzt: Einerseits ihrer Instrumentalisierung durch die Ökonomie (Entgeistigung), und andererseits ihrer Ästhetisierung durch die Konsumgesellschaft mit ihrer Dominanz des Visuellen (Entkörperlichung).

Pallasmaas enge Verschränkung der Imagination mit der sinnlichen Ebene verdient Beachtung, da sie verlorenes Terrain der Architekturtheorie zurückerobert. Die vielschichtigen körperlichen sowie mentalen Qualitäten des Bildes werden in den gleichnamigen Unterkapiteln durchdekliniert: „Bilder der Materie", „Das multisensorische Bild", „Das unbewusste Bild", „Das ikonische Bild", „Das epische Bild" und viele andere.

Die *primären Bilder der Architektur* (S. 128 f.), von Pallasmaa in Anlehnung an C. G. Jung als die *archetypischen Bilder* bezeichnet, entstammen nach wie vor dem unmittelbaren Kontext des Wohnens als die Urform der Architektur: Boden, Dach, Wand, Tür, Fenster, Herd, Treppe, Bett, Tisch, und

Bad. Sie verstehen sich nicht als geometrische Elemente, sondern als Bilder die den Körper unmittelbar einbeziehen und zu einer Handlung einladen: das Durchschreiten einer Tür, das Emporsteigen einer Treppe, der Blick aus dem Fenster etc. (S. 123).

Die Rückverankerung der Architektur in den Sphären des poetischen Bildes ist für Pallasmaa eine Frage der (verkörperten) künstlerischer Sensibilität des Entwerfers. Der Architekt muss die Bilder unserer biologischen Geschichte reaktivieren und neu thematisieren anstatt mit konzeptionellen und formalen Erneuerungen aufzuwarten. Viel deutlicher wird die bis zu diesem Schritt durchaus überzeugende Argumentation leider nicht, und verbleibt bei einer Beispielsammlung diverser einigermaßen aktueller Architekturen, wobei keine davon einer tieferen Analyse unterzogen wird. Die Beispiele reichen von der stark bildhaften Architektur eines Louis Kahn, die neue Potenziale der Expression innerhalb ursprünglicher Geometrien entdeckt, bis hin zu Architekturen des *fragilen Bildes* abseits eindeutig artikulierter Formen, wie sie Pallasmaa Carlo Scarpa adjustiert (S. 101, 132). Dabei ist auch das Bildmaterial wirkungsvoll platziert, und verkommt nicht zur bloßen Erklärung des Textes.

Der aktuelle Kontext digitaler Architekturproduktion findet dann gar keine Auseinandersetzung mehr und wird vom Autor pauschal in den Bereich des Spektakulären gerückt, indem er nur formal virtuose sowie vordergründig den Sehsinn verführende Negativbeispiele anführt. Spätestens hier wäre die biohistorische und die kulturhistorische Perspektive Pallasmaas um eine medienhistorische Sichtweise zu ergänzen gewesen, insofern die Bedeutung zeitgenössischer computerisierter Bildpraktiken als Vermittlungsebene zwischen Entwerfer und physischem Werk in ihrer die Realität strukturierenden Wirkung nicht überschätzt werden kann. Das Thema Bildlichkeit und Imagination lässt sich ohne diese Auseinandersetzung kaum auf die zeitgenössische Architekturproduktion beziehen.

Zusammenfassend lässt sich sagen, dass sich die Lektüre des Buches jedenfalls lohnt. Es wird ein vielschichtiger Bildbegriff erarbeitet und in seiner Relevanz für Kunst und Architektur schlüssig dargelegt. Ein gangbarer Weg der Rückverankerung der Architektur in den Sphären des poetischen Bildes kann jedoch nicht zufriedenstellend skizziert werden.

Magnus Griesbeck

beings, and it is an extension of body and mind. Today, architecture finds itself subjected to two opposing threats: on the one hand, to instrumentalization by the economy (despiritualization) and, on the other, to aestheticization by consumer society with its dominance of the visual (disembodiment).

The tight entanglement of the imagination with the sensory plane as asserted by Pallasmaa is noteworthy, for it reconquers lost terrain within architectural theory. The multilayered physical and mental qualities of the image are run through in the eponymous subchapters: "Images of matter," "The multi-sensory image," "The unconscious image," "The iconic image," "The epic image," and many more.

The "primal architectural images" (p. 128), which Pallasmaa calls "archetypal images" with reference to C. G. Jung, still originate within the immediate context of housing as the archetype of architecture: floor, ceiling, wall, door, window, hearth, stairway, bed, table, and bath. These are

understood not as geometric elements, but as images that directly address the body and invite it to act: to walk through a door, to ascend a stairway, to look out a window, and so forth (p. 123).

The anchoring of architecture in the spheres of the poetic image is, for Pallasmaa, a question of the (embodied) artistic sensibility of the designer. The architect is called upon to reactivate and rethematize images from our biological history instead of coming up with conceptional and formal innovations. This line of argumentation, which up to this point has certainly been convincing, is unfortunately not carried further but instead evolves into a collection of examples of various more or less current architectures, though none are granted more in-depth analysis. The examples range from the strongly pictorial architecture of Louis Kahn that discovers new potentiality of expression within primary geometries to architectures of the "fragile image" beyond clearly articulated forms as attributed to Carlo Scarpa by Pallasmaa (pp. 101 and 132). Here the graph-

ical material is effectively situated and does not deteriorate to simply explaining the text.

The current context of digital architecture production thus fails to enter the discussion and is instead generally positioned within the realm of the spectacular by the author in that he only cites negative examples of a formally virtuosic nature or those that ostensibly seduce the sense of sight. Here, at the latest, Pallasmaa's biohistorical and cultural-historical perspective would have benefited from being complemented by a media-historical viewpoint, considering that the importance of contemporary computerized image practices, as a mediating level between designer and physical work, cannot be overrated in terms of reality-structuring agency. The topic of imagery and imagination can hardly be related to contemporary architecture production without stepping into this particular discussion.

It may be noted in summary that reading the book is definitely worthwhile. A multifaceted concept of the image is elaborated and its relevance

Das Kaleidoskop des Dr. CIAM

Sigfried Giedion und die Fotografie.
Bildinszenierungen der Moderne (9)
Werner Oechslin/Gregor Harbusch (Hg.)
Zürich: gta Verlag, 2010
Deutsch, 304 Seiten, 624 Farbabbildungen,
Hardcover mit Schutzumschlag
ISBN 978-3-85676-252-0
EUR 58,00

„Ich selbst ‚photographiere' ja nicht, ich mache Aufnahmen lediglich aus sachlichen Gründen, damit ich mit meinen Aufsätzen rascher argumentieren kann" (S. 18).

Der Schweizer Kunsthistoriker Sigfried Giedion (1888–1968) legte mit seinen Publikationen nicht nur den Grundstein für die Rezeption des modernen Bauens in der westlichen Welt, sondern auch für den heute inflationären Einsatz von Bildern in den gängigen Medien der Architekturvermittlung. Giedions architekturtheoretisches Werk, wie *Bauen in Frankreich* (1928), *Befreites Wohnen* (1929), *Space, Time, and Architecture* (1941) und *Mechanization Takes Command* (1948), zementierte einen Kanon von Bauten und Bildern der Moderne, der bis heute Gültigkeit hat. Mit dem präzisen Einsatz von assoziativ zusammengestellten Fotografien veranschaulichte Giedion das neue Bauen; setzte Bild und Text gleichwertig nebeneinander und verwendete Architekturaufnahmen und Bildvergleiche als augenfälliges Argument. Die bildgewaltige Überzeugungskraft seiner Publikationen veranlasste unter anderem Kritiker dazu, Giedion als Propagandisten der Moderne zu bezeichnen.

Die vorliegende Publikation geht aus einem Forschungsprojekt des Instituts für Geschichte und Theorie der Architektur der ETH Zürich zum Nachlass Giedions hervor, der mehr als 2.500 Fotografien, Negative und Diapositive von eigenen und fremden Aufnahmen umfasst. Wie bedeutsam die Fotografie und deren Verwendung für den Wissenschaftler, Autor, Buchproduzenten, Kurator, CIAM-Generalsekretär, Lehrer und entgegen seiner eingangs zitierten Selbsteinschätzung eben auch ambitionierten Fotografen war, lässt sich an den Resultaten der kritischen Sichtung ablesen.

Sieben längere und zahlreiche kurze Texte, Fallstudien genannt, geben fundiert und detailreich Einblick in das Denken und die Arbeitsweise Giedions. Die Forschungsberichte glänzen durch Genauigkeit und eine versierte und vielschichtige thematische Auswahl: Martin Gasser fokussiert die neue Fotografie in der Schweiz und Giedions eigene fotografische Praxis. Giedion beschäftigte sich vor 1926 kaum mit dem Medium Fotografie, erst durch Anregung seines Freundes László Moholy-Nagy greift er im Sinne des *Neuen Sehens* der Bauhaustradition zur Kamera, setzt sich für Ausstellungen zur Fotografie ein und verwendet eigens aufgenommene Fotos prominent in seinen Texten. Giedions Kuratorentätigkeit und ausgeprägte Fähigkeiten als Kommunikator im Zusammenhang mit der Ausstellung *Film und Foto* (Berlin, 1929) beschreibt Olivier Lugon anschaulich im Artikel „Neues Sehen, Neue Geschichte". In dieser Zeit klärt sich Giedions Selbstbild als „Typ eines neuen Historikers", der anhand einer modernen Kunstgeschichte „die Vergangenheit für den Blick in die Zukunft auswertet" (S. 102).

Der hochspezifische Text Werner Oechslins führt weit weg in andere Bibliotheken als in die Siegfried Giedions und setzt zudem ein polyglottes Multitalent als Leser voraus, denn sämtliche Zitate in toten und lebenden Sprachen bleiben unübersetzt. Darüber tröstet auch die luxuriöse Bebilderung in Form von Buchumschlägen im Vierfarbdruck nicht hinweg, deren Relevanz for art and architecture convincingly presented. Nevertheless, a practicable way of anchoring architecture in the spheres of the poetic image is not sketched in a satisfactory manner.

Magnus Griesbeck
(translation Dawn Michelle d'Atri)

The Kaleidoscope of Dr. CIAM

Sigfried Giedion und die Fotografie:
Bildinszenierungen der Moderne (9)
Werner Oechslin and Gregor Harbusch (eds.)
Zurich: gta Verlag, 2010
German, 304 pages, 624 color illustrations,
hardcover with jacket
ISBN 978-3-85676-252-0
EUR 58.00

"I myself do not 'photograph,' of course; I merely take pictures for factual purposes, so that I may be better able to bring forward an argument in my essays" (p. 18).

With his publications, Swiss art historian Sigfried Giedion (1888–1968) was laying the foundation not only for the reception of modern building in the Western world, but also for the implementation of images in the usual media for presenting architecture, a custom that has recently become inflationary. Giedion's architectural-theoretical work, including *Bauen in Frankreich* (1928), *Befreites Wohnen* (1929), *Space, Time, and Architecture* (1941), and *Mechanization Takes Command* (1948), cemented a canon of buildings and images of modernity that still retains relevance today. Through a precise approach involving associatively compiled photographs, Giedion illustrated modern building practices; he equipollently juxtaposed image and text, using photographs of architecture and image comparisons as visual argumentation. The visually stunning cogency of his publications was one of the reasons Giedion was declared by critics to be a propagandist of modernism.

The publication at hand originates from a research project conducted by the Institute for the History and Theory of Architecture at the Swiss Federal Institute of Technology Zurich on Giedion's bequest, which encompasses more than 2,500 photographs, negatives, and diapositives of pictures taken both by him personally and by others. The results of this critical inspection conveys how important photography and its application was for Giedion, who was a scientist, author, producer of books, curator, CIAM general secretary, teacher, and (contrary to his assertion cited above) also an ambitious photographer, as is evidenced here.

Seven long and numerous short texts, with the latter called *Fallstudien* (case studies), provide substantiated and detailed insight into Giedion's thoughts and working approach. The research reports shine thanks to their precision and to an adept, multifaceted thematic selection. Martin Gasser for instance focuses on new photography in Switzerland and on Giedion's own photographic

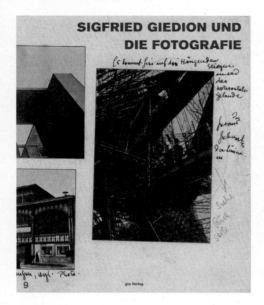

SIGFRIED GIEDION UND DIE FOTOGRAFIE

9   gta Verlag

zum Thema sich teilweise nicht erschließen mag. Gregor Harbusch erläutert Giedions *Arbeiten an Wort, Bild und Buch* anhand der Entstehung von *Space, Time, and Architecture* aus den Vorlesungen an der Harvard University in Cambridge, Massachusetts. Er beschreibt eindrücklich die Arbeitsweise des präzisen Editors, der die Möglichkeiten der Gestaltung eines Buches durch ein raffiniertes Layout mit zahlreichen Illustra-

tionen und Textebenen zu nutzen wusste. Die *Lesegefälligkeit* durch eine schlüssige Verbindung von Bild und Text war Giedion sehr wichtig – eine Qualität, die gegenwärtige wissenschaftliche Publikationen häufig vermissen lassen. Die Produktionskosten von *Space, Time, and Architecture* betrugen mit $ 9.000 ein Vielfaches der üblichen Ausgaben der Harvard University Press, jedoch machte sich der Aufwand bezahlt: „Getting it out ,caused more difficulty than a dozen ordinary books‘ […], and when it appeared in 1941 it was already a Press legend".[1] Die gegenwärtige Bedeutung von Bildern in der Architekturvermittlung, in der Giedions dokumentarisch-analytischer Ansatz zunehmend von glatten Architekturaufnahmen mit Werbeeffekt verdrängt wurde, bleibt in Harbuschs Text leider unreflektiert. Reto Geiser spürt der Arbeit am Bild in Giedions Jahren in den USA ab 1938 nach. Er verfolgt den Versuch einer *Erziehung zum Sehen*, die Giedion gerne als Institutsleiter des von Le Corbusier 1964 gebauten Carpenter Center der Harvard University umgesetzt hätte. Erfolglos dieses Projekt – umso fruchtbarer jedoch andere Kollaborationen, wie etwa jene mit Marshall McLuhan, der im Text ausführlich nachgegangen wird.

Neben den ausführlichen Forschungsberichten bieten mehr als vierzig ein- bis zweiseitige *Fallstudien* Einblicke in das Kaleidoskop des Giedion'schen Schaffens. In anekdotischer Kürze beschreiben sie etwa die Begegnungen mit Le Corbusier, die 2300 Glasdiapositive umfassende Diathek, die Freundschaft zu Alvar Aalto oder die Reise nach Chicago und in den Mittleren Westen. Die Texte ergänzen zahlreiche kleinere und wenige größere Abbildungen aus dem Archiv. Die letzten beiden Seiten des Buches sind zugleich die eindrucksvollsten: Fotografien Giedions von Mies van der Rohe und der St. John's Church von Marcel Breuer. Man wünscht sich mehr dieser – wenn auch nicht künstlerischem Selbstzweck dienenden, so doch treffenden – Aufnahmen als großformatige Abbildungen.

Dem Buch fehlen eine Einführung in die Thematik und ein rahmender Text, der die Einzelerkenntnisse resümierend zusammenführt, ebenso eine Biografie Giedions und der Autoren. Irritierend für die Leser erscheinen gegensätzliche Ansichten zum fotografischen Talent

1   Max Hall, *Harvard University Press. A History*, Cambridge, MA/London 1986, S. 80.

practice. Prior to 1926, Giedion was hardly concerned with the medium of photography; it was his friend László Moholy-Nagy who encouraged him to take up the camera along the lines of *Neues Sehen* (new perception) in the Bauhaus tradition. Giedion thus promoted exhibitions on photography and prominently integrated his own photos into his texts. Giedion's curating activities and pronounced talents as a communicator are vividly described, in relation to the exhibition *Film und Foto* (Berlin, 1929), by Olivier Lugon in his article "Neues Sehen, Neue Geschichte." Giedion's self-conception during this period can be construed as a "new kind of historian" who, based upon modern art history, "evaluates the past in order to arrive at a view of the future" (p. 102).

Werner Oechslin's highly specific text, in turn, leads us far astray to libraries other than that of Siegfried Giedion. It also presupposes that the reader is a multitalented polyglot, for various quotations remain untranslated from both dead and living languages, a circumstance that is not suc-

cessfully counteracted by the luxurious illustrations taking the form of four-colored book jackets, the relevance of which cannot always be ascertained. In his essay "Arbeiten an Wort, Bild und Buch," Gregor Harbusch expounds upon Giedion's preoccupation with text, image, and book by referencing the creation of *Space, Time, and Architecture* as part of lectures held at Harvard University in Cambridge, Massachusetts. Harbusch impressively describes Giedion's working methods as those of a precise editor who knows how to make use of opportunities for designing a book with a refined layout and numerous illustrations and layers of text. Of great importance to Giedion was the readibility facilitated by coherently associating image and text—a quality that is often missing in many present-day academic publications. The costs of publishing *Space, Time, and Architecture* amounted to $US 9,000, considerably more than a typical book issued by the Harvard University Press, yet the effort paid off: "Getting it out caused more difficulty than a dozen ordinary

books …, and when it appeared in 1941 it was already a Press legend."[1] Sadly, the present-day importance of images in the presentation of architecture—where Giedion's documentary-analytical approach is increasingly being supplanted by sleek pictures of architecture accompanied by advertising effects—remains unreflected in Harbusch's text. In a further essay, Reto Geiser traces the way in which images were worked with during Giedion's years in the United States, starting with 1938. He follows an attempt, which Giedion would've liked to have pursued as institute director of the Harvard University's Carpenter Center that was built in 1964 by Le Corbusier, at educating through perception ("Erziehung zum Sehen"). As unsuccessful as this project was, other collaborations proved considerably more fruitful, for example one with Marshall McLuhan, which is thoroughly elaborated upon in the essay.

1   Max Hall, *Harvard University Press: A History* (Cambridge, MA, and London, 1986), p. 80.

Giedions. So schreibt Martin Gasser: „Auch schräge Horizonte gibt es – außer in ganz wenigen, bewusst komponierten Aufnahmen – in Giedions Fotografien nicht. Unnatürlich tiefe Standpunkte, optische Verzerrungen oder eigentliche Nahaufnahmen kommen ebenfalls nicht vor" (S. 71). Dagegen Andreas Haus: „Im Vergleich zu professionellen Architekturfotografien […] erscheinen seine Fotos […] durchgängig recht unkritisch gegenüber fotografischen Bildfehlern wie leicht verkanteten Vertikalen, schrägen Horizonten oder nach oben ‚zusammenfallenden' Fluchtlinien" (S. 74). Was soll man in Unkenntnis der Sammlung nun glauben? Diese Widersprüchlichkeiten und mehrfache Wiederholungen gleicher Informationen, wohl entstanden durch die Vielzahl von Autoren, hätte ein genaueres Lektorat vermieden. Einen weiteren interessanten Aspekt böte ein Blick auf die Diskurse der *Visual Studies*, denn lange vor dem *Iconic Turn* und W. J. T. Mitchells *Picture Theory* (1994) plante Giedion bereits 1956 ein *Visual Studies Program*. Überfakultär, interdisziplinär und an die Architekturfakultät der Harvard University angegliedert – *how visionary*!

Margareth Otti

Erratum

In Marena Marquets Rezension des Buches *Clemens Holzmeister. Architekt zwischen Kunst und Politik* von Wilfried Posch in *GAM.07* hat sich leider ein sinnentstellender Fehler eingeschlichen. Es wird dort auf Seite 322 kritisiert, der NS-Kunsthistoriker Hubert Schrade erscheine bei Posch „als ein wichtiger Deuter der nationalsozialistischen Architektur". In Poschs Buch heißt es aber, dieser sei ein „wichtiger zeitgenössischer Deuter der nationalsozialistischen Architektur" gewesen. Die Redaktion bedauert diesen Fehler.

In addition to these extensive research reports, more than forty one- to two-page *Fallstudien* offer insight into the kaleidoscope of Giedion's creations. With anecdotal brevity, they for instance detail Giedion's encounters with Le Corbusier, his library filled with 2,300 glass diapositives, his friendship with Alvar Aalto, or his trip to the Midwest, particularly Chicago. The texts complement various other small, or less large, pictures from the archive. The last two pages of the book are incidentally the most impressive: photographs Giedion took of Mies van der Rohe and of St. John's Church, which was designed by Marcel Breuer. It leaves us wishing for more of these photographs—that are fitting even without yielding to artistic autotelism—as large-format prints.

Missing from the publication is both an introduction to the subject matter and a framework-providing text that resumptively compiles the individual findings; also lacking are biographies for Giedion and the various authors. And irritating to the readers are contradictory viewpoints on Giedion's photographic talent. For one, Martin Gasser writes: "Neither do slanted horizons exist—except in a few select, purposely composed pictures—in Giedion's photographs. Nor can angles of unnatural depth, optical distortions, or real close-ups be found" (p. 71). Andreas Haus, meanwhile, asserts the contrary: "As compared to professional photographs of architecture … his photos consistently appear to be quite open to photographic image errors, such as slightly tilted verticals, slanted horizons, or 'coinciding' vanishing lines toward the top" (p. 74). So, being unfamiliar with the collection, what are we to believe? Such contradictions along with multiple repetitions of the same information, likely resulting from the plurality of authors, could have been avoided had more thorough editing been conducted. A further interesting aspect would have been a review of the Visual Studies discourse, for long before the *Iconic Turn* and W. J. T. Mitchell's *Picture Theory* (1994), Giedion planned a *Visual Studies Program* back in 1956. Spanning faculties and disciplines while likewise associated with the architecture faculty of Harvard University—*how visionary*!

Margareth Otti
(translation Dawn Michelle d'Atri)

Erratum

An error has unfortunately crept into Marena Marquet's book review of *Clemens Holzmeister: Architekt zwischen Kunst und Politik* by Wilfried Posch in *GAM.07*. On page 322, it is mentioned that for Posch the NS-art historian Hubert Schrade appears to be "an important interpreter of National Socialist architecture." In Posch's book, however, it is indicated that Schrade is "an important contemporary interpreter of National Socialist architecture." The editors regret any confusion this error has caused.

Publikationen/ Forschung

Chronotopes of the Uncanny

Time and Space in Postmodern New York Novels. Paul Auster's *City of Glass* **and Toni Morrison's** *Jazz* (10)
Petra Eckhard
Bielefeld: transcript, 2011
Englisch, 206 Seiten, kartoniert
ISBN 978-3-8376-1841-9
EUR 29,80

In kritischer Auseinandersetzung mit den Theorien von Freud, Todorov und Bahktin untersucht dieses Buch, wie das psychoanalytische Konzept des „Unheimlichen" von amerikanischen Schriftstellern des späten 20. Jahrhunderts in novellistische Diskurse übertragen wurde. Die exemplarisch zur Analyse gewählten Stadtromane – Paul

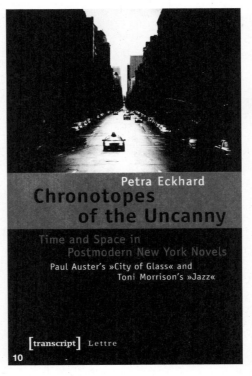

Austers *City of Glass* und Toni Morrisons *Jazz* – zeigen deutlich, dass das Unheimliche im 20. Jahrhundert zum entscheidenden Tropus wird, der auf zunehmende individuelle und kollektive Unsicherheiten verweist, die auf einer postmodernen Auflösung von raumzeitlichen Kontinuitäten und Kohärenzen basieren.

Publications/ Research

Chronotopes of the Uncanny:

Time and Space in Postmodern New York Novels. Paul Auster's *City of Glass* **and Toni Morrison's** *Jazz* (10)
Petra Eckhard
Bielefeld: transcript, 2011
English, 206 pages, paperback
ISBN 978-3-8376-1841-9
EUR 29.80

Using the theoretical frameworks of Freud, Todorov, and Bahktin, this book explores how American writers of the late twentieth century have translated the psychoanalytical concept of "the uncanny" into their novelistic discourses. The two texts under scrutiny—Paul Auster's *City of Glass* and Toni Morrison's *Jazz*—show that the uncanny has developed into a crucial trope to delineate personal and collective fears that are often grounded on the postmodern disruption of spatio-temporal continuities and coherences.

Architektur. Vergessen

Jüdische Architekten in Graz (11)
Antje Senarclens de Grancy and Heidrun Zettelbauer (eds.)
Vienna/Cologne/Weimar: Böhlau, 2011
German, 300 pages, paperback
ISBN 978-3-205-78472-2
EUR 35.00

Five buildings in Graz, constructed between 1910 and 1934, open a perspective onto forgetting as a cultural practice in the field of architecture. The

Architektur. Vergessen

Jüdische Architekten in Graz (11)
Antje Senarclens de Grancy/Heidrun Zettelbauer (Hg.)
Wien/Köln/Weimar: Böhlau, 2011
Deutsch, 300 Seiten, kartoniert
ISBN 978-3-205-78472-2
EUR 35,00

Fünf Grazer Bauten aus der Zeit von 1910 bis 1934 bilden den Ausgangspunkt für den Blick auf das Vergessen als kulturelle Praxis im Feld der Architektur. Die Autorinnen zeichnen ein Spannungsfeld zwischen alltäglichen Prozessen der Überbau-

authors describe a range of strategies from (an area of tension between) the quotidian processes of renovating and rebuilding, functional changes, and spatial redesign to the violent actions of political recoding or demolition.

The examination of an employment office, a swimming pool, a Jewish ceremonial hall, a children's home, and a suburban settlement reveals different dimensions of forgetting: accidental, intentional, private, public, non-narrated, (in-)visible.

What ties the four architects of the buildings together is not their Jewish origin or identity, but

ung, Funktionsveränderung und räumlicher Neukonzeption sowie gewaltsamen Eingriffen wie politischer Neukodierung und Zerstörung nach.

Am Beispiel von Arbeitsamt, Freibad, Jüdischer Zeremonienhalle, Kinderheim und Stadtrandsiedlung werden vielschichtige Dimensionen des Vergessens freigelegt: Zufälliges, Intentionales, Privates, Öffentliches, Nicht-Erzähltes, Un-/Sichtbares.

Die Klammer, welche die vier Architekten und Baumeister zusammenhält, ergibt sich nicht aus ihrer jüdischen Herkunft oder Identität, sondern erst aus der nationalsozialistischen Verfolgungsgeschichte als einem Aspekt des Vergessens.

Dissertationen 2011

A Methodology for Acoustically Superior Spaces or An Acoustics Handbook for Architects (Methodik zum Bau von Räumen bester Klangqualität oder das Akustikhandbuch für Architekten), Vesna Balta; 229 Seiten, Englisch (Institut für Architekturtechnologie; Beurteiler: Roger Riewe/Hrvoje Domitrovic).

rather the history of Nazi persecution as an aspect of oblivion.

Doctoral Theses: 2011

A Methodology for Acoustically Superior Spaces or An Acoustics Handbook for Architects, Vesna Balta; 229 pages, English (Institute of Architecture Technology; assessors: Roger Riewe/Hrvoje Domitrovic).

Development of design approach for the optimal model of an energy-efficient timber house, Vesna Zegarac Leskovar; 120 pages, English (Institute of Urbanism; assessors: Grigor Doytchinov/Miroslav Premov).

Doctoral Theses: 2010

Corporate Urban Responsibility, Corporate Social Responsibility als Element der Stadt-

Development of design approach for the optimal model of an energy-efficient timber house (Entwicklung eines optimalen Modells für energieeffiziente Holzbauten), Vesna Zegarac Leskovar; 120 Seiten, Englisch (Institut für Städtebau; Beurteiler: Grigor Doytchinov/Miroslav Premov).

Dissertationen 2010

Corporate Urban Responsibility, Corporate Social Responsibility als Element der Stadtentwicklung, Hans-Hermann Albers; 430 Seiten, Deutsch (Institut für Städtebau; Beurteiler: Joost Meuwissen/Philipp Oswalt).

Raumauflösung. Mies van der Rohe und Japan. Eine Vernetzung, Inge Maria Andritz; 306 Seiten, Deutsch (Institut für Raumgestaltung; Beurteiler: Irmgard Frank/Adrian Meyer).

The Peasant House: Contemporary Meanings, Syntactic Qualities and Rehabilitation Challenges, Shaden Awad; 216 Seiten, Englisch (Insti-

entwicklung ("Corporate Urban Responsibility", Corporate Social Responsibility as Element of Urban Development), Hans-Hermann Albers; 430 pages, German (Institute of Urbanism; assessors: Joost Meuwissen/Philipp Oswalt).

Raumauflösung: Mies van der Rohe und Japan. Eine Vernetzung (Dissolving Space: Mies van der Rohe and Japan. An Association), Inge Maria Andritz; 306 pages, German (Institute of Spatial Design; assessors: Irmgard Frank/Adrian Meyer).

The Peasant House: Contemporary Meanings, Syntactic Qualities and Rehabilitation Challenges, Shaden Awad; 216 pages, English (Institute of Urban and Architectural History; assessors: Hasso Hohmann/Grigor Doytchinov).

Urban Form Interrelations to Social Behaviour; Toward Humanizing Ramallah City Centre, Yazeed Elrifai; 150 pages, English (Institute of Urbanism; assessors: Grigor Doytchinov/Hasso Hohmann).

tut für Stadt- und Baugeschichte; Beurteiler: Hasso Hohmann/Grigor Doytchinov).

Urban Form Interrelations to Social Behaviour; Toward Humanizing Ramallah City Centre, Yazeed Elrifai; 150 Seiten, Englisch (Institut für Städtebau; Beurteiler: Grigor Doytchinov/ Hasso Hohmann).

Carlo von Boog: Die Planung der Kaiser Franz Joseph-Landes-Heil- und Pflegeanstalt Mauer-Öhling , Peter Kunerth; 195 Seiten, Deutsch (Institut für Stadt- und Baugeschichte; Beurteiler: Peter Schurz/Karl-Friedrich Gollmann).

Impact of the World Exhibition on Urban and Regional Development (Auswirkung der Weltausstellung auf Stadt- und Regionalentwicklung), Lea Petrovic; 374 Seiten, Englisch (Institut für Städtebau; Beurteiler: Grigor Doytchinov/ Srecko Pegan).

Der Versuch einer authentischen Betrachtung des sozialen Wohnbaus an zwei Beispielen von Roland Rainer, Isa Stein; 159 Seiten, Deutsch (Institut für Städtebau; Beurteiler: Joost Meuwissen/ Anselm Wagner).

Carlo von Boog: Die Planung der Kaiser Franz Joseph-Landes-Heil- und Pflegeanstalt Mauer-Öhling (Carlo von Boog and the Design of the Kaiser Franz Joseph-Landes-Heil- und Pflegeanstalt Mauer Öhling), Peter Kunerth; 195 pages, German (Institute of Urban and Architectural History; assessors: Peter Schurz/Karl-Friedrich Gollmann).

Impact of the World Exhibition on Urban and Regional Development, Lea Petrovic; 374 pages, English (Institute of Urbanism; assessors: Grigor Doytchinov/Srecko Pegan).

Der Versuch einer authentischen Betrachtung des sozialen Wohnbaus an zwei Beispielen von Roland Rainer (The Attempt of an Authentic View on Social Housing by Using Two Examples of Roland Rainer), Isa Stein; 159 pages, German (Institute of Urbanism; assessors: Joost Meuwissen/ Anselm Wagner).

Preise

GAD-Awards 2011 – Grazer Architektur Diplompreis

Im Rahmen der GAD-Awards werden jährlich die besten Diplomarbeiten der Fakultät für Architektur von einer internationalen Fachjury ausgezeichnet. 2011 fand dieses Event bereits zum neunten Mal statt. Die prämierten Arbeiten wurden außerdem vom 4. bis 11. November 2011 im Foyer des Mumuth in Graz (12 © Martin Slobodenka) ausgestellt.

Insgesamt 54 Arbeiten aus dem vergangenen Studienjahr hatten die jeweiligen Betreuer für den Preis vorgeschlagen. Eine internationale Fachjury, bestehend aus Thomas Pucher (Atelier Thomas Pucher), Laurent Stalder (ETH Zürich), Markus Tomaselli (TU Wien), Tobias Wallisser (ABK Stuttgart) und Tina Wolf (TU München)

Awards

GAD Awards 2011—Graz Architecture Diploma Awards

At the GAD Awards, every year the best architecture diploma theses of TU Graz are selected by an international panel of experts. The winning projects were also exhibited in the foyer of the Mumuth in Graz (12 © Martin Slobodenka) from November 4 to 11, 2011.

A total of 54 theses projects from the past academic year had been nominated by the supervisors to compete for the prizes. An international jury, consisting of Thomas Pucher (Atelier Thomas Pucher), Laurent Stalder (ETH Zurich), Markus Tomaselli (Vienna University of Technology),

wählte aus den nominierten Beiträgen ihre Favoriten und kürte die Gewinner der GAD-Awards 2011. Zusätzlich zu den drei Hauptpreisen wurden außerdem der Tschom-Wohnbaupreis und das Hollomey-Reisestipendium vergeben.

Die Auswahlkriterien der Jury bezogen sich in erster Linie auf die Klarheit von Fragestellung, Umsetzung und Resultat der eingereichten Projekte. Das Hollomey-Reisestipendium wird für geplante Diplomarbeitsprojekte vergeben, deren Durchführung eine Reise in ein anderes Land erfordert.

Bereits im Vorfeld der Veranstaltung hielt Jurymitglied Tobias Wallisser am Donnerstag, dem 13. Oktober 2011 einen Werkvortrag mit dem Titel „Learning from the Desert".

Die festliche Preisverleihung fand dann am Freitag, dem 14. Oktober 2011 um 19.00 Uhr im Foyer vor dem Hörsaal I der Alten Technik statt. Das Fest endete bei Musik, Speis und Trank mit der traditionellen GAD-Award-Party, welche bei Studierenden, Lehrenden und Vertretern aus der Wirtschaft gleichermaßen beliebt ist.

Organisiert wurden die diesjährigen GAD-Awards vom Institut für Tragwerksentwurf der TU Graz, dessen Leiter Stefan Peters auch durch die Preisverleihung führte.

Tobias Walliser (Stuttgart State Academy of Art and Design) and Tina Wolf (Munich University of Technology) selected their favorites and chose the winners of the GAD Awards 2011. In addition to the three main prizes, the jury also awarded the Tschom Housing Prize and the Hollomey Travel Prize.

The selection criteria of the jury focused primarily on the clarity of the question, implementation, and results of the projects submitted. The Hollomey Prize is awarded to thesis projects that cannot be conducted without traveling to a foreign country.

One of the members of the jury, Tobias Walliser, gave a lecture about his design work, entitled "Learning from the desert," on the evening before the diploma event, on Thursday, October 13, 2011. The festive ceremony took place on the following Friday at 7 pm in the foyer outside lecture hall I in the Old University. The event ended with music, food, and drink: the traditional GAD Award party—popular with students, teachers, and industry representatives alike.

Andrea Plank

Herbert-Eichholzer-Förderungspreis 2011
Architektur des Architekturstudiums
… wenn ich es selbst entwerfen könnte …

Der alle zwei Jahre im Auftrag des Kulturamtes der Stadt Graz vergebene „Herbert-Eichholzer-Förderungspreis" für Architekturstudierende an der TU Graz wurde im Jahr 2011 vom Institut für Architekturtheorie, Kunst- und Kulturwissenschaften konzipiert und organisiert. Das spezifische Thema des diesjährigen Wettbewerbs hieß „Architektur des Architekturstudiums … wenn ich es selbst entwerfen könnte …". Mit diesem Thema wurden die teilnehmenden Studierenden aufgefordert, in den Zeiten der laufenden Universitätsreformen und massiven Umstrukturierung der Studienpläne selbst darüber nachzudenken, wie sie Architektur studieren möchten und wie sich ihre Vorstellung vom Studium räumlich denken ließe.

Von vierzehn eingereichten Beiträgen hat die Wettbewerbsjury drei Projekte zur Vergabe des mit insgesamt EUR 6.600 dotierten Förderungspreises empfohlen. Die offizielle Preisverleihung und die Eröffnung der Wettbewerbsausstellung fanden am 11. Januar 2012 im Haus der Architektur Graz statt (13 © HDA/Georg Kaulfersch). In der zweiwöchigen Ausstellung wurden alle in die engere Wahl gekommenen Projekte dem architekturinteressierten Publikum gezeigt.

13

Preisträger: der Entwurf von **Andreas Draxl** teilt sich mit dem Entwurf von **Stefan Jos**, **Christian Buresch** und **Alexander Gebetsroither** ex aequo den zweiten Preis, während der Entwurf von **Toni Levak**, **René Märzendorfer**, **Christian Repnik** und **Reinhold Weinberger** mit dem dritten Preis ausgezeichnet wurde.

Ana Jeinić

Herbert Eichholzer Prize 2011
The Architecture of Architectural Studies
… If I Could Design It Myself …

The "Herbert Eichholzer Prize" for students of architecture at the TU Graz, awarded every two years on behalf of the Cultural Office of the City of Graz, was conceived and organized in 2011 by the Institute of Architectural Theory, History of Art and Cultural Studies. The specific theme of this year's contest was "The architecture of architectural studies … if I could design it myself …" The theme provoked the participating students to think how they want to study architecture in these times of ongoing university reforms and a massive restructuring of the curricula and what spatial implications their concept would have.

Of the fourteen projects submitted, the jury recommended three entries for the EUR 6,600 award. The official awards ceremony and the opening of the exhibition took place on January 11, 2012 at Graz House of Architecture

12

This year's GAD Award ceremony was organized by the Institute for Structural Design of TU Graz, whose director Stefan Peters presided over the event.

Andrea Plank

14

(Ingo Feichter, Manuel Margesin, Jaco Trebo) und „Seerose" (Christian Fischer, Julian Gatterer, Jürgen Holl), beide betreut von Franz Forstlechner und Günther Illich, überzeugten die Jury durch hohe Innovationskraft und Einfallsreichtum. Die Aufgabenstellung war heuer sehr knifflig, denn verlangt waren mehrere Funktionen vereint in einem Projekt: die ökologische Komponente, Barrierefreiheit wie auch der innovative Einsatz von Beton. „Hier sehen wir eine klare Entwicklung der Universitäten, eine Offenheit aber auch den professionellen und selbstverständlichen Umgang mit dem ökologischen Werkstoff Beton", erklärt Felix Friembichler, Geschäftsführer der Vereinigung der Österreichischen Zementindustrie. Die Auslober der Concrete Student Trophy, ein Konsortium bestehend aus der Vereinigung der Österreichischen Zementindustrie und der Bauwirtschaft, vergaben insgesamt Preisgelder von EUR 13.000. Bewertet wurden der visuelle Gesamteindruck, der innovative Umgang mit Beton unter Einbeziehung der nachhaltigen Aspekte Umwelt, Soziales und Wirtschaft. Zu den Beurteilungskriterien zählte aber auch die Präsentation der Wettbewerbsbeiträge.

(Quelle: VÖZ/Vereinigung der Österreichischen Zementindustrie)

Concrete Student Trophy 2011. Urbane Gartenwege über die Neue Donau

„BEETon" (14 © VÖZ) und „Seerose"
überzeugen mit Teamplaying

Eine schwimmende, barrierefreie Wegeverbindung mit integrierter Gastronomie als Verbindungsglied zwischen der Wiener Brigittenauer Bucht und der Donauinsel über die Neue Donau war die Aufgabenstellung der sechsten „Concrete Student Trophy", einem etablierter Architektur- und Konstruktionswettbewerb, der als ein interdisziplinäres Kräftemessen für Studententeams aus den Fachrichtungen Architektur und Bauingenieurwesen gilt. Im Rahmen der Preisverleihung am 17. November 2011 im Haus der Zementindustrie in Wien wurden zwei erste Preise an zwei Teams der TU Graz vergeben. Die Projekte „BEETon"

(13 © HDA/Georg Kaulfersch). All the shortlisted projects were shown to the interested public in the two-week exhibition.

Award winners: the design by **Andreas Draxl** shares the second prize *ex aequo* with the entry by **Stefan Jos**, **Christian Buresch** and **Alexander Gebetsroither** while the project by **Toni Levak**, **René Märzendorfer**, **Christian Repnik** and **Reinhold Weinberger** received the third prize.

Ana Jeinić

Concrete Student Trophy 2011: Urban Garden Paths across the Danube

"BEETon" (14 © VÖZ) and "Seerose"
convince with team play

A floating, accessible pathway with a café/restaurant crossing the New Danube river from the Brigittenau Bay to the Danube Island was called for by the brief for the sixth "Concrete Student Trophy," an established architectural and structural design competition known as an interdisciplinary trial of strength for student teams from the disciplines of architecture and civil engineering. During the awards ceremony on November 17, 2011 in the building of the cement industry in Vienna, two first prizes were awarded to teams from Graz University of Technology. The projects "BEETon" (Ingo Feichter, Manuel Margesin, Jaco Trebo) and "Seerose" (Christian Fischer, Julian Gatterer, Jürgen Holl), both advised by Franz Forstlechner and Günther Illich, convinced the jury with their innovativeness and wealth of ideas. This year the task was very tricky, because the projects were to combine several aspects: ecological concerns, universal accessibility, as well as the innovative use of concrete. "Here we see a clear development of the universities, an openness as well as a professional and confident use of the ecological material, concrete," explains Felix Friembichler, director of the Association of the Austrian Cement Industry. The organizers of the Concrete Student Trophy, a consortium representing cement and construction industries, awarded prizes totaling EUR 13,000. The jury focused on overall visual impression, innovative use of concrete as well as environmental, social, and economic sustainability. Also the presentation of the competition entries counted as one of the criteria.

(Source: VÖZ/Vereinigung der Österreichischen Zementindustrie)

Piranesi Awards 2011

The 29th edition of the Piran Days of Architecture took place on November 26, 2011. That day the center of the medieval port city in Slovenia was taken over by architects and students from the neighboring countries that participated. In

Piranesi Awards 2011

Am 26. November fand die 29. Ausgabe der Piran Days of Architecture statt. Das Zentrum der mittelalterlichen slowenischen Hafenstadt wurde an diesem Tag von Architekten und Studierenden der teilnehmenden Nachbarländer in Beschlag genommen. Zum Programm gehörte neben zahlreichen Ausstellungen und Vorträgen (z.B. Bergmeisterwolf architekten, abiro, Govaert & Vanhoutte, Bearth & Deplazes) auch die Verleihung der Piranesi Awards 2011 (15 © Piran Days of Architecture). In der Kategorie Piranesi Student's Award hat die Architekturfakultät der TU Graz einen doppelten Erfolg zu feiern:

der Preis ging ex aequo an Stefan Jos mit seinem Projekt „The Berlin Stage" (Projektübung im SS 2011 am Institut für Architekturtechnologie) und an Michael Lammer mit dem „Auditorium und Kongresszentrum in Terezin" (Projektübung SS 2011 am Institut für Raumgestaltung). Die Jury hob in ihrem Protokoll den selbstbewussten und sensiblen Umgang mit dem Kontext, die neu geschaffene Raumqualität und die schlüssige Materialwahl der beiden Projekte hervor. Teilnahmeberechtigt waren Studierende der Architekturfakultäten in Graz, Ljubljana, Maribor, Pescara, Split, Triest, Wien und Zagreb. Mehr Info: http://pida.si

Marisol Vidal Martinez

15

addition to numerous exhibitions and lectures (e.g. Bergmeister Wolf Architects, Abiro, Govaert & Vanhoutte, Bearth & Deplazes) the program also featured the Piranesi Awards 2011 (15 © Piran Days of Architecture). The Faculty of Architecture of Graz University of Technology celebrated a double success in the category of Piranesi Student's Honorable Mention, as the prizes went *ex aequo* to Stefan Jos with his project "The Berlin Stage" (Architecture Technology studio in the summer semester of 2011) and Michael Lammer

with "Terezin Auditorium and Congress Center" (Spatial Design studio in the summer semester of 2011). In the protocol, the jury praised both projects for their confident and sensitive response to the context, their new spatial qualities, and their convincing choice of materials. Eligible for the prize were students at the architecture faculties in Graz, Ljubljana, Maribor, Pescara, Split, Trieste, Vienna, and Zagreb. More info: http://pida.si

Marisol Vidal Martinez

Projekte/ Ausstellungen/ Öffentliche Veranstaltungen

Räume anders denken

Andreas Lichtblau (AL), zum Wintersemester 2011 neu berufener **Professor für Wohnbau** an der Architekturfakultät der TU Graz im Gespräch mit **Ute Angeringer-Mmadu** (UAM).

UAM: Herr Professor (16 © Andreas Lichtblau), *Sie sind in Graz relativ unbekannt, bitte stellen Sie sich selbst kurz vor.*

AL: Ich habe in Graz und Wien Architektur studiert. Ich erzähle immer, weil ich in Wien begonnen habe, habe ich in Graz fertig studiert; denn eigentlich wollte ich nur ein Semester bleiben. Ich habe das System an der TU in Graz gut gefunden, wo man verschiedene Entwerfen und auch die Grundlagen bei verschiedenen Instituten absol-

Projects/Exhibitions/ Public Events

Thinking Spaces Differently

Ute Angeringer-Mmadu (UAM) interviews **Andreas Lichtblau** (AL), who started his tenure as **Professor of Housing** at the Faculty of Architecture of Graz University of Technology in the winter semester 2011.

UAM: Professor Lichtblau (16 © Andreas Lichtblau), *in Graz you are not so well known. Could you please introduce yourself briefly?*

AL: I studied architecture in Graz and Vienna. I always say that I finished my studies in Graz because I had started in Vienna; for originally I had planned to stay for only one semester. I liked

vieren konnte, in einem Mischsystem zwischen Akademie und Technischer Universität. In Wien war das sehr stark reglementiert, sodass man alle Professoren einmal durchlaufen musste. Ich habe etwa ähnliche Themen bei Klose und bei Domenig eingereicht, um kontroversielle Meinungen einzuholen. Ich war dann eine Zeit lang Assistent bei Domenig am Institut für Gebäudelehre und Wohnbau [1990–1994, Anm. d. Red.] und habe seit einigen Jahren [seit 1987, Anm. d. Red.] ein Büro in Wien mit meiner Partnerin Susanna Wagner. Wir decken in unserem Büro ein relativ breites Spektrum ab. Wir bauen Kirchen, Büros, Schulen und Wohnungen, wobei sich einige „rote Fäden" durch alle unsere Arbeiten ziehen: zum Beispiel der Aspekt der Niedrigenergie, aber nicht so wie er im Lehrbuch steht. Wir haben einige spannende Luftheizungskonzepte wieder aufgegriffen, die verlorengegangen sind. Wir schlagen andere Wege ein, etwa eine Kombination aus Luftheizung, großflächigen Glasfassaden und Bäumen. Diese funktionieren über die Jahreszeiten als selbstregulierender Sonnenschutz, sind kostengünstig und verleihen dem Gebäude zusätzlich eine poetische Komponente. Als weiterer Aspekt ist für uns die Relation des Gebäudes in seinem Umfeld wichtig. Für uns hört ein Gebäude nicht an den Außen-

wänden auf, sondern es gibt ein weiter definiertes Gebäudeumfeld, sowohl ein bauliches als auch ein soziologisches. Was uns ebenfalls interessiert sind Innenraumqualitäten, Akustik, Lüftung, Luftqualitäten.

UAM: *Im Wohnbau setzen lichtblau.wagner architekten auf „pulsierende Wohnungen", keine rein funktionalistischen Grundrisse, sondern auf sich ändernde Bedürfnisse der Bewohner reagierende Räume. Ein solches Konzept funktioniert im „Eigenversuch".*

AL: Wie schwierig es nach wie vor ist, solche Konzepte umzusetzen, zeigt die Praxis, wo das Diktum vom „sozialen" Wohnbau durch Gesetzgeber und Bauträger sehr leicht verunklart werden kann.

UAM: *Noch gibt es keine institutionelle Verankerung für solche erweiterten, praxiserprobten Projekte. Wie werden diese Erkenntnisse in Ihre Lehre einfließen?*

AL: Die Mehrfachdefinitionen von Grundrissen und der Räumlichkeiten von Wohnungen werden ein grundlegendes Thema sein. Ich habe ein paar fundamentale Themen, die ich als Grundlage für jeden Entwurf stellen möchte. Dazu gehört, dass eine Wohnung nicht mehr nur funktionalistische Raumbezeichnungen hat, sondern dass

es nutzungsneutrale Räume gibt, die alle gleich groß sind, damit man die Möblierung ändern kann – eigentlich alte Geschichten, die aber im aktuellen Wohnbau nicht selbstverständlich sind, weil da die Zimmerzuschnitte sehr determiniert sind. Wir arbeiten daran, wie man in eine harte bauliche Struktur in verschiedenen graduellen Unterschieden weichere Strukturen einschreiben kann, etwa mit Trockenbauwänden, Leichtbauwänden, Möbeln, Stoffwänden. Mit solchen Mitteln kann man verschiedene Raumbildungen und atmosphärische Situationen herstellen. Solche

---

the Graz model where you could take studios and basic courses at different institutes, as in a hybrid between an Academy and a University of Technology. The program in Vienna was strictly regulated, and one had to take at least one class with each professor. I turned in rather similar projects to Klose and to Domenig in order to get different opinions. Subsequently I was Domenig's assistant at the Institute of Architectural Typologies and Housing for a while [1990–1994, editor's note].

In Vienna I have been running a practice with my partner Susanna Wagner for several years [since 1987, editor's note]. In our office we cover a relatively wide range of issues: we plan churches, offices, schools and residential buildings, but there are common themes running through all our designs: for instance, the issue of low energy, but not the way it is understood in textbooks. We have revived some exciting heating concepts that have by and large been forgotten. We combine air heating, large glass façades and trees to make a sun protection system that regulates itself with

the seasons, that is inexpensive and also affords the building a poetic dimension. Another aspect that is important to us is the relation of the building to its surroundings. In our mind, a building does not stop existing where the exterior walls are; it is part of a larger environment, both architectural and sociological. In addition, we are interested in interior atmospheres, acoustics, ventilation, and the quality of air.

UAM: *In their housing projects lichtblau. wagner architects work with "pulsating apartments": instead of drawing purely functionalist plans they create spaces that respond to the changing needs of the inhabitants. Such a concept does work in a "self-test."*

AL: Practical experience shows just how difficult it still is to implement such concepts in the real world where the dictum of "social" housing is often undermined by legislators and developers.

UAM: *There is still no institutional basis for such expanded projects that are tested in practice.*

How are you going to incorporate your findings in your teaching?

AL: Multiple definitions of plans and living spaces will be a fundamental issue. There are a few basic ideas that I am going to define as the foundation for every design project. One of them is that an apartment should not only feature spaces with a predefined function but also neutral spaces of equal size so that you can rearrange the furniture—this is really traditional wisdom but it is no longer self-evident in today's housing projects where rooms are precisely determined. We are working on how to insert a range of soft divisions—such as drywall, walls out of lightweight materials, including fabric, or furniture elements—in a hard construction. By such means different spatial formations and atmospheric situations can be created. These considerations should be obvious in every design project.

Thinking about spaces in a different way: one can draw valuable conclusions from the juxtaposition of historical and current models. It is impor-

Überlegungen sollen für jeden Entwurf selbstverständlich sein.

Dass man Räume anders denkt: In der Gegenüberstellung von historischen und gegenwärtigen Modellen kann man wertvolle Schlüsse ziehen. Es ist mir wichtig, die Funktionalität der 1930er Jahre, die Eindeutigkeit der Räume aufzulösen. Wir haben das Thema in einigen Wohnungen von uns erweitert, indem wir das Bad direkt in den Wohnraum integriert haben. So gibt es sehr kleine Wohnungen, wo das Bad auch ein Teil der Wohnung sein kann – ohne fixe Wände, mit japanischen Schiebewänden (17 © Margherita Spiluttini). Das kann einerseits eine schöne Qualität der Belebung sein, aber auch eine Raumersparnis an Allgemeinflächen bringen. Poesie und Ökonomie gehen Hand in Hand.

UAM: Ihr Ansatz von Energie?

AL: Solche Überlegungen sind für mich schon eine Selbstverständlichkeit, wenn ich an Wohnbau denke. Für mich sind Fassaden immer dann wertvoll, wenn sie eine Mehrschichtigkeit aufweisen: Auf der einen Seite steht die Benutzbarkeit der Fassade als Raumfigur, die das Innen und Außen erlebbar macht, auf der anderen Seite wird es spannend, wenn eine Fassade auch dazu dient, die Energiegewinnung sichtbar zu machen. Die

Möglichkeiten dazu sind vielfältig; die Idee, dass Gebäude Kraftwerke sind, ist auch nicht mehr neu. Ein Aspekt solcher sichtbaren Energiegewinnung ist auch der sorgsamere Umgang damit, wenn man ihn unmittelbar „körperlich" wahrnimmt.

UAM: Eine Frage zur Architekturausbildung: Sie sprachen eingangs über die Vorteile der Unterschiedlichkeit und Wahlfreiheit an der TU Graz. Mittlerweile ist es so, dass es ein eigenes Institut für Grundlagen der Konstruktion und des Entwerfens geben soll, was halten Sie davon?

AL: Die alten „Grundlagen der Gestaltung" sind ja aus dem Vorkurs des Bauhauses abgeleitet, der relativ dezidiert auf die Architekturausbildung abgestimmt war. Das hat in der Präzision an der TU Graz nicht funktionieren können. Es war für uns als Assistenten damals eine spannende Arbeit, auch für die Studenten, aber es hat kein akkordiertes Ausbildungsziel gegeben. Das zu bündeln wird jetzt das Thema sein.

UAM: Wie könnte man Zugangsbeschränkungen, an denen kein Weg vorbeizuführen scheint, sinnvoll gestalten?

AL: Über Qualifikationsnachweise, je länger man diese dehnen kann, desto besser – ein bis zwei Semester wären wünschenswert. Was mir aus der Sicht des praktizierenden Architekten

nicht gut gefällt, ist, dass sehr viele Leute von der Uni mit relativ wenig Büropraxis kommen. Ein verpflichtendes Semester Büropraxis wie in Holland erscheint mir sinnvoll, weil es einen Blick darauf wirft, wie der Büroalltag aussieht. Studierende kommen zu uns ins Büro und wollen entwerfen. Entwerfen beträgt 2–3 Prozent des Büroalltages. Es gibt immer noch die Zielvorstellung, der große Künstler zu sein, wenn man von der Uni kommt. Es scheint mir wichtig, Leute auszubilden, die auch in die Politik gehen, die auch

17

tant to me to dissolve the 1930s concept of functionality with its univocal space. We have expanded the theme in some of our apartments by integrating the bathroom within the living room. Because of that there are very small apartments where the bathroom is a part of the home—with sliding Japanese partitions (17 © Margherita Spiluttini) instead of heavy walls. Such solutions can both animate the atmosphere and bring savings in the shared areas. Poetry and economy go hand in hand.

UAM: What is your take on energy?

AL: When I think about housing, it goes without saying that one has to consider energy issues. For me, façades have a plurality of functions: on the one hand the façade is a spatial figure that defines the inside and the outside; on the other hand, it gets exciting when the façade also makes the generation of energy visible. This can be done in many ways, and the idea of buildings as power plants is not new either. One aspect of such a visualization of energy management is that a corporeal awareness of energy makes one use it with more care.

UAM: A question about architectural education: you just praised the diversity and freedom of choice at Graz University of Technology. Now there are even plans for a specific institute for basic construction and design. What is your view?

AL: The old basics of design were derived from the preliminary course at the Bauhaus, which was relatively decidedly adapted to architectural education. Exactly the same could not have worked at Graz University of Technology. It was an exciting time for us working as assistants, and for the students as well, but there was no specific educational goal. The challenge now is to form such a goal.

UAM: There does not seem to be any way of retaining open access to the studies. What kind of restrictions would make sense to you?

AL: A measuring of qualifications. The longer you can stretch this, the better—desirable would be one to two semesters. As a practicing architect, what I dislike is that many people graduate from the architecture program with relative-

ly little office practice. To require one semester of office practice, as in the Netherlands, seems reasonable because it would let one see a normal day at the office. Students come to our office and want to design. Design makes up only 2–3 percent of normal office work. Coming fresh out of the university, people still hold on to the vision of being great artists. I find it important to prepare people to go into politics or work with developers, to areas where no lobby is working for architects. Students must learn to remain doggedly on an issue, even if it seems unspectacular.

UAM: How do you explain people that the cherished single-family house is not the mother of all good things?

AL: This is a research topic on which we work. I refuse to engage in a dispute on taste or indulge in moralization. We will articulate the expenses and determine what the total cost will be if people live in affluent suburbs or peripheries, i.e., how much the republic has to pay to connect and operate a house on a remote site, including inhabi-

zu den Bauträgern gehen, wo Architekten bislang wenig Lobby haben. Studierende müssen lernen, hartnäckig an einem Thema zu bleiben, auch wenn es unspektakulär scheint.

UAM: Wie erklärt man Leuten, dass das immer noch propagierte Einfamilienhaus nicht der Weisheit letzter Schluss ist?

AL: Das ist ein Forschungsthema, an dem wir arbeiten. Ich werde mich dabei nicht auf eine Geschmacks- oder moralisierende Diskussion einlassen. Wir werden die Kosten aufgliedern und werden zusammentragen, was es tatsächlich kostet, wenn die Leute im Speckgürtel oder in peripheren Gegenden wohnen: Was die Republik zahlen muss, damit ein abgelegener Baugrund aufgeschlossen und betrieben werden kann, inklusive dem individuellen Transport und der Wartung dieser Infrastruktur. Da wird man auf Preise kommen, die höher liegen als in der Innenstadt. Wir werden das herunterbrechen auf einen Preis pro m² Eigenheim im Speckgürtel.

UAM: Haben Sie schon einmal ein Einfamilienhaus gebaut?

AL: Wir bauen keine Einfamilienhäuser!
UAM: Danke für das Gespräch!

Ute Angeringer-Mmadu

Was bleibt von der Grazer Schule?

Symposium; **Institut für Architekturtheorie, Kunst- und Kulturwissenschaften**; TU Graz; November 2010

Die sogenannte „Grazer Schule" zählt bis heute zu den bekanntesten Phänomenen der österreichischen Architektur des 20. Jahrhunderts. „Sogenannt" deshalb, weil sie weder eine zentrale Lehrerfigur, noch ein gemeinsames Programm, noch stilistische Gemeinsamkeiten aufweist. Der kleinste gemeinsame Nenner besteht lediglich darin, dass die Mitglieder der „Grazer Schule" an der Architekturfakultät der TH bzw. TU Graz studiert haben.

Aus der zeitlichen Distanz schien es angebracht, dass sich die Grazer Architekturfakultät wieder mit ihrer eigenen Geschichte, die bis heute zu ihrer internationalen Reputation beiträgt, befasst. Dabei sollte es nicht um eine bloß historiografische Aufarbeitung um ihrer selbst willen gehen, sondern um die zentrale – und sehr kontrovers zu diskutierende – Frage, welche Programme, Ideen und Konzepte heute noch Relevanz besitzen.

Der Fokus des Symposiums (18 © AKK) lag weniger auf den 1980er Jahren, in denen der Begriff „Grazer Schule" vom Wiener Architekturkritiker Friedrich Achleitner geprägt wurde und dieses Phänomen seine größte Bekanntheit erreichte, sondern bereits auf den 1960ern, und

---

tants' transportation and the maintenance of the infrastructure. One will arrive at a price higher than in the city center. We will calculate the price per square meter of a home in the affluent suburbs.

UAM: Have you ever built a single-family house?

AL: We never do single-family houses!
UAM: Thank you for your time!

Ute Angeringer-Mmadu

What Remains of the Graz School?

Symposium, organized by the **Institute of Architectural Theory, History of Art and Cultural Studies** at Graz University of Technology in November, 2010

The so-called "Graz School" remains one of the best-known phenomena of twentieth century Austrian architecture; "so-called" because it was not unified by a leading figure, a joint program, or stylistic similarities. The lowest common denominator is simply the fact that the members of the Graz School studied architecture in Graz at the Institute of Technology or later University of Technology.

The distance of a few decades prompted the present architecture faculty at Graz to confront its own history again, a past that still contributes to its reputation worldwide. The goal was not just to do academic historical research for its own sake to address the central—and very controversial—question of which programs, ideas, and concepts of the Graz School continue to have relevance today.

The symposium (18 © AKK) focused less on the 1980s, the time when the Viennese architecture critic Friedrich Achleitner coined the term "Graz School" for the phenomenon then at its peak, and concentrated instead on the 1960s and especially on the autonomous ateliers of the Institute of Technology, where radical architectural and social utopias emerged in the designs of the students.

The contributions ranged from first-hand reports by original members of the Graz School to the confrontations of a younger generation of architects with the ideas and historical benchmarks and presentations of current research. The proceedings of the symposium will be published in 2012 by the Institute of Architectural Theory, History of Art and Cultural Studies.

The full version of the text was published on www.gat.st (author: Martin Grabner).

Contributors: Peter Blundell Jones, Konrad Frey, Andri Gerber, Daniel Gethmann, Volker Giencke, Bettina Götz, Eugen Gross, Simone Hain, Gabu Heindl, Eilfried Huth, Dörte Kuhlmann, Winfried Ranz, Karin Tschavgova-Wondra, Tomáš Valena, Anselm Wagner, Christoph Wiesmayr, Claudia Wrumnig.
Comment/Moderation: Ingrid Böck, Wolfdieter Dreibholz, Bernhard Hafner, Ana Jeinić, Antje Senarclens de Grancy, Manfred Wolff-Plottegg.

Martin Grabner, Antje de Senarclens Grancy

hier insbesondere auf den autonomen Zeichensälen der TH, wo in den Entwürfen der Studierenden radikale architektonische und gesellschaftliche Utopien entwickelt wurden.

Die Beiträge reichten von „Zeitzeugen"-Berichten von den Vertretern der „Grazer Schule" selbst über Auseinandersetzungen einer jüngeren Generation mit den Ideen und historischen Eckpunkten bis zu aktuellen Forschungsberichten. 2012 wird am Institut für Architekturtheorie, Kunst- und Kulturwissenschaften eine Publikation zum Symposium und dessen Ergebnissen erscheinen.

Der Text ist in einer ungekürzten Fassung auf www.gat.st erschienen (Autor: Martin Grabner).

Beiträge von: Peter Blundell Jones, Konrad Frey, Andri Gerber, Daniel Gethmann, Volker Giencke, Bettina Götz, Eugen Gross, Simone Hain, Gabu Heindl, Eilfried Huth, Dörte Kuhlmann, Winfried Ranz, Karin Tschavgova-Wondra, Tomáš Valena, Anselm Wagner, Christoph Wiesmayr, Claudia Wrumnig. **Kommentar/Diskussionsleitung**: Ingrid Böck, Wolfdieter Dreibholz, Bernhard Hafner, Ana Jeinić, Antje Senarclens de Grancy, Manfred Wolff-Plottegg.

Martin Grabner, Antje Senarclens de Grancy

Dust

Symposium organized by the Austrian Research Association (ÖFG), Working Group "Science and Art" at the **Institute of Architectural Theory, History of Art and Cultural Studies** at Graz University of Technology from May 20–21, 2011

The ÖFG symposium at Graz University of Technology was dedicated to the topic of dust, as researched in a variety of disciplines from the natural sciences to engineering and from the humanities to architecture. This interdisciplinary approach enabled the symposium to pursue the goal of relating scientific research to artistic projects emanating from the same subject, dust (19 © AKK).

The three sections of the symposium thematized dust as the material of art and science, analyzed the different orders of dust in terms of classification and distribution systems, and examined specific cognitive processes and epistemologies that let one think of and in dust.

Staub

Symposium der Österreichischen Forschungsgemeinschaft, Arbeitsgemeinschaft „Wissenschaft und Kunst" am **Institut für Architekturtheorie, Kunst- und Kulturwissenschaften** der TU Graz, 20. und 21. Mai 2011

Das ÖFG-Symposium an der TU Graz widmete sich dem Thema Staub, dessen Erforschung die Angelegenheit vieler Disziplinen von den Natur-, Ingenieur- und Geisteswissenschaften bis zur Architektur ist. Dieser interdisziplinäre Zugang zum Thema Staub (19 © AKK) ermöglichte es dem Symposium, das Ziel zu verfolgen, wissenschaftliche Staubforschung und künstlerische Projekte miteinander in Beziehung zu setzen, die vom gleichen Gegenstand ausgehen.

Die drei Sektionen des Symposiums thematisierten Staub als Material von Kunst und Wissenschaft, analysierten die unterschiedlichen Ordnungen des Staubs hinsichtlich ihrer Klassifikations- und Verteilungssysteme und nahmen schließlich spezifische Erkenntnisprozesse und Epistemologien in den Blick, die sich am und im Staub zu denken geben.

Die Publikation der überarbeiteten Beiträge des Symposiums in der Schriftenreihe der Arbeitsgemeinschaft „Wissenschaft und Kunst" der Österreichischen Forschungsgemeinschaft ist im Jahr 2012 vorgesehen.

Beiträge von: Julia Feldtkeller, Daniel Gethmann, Anna Gorbushina, Andrés Gutiérrez Martínez, Roland Meyer, Bertl Mütter, Otto Neumaier, Gerhard Nierhaus, Ernst Stadlober, Wladyslaw Szymanski, Klaus Torkar, Bettina Vismann, Anselm Wagner, Monika Wagner. **Idee und Konzeption**: Daniel Gethmann, Anselm Wagner.

Daniel Gethmann

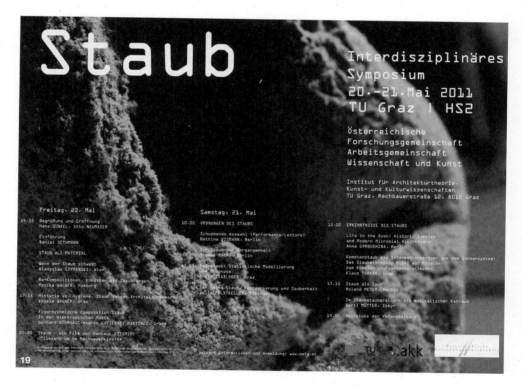

The publication of the revised contributions of the symposium are scheduled to appear in 2012 in the series of the Working Group "Science and Art" by the Austrian Research Association.

Contributors: Julia Feldtkeller, Daniel Gethmann, Anna Gorbushina, Andrés Gutiérrez Martínez, Roland Meyer, Bertl Mütter, Otto Neumaier, Gerhard Nierhaus, Ernst Stadlober, Wladyslaw Szymanski, Klaus Torkar, Bettina Vismann, Anselm Wagner, Monika Wagner. **Idea and Concept**: Daniel Gethmann, Anselm Wagner.

Daniel Gethmann

Urbanistische Planungs-instrumente (Wien)

Symposien; **Institut für Städtebau**; Dezember 2010, Mai 2011

Ziel der Veranstaltungsreihe war die Vorstellung verschiedener Planungsmodelle, eine diskursiv-kritische Auseinandersetzung damit und die Diskussion alternativer Möglichkeiten. Der Schwerpunkt lag zu Beginn hauptsächlich auf Wiener Planungsinstrumenten, es wurde aber versucht, eine Diskussion mit der Grazer Planungsszene sowie Anregungen, Vergleiche, Gegenüberstellungen und Kritik zu fördern.

Während sich der erste Block hauptsächlich mit dem Modell der Wiener „Bauträgerwettbewerbe" auseinandersetzte, wurde im zweiten Block ein weiterer Bogen gespannt und der Versuch gestartet, Planungsinstrumente von städtebaulichen Expertenverfahren, Gutachterverfahren und Ideenwettbewerben bis hin zu den schon besprochenen Bauträgerwettbewerben vorzustellen, welche schließlich in Architekturentwurf, Einreichung und Ausführung enden.

Der wichtige Versuch, diesen Bogen anhand verschiedener Beiträge zu zeichnen, wird nur selten unternommen. Meist beschäftigen sich lediglich bestimmte Architekturbüros mit Städtebau, doch der Übergang zur Architektur bleibt für viele, auch erfahrene Architekten und Planer oft verdeckt. Aufgrund dessen ist eine Diskussion darüber, was die eine Seite für die andere bedeuten und bewirken kann, üblicherweise sehr selten.

Es wurde bewusst die Möglichkeit wahrgenommen, unterschiedliche Beteiligte im Planungsprozess einzuladen: Beamte der Stadt, Planende, Universitätsprofessoren und Organisationen wie z.B. den Wohnfonds Wien, damit eine Diskussion auch über institutionelle Grenzen hinweg möglich wird. Die Vortragsreihe richtete sich an Studierende und Architekten sowie an Bewohner und Planende.

Beiträge von: Dieter Groschopf, Markus Kaplan, Rudolf Kohoutek, Joost Meuwissen, Volkmar Pamer, Georg Poduschka, Heidi Pretterhofer, Michael Rieper, Evelyn Rudnicki, Rudolf Scheuvens, Alexander Schmöger, Klaus Stattmann, Karoline Streeruwitz, Juri Troy, Daniela Walten, Albert Wimmer, Johnny Winter. **Diskussionsteilnehmer**: Alle Vortragenden und Grigor Doytchinov, Kai-Uwe Hoffer, Wolfgang Köck, Klaus Loenhart, Erica Petric. **Moderation und Konzept**: Susan Kraupp.

Susan Kraupp

Urban Planning Instruments (Vienna)

Symposia organized by the **Institute of Urbanism**, December 2010/May 2011

The series of events featured a presentation of different planning models, a discursive and critical engagement with them and the discussion of alternative possibilities. At the beginning, the focus was primarily on Viennese planning instruments, but attempts were made to promote a discussion about the condition of planning in Graz as well as invite suggestions, comparisons, contrasts and critique.

While the first block concentrated on the Viennese model of the "developer competitions," the second block covered a broader spectrum of topics also including such planning instruments as the urban expert competition, the review process and the idea competition, all of which ultimately prepare the ground for architectural design, the submission of plans and construction.

It is only rarely that the important attempt is made to span this variety of approaches with regard to diverse contributions. In most cases, only certain architectural firms are involved with urban planning, while the transition to the level of architecture remains obscure for many architects and planners, even the most experienced ones. Consequently, there is seldom a discussion about what one side can mean and contribute to the other.

The opportunity was deliberately taken to invite different stakeholders in the planning process: city officials, planners, university professors, and organizations such as the Viennese housing funds, in order to enable a discussion across institutional boundaries. The lecture series was aimed at students and architects as well as residents and planners.

Contributors: Dieter Groschopf, Markus Kaplan, Rudolf Kohoutek, Joost Meuwissen, Volkmar Pamer, Georg Poduschka, Heidi Pretterhofer, Michael Rieper, Evelyn Rudnicki, Rudolf Scheuvens, Alexander Schmöger, Klaus Stattmann, Karoline Streeruwitz,

Stadt und Psyche

Symposium; **Institut für Städtebau**; TU Graz; 24. und 25. März 2011

Was hat die psychische Konstitution eines Individuums mit der Stadt und der urbanen Kultur zu tun? Das war eine der wichtigsten Fragen beim Symposium, das von Joost Meuwissen, Leiter des Instituts für Städtebau, in Zusammenarbeit mit dem Institut für Philosophie der Universität für Angewandte Kunst in Wien ausgerichtet wurde. Zu Gast waren Wissenschaftler und Forscher aus den Bereichen Philosophie, Psychoanalyse, Kulturwissenschaften und Medientheorie, Architektur und Stadtplanung. Die Vielfalt der Disziplinen spiegelt die Vielschichtigkeit der Diskurse über den Gegenstand und seine Strukturen wider. Ziel war es, durch diesen multidisziplinären Ansatz neue Erkenntnisse für die urbane Theorie zu gewinnen und ein neues Forschungsfeld zu eröffnen, in dessen Zentrum das Verhältnis von Individuum und Stadt steht.

Seit jeher wurde psychoanalytische Literatur auch von Künstlern und Architekten rezipiert, wie z.B. vom Kreis holländischer Architekten und Architekturtheoretiker um Aldo van Eyck.

Juri Troy, Daniela Walten, Albert Wimmer, Johnny Winter. **Discussion Participants**: All contributors and Grigor Doytchinov, Kai-Uwe Hoffer, Wolfgang Köck, Klaus Loenhart, Erica Petric. **Moderation and Concept**: Susan Kraupp.

Susan Kraupp

City and Psyche

Symposium, organized by the **Institute of Urbanism** at Graz University of Technology, from March 24–25, 2011

What does the mental constitution of an individual have to do with the city and urban culture? That was one of the most important questions at the symposium conceived by Joost Meuwissen, director of the Institute of Urbanism, in collaboration with the Institute of Philosophy at the University for Applied Arts in Vienna. Guests included academics and researchers from the fields of philosophy, psycho-

Dieser Einfluss hat sogar in konkreten städtebaulichen Konzeptionen seinen Niederschlag gefunden, wie Joost Meuwissen nachweisen konnte.

Ein wichtiges Thema war auch der Film, der eine wesentliche Rolle bei der Bildung von Vorstellungen über die Stadt gespielt hat. Anna Schober, Gastprofessorin am Institut für Philosophie der Universität Verona, hat mit zahlreichen Ausschnitten aus Filmen von Rainer Werner Fassbinder Belege für das Ineinandergreifen der Strukturen im Film gebracht.

Seit jeher hat das Abweichende, das Fremde Abgrenzung und Ausgrenzung erfahren. Mit dem Devianten der Gesellschaft, das besonders in der Figur des „Verbrechers" Gestalt annimmt, hat sich Michael Zinganel in seinem Buch *Real Crime. Architektur, Stadt und Verbrechen* beschäftigt, das zeigt, wie sich auf allen Ebenen der Stadt die Angst vor dem Verbrechen produktiv niederschlägt.

Peter Mörtenböck vom Institut für Kunst und Gestaltung der TU Wien entwickelte den Begriff der inneren Sicherheit in einem doppelten Sinn: als die Sicherheit des psychischen Apparats und jene des Staatsapparats. Am Beispiel von London stellte Mörtenböck subtile Strategien in der Stadtgestaltung vor, die sich in Antizipation möglicher Verbrechen und terroristischer Aktivitäten entwickelt haben.

Die Ökopsychologie betrachtet das Individuum hinsichtlich seiner Wirkung und Wechselwirkung mit der (urbanen) Umwelt. Um herauszufinden, was der einzelne Stadtbewohner will, wurden verschiedene diagnostische Verfahren entwickelt, z.B. die aktivierende Stadtdiagnose von Cornelia Ehmayer, die von Tanja Gerlich, einer Mitarbeiterin Ehmayers, vorgestellt wurde. Ziel ist letztendlich, konkrete Vorschläge für städtebauliche Veränderungen und Planungsmaßnahmen herauszuarbeiten.

Helge Mooshammer hat in seinem Vortrag von einer „kollektiven Psyche" gesprochen. Darunter versteht er die psychische Struktur der Stadt in einer für alle offenen, aufgeschlossenen Konfiguration.

Aus diesen theoretischen Überlegungen über die psychische Struktur sollten praktische Auswirkungen auf die bauliche Struktur der Stadt folgen.

Beiträge von: Tanja Gerlich, Helge Mooshammer, Peter Mörtenböck, Anna Schober. **Begrüßung und Einführung**: Michael Zinganel.

Albrecht Kreuzer

Meta-Methoden in der (Post-) Moderne. On Synthesis in Architecture and Urbanism

Symposium; **Institut für Städtebau**; Generali Foundation, Wien; 9.–11. November 2010

Als übergreifende Reflexion werden Meta-Methoden vor allem zu Krisenzeiten oder während eines Paradigmenwechsels verwendet, um die stattfindenden Änderungen in der Anwendung der Methoden verstehen zu können. Die Vortragenden auf dem lebhaften internationalen Symposium wurden gebeten, ausgehend von Texten zur „ostranenie"/ Verfremdung (Šklovskij), zur „Bricolage" (Lévi-Strauss) und zum „Leeren Feld" (Deleuze) das Konzept der Meta-Methoden zu interpretieren, sie historisch einzuordnen und anhand von Projektbeispielen ihre Relevanz in der Praxis zu untersuchen.

Das überraschende Ergebnis war in allen Fällen eine Art heuristischer Methode, welche die Inkongruenzen eines Gegenstandes, sei es eines noch zu entwickelnden Projektes oder einer bestimmten Synthese aus der Vergangenheit, darstellt und bestätigt. In der abschließenden Debatte wurde

---

analysis, cultural studies and media theory, architecture and city planning. The variety of disciplines reflects the diversity of discourses on the object and its structures. The goal of this multidisciplinary effort was to gain new insights for urban theory and to open a new research field, centering on the relationship between the individual and the city.

Since time, immemorial psychoanalytic literature has been reviewed by artists and architects, for example the group of Dutch architects and theorists around Aldo van Eyck. This influence has affected even concrete urbanist concepts, as Meuwissen demonstrated.

Another important topic was the cinema that has significantly formed our ideas about the city. Anna Schober, a visiting professor at the Institute of Philosophy at the University of Verona, showed with numerous excerpts from films by Rainer Werner Fassbinder how filmic structures are intertwined.

The Other or the foreign has always been demarcated and excluded. In his book *Real Crime: Architektur, Stadt und Verbrechen*, Michael Zinganel examines social deviancy, in particular as it is crystallized in the figure of the criminal, and shows how the fear of crime has produced urban form.

Peter Mörtenböck from the Institute of Art and Design at Vienna University of Technology developed the concept of inner security in a double sense: as the security of the psychic apparatus or that of the state apparatus. Using London as an example, he presented subtle urbanist strategies that anticipate possible crimes and terrorist activities.

Ecopsychology considers a person in terms of her impact and interaction with the (urban) environment. To find out what an individual city dweller wants, different diagnostic methods have been developed, including Cornelia Ehmayer's "Activating Community Diagnosis," a method that was presented by her assistant Tanja Gerlich. The ultimate goal is to work out concrete proposals for urban change and urban planning measures.

Helge Mooshammer spoke in his presentation of a "collective psyche." By this he means the psychological structure of the city in a configuration that is open to all.

Such theoretical considerations about the psychological structure of the city can be expected to entail practical conclusions about its built structure.

Contributors: Tanja Gerlich, Helge Mooshammer, Peter Mörtenböck, Anna Schober. **Welcoming and Introduction**: Michael Zinganel.

Albrecht Kreuzer

Meta-Methods in (Post-) Modernity: On Synthesis in Architecture and Urbanism

Symposium, organized by the **Institute of Urbanism** at the Generali Foundation in Vienna on November 9–11, 2010

Meta-methods represent a form of all-encompassing reflection that in times of crisis or a para-

klar, dass die vortragenden Architekten eine solche Bestätigung durch einen bescheidenen und höflichen Subjektivismus zu realisieren versuchen, während die Theoretiker sich eher mit einer reinen, mithin schwierigen Darstellung der Unbestimmtheit befassen. So erklärte der Architekt Ernst J. Fuchs, sein „Provozieren von Zufällen und dem Unvorhersehbaren" ziele darauf ab, „alles aufzuspüren, was über das reine Funktionieren hinausgeht", wobei, wie Anna Popelka meinte, „die Überprüfung durchaus im Selbstversuch erfolgt". Statt eines solchen Selbstversuchs schlugen die Theoretiker ohne Ausnahme eine Neuformulierung der von Susan Kraupp ins Spiel gebrachten strukturalistischen Ideen vor, welche laut Martin Guttmann als „Versuche, hinter den variierten Formen des Lebens die Logik zu finden" betrachtet werden könnten.

Beiträge von: Tom Avermaete, Ernst J. Fuchs, Yair Martin Guttmann, Joost Meuwissen, Anna Popelka, Angelika Schnell, Christian Teckert. **Begrüßung und Einführung**: Susan Kraupp, Andreas Ruby (auch Leitung der Diskussion mit allen Vortragenden).

Joost Meuwissen

Baugruppen – Qualität für die Stadt

Tagung; **Institut für Städtebau**/Grazer Arbeitsgemeinschaft „Wohnbau: Alternative: Baugruppen" (Arge W:A:B)/Kammer der ZiviltechnikerInnen für Steiermark und Kärnten; TU Graz; 13. Mai 2011)

Teilnehmer aus Österreich, Deutschland und der Schweiz berichteten auf der internationalen Tagung über Baugruppenprojekte und städtische Planungen, bei denen Baugruppen den Ausgangspunkt bilden. Als „Zweckgemeinschaften von Privatpersonen mit dem Ziel individueller und kostengünstiger Realisierung von Wohnraum" (Arge W:A:B) können Baugruppen von Anfang an als zielführend für die Stadtentwicklung aufgefasst oder als kaum erwünschte Ausnahme gegen Ende der Umsetzung der Planung nur geduldet werden. Die Tagung zeigte die ganze Bandbreite dieser Möglichkeiten. Somit stellte sich die prinzipielle Frage, wie sich öffentliche Planungsvorhaben zukünftig zu kleinmaßstäblichen Privatinitiativen verhalten könnten. In Wien werden Frauenbaugruppen noch von den allgemeinen Zuweisungsregeln des Sozialwohnbaus, in diesem Fall des Wohnfonds, behindert. In Zürich sind die – neben

traditionellen Privatinitiativen vorhandenen – größeren Schweizer Baugenossenschaften innerhalb der großmaßstäblichen Stadtplanung noch zu klein, um zur Außenraumentwicklung beizutragen. Der Wunsch nach Gemeinschaftsräumen wurde eher in der Zusammensetzung der Wohnungsgrundrisse als im Außenraum umgesetzt.

Der Tübinger Baubürgermeister stellte fest, dass eine Stadtplanung, die Baugemeinschaften von vornherein miteinbezieht, nicht nur wirtschaftliche Vorteile bietet (die Errichtung eines Stadtteils durch Gruppenbauten wäre ihm zufolge 15 bis 20 Prozent billiger), sondern auch zur innerstädtischen Verdichtung beiträgt. Seine Idee einer städtischen Innen- und Außenentwicklung basiert deshalb auf Parzellierung, der Vision des „Stadthauses" und „kleinteiliger Grundstücke" sowie einer klaren Trennung zwischen öffentlicher und privater Verantwortung. Eigentümergemeinschaften sollen als *Akteure* und nicht als *Opfer* früh eingebunden werden.

Das Institut für Städtebau hält eine Analyse der durch Baugruppeninitiativen entstandenen städtischen Räume für wichtig, um damit die Qualität derselben auch für andere Planungsprozeduren verfügbar zu machen. Eine Mischung aus gemeinschaftlichen und privaten Außenräumen auf Grundstücken könnte zu einer gestaltungstypolo-

---

digm shift offers a way to comprehend changes taking place in working methods. Prompted by papers on Shklovsky's ostranenie or defamiliarization, Lévi-Strauss's bricolage and Deleuze's "empty box," the speakers at the vibrant international symposium were asked to interpret the concept of meta-methods, classify them historically and examine their relevance to practice in the light of actual projects.

Surprisingly, what was discovered in all cases was a heuristic method that revealed and confirmed the incongruencies of the object, whether it was a project to be developed or a specific synthesis of the past. In the closing debate, the designing architects attempted such a confirmation through a modest and polite subjectivism, while the theorists were concerned with a pure, and therefore difficult, representation of undecidability. Thus the architect Ernst J. Fuchs declared that by "provoking coincidences and the unpredictable" he aims to "trace everything that goes beyond simply functioning;" in this effort, as Anna Popelka

pointed out, "the final proof depends entirely on the self." Instead of such a self-test, all the theorists suggested a reformulation of structuralist ideas, brought up by Susan Kraupp, which "attempted to detect a specific logic behind the varied forms of life," in the words of Martin Guttmann.

Contributors: Tom Avermaete, Ernst J. Fuchs, Yair Martin Guttmann, Joost Meuwissen, Anna Popelka, Angelika Schnell, Christian Teckert. **Welcoming and Introduction**: Susan Kraupp, Andreas Ruby (who also led the discussion with all contributors).

Joost Meuwissen

User Planning Groups—Quality for the City

A conference, organized by the **Institute of Urbanism**/Graz Team "Housing: Alternative: User Planning Groups" (Team W: A: B)/Chamber of Civil

Engineers for Styria and Carinthia, held at Graz University of Technology, May 13, 2011

The international conference featured participants from Austria, Germany, and Switzerland reporting on housing projects by groups of users and urban projects in which such groups formed the starting point. As "societies formed for the purpose of individual and cost-effective construction of housing" (Team W: A: B) user groups can be viewed as an effective model for urban development or merely tolerated as an undesirable exception as the plan is being finally implemented. The conference demonstrated the wide range of such possibilities. They pose the fundamental question of how public planning projects in the future should deal with small-scale private initiatives. In Vienna, women's planning groups are still hampered by the general rules concerning the allocation of funds for social housing. In Zurich there are along traditional private initiatives also larger building cooperatives that nonetheless remain too small to con-

gischen Unbestimmtheit oder Unterdeterminiert-heit bzw. Offenheit führen, die auf den umgeben-den öffentlichen Raum ausstrahlt. Dies ist nötig, um eine Vielfalt an Funktionen in der Kleinheit zu er-möglichen. Ein derartiger „Städtebau der Freiheit" ist schwierig und bislang selten gefordert. Bau-gruppen können aber ein Zukunftsmodell sein, so-fern die Parzellierung in den städtischen Raum-planungsprozederen wieder an Gewicht gewinnt.

Beiträge von: Mathias Heyden, Joost Meuwissen, Cord Soehlke, Claudia Thiesen, Constance Weiser.
Begrüßung: Elisabeth Anderl, Martin Gruber, Joost Meuwissen, Lisa Rücker

Joost Meuwissen

Dense Cities. Architecture for Living Closer Together

Symposium; **Institut für Gebäudelehre**, TU Graz, 26.–28. Mai 2011

„Cities are Great. Density is Great." Im Rahmen des internationalen Symposiums polarisierte der Spanier Luis Fernández Galiano mit einem feu-rigen Manifest für urbane Dichte. Doch weder er noch die Veranstaltung als Gesamtes priesen Dichte kritiklos als Allheilmittel an. Vielmehr wurde die Frage nach deren sozialer Verträglich-keit und nach qualitativen Aspekten quantitativer Dichte (20 © Institut für Gebäudelehre) gestellt.

Weltweit (und leider auch besonders ausge-prägt rund um Graz) stellt die Zersiedelung als Folge des unkontrollierten Flächenwachstums von Städten ein zunehmendes Problem dar. Die Hauptursache ist ein gesellschaftliches Phänomen: die irrationale Faszination der Menschen von ei-nem Objekt: dem Einfamilienhaus. Multipliziert mit mehreren Millionen ist es unser größter Feind. Die Stadt Graz steht angesichts des prognostizier-ten Wachstums vor einer Entscheidung: einen Di-mensionssprung in Richtung Urbanität zu wagen oder in selbstverordneter Provinzialität zu verhar-ren. Einige Vortragende präsentierten für ersteres erfolgreiche Beispiele, etwa aus der Schweiz oder den Niederlanden, deren Landesarchitekt für ein unmittelbares Nebeneinander von dichter Stadt und grüner Natur warb.

Aber Dichte ist nicht gleich Dichte, wie in vielen Beiträgen betont wurde: Ausschlaggebend ist nicht die Masse an Baukörpern, sondern die

20

Intensität der sozialen Beziehungen im (öffentli-chen) Raum, die mit verschiedenen Mitteln – Dich-te ist eines davon – ermöglicht und gestärkt wer-den müssen.

Der Tradition der europäischen Stadt folgend und in Opposition zum dogmatisch-funktionalis-tischen Städtebau der Moderne sind es Heteroge-

tribute to urban planning. The desire for more com-munity facilities affects the composition of the floor plans more than the organization of exte-rior space.

According to the Senior Planning Officer of Tübingen, city planning processes that involve building communities from the outset enjoy not only economic benefits (building groups would make the construction of an urban district 15 to 20 percent cheaper), but also leads to higher den-sity in the inner city area. His idea of an inner and outer urban development is therefore based on parceling, the vision of a "city house" and small building sites as well as a clear separation between public and private responsibilities. The associa-tions of owners should be involved from early on as *actors* rather than *victims*.

The Institute of Urbanism stresses the impor-tance of analyzing the urban spaces that result from group initiatives and making the same qualities available also for other planning processes. A mix-ture of common and private outdoor spaces on the properties could lead to typologically undecided or under-determined openness that would radiate to the surrounding public space. This is required to make a variety of functions possible in small spaces. "Free urban design" in this sense is both difficult and seldom requested. If parceling re-gains prominence in urban planning processes, user groups can be a model for the future.

Contributors: Mathias Heyden, Joost Meuwissen, Cord Soehlke, Claudia Thiesen, Constance Weiser.
Welcoming: Elisabeth Anderl, Martin Gruber, Joost Meuwissen, Lisa Rücker.

Joost Meuwissen

Dense Cities: Architecture for Living Closer Together

Symposium, organized by the **Institute for Architectural Typologies** at Graz University of Technology, May 2011

"Cities are great. Density is great." In this inter-national symposium, Spanish architect Luis Fernández Galiano polarized the debate with his fiery manifesto for urban compactness. Still, nei-ther Galiano nor the event as a whole uncritically praised density as a universal panacea. Questions were posed in particular with regard to its social sustainability and the qualitative effects of quan-titative densification (20 © Institute for Architec-tural Typologies).

Resulting from the uncontrolled growth of cit-ies, urban sprawl has become a growing problem all across the world (and, alas, strikingly around Graz). Its main cause can be traced back to a so-cial phenomenon: the irrational fascination of peo-ple with the single-family house. Multiplied in the millions, it is our greatest enemy. The projected population growth prompts the city of Graz to make a decision: either dare a leap into a dimen-sion of urbanity or persist in self-imposed provin-cialism. Several speakers presented successful examples of the former from Switzerland or the

nität und die funktionale Durchmischung sowie Kompaktheit und Dichte, die einen qualitativen öffentlichen Raum und eine kulturelle Produktivität hervorbringen. Die gründerzeitliche Blockrandbebauung als *die* charakteristische Typologie der Stadt des 19. Jahrhunderts ist hauptverantwortlich für die erfolgreiche Balance zwischen komprimiertem Volumen und großzügigem Stadtraum, zwischen einer urbanen öffentlichen Straße und einem ruhigen privaten Hof. Anhand zeitgenössischer Interpretationen, etwa Ergänzungen der typischen Cerdà-Blocks in Barcelona oder spektakulären, an schimmernde Eisberge erinnernden Gebäuden, zeigten mehrere Architekten, wie sich der urbane Block weiterentwickeln und um zusätzliche Qualitäten ergänzen lässt.

Die bauliche soziale Verdichtung unserer Städte wird, darin waren sich alle Teilnehmer einig, nicht immer ohne Konflikte ablaufen und das ist auch gut so. Denn was bringt Weiterentwicklung und Neues besser hervor als kulturelle Divergenz?

Der Text ist in einer ungekürzten Fassung auf www.gat.st erschienen.

Beiträge von: Dietmar Eberle, Aurora Fernandez & Javier Mozas, Stefan Forster, Luis Fernández Galiano, Fabian Hörmann, Benoit Jallon & Umberto Napolitano,

Allard Jolles, Reinhard Kropf, Rüdiger Lainer, Vittorio Magnago Lampugnani, Judith Leclerc, Umberto Napolitano & Franck Boutté, Markus Penell, Khoo Peng Beng & Belinda Huang, Bernardo Secchi & Paola Viganò, Henning Stüben, Peter Trummer. **Moderation/Diskussion**: Hubertus Adam, Hans Gangoly, Christoph Luchsinger/Harald Grießer, Andreas Tropper, Bertram Werle. **Initiator**: Hans Gangoly. **Wissenschaftliche Leitung/Konzeption**: Markus Bogensberger. **Organisation/Assistenz**: Yvonne Bormes.

Martin Grabner

ENERGYCITY
Konferenz; **Institut für Gebäude und Energie**; 10. Juni 2011

Im Mittelpunkt der Konferenz stand die Präsentation der Ergebnisse des interdisziplinären Forschungsprojekts „UTE" (21 © ige) unter der Leitung des Instituts für Gebäude und Energie der TU Graz, gefördert von der FFG.

Das Projekt untersucht Wege zur Restrukturierung und Rekonfigurierung der baulichen Struktur von Städten, um deren Energieeffizienz erheblich zu steigern. Besonderes Augenmerk wurde auf eine effizientere Nutzung von Gebäudeflächen und die Nutzung von Synergien zwischen baulicher und virtueller Infrastruktur, Wohn- und Arbeitsplatz, Telearbeit etc. gelegt, also auf Strategien zur räumlichen, zeitlichen und digitalen Verdichtung. Im Rahmen des Projekts wurden neue Typologien für vertikale Strukturen mit allen erforderlichen Infrastrukturelementen der Gesellschaft, wie beispielsweise auch Industrie und Nahrungsmittelproduktion etc. entwickelt. Einer der Schwerpunkte lag hierbei auf gebäudeintegrierter Energieproduktion. Ziel war es, Lösungen für die bevorstehenden Energieprobleme aufzuzeigen und gleichzeitig die Lebensqualität in unseren Städten deutlich zu verbessern.

Zusätzlich zum Kernteam wurden Fachleute aus verschiedenen Disziplinen eingeladen, einen umfassenden Überblick über das komplexe Forschungsthema zu geben.

Kas Oosterhuis, Professor an der Architekturfakultät der TU Delft und Leiter von Hyperbody und dem Protospace Laboratory for Collaborative Design and Engineering, hielt einen interaktiven Vortrag über seine Forschung im Bereich Echtzeitverhalten von Gebäuden auf deren Umgebung,

---

Netherlands; Allard Jolles, historian and senior advisor to the Dutch Chief Government Architect, made a plea for the immediate juxtaposition of dense urban fabric and green nature.

But not all kinds of density are equal, as many presentations stressed: What matters is not the built mass per se, but the intensity of social relations in (public) spaces. This can be achieved and strengthened through various methods, one of them being density.

As in the tradition of European cities but contrary to the dogmatic functionalist urbanism of modernity, quality public space and cultural productivity are generated by heterogeneity, the mixing of functions as well as compactness and density. The typical perimeter block typology of the nineteenth century city is largely responsible for the successful balance between compressed volume and generous public space, or between an urban public street and a quiet private courtyard. By showing contemporary interpretations of the typology, from additions to the typical

city blocks of Cerdà's Barcelona to spectacular buildings reminiscent of shimmering icebergs, the participating architects demonstrated how the perimeter block can be further developed and enhanced with new qualities.

The participants agreed that as cities get denser there will occasionally be social conflicts—and that's a good thing. What would further continue development and the emergence of the new better than cultural diversity?

An unabbreviated version of the text has appeared on www.gat.st.

Contributors: Dietmar Eberle, Aurora Fernandez & Javier Mozas, Stefan Forster, Luis Fernández Galiano, Fabian Hörmann, Benoit Jallon & Umberto Napolitano, Allard Jolles, Reinhard Kropf, Rüdiger Lainer, Vittorio Magnago Lampugnani, Judith Leclerc, Umberto Napolitano & Franck Boutté, Markus Penell, Khoo Peng Beng & Belinda Huang, Bernardo Secchi & Paola Viganò, Henning Stüben, Peter Trummer. **Discussion Participants**: Hubertus Adam, Hans

Gangoly, Christoph Luchsinger/Harald Grießer, Andreas Tropper, Bertram Werle. **Initiator**: Hans Gangoly. **Concept**: Markus Bogensberger. **Organisation/Support**: Yvonne Bormes.

Martin Grabner

ENERGYCITY
Conference; **Institute of Buildings and Energy**; June 10, 2011

The central focus of the conference was the presentation of the results of an interdisciplinary research project led by the Institute of Buildings and Energy at Graz University of Technology and funded by the Austrian FFG (21 © ige).

The project examines ways of restructuring and reconfiguring the physical infrastructure of cities to radically increase their energy performance. Particular emphasis was put on more effective use of building space and the use of

21

das Konzept des „Living Building", Collaborative Design, File-to-factory-Produktion und parametrisches Design.

Alejandro Gutierrez, Direktor bei Arup Urban Design, sprach über nachhaltige urbane Entwurfsstrategien. Er ist für den Entwurf des Dongtan Eco City Projekts in Shanghai verantwortlich und leitet derzeit einige innovative Projekte wie das Low2no Projekt in Helsinki, das Projekt Manifattura Domani und ein Projekt in Santiago, Chile.

Roger Riewe, Leiter des Instituts für Architekturtechnologie der TU Graz sowie Mitbegründer und Geschäftsführer von Riegler Riewe Architekten, illustrierte das Potenzial für flexible, anpassungsfähige Räume anhand seiner eigenen Projekte und nahm zu den gegenwärtigen österreichischen Bauvorschriften kritisch Stellung.

Klaus Bollinger, Professor an der Universität für angewandte Kunst Wien und Leiter des Ingenieurbüros für Tragwerks- und Fassadenplanung Bollinger + Grohmann, präsentierte Projekte aus seinen Forschungsschwerpunkten, wie unter anderem der Entwicklung flexibler, anpassungsfähiger Räume mithilfe rekonfigurierbarer Tragwerke.

Abschließend wurde der „Energy City Award 2011" für die besten Studierendenprojekte am Institut für Gebäude und Energie der TU Graz und der Angewandten in Wien an Joseph Hofmarcher, Rangel Karaivanov, Martina Lesjak, Verena Lihl, Christoph Pehnelt, Sille Pihlak, Maximin Rieder, Harry Spraiter, Emanuel Tornquist und Siim Tuksam vergeben.

Beiträge von: Klaus Bollinger, Alejandro Gutierrez, Kas Oosterhuis, Roger Riewe. **Projektleitung**: Brian Cody. **Projektteam**: Andreas Ampenberger, Wolfgang Löschnig, Eduard Petriu, Daniel Podmirseg, Bernhard Sommer. **Consulting**: Volker Buscher/Kin Puan Wong (IT), Martin Fellendorf (Verkehr), Raimund

synergies between physical and virtual infrastructure, living and working spaces, teleworking etc.; in short, strategies for spatial, temporal, and digital densification. In the course of the project, new typologies for vertical structures incorporating all the necessary infrastructural elements of society including industrial and agricultural usages, food production etc. were developed. Building integrated energy production was one of the focal points thereby. The aim was to provide solutions for the impending energy issues and at the same time radically improve the quality of life in our cities.

In addition to the core team, an interdisciplinary selection of lecturers was invited to give a holistic view to the complex research question.

Kas Oosterhuis, professor at the architectural faculty at Delft University of Technology and director of Hyperbody and the protospace laboratory for collaborative design and engineering, gave an interactive lecture about his research in the areas of real time behavior of buildings and environments, living building concepts, collaborative design, file to factory production and parametric design.

Alejandro Gutierrez, associate director at Arup Urban Design, was talking about sustainable urban design strategies. He led the design of the Dongtan Eco City project for Shanghai and is currently leading several innovative projects that include the Low2no project in Helsinki, the Manifattura Domani project, and a project in Santiago, Chile.

Roger Riewe, director of the Institute of Architectural Technology at Graz University of Technology and co-founder and managing director of Riegler Riewe Architects, illustrated the potential for flexible adaptable space, based on own projects and discussed critically the current situation of building regulations in Austria.

Klaus Bollinger, professor at the architectural faculty of the University of Applied Arts in Vienna and director of the structural engineering consulting firm "Bollinger + Grohmann," presented projects of his research interests in the use of structure to create flexible adaptable spaces.

Finally, the results of the "Energy City Award 2011" for the best student projects of the studio work at the Institute of Buildings and Energy at Graz University of Technology and the "Angewandte" in Vienna were awarded to Verena Lihl, Christoph Pehnelt, Emanuel Tornquist, Sille Pihlak, Maximin Rieder, Siim Tuksam, Joseph Hofmarcher, Rangel Karaivanov, Martina Lesjak, Harry Spraiter.

Contributors: Klaus Bollinger, Alejandro Gutierrez, Kas Oosterhuis, Roger Riewe. **Project Leader**: Brian Cody. **Project Team**: Andreas Ampenberger, Wolfgang Löschnig, Eduard Petriu, Daniel Podmirseg, Bernhard Sommer. **Consulting**: Volker Buscher/ Kin Puan Wong (IT), Martin Fellendorf (Transport), Raimund Gutmann (Sociology). **Support**: Andrea Cavagna, Doris Damm, Alexander Eberl, Christian Schneeberger, Gregor Thiel.

Brian Cody, Wolfgang Löschnig

Gutmann (Soziologie). **Support**: Andrea Cavagna, Doris Damm, Alexander Eberl, Christian Schneeberger, Gregor Thiel.

Brian Cody, Wolfgang Löschnig

Sustainable Smart Cities
Winterschool 2011; **Institut für Architekturtechnologie** und Styrian Academy for Sustainable Energies

Nachhaltige und energieeffiziente Planung findet Anwendung in übergreifenden städtebaulichen Konzepten bis hin zum konstruktiven Detail. Die Winterschool „Sustainable Smart Cities" (22 © Institut für Architekturtechnologie) führte

vom „großen" bis zum „kleinen" Maßstab. Die „Makro-, Meso-, Mikro-Ebene" wurde auf dem Symposium ganzheitlich thematisiert.

Hierzu wurden Spezialisten aus der ganzen Welt eingeladen, um in Vorträgen und Workshops diverse Themen zu vertiefen und durch den fachlichen Austausch Synergieeffekte zu erzielen. 18 Doktoranden konnten sich hierfür bewerben und nahmen an dieser einwöchigen Veranstaltung teil.

Höhepunkt war ein öffentlicher Vortrag mit Podiumsdiskussion. Bei diesem „Fireside Chat" in der Aula der TU Graz waren WOHA Architekten aus Singapur eingeladen. Andreas Ruby (textbild, Berlin) moderierte alle Veranstaltungen auf hervorragende Art und Weise.

Beiträge von: Laura Baird, Brian Cody, Johannes Fiedler, Hans Gangoly, Richard Hassell und Wong

Mun Summ, Hyeong-Il Kim, David Müller, Edward NG, John C. Y. NG, Roger Riewe, Werner Sobek.

Ferdinand Oswald

Das Roboter Design Labor (RDL) stellt sich vor

Mit der Umsetzung des Projekts „Resource Efficient Non Standard Structures" gelingt es den Fakultäten für Architektur und Bauingenieurwissenschaften der TU Graz in Zukunft entlang der gesamten Prozesskette bei der Entwicklung von Prototypen neue Wege zu gehen.

Im Roboter Design Labor wurde eine flexible Bearbeitungszelle eingerichtet, die vom Modellbau aus Schaum oder Holz bis hin zur Nachbearbeitung von Betonfertigteilen zur Verfügung steht. Auch für Handlings- bzw. additive Prozesse soll das Labor genutzt werden (23 © ite).

Die Anlage setzt neue Maßstäbe im Bereich der Bearbeitungsgenauigkeit und stellt die Basis für Beiträge im internationalen Diskurs zum Thema „Manufacturing and Fabrication in Architecture und Civil Engineering" dar.

22　Copyright: WOHA architects | Foto: Kirsten Bucher

Sustainable Smart Cities
Winter School 2011, organized by the **Institute of Architecture Technology** and the Styrian Academy for Sustainable Energies

Sustainable and energy efficient designs are needed across the board from city planning to construction details. The Winter School, titled "Sustainable Smart Cities," proceeded from the large to the small scale. The continuum from the macro to the meso and further to the micro level was comprehensively discussed at the symposium (22 © Institute of Architecture Technology).

Experts from around the world were invited to give lectures and hold workshops on a variety of topics in order to delve into various topics and

to produce synergies through the exchange of ideas. Doctoral students could apply for this week-long event and eighteen were able to participate.

The highlight was a public lecture by WOHA architects from Singapore, followed by a panel discussion, a "Fireside Chat" in the Old Hall of Graz University of Technology. Andreas Ruby (textbild, Berlin) did an excellent job in hosting all events.

Contributors: Laura Baird, Brian Cody, Johannes Fiedler, Hans Gangoly, Richard Hassell und Wong Mun Summ, Hyeong-Il Kim, David Müller, Edward NG, John C. Y. NG, Roger Riewe, Werner Sobek.

Ferdinand Oswald

Presenting the Robotic Design Laboratory (RDL)

With the implementation of the project "Resource Efficient Non-Standard Structures," the Faculties of Architecture and Civil Engineering at Graz University of Technology are opening new ways across the entire process chain for the development of prototypes (23 © ite).

The robotic design lab was provided with a flexible machining unit that serves all stages of the process from the construction of models out of foam or wood up to the post-processing of pre-cast concrete parts. The laboratory can also be used for handling or additive processes.

The facility sets new standards in machining accuracy and provides the basis for contributions to the international discourse on the manufacture and fabrication in architecture and civil engineering.

Concept. In the last 15 to 20 years, the digital revolution has had a lasting effect on design, planning, and building.

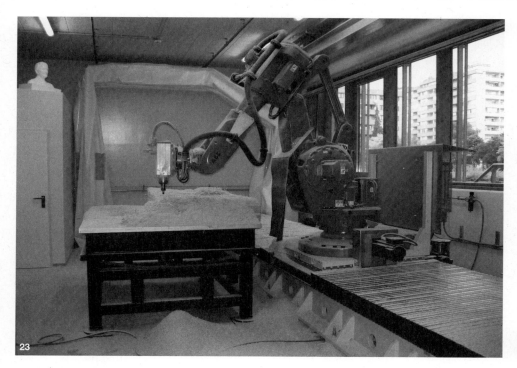
23

sende Betrachtung des Bauprozesses vom digitalen Design über den Modellbau bis zur Fertigung von Prototypen und deren Überprüfung durch entsprechende Messtechnik.

Fertigung. Für die Herstellung von Prototypen im großen Maßstab steht nun ein Industrieroboter zur Verfügung, der auf einer hochpräzisen Verfahrschiene montiert ist und neue Maßstäbe in der Bearbeitungsgenauigkeit bei höchster Flexibilität setzt. Bearbeitungsmöglichkeiten wie Trocken- und Nassbearbeitung sowie eine hohe Flexibilität für weitere Aufgaben wie Spritzen, Cutten oder Handlingaufgaben sind in einer Anlage vereint. Online unter: www.ite.tugraz.at

Andreas Trummer

Konzept. Die digitale Revolution hat in den letzten 15 bis 20 Jahren das Entwerfen, Planen und Bauen nachhaltig verändert.

Workflow. An Universitäten und in Planungsbüros werden zusätzlich die neuen gestalterischen Möglichkeiten der digitalen Planungswerkzeuge und deren Auswirkungen auf die Fertigung von Bauwerken untersucht.

Umsetzung. Im Rahmen eines fakultätsübergreifenden Infrastrukturprojekts wurde der Forschungsantrag „Resource Efficient Non Standard Structures" gestellt. Dieser beinhaltet die umfas-

Solar Energy in the City:
Analysis and Evaluation of Economic, Energy and Architectural Quality in Urban Solar Energy Buildings.
two-year research project

Workflow. New creative possibilities of digital design tools and their impact on the building production are further investigated in universities and design offices.

Implementation. The research proposal on "Resource Efficient Non-Standard Structures" was submitted as part of a cross-faculty infrastructure project. The proposal includes the comprehensive analysis of the construction process from digital design to model building and further to the manufacturing of prototypes and their testing through the appropriate measurement techniques.

Production. Large-scale prototypes can now be produced by an industrial robot, mounted on precision rails, that combines extreme accuracy with maximum flexibility. The facility enables dry and wet machining and provides a high flexibility for other tasks such as spraying, cutting, and handling. Online at: www.ite.tugraz.at

Andreas Trummer

The interdisciplinary research project, "Solar Energy in the City" examined four typical multistory residential buildings in Graz and Vienna—one from the late nineteenth century, an apartment tower from the 1960s and two new constructions—in terms of economic, energetic, architectural and technical aspects of integrated solar thermal systems (24 © Institute of Architectural Typologies: Sophie Grünewald and Andreas Lechner). Energy gain and design scenarios for the ecologically and economically crucial integration of renewable energy production systems in dense urban housing were explored from different perspectives. It became clear that currently available, technically and economically mature technologies provide few solutions for the architecturally sophis-

 Solarenergie Urban.
Analyse und Bewertung der ökonomischen, energetischen und architektonischen Qualität urbaner Solarenergiebauten.
zweijähriges Forschungsprojekt

24

ticated integration of solar thermal energy systems (as opposed to photovoltaics). One can only hope that in the future architects will be much more involved in this field of research and development, since their imaging, visualization, and

313

Das interdisziplinäre Forschungsprojekt „Solarenergie Urban" untersuchte vier typische Mehrgeschoßwohnbauten in Graz und Wien – ein Gründerzeitobjekt, ein Wohnhochhaus aus den 1960ern und zwei neue Wohnbauten – hinsichtlich ökonomischer, energetischer, architektonischer und bautechnischer Aspekte gebäudeintegrierter Solarthermie (24 © Institut für Gebäudelehre: Sophie Grünewald und Andreas Lechner). Ziel des Projekts war es, im ökologisch und ökonomisch hochrelevanten Spannungsfeld aus städtisch-dichten Wohnformen und gebäudeintegrierter Energiegewinnung mögliche Ertrags- und Gestaltungsszenarien aus allen relevanten Fachperspektiven auszuloten. Der Fokus auf Solarthermie verdeutlicht dabei, dass eine technisch und ökonomisch ausgereifte Technologie gegenwärtig noch kaum Produktlösungen für gestalterisch einigermaßen solide handzuhabende Gebäudeintegration liefert (im Gegensatz zur Fotovoltaik). In diesem Forschungs- und Entwicklungsfeld wäre zukünftig auf noch wesentlich stärkere Forschungsbeteiligung der Architektur zu hoffen, da erst deren Bild-, Visualisierungs- und Gestaltungskompetenzen mögliche und dringliche gestalterische Qualitäten im sichtbaren Bereich künftiger Stadt- und Wohnformen ins Blickfeld sowohl der Entwurfs- und Fachplanungsabteilungen als auch der Produkthersteller, der Politik und Fördergeber sowie beteiligter Fachdisziplinen, rücken können.

In den vier Case Studies des Forschungsprojekts folgen der energetischen Analyse urbaner Randbedingungen (Verschattungsanalysen, Verfügbarkeit der Hüllenflächen, saisonale Deckungsbeiträge) dementsprechend die Analyse und Bewertung architektonisch relevanter Aspekte (Formen, Positionierungs- und eventuelle Mehrfachnutzungsmöglichkeiten aktiver Solartechnologieelemente samt Visualisierung) und die bautechnische Analyse und Bewertung der Nutzbarkeit und Integrationsfähigkeit dieser Vorschläge sowie die Auslegung und Simulation der thermischen Solaranlagen.

Die aktuell anlaufenden Forschungsprogramme im Bereich von Energie und Stadt (etwa Fit4Set, www.smartcities.at etc.) verdeutlichen die dringliche Einbringung architektonischer Gestaltungs- und Darstellungsexpertise – nicht nur im Fall exaltiert-innovativer Leuchtturmprojekte, sondern auch für die Hebung des Qualitätsanspruchs an jene Alltagsbauten, die erst das bindende Gewebe des Nachhaltigkeitsdesiderats dicht-städtischer Bebauungen bilden. Im Gegensatz zur Energie(-Performanz) eines Gebäudes ist dessen gestalterische Qualität durchgängig an die sichtbare Welt gebunden – sowohl mit als auch ohne sichtbare Solarkollektorflächen.

Die Ergebnisse werden demnächst auf der BMVIT-Homepage des Forschungsprogramms www.HAUSderZukunft.at publiziert.

Beteiligte: Österreichische Forschungsförderungsgesellschaft, FFG (Programmlinie „Haus der Zukunft Plus"); International Energy Agency, IEA (Task 41 Architecture & Solar Energy, www.iea-shc.org/task41); Österreichische Energieagentur, AEA (Projektleitung, Wirtschaftlichkeit und WLC-Bewertung); Austrian Institute of Technology, AIT (Verschattungsanalysen und Gebäudesimulationen); TU Graz, Institut für Wärmetechnik (Energetische Erträge und Deckungsgrade); TU Graz, Institut für Gebäudelehre (Erarbeitung, Visualisierung und Bewertung gestalterischer Bandbreiten; Projektleitung: Andreas Lechner); Dr. Ronald Mischek ZT GmbH (Bauphysik und Bautechnik).

Andreas Lechner

design skills are needed to make the design and technical planning departments as well as product manufacturers, political decision makers, and funding bodies aware of the possible and urgent artistic qualities in what can be seen of our future urban living.

In the four case studies of the research project the energetic analysis of given urban conditions (shading analysis, building envelope availability, seasonal solar coverage) is followed, accordingly, by the analysis and evaluation of architecturally relevant aspects (shapes, positioning and possible multiple uses of active solar technology elements, as well as visualization), the structural analysis and evaluation of the usability and integration capability of these proposals, and the interpretation and simulation of solar thermal systems.

The current research programs in the incipient field of energy and the city (e.g., Fit4Set, www.smartcities.at) clearly illustrate the urgency of bringing in architectural design and visualization expertise—not only in the case of exceptional and innovative flagship projects, but also with the intention of raising the quality standards for the general urban fabric that forms the basis for sustainable urbanism.

In contrast to the energy performance of a building, its design quality is part of the visible world—with or without visible solar panels.

The results will be published soon on the BMVIT homepage of the research program: www.HAUSderZukunft.at

Participants: Austrian Research Promotion Agency, FFG (Program "House of the Future Plus"); International Energy Agency IEA (Task 41 Solar Architecture & Energy, www.iea-shc.org/task41); Austrian Energy Agency AEA (project management, cost and WLC evaluation); Austrian Institute of Technology, AIT (shading analysis and building simulations); Graz University of Technology, Institute of Thermal Engineering (Energy gains and levels of coverage); Graz University of Technology, Institute of Architectural Typologies (development, visualization and evaluation of design solutions; Project Director: Andreas Lechner); Dr. Ronald Mischek ZT GmbH (Building physics and building technology).

Andreas Lechner

INTEGRAL E+, Integral Energy Landscape Eastern Styria

A research project at the LANDLAB of the **Institute of Architecture and Landscape** 2010–2012, funded by the Climate and Energy Fund and carried out as part of the program "New Energies 2020"

The shift to sustainable forms of energy represents a significant decentralization of energy production and a move towards networking and interconnections. When everyone in the future will be producing energy, its generation will be organized in many individual ways all of which, however, will depend on the interplay between the actors.

INTEGRAL E+, Integrale Energie-landschaft Oststeiermark

Forschungsprojekt am LANDLAB des **Instituts für Architektur und Landschaft** 2010–2012, gefördert aus Mitteln des Klima- und Energiefonds und durchgeführt im Rahmen des Programms „Neue Energien 2020"

Die Wende hin zu nachhaltigen Energieformen bedeutet eine deutliche Dezentralisierung der Energiegewinnung und eine stärkere Vernetzung und Verschaltung. Wenn in Zukunft jedermann Energie erzeugt, wird die Energiegewinnung sehr individuell erfolgen, jedoch auf das Zusammenspiel der einzelnen Akteure angewiesen sein. Die Technologien – seien es Solarenergieanlagen über einem Parkplatz, Biogas aus Speiseresten oder piezo-elektrische Energie aus Schwingungen – sind seit langem bekannt und weit verbreitet. Auch Mobilität mittels Elektro- oder Gasmotoren wird schon seit Jahrzehnten erprobt bzw. angewandt. Eine sinnvolle Verschränkung dieser Technologien im Rahmen regional verfügbarer Ressourcen

findet bis heute dennoch kaum statt, bürokratische Strukturen und mangelnde gesellschaftliche Akzeptanz verhindern dies allzu oft. Nach wie vor fehlen starke Bilder und Modelle einer zukünftigen Umwelt und Lebenspraxis.

Mit dem Projekt „Integral E+" versuchen wir einen umfassenden Wandel der Kulturlandschaft in der Oststeiermark voranzubringen. Zukünftige Prosumenten (also Produzenten und Konsumenten gleichzeitig) werden sich in einer immer stärker hybridisierenden Umwelt bewegen. Dabei beschäftigen uns folgende Fragen: Wie können funktionale Trennungen überwunden werden? Auf welche Weise wird Energiegewinnung in der Landschaft wirksam? Was bedeutet das für unsere Lebenspraxis?

Wesentlicher Bestandteil des Projektes „Integral E+" ist eine integrale Lehre. Über den gesamten Projektzeitraum sind wir mit Studierendengruppen in der Region um Bad Blumau unterwegs, um gemeinsam mit den Akteuren vor Ort lokale Ressourcen, soziale Zusammenhänge und Potenziale zu untersuchen und mögliche Energie-Akteurs-Landschaften zu entwickeln. Online unter: www.integral-e.at

Bernhard König

Scenarios on the Megalopolitan Future

Projektübung, Podiumsdiskussion und Ausstellung WS 2010; **Institut für Städtebau**

Stadt ist nicht mehr gleich Stadt: Die neuen, rasant wachsenden Großstädte (Megalopolis) haben nur wenig mit der mitteleuropäisch geprägten Großstadt zu tun. Riesige Metropolregionen, die nun fast alle auf der Südhalbkugel liegen, sind die Brennpunkte der aktuell stattfindenden Urbanisierung. Urbane Transformationsprozesse finden vor allem in Metropolen der Dritten Welt wie Dhaka (Bangladesch) oder Lagos (Nigeria) statt, die gemeinsam mit dem auch an einer Küste liegenden Großraum Rotterdam von Studierenden von Joost Meuwissen und Martin Zettel in der Projektübung „Scenarios On The Megalopolitan Future: The Recreated Utopia" am Institut für Städtebau der TU Graz näher untersucht wurden. Ausgehend von intensiven Recherchen zu den Themenkomplexen *Economy, Disaster und Hinterland* wurden Konzepte und Strategien entwickelt, die im Grazer Haus der Architektur in Form von Modellen, Projektionen und Filmen zu sehen waren.

The technologies—whether solar cells spread over a parking lot, biogas derived from food waste, or piezo-electric energy generated by vibrations—are well known and widely disseminated. Mobility by means of electric or gas motors has also been tested or used for decades. Still, an effective combination of these technologies with regionally available resources is to this day seldom achieved, due to bureaucratic structures and lack of social acceptance. As before, we still lack strong images and models of the future environment and life forms.

The project "Integral E+" seeks to promote comprehensive change in the cultural landscape of Eastern Styria. The "prosumers" (i.e., simultaneously producers and consumers) of the future will be confronted with an increasingly hybridized environment. Here, we address the following questions: How can functional divisions be overcome? How can energy be effectively generated in the rural environments? What does this mean for our way of life?

An essential component of the project "Integral E+" is its integrated nature. Over the entire project period, we will be traveling with groups of students around Bad Blumau to investigate with local actors the available resources, social relationships, and opportunities as well as develop potential networks of energy-actor-landscapes. Online at: www.integral-e.at

Bernhard König

Scenarios on the Megalopolitan Future

Master studio, panel discussion and exhibition, winter semester 2010, organized by the **Institute of Urbanism**

The city no longer remains the city: the new, rapidly growing megalopoleis have little to do with the central European city. Huge metropolitan areas, almost all of which are now located in the south-

ern hemisphere, are the focal points of current urbanization. Urban transformation processes take place mainly in Third World cities, such as Dhaka in Bangladesh or Lagos in Nigeria, which, along with the coastal Greater Rotterdam area, were scrutinized by students of Joost Meuwissen and Martin Zettel in the Master studio "Scenarios on the Megalopolitan Future: the Recreated Utopia" at the Institute of Urbanism at Graz University of Technology. Based on intensive research on the topics of *economy, disaster, and hinterland*, the participants developed concepts and strategies that were exhibited in the Graz House of Architecture in the form of models, projections, and films.

The exhibition opened with a panel discussion on urban utopias. The central question was whether utopias are possible in complex locations whose functioning is not yet fully understood by researchers. Who would be able to create such utopias? And what is their relevance in the future?

Zur Ausstellungseröffnung fand eine Podiumsdiskussion zum Thema „Urbanistische Utopien" statt. Die zentrale Frage war, ob Utopien an komplexen Orten, deren Funktionsweise trotz aller Forschung noch nicht endgültig verstanden werden kann, überhaupt möglich sind, wer sie erschaffen könnte und welche Relevanz sie in ihrer weiteren Folge überhaupt haben.

Aufgrund der Aufgabenstellung des Seminars – ein ferner Ort, den keine(r) der Studierenden selbst besucht hat, und ein Katastrophenszenario, das eine tabula rasa-ähnliche Ausgangssituation schafft – war es möglich, Entwürfe losgelöst von kulturellem Ballast und früheren Utopien zu entwickeln. So entstanden sehr unterschiedliche Projekte, die nicht versuchen Bekanntes zu kopieren, sondern mit Fokus auf einzelne Aspekte der Stadt neue, eigene Utopien schaffen wollen. Durch die Verlagerung an einen Ort in der Ferne (gewissermaßen einen Nicht-Ort für die Studierenden) und die damit einhergehende Entfernung von der eigenen Realität werde das Denken einer Utopie vielleicht erst möglich, kommentierte Hannes Mayer die Aufgabenstellung.

Der Text ist in einer ungekürzten Fassung auf www.gat.st erschienen.

The brief of the seminar — providing a remote place that none of the students have ever visited and a disaster scenario that created a tabula rasa — made it possible to develop projects unburdened with cultural baggage or utopian predecessors. This resulted in radically different projects that did not try to copy familiar paradigms, but created new utopias of their own by focusing on specific aspects of the city. Perhaps a utopia can only be conceived through the displacement of the site to a distant location (a non-place for the students) and the resulting removal of one's own reality, as Hannes Mayer observed.

The text was published in an unabbreviated version on www.gat.st.

Exhibition participants (February 2–13, 2011, HDA): Matej Banozic, Bettina Domenig, Patrick Ebner, Christoph Haidacher, Claudia Huber, Pia Hundhammer, Jasna Kuljuh, Anja Leinich, Peter Mayrhofer, Nedzad Sabanovic, Pacome Soissons,

Teilnehmer Ausstellung (2.–13. Februar 2011, HDA): Matej Banozic, Bettina Domenig, Patrick Ebner, Christoph Haidacher, Claudia Huber, Pia Hundhammer, Jasna Kuljuh, Anja Leinich, Peter Mayrhofer, Nedzad Sabanovic, Pacome Soissons, Michaela Wallner, Henri Winter. **Podiumsdiskussion**: Eilfried Huth, Hannes Mayer, Joost Meuwissen, Martin Zettel (Moderation).

Martin Grabner

Campus 2011. RAUM – ZEIT – SPUREN. Technische Universität Graz 1811–2011

Ein Systemtrailer als Machbarkeitsstudie; Film; **Institut für Stadt- und Baugeschichte** im Auftrag des Rektorats

Der Film zeigt Ausschnitte der Fülle an Möglichkeiten, die das System „Campus 2011" (25 © TU Graz) bereithält. Erdacht als Ausstellung im virtuellen Raum anlässlich des 200-jährigen Jubiläums der TU Graz werden „200 Jahre Wissen, Technik, Leidenschaft" zu Geschichten geformt und mit-

tels neuester Technologien erzählt. Campus 2011 eröffnet damit neue Möglichkeiten der Wissenschaftsvermittlung, darüber hinaus fungiert die Methode als umfassendes Informationssystem der TU Graz, das sich nicht bloß auf die Zugänglichkeit der drei Campi der TU Graz beschränkt, sondern Verbindungen durch Räume und Zeiten kreiert. In enger Zusammenarbeit mit den beteiligten Instituten (Stadt- und Baugeschichte, Geoinformation, Navigation und Satellitengeodäsie, Fernerkundung und Photogrammetrie, Computer Graphik und Wissensvisualisierung CGV, Maschinelles Sehen und Darstellen ICG, Institut für Informationssysteme und Computer Medien, Insti-

Michaela Wallner, Henri Winter. **Panel discussion**: Eilfried Huth, Hannes Mayer, Joost Meuwissen, Martin Zettel (moderation).

Martin Grabner

Campus 2011: TRACES IN SPACE AND TIME Graz University of Technology 1811–2011

A film, produced by the Institute of **Institute of Urban and Architectural History** on behalf of the Rector

The film shows glimpses of the many possibilities provided by the system "Campus 2011" (25 © TU Graz). Celebrating the bicentennial of Graz University of Technology, this exhibition in virtual space uses the latest technologies to narrate "200 years of knowledge, technology, passion." Campus 2011 not only opens up new possibilities of knowledge

transfer but also acts as a comprehensive information platform for the university. Instead of being confined to the three campus locations, it connects them across space and time. In close cooperation with the participating institutes — Urban and Architectural History, Geoinformation, Navigation, Remote Sensing and Photogrammetry, Computer Graphics and Knowledge Visualisation (CGV), Computer Vision and Graphics (ICG), Information Systems and Computer Media (IICM), Architecture and Media (IAM) — new opportunities have been developed for visitors to access the science, technology, and history of Graz University of Technology and beyond at many different levels. An essential aspect of the project is the trans-disciplinary collaboration between natural science, technology, and the humanities.

The latest technologies are combined with historical findings to enable multidimensional, interactive historiography. Information concerning persons and events is organized with regard to location and date in a space-time matrix; con-

tut für Architektur und Medien) wurden Möglichkeiten ausgelotet und entwickelt, die den Besuchern auf unterschiedlichsten Ebenen Zugänge zu Wissenschaft, Technik, Geschichte der TU Graz und darüber hinaus ermöglichen. Ein wesentlicher Aspekt des Projekts ist die transdisziplinäre Zusammenarbeit von Natur-, Technik- und Geisteswissenschaft.

Neueste Technologien verknüpft mit historischen Erkenntnissen generieren eine multidimensionale, interaktive Geschichtsschreibung. In der Raum-Zeit-Matrix sind Daten von Personen und Ereignissen verortet und in die Zeit eingebettet; Verbindungen von Personen und Ereignissen ergeben ein komplexes Netzwerk an Wissen, intelligente Verknüpfungen werden zu Geschichten, die Spuren in der Matrix erzeugen. Die Besucher können vorgezeichneten Spuren folgen, aber auch eigene Pfade beschreiten und Spuren in der Matrix hinterlassen.

Als Informationsquellen dienen sowohl die umfangreichen Bild- und Textarchive der TU Graz als auch externe Datenbanken. Die Informationen können über mobile Smartphones bezogen werden oder stationär z.B. an den TU-Terminals in Form einer virtuellen Campus-Tour erlebt werden. Die Georeferenzierung des gesamten Campusbereiches bietet eine Einstiegsmöglichkeit in das System, die Anbindung an externe Geoinformationssysteme wie Earth Viewer (Google Maps und Earth, Microsoft Bing u.a.) verorten Ereignisse außerhalb der TU und machen sie damit sichtbar.

Idee und Konzept: Ute Angeringer-Mmadu, Simone Hain, Oliver Jungwirth. **Technische Projektleitung**: Norbert Bartelme. **Content**: Andrea Contursi, Eugen Gross, Volker Pachauer, Bettina Paschke, Emina Poljac, Elisabeth Seuschek, Marion Starzacher, Alexander Waldhör, Wolfgang Wallner. **Umsetzung Film**: Ute Angeringer-Mmadu (Produktionsleitung), Philipp Erkinger (3D-Animation), Oliver Jungwirth (Datenarchitektur). Der Film auf youTube: http://www.youtube.com/watch?v=FHAeVCiDPEk Link zum Manual: http://www.stadt-geschichte.tugraz.at/home/110127_manual.pdf

Ute Angeringer-Mmadu

 ## Bilder im Steinhaus
Ausstellung von Annemarie Dreibholz-Humele, Dezember 2010

nections between people and events build up a complex network of knowledge; intelligent links turn into stories that generate traces in the matrix. Visitors can either follow pre-recorded tracks or choose their own path and leave their own traces.

The information is sourced from the large image and text archive of the university as well as from external databases. The information can be accessed via smartphones or viewed as a virtual campus tour from fixed terminals at university locations. The geographical referencing of the entire campus area offers an entry point into the system, while a connection to external geographic information systems such as Earth Viewer (Google Earth and Maps, Microsoft Bing, etc.) locate events outside the university and make them visible.

Idea and concept: Ute Angeringer-Mmadu, Simone Hain, Oliver Jungwirth. **Technical project management**: Norbert Bartelme. **Content**: Andrea Contursi, Eugen Gross, Volker Pachauer, Bettina Paschke, Emina Poljac, Elisabeth Seuschek, Marion Starzacher, Alexander Waldhör, Wolfgang Wallner. **Implementation of the film**: Ute Angeringer-Mmadu (production management), Philipp Erkinger (3D-animation), Oliver Jungwirth (data architecture). The film on youTube: http://www.youtube.com/watch?v=FHAeVCiDPEk Link to the manual: http://www.stadt-geschichte.tugraz.at/home/110127_manual.pdf

Ute Angeringer-Mmadu

Images in the Steinhaus
An exhibition of paintings by Annemarie Dreibholz-Humele, December 2010

The Steinhaus nestled in soft snow, a rare day in December 2010. An exhibition provoked Styrians and Carinthians interested in architecture to re-

26

Das Steinhaus eingebettet im weichen Schnee, ein seltener Tag im Dezember 2010. Eine Ausstellung motivierte Architekturinteressierte aus der Steiermark und Kärnten, dieses gebaute Manifest der Architektur von Günther Domenig wieder aufzusuchen. Glitzerndweißer Schnee umarmte die kaltgraue Betonkonstruktion des Gebäudes. Meterhohe Eisstalaktiten hingen vom Dach und die Sonne drängte sich über den Ossiachersee durch die großzügigen Glasflächen ins Haus.

Ohne Rahmen, ohne Nagel standen die Ölbilder selbstständig in den Ausnehmungen der Glaskonstruktion oder frei in den Nischen und

visit the manifesto of architecture built by Günther Domenig. Shiny white snow hugged the cold gray concrete of the building. Meter-long icicles were hanging from the roof as the sunlight over the Ossiachersee squeezed through the large glass surfaces into the house.

Without the support of frames or nails, the oil paintings were standing on their own in the recesses of the glass structures, in the niches, and along the smooth walls of gray concrete. The paintings merged with the interior as if it had always been the plan. In this exhibition the painter showed her latest pictures (26 © Annemarie Dreibholz-Humele) which deal with organic shapes, body language, and bodily communication.

University professor Linda Pelzmann, a Carinthian herself, opened the show with a humorous speech. On behalf of the landlord and the Steinhaus Foundation, architect Wallner led visitors through the complex.

Annemarie Dreibholz-Humele

an den betongrauen glatten Wänden. Die Formate fügten sich in den Innenraum ein, als hätte man es so geplant. Die Malerin zeigte in dieser Ausstellung ihre neuesten Bilder (26 © Annemarie Dreibholz-Humele), in denen sie sich mit Körperformen, Körpersprache bzw. Körperkommunikation beschäftigt.

Universitätsprofessorin Linda Pelzmann, selbst Kärntnerin, hielt eine humorvolle Eröffnungsansprache. Architekt Wallner war in Vertretung des Hausherrn bzw. der Steinhaus-Stiftung anwesend und führte Interessierte durch die Anlage.

Annemarie Dreibholz-Humele

Masterstudios

Mit dem Wintersemester 2009/2010 wurde das zweijährige Master-Curriculum an der Fakultät eingeführt. Das zentrale Fach des neu konzipierten Studiums ist das Masterstudio, welches aus einer Projektübung und zwei obligatorischen integrierten Seminaren besteht. Wir sind der Mei-

Master Studios

In the winter semester 2009/10 the new biennial Master-Curriculum was introduced at the faculty. The central subject of the completely revamped course program is the Master studio, which combines a main project exercise with two obligatory integrated seminars. With this structure we think that we have found an adequate answer to the challenges that face architectural education today. The format allows for interdisciplinary and in-depth investigations into a subject-matter. Current problems and research topics can be taken up and dealt with in far greater complexity than in previous design studio formats. The Master studios that have taken place up to now have demonstrated that this concept is successful. All institutes are offering studios. This leads to an astonishing breadth and variety of course topics—besides architectural, urban, and landscape designs, also technical and theoretical topics are dealt with.

nung, dass wir damit eine zeitgemäße Antwort auf die Herausforderungen gefunden haben, vor denen die Architekturausbildung heute steht. Das Format erlaubt das vertiefte und fächerübergreifende Bearbeiten einer Aufgabenstellung. Aktuelle Fragen und Forschungsthemen können aufgegriffen und in weit größerer Komplexität behandelt werden, als dies in den bisherigen Entwurfsformaten möglich war. Die bisher veranstalteten Masterstudios haben gezeigt, dass das Konzept funktioniert. Alle Institute bieten Masterstudios an. Dadurch entsteht eine erstaunliche Breite und Vielgestaltigkeit in den Lehrangeboten – neben architektonischen und städtebaulichen Entwürfen auch spezialisierte und theoretische Themenstellungen.

Im Folgenden werden vier Masterstudios vorgestellt, die einen Eindruck dieser Vielfalt zu geben vermögen. Im Anschluss daran befindet sich ein tabellarischer Überblick über das gesamte Angebot an Masterstudios im Studienjahr 2010/2011. Obwohl die Faculty News-Seiten von *GAM* üblicherweise nicht über Inhalte von Lehrveranstaltungen berichten, behandeln wir die Masterstudios dennoch, weil sie das wichtigste Fach des Master-Curriculums sind und dokumentieren, dass die Architekturfakultät der TU Graz die Ausbildung

On the following pages four Master studios that give an impression of this diversity are presented. Subsequently there is a table showing the whole range of Master studios during the academic year 2010/11. Although the Faculty News pages of *GAM* usually don't report on the contents of individual courses, we present the Master studios, because they are the most important course in the Master-Curriculum. They show that the Faculty of Architecture of Graz University of Technology strives to offer an architectural education, which on the broadest disciplinary basis is as close to practice and as research oriented as possible.

Urs Hirschberg

Density +:
BIG BANG Seoul
Master studio summer semester 2011,
organized by the **Institute of
Architecture Technology**

auf breiter disziplinärer Basis so praxisnah und forschungsorientiert wie möglich gestaltet.

Urs Hirschberg

Density +:
BIG BANG Seoul
Masterstudio SS 2011;
Institut für Architekturtechnologie

In einer Metropolis ist alles in Veränderung – urbane Form, Funktion und Raum. Dichte ist keine Ausnahme. Durch neue Möglichkeiten der Dichte kann die Evolution einer Stadt sich fortsetzen. Das bedeutet density + … Funktion, Infrastruktur, Institution, Menschen, Event usw.

Im Sommersemester 2011 bot das Institut für Architekturtechnologie in Kooperation mit der Seoul National University (SNU) und Prof. Seung Hoy Kim das Masterstudio BIG BANG SEOUL an. Aufgabe der Studierenden war es, die Megastruktur Seun Sanga neu zu definieren – ein länglicher, mehrgeschossiger Komplex bestehend aus vier Blöcken, welcher zum Zeitpunkt der Entstehung in den späten 1960er Jahren eine neue

In a Metropolis everything is changing—urban fabric, program, and space. Density is no exception. Through finding new solutions for density the evolution of a city can continue. That's what density + means … program, infrastructure, institution, people, event, and so on.

In the summer term 2011, the Institute of Architecture Technology ran the Master studio BIG BANG SEOUL in cooperation with Seoul National University (SNU) and Prof. Seung Hoy Kim. Students were asked to rethink the megastructure Seun Sanga—an elongated high-rise building consisting of four blocks which provided Seoul with a new dense setting in the late 1960s but is now facing the fatal destiny of "to be or not to be." Seun Sanga has failed to evolve for the new conditions of urban life (27 © Uta Gelbke), which students needed to take into account when establishing a new density: changing or adding program(s), movement systems, volumes, etc.

The studio work involved a trip to Seoul, a joint workshop with students and lecturers from

dichte Struktur für Seoul darstellte, aber nun der endgültigen Bestimmung „sein oder nicht sein" entgegensieht. Seun Sanga konnte nicht auf die neuen Konditionen urbanen Lebens reagieren. (27 © Uta Gelbke) Dies sollten die Studierenden bei der Entwicklung einer neuen Definition von Dichte beachten: Veränderung oder Addition von Funktion(en), Bewegungssystemen, Volumen etc.

Das Projekt beinhaltete eine Reise nach Seoul und einen gemeinsamen Workshop mit Studierenden und Lehrenden der SNU sowie deren Gegenbesuch in Graz zur Abschlusspräsentation der Arbeiten. Die Kooperation zwischen SNU und TU Graz wird durch ein Student & Staff Exchange Agreement fortgesetzt, das die Erfahrung einer anderen architektonischen und kulturellen Perspektive ermöglicht.

Roger Riewe, Uta Gelbke

27

Seoul National University and their return visit to Graz for the final presentation of the projects. The cooperation between SNU and TU Graz will continue due to a Student & Staff Exchange Agreement that allows experiencing a different architectural as well as cultural perspective.

Roger Riewe, Uta Gelbke

Arizona Dream: New Realities for Broadacre City

Master studio at the **Institute of Architecture and Landscape**, summer semester 2011

In 2011, the Institute of Architecture and Landscape thematized Frank Lloyd Wright's urban

Arizona Dream: New Realities for Broadacre City

Masterstudio SS 2011;
Institut für Architektur und Landschaft

2011 thematisierte das Institut für Architektur und Landschaft die Stadtvision von Frank Lloyd Wright – BROADACRE CITY. Im Projektstudio erforschten und entwickelten wir dessen prototypisches Potenzial für eine zukünftige urbane Landschaft aus heutiger Sicht weiter.

Basierend auf der vorangegangenen Lehrveranstaltung CASE 05 – REACTIVATING BROADACRE CITY, in der die systemischen Grundlagen des Stadtmodells erarbeitet wurden, erweckten wir nun Broadacre City zu neuem Leben. Ausgangspunkt für die Untersuchung war die Notwendigkeit der Umstellung von fossilen

vision: BROADACRE CITY. In the project studio, we further explored and developed its prototypical potential for future urban landscapes from today's perspective.

Based on the previous course CASE 05 — REACTIVATING BROADACRE CITY, where the systemic foundations of Wright's urban model were articulated, we now awakened Broadacre City to new life. The starting point for the new study was the need to switch from fossil fuels to renewable energy sources and the question of possible regional resources (28 © Sebastian H. Jenull, Sandra I. Tantscher).

Consequently, the related elective course CASE 06—CULTIVATING SYNERGIES aimed at providing an understanding of the relationships between products, culture, and regional landscape.

auf regenerative Energieträger und die Frage nach möglichen regionalen Ressourcen.

Das zugehörige Wahlfach CASE 06 – CULTIVATING SYNERGIES fokussierte deshalb auf der Vermittlung eines Verständnisses von Bezüglichkeiten zwischen Produkten, Kultur und regionaler Landschaft. Dafür wurde eine Auswahl von verschiedenen Kulturpflanzen, Kultivierungsmethoden und Produkten untersucht, die potenziell eine signifikante Rolle bei der Umstellung von fossilen auf erneuerbare Energieträger spielen werden (28 © Sebastian H. Jenull, Sandra I. Tantscher).

Entwickelt wurde eine „Post-Oil-Broadacre City" und wir gingen dabei von der These aus, dass die dezentrale Stadt mit ihrer heterogenen Nutzungsmischung ein zu entdeckendes Potenzial besitzt, urbane und landwirtschaftliche Praktiken gleichermaßen in interagierende ökonomische, kulturelle wie gestaltende Beziehung zu setzen und damit, im Gegensatz zu einer funktional gegliederten Stadt, Synergieeffekte kulturell nutzbar zu machen.

Die entstandenen Entwürfe zeigen auf, dass es mittels moderner, kleinmaßstäblicher Technologien möglich ist, Prozesse der Energieerzeugung, der Abfallbewirtschaftung, der Wasseraufbereitung sowie der Lebensmittel- und Rohstoff-

To this effect, the investigation focused on a variety of different crops, cultivation methods, and products that potentially play a significant role in the transition from fossil to renewable energy sources.

The result was a "post-oil Broadacre City." We proceeded from the premise that the decentralized city with its heterogeneous mix of functions boasts untapped potential to set urban and agricultural practices in interactive economic, cultural, and creative relationships and thus release synergy effects unavailable to a city structured in terms of functions.

As the resulting design projects demonstrate, it is possible with modern, small-scale technologies to effectively initiate local processes of energy generation, waste management, water treatment and food and raw material production and thereby strengthen the energy and cultural resources of the locality and the region.

*Klaus K. Loenhart, Andreas Goritschnig,
Ania V. Zdunek, Anne Oberritter*

28

produktion effektiv direkt vor Ort zu initiieren und damit lokale und regionale Ressourcen – seien sie energetisch oder kulturell – zu stärken.

Klaus K. Loenhart, Andreas Goritschnig, Ania V. Zdunek, Anne Oberritter

Papier Peint
Masterstudio WS 2010,
Institut für Architektur und Medien

Am 13. Jänner 2011 wurde feierlich das „Roboter Design Labor" im Bautechnikzentrum Inffeldgasse eröffnet. Diese große Infrastrukturinvestition ist eine beispielhafte Kooperation der beiden Fakultäten für Architektur und Bauingenieurwissenschaften. Der zukunftsträchtige Bereich der digitalen Fabrikationstechniken, der uns am Institut für Architektur und Medien besonders interessiert, erhält dadurch ein perfektes Experimentierfeld für aktuelle Forschungsagenden, aber auch für die forschungsgeleitete Lehre im Masterstudio.

Reine Technologie ohne kreativen Input ist für den Architekturentwurf uninteressant. Den Einsatz der Robotertechnik im Rahmen unseres Masterstudios „Papier Peint" haben wir deshalb als Pilotprojekt entwickelt. Das „Digitale Handwerk" wird als Forschungsthema aufgefasst, welches aus der intensiven Beschäftigung mit den Möglichkeiten des Roboters, aber auch der Gestaltung durch digitale Codes, dem Scripting, entsteht. Die Studierenden bekamen Gelegenheit, algorithmische Entwürfe von einem ABB Roboter umsetzen zu lassen. „Papier Peint" – französisch für bemaltes Papier, oder einfach Tapeten – war dabei nur die Leitidee. Gemäß Sempers Theorie, dass die Oberflächen von Wänden unsere Raumwahrnehmung am nachhaltigsten prägen, ging es um flächige, superfizielle Effekte und deren Produktion mit Robotern, mit dem Ziel eine architektonische Situation räumlich zu definieren. Die Studierenden mussten entsprechend ihrer Entwürfe parallel eigene Programme (in Rhino/Grasshopper bzw. Java/Processing) schreiben, passende Werkzeuge für den Roboter entwickeln

Papier Peint
Master studio, winter semester 2010,
Institute of Architecture and Media

On January 13, 2011 the "Robot Design Laboratory" at the Building Technology Center Inffeldgasse was ceremoniously opened. This large infrastructure investment is the result of an exemplary collaboration between the two faculties of civil engineering and architecture. The seminal field of digital fabrication technology, which has long been a special focus of the Institute of Architecture and Media, is thereby getting a perfect environment not only for experiments and research activities, but also for the research-oriented teaching in the Master studio.

Pure technology without creative input is not interesting for architectural design. We have therefore developed the application of robot technology in our Master studio "Papier Peint" as a pilot project. "Digital crafting" is treated as a research subject, which results from the intensive investigation of the possibilities of the robot, but also of designing by means of digital code, of the art of generative scripting. Students had the opportunity to have their algorithmic designs realized by an ABB robot. "Papier Peint"—French for painted paper or simply tapestry—was merely the leading idea. Based on Semper's notion that it is the surface of walls that most strongly influences our spatial perception, the studio was about developing surface effects and their prototypical production with the help of robots, with the aim of redefining a precise architectural setting. According to their designs, students had to write their own programs (in Rhino/Grasshopper resp. Java/Processing), find or construct the proper tools for the robot, and finally have the robot (we used an ABB IRB 140) turn them into physical reality at 1:1 scale. The excellent results of the studio were the result of numerous virtual, haptic, digital and analogue tests (see image 29 © Philipp Sackl, the presentation video, resp. the full documentation online at https://iam2. tugraz.at/studio/w10/). To enable this intensity of investigation took a lot of preparation and development work also on part of the teachers. As there was no appropriate software for the students available, the IAM team led by Richard Dank wrote the program "Boot the Bot" (BTB), which allows the robot to be controlled in a straightforward fashion. This extensive development will be valuable for future projects, but it already created interesting spin-offs during the semester. At the press-conference and the Open Labs exhibition the TU Graz held on the occa-

29

respektive selber bauen und diese schlussendlich mit dem Roboter (zum Einsatz kam ein ABB IRB 140) realisieren. Die hervorragenden Ergebnisse waren das Resultat von vielen virtuellen, haptischen, digitalen und analogen Versuchen (siehe Abbildung 29 © Philipp Sackl, das Präsentationsvideo und die volle Dokumentation online unter https://iam2.tugraz.at/studio/w10/). Um diese Intensität der Studierendenarbeiten zu ermöglichen war auch sehr viel Vorbereitung bzw. Entwicklungsarbeit von Betreuerseite notwendig. Da keine geeigneten Programme für die Studierenden verfügbar waren, hat das IAM-Team um Richard Dank die Software „Boot the Bot" (BTB) entwickelt, mit welcher der Roboter auf einfache Weise angesteuert werden kann. Diese aufwändige Entwicklungsarbeit wird sich bei zukünftigen Projekten auszahlen, hat aber auch schon zu Spin-offs während des Semesters geführt. Bei der Pressekonferenz und in der Open Labs-Ausstellung im Dom im Berg, welche anlässlich der 200-Jahr-Feier der TU Graz organisiert wurden, standen jeweils durch BTB gesteuerte Anwendungen des kleinen Industrieroboters im Zentrum des Publikumsinteresses. Viele Ausstellungsbesucher waren fasziniert, dass der Roboter Porträts von ihnen zeichnete, aber auch von der Tatsache, dass

sion of its bicentennial celebration, BTB-controlled applications of the small industrial robot were at the center of public interest. Visitors were fascinated by the robot drawing portraits of them and by the fact that it was from the architecture faculty that these virtuosic applications of technology originated. Online at: https://iam2.tugraz.at/studio/w10/

Richard Dank, Urs Hirschberg

"A Laboratory for …"

Master studio at the **Institute of Urban and Architectural History** with an exhibition as a contribution to the anniversary year of Graz University of Technology, summer semester 2011

To celebrate the anniversary of the Graz University of Technology, students who did the Master studio at the Institute of Urban and Architectural

diese virtuose Anwendung von Technik an der Architekturfakultät entwickelt wurde. Online unter: https://iam2.tugraz.at/studio/w10/

Richard Dank, Urs Hirschberg

30

History traced the footsteps of nineteen remarkable personalities and designed for them optimal working environments.

Based on intensive research into the life stories of these individuals, the places where they worked and their possible architectural expectations, the students developed spaces of work and research for the people who had left their mark on Graz University of Technology in its two hundred years of existence.

The exhibition brought together the results of these studies, featuring biographical notes, models, plans and images—forming at the same time a tribute to the scientists whose fascinating life stories often remain hidden behind their inventions.

„Ein Labor für …"

Masterstudio, SS 2011, **Institut für Stadt- und Baugeschichte** mit Ausstellung als Beitrag zum Jubiläumsjahr der TU Graz

Anlässlich des Jubiläumsjahres der TU Graz folgten Studierende der Architektur im Rahmen ihres Masterstudios am Institut für Stadt- und Baugeschichte den Spuren von 19 bemerkenswerten Persönlichkeiten und entwarfen für diese optimale Arbeitsumgebungen.

Basierend auf der intensiven Recherche der Lebensgeschichten der jeweiligen Personen, der Orte, an denen diese gewirkt haben und ihren möglichen baukulturellen Ansprüchen entwickelten die Studierenden Gebäude des Arbeitens und des Forschens für Personen, die in den 200 Jahren des Bestehens der TU Graz hier gewirkt haben.

Die Ausstellung versammelte die Ergebnisse dieser Auseinandersetzung anhand von biografischen Notizen, Modellen, Plänen und Bildern – gleichsam eine Hommage an Wissenschaftlerinnen und Wissenschaftler, deren spannende Lebensgeschichten oft hinter ihren Erfindungen verborgen bleiben.

Integraler Bestandteil dieses Masterstudios war darüber hinaus die Auseinandersetzung mit

Other integral elements of this Master studio included a discussion of how spaces and laboratories have changed in the course of history, the exploration of what the structural possibilities were at different times, as well as the design of the exhibition system.

The intention of the project was to connect the arts, technology, and the natural sciences as a contribution of a comprehensive knowledge transfer in the context of the anniversary year of Graz University of Technology "200 years of knowledge, technology and passion."

During the four phases of the studio, the students were advised by an **interdisciplinary team** consisting of Simone Hain, Ute Angeringer-Mmadu, Marion Starzacher (project exercise), Volker Pachauer (AK architectural history), Mabel Altmann (Curatorial Practices). **Students**: Marlene Bartelme, Ernst Dengg, Sabine Forstinger, Christoph Gradauer, Stefan Höll, Thomas Koch, Miriam Leitner, Christof Lösch, Lucija Lukas, Michael Martinelli, Simone

Räumen und Labors im Wandel der Geschichte, das Erforschen von baukonstruktiven Möglichkeiten der jeweiligen Zeit sowie die Erarbeitung eines Ausstellungskonzeptes.

Intention des Projektes ist die Vernetzung von Geistes-, Technik- und Naturwissenschaften als Beitrag einer umfassenden Wissensvermittlung im Rahmen des Jubiläumsjahres der TU Graz „200 Jahre Wissen, Technik und Leidenschaft".

Begleitet wurden die Studierenden während der vier Phasen von einem **interdisziplinär arbeitenden Team**: Simone Hain, Ute Angeringer-Mmadu, Marion Starzacher (Projektübung), Volker Pachauer (AK Architekturgeschichte), Mabel Altmann (Kuratorische Praktiken). **Studierende**: Marlene Bartelme, Ernst Dengg, Sabine Forstinger, Christoph Gradauer, Stefan Höll, Thomas Koch, Miriam Leitner, Christof Lösch, Lucija Lukas, Michael Martinelli, Simone Mayr, Neira Mehmedagic, David Pfister, Nicole Ploschnik, Carina Prasser, Beatrice Reinbacher, Melinda Temesi, Martina Thaller, Stephan Zotter.

Ute Angeringer-Mmadu, Marion Starzacher

Mayr, Neira Mehmedagic, David Pfister, Nicole Ploschnik, Carina Prasser, Beatrice Reinbacher, Melinda Temesi, Martina Thaller, Stephan Zotter.

Ute Angeringer-Mmadu, Marion Starzacher

Masterstudios 2010/2011 Master Studios 2010/2011

Institut Institute | Semester | **Titel** | Vortragende Lecturer

Tragwerksentwurf Structural Design | WS 2010
Sub//Add | Peter Kaschnig, Stefan Peters, Andreas Trummer

Tragwerksentwurf Structural Design | SS 2011
Footprint | Peter Kaschnig, Stefan Peters, Andreas Trummer

Stadt- und Baugeschichte Urban and Architectural History | WS 2010
Jugend(t)räume Eisenerz – In einer schrumpfenden Stadt | Simone Hain, Oliver Jungwirth, Manfred Omahna

Stadt- und Baugeschichte Urban and Architectural History | SS 2011
Jet back – Ein Labor für ... | Ute Angeringer-Mmadu, Simone Hain, Marion Starzacher

Architekturtheorie, Kunst- und Kulturwissenschaften
Architectural Theory, History of Art and Cultural Studies | WS 2010
Das Haus Zankel in Genf von Konrad Frey | Ingrid Böck, Anselm Wagner

Architekturtheorie, Kunst- und Kulturwissenschaften
Architectural Theory, History of Art and Cultural Studies | SS 2011
Rethinking Designing Infrastructure | Daniel Gethmann, Bernhard Hafner

Städtebau Urbanism | WS 2010
Scenarios on the Megapolitan Future: The Recreated Utopia | Joost Meuwissen, Martin Zettel

Städtebau Urbanism | WS 2010
„Olympiade 2020 – Budapest"/Großevent und nachhaltige Stadtentwicklung | Johann Zancanella

Städtebau Urbanism | SS 2011
New Urban Models for Aging | Silke Fischer, Joost Meuwissen

Städtebau Urbanism | SS 2011
Sao Paolo | Wolfgang Dokonal

Gebäudelehre Architectural Typologies | WS 2010
Nachverdichtung Gründerzeitblock | Sonja Frühwirt, Hans Gangoly, Andreas Lechner

Gebäudelehre Architectural Typologies | SS 2011
Plüddemanngasse – McBoulevard 2.0 | Markus Bogensberger, Hans Gangoly, Christian Andreas Mueller Inderbitzin

Architekturtechnologie Architecture Technology | WS 2010
Rijeka Waterfront | Tim Lüking, Roger Riewe

Architekturtechnologie Architecture Technology | SS 2011
BIG BANG Berlin | Uta Gelbke, Roger Riewe

Architekturtechnologie Architecture Technology | SS 2011
BIG BANG Seoul | Uta Gelbke, Seung Hoy Kim, Roger Riewe

Raumgestaltung Spatial Design | WS 2010
PTUJ – UFERLOS! | Irmgard Frank

Raumgestaltung Spatial Design | SS 2011
diverseIdentity Theresienstadt (CZ) – Entwurf für ein europäisches Kongress und Tagungszentrum | Claudia Gerhäusser, Gottfried Prasenc

Architektur und Landschaft Architecture and Landscape | WS 2010
Rurban Stories: Wie Mikropraktiken den rurbanen Raum formen | Andreas Goritschnig, Klaus K. Loenhart, Anne Oberritter

Architektur und Landschaft Architecture and Landscape | SS 2011
Arizona Dream: New Realities for Broadacre City | Andreas Goritschnig, Klaus K. Loenhart, Anne Oberritter, Ania Viktoria Zdunek

Zeitgenössische Kunst Contemporary Art | WS 2010
Kunst und Energie | Brigitte Kovacs, Hans Kupelwieser, Nicole Pruckermayr

Wohnbau Housing | WS 2010
Urban Renewal of Industrial Zones am Beispiel einer Industriebrache in Berlin | Marlis Nograsek

Wohnbau Housing | SS 2010
INFERNO/Kap Verde im Rahmen des Forschungsprojektes InforCidade – Die informelle Stadt | Marlis Nograsek

Gebäude und Energie Buildings and Energy | WS 2010
Touching the ground lightely | Brian Cody, Daniel Podmirseg

Gebäude und Energie Buildings and Energy | SS 2011
Touching the ground lightely | Brian Cody, Daniel Podmirseg

Architektur und Medien Architecture and Media | WS 2010
Papier Peint | Richard Dank, Urs Hirschberg

Architektur und Medien Architecture and Media | SS 2011
Sensitive Wall | Urs Hirschberg, Martin Kaftan, Ingrid Maria Pohl

Mobilitätsprogramme

Seit 1992 nehmen österreichische Hochschulinstitutionen am Erasmusprogramm teil. In diesen beinahe 20 Jahren sind Auslandsaufenthalte zu einem selbstverständlichen Teil des Studiums geworden.

Die Architekturfakultät der TU Graz zählt zu den beliebten Zielen für Studierenden aus aller Welt und so dürfen wir jährlich um die 55 Incoming Studierende bei uns begrüßen. Um das Angebot an Partneruniversitäten zu erweitern, werden derzeit weitere Abkommen mit ausgewählten Partnern unterschrieben. So freuen wir uns, ab dem Studienjahr 2011/2012 die Architekturfakultäten der *University of Cyprus*, der *Estonian Academy of Arts* und der *Iceland Academy of the Arts* zu unseren Erasmuspartnern zählen zu dürfen.

Aber Erasmus ist nicht das einzige Austauschprogramm der Architekturfakultät und so richtet sich unser Blick unter anderem auch nach Asien. Im Rahmen von Joint Study wurden auf Initiative des Instituts für Architekturtechnologie Verträge mit der *Seoul National University* (Südkorea), der *Chinese University of Hong Kong* und der *Tongji University in Shanghai* (China) unterschrieben. So konnten wir uns im vorigen Studienjahr darüber freuen, die ersten chinesischen Architekturstudierenden aus Hong Kong in Graz zu begrüßen. Die ersten Grazer Studierenden sind inzwischen aus Hong Kong zurückgekehrt und das Feedback der Studierenden ist überwältigend. Im Wintersemester 2011/2012 freuen wir uns, die ersten Studierenden aus Seoul an unserer Fakultät begrüßen zu dürfen. Das Abkommen mit dem CAUP (College of Architecture and Urban Planning) der Tongji University sieht auch einen Austausch im Bereich der Lehre und Forschung vor. Der Vertrag dafür wurde schon von den Rektoren der beiden Universitäten unterschrieben und so wird der erste Austausch von Studierenden und Lehrenden voraussichtlich ab 2012/2013 stattfinden.

Weiters nehmen pro Jahr ca. 60 Studierende unserer Fakultät ein Stipendium für kurzfristige wissenschaftliche Arbeiten und fachspezifische Kurse im Ausland (KUWI) in Anspruch, meistens im Rahmen ihrer Diplomarbeit oder Dissertation.

Für weitere Informationen stehen das Büro für Internationale Beziehungen und Mobilitätsprogramme der TU Graz und Marisol Vidal Martinez als Koordinatorin der Architekturfakultät gerne zur Verfügung.

Marisol Vidal Martinez

Exchange Programs

Since 1992, Austrian higher education institutions have taken part in the Erasmus program. During these almost twenty years, sojourns abroad have become a natural part of the curricula.

The Faculty of Architecture of Graz University of Technology counts as one of the more popular destinations for students from around the world and so we welcome up to 55 incoming students annually. To expand the range of partner universities, new agreements are currently being signed with selected partners. Starting with the academic year 2011/2012, we are fortunate to include the architecture faculties of the *University of Cyprus*, the *Estonian Academy of Arts* and the *Icelandic Academy of the Arts* as our Erasmus partners.

But Erasmus is not the only exchange program of the Faculty of Architecture; we also look, for example, towards Asia. At the initiative of the Institute of Architecture Technology, joint study contracts were signed with the *Seoul National University* (South Korea), the *Chinese University of Hong Kong* and the *Tongji University in Shanghai* (China). As a result, we welcomed the first Chinese architecture students from Hong Kong in the previous academic year. The first Graz students have now returned from Hong Kong and the students' feedback has been overwhelming. In the winter semester 2011/2012, we are looking forward to the first students from Seoul to visit our faculty. The agreement with the CAUP (College of Architecture and Urban Planning) of Tongji University also envisages an exchange program in the field of teaching and research. The contract was already signed by the rectors of both universities and the first exchange of students and teachers is expected to take place in 2012/2013.

Furthermore, approximately sixty students per year receive a scholarship for short-term scientific work and specialized courses abroad (KUWI), usually as part of their Master's thesis or Ph.D. dissertation.

For more information, please contact the Office of International Relations and Mobility Program of the University of Graz or Marisol Vidal Martinez, the coordinator of the architecture faculty.

Marisol Vidal Martinez

GAM.
ARCHITECTURE MAGAZINE 09

GAM.09 beschäftigt sich mit dem Thema der Schichtungen von Wänden in der Architektur. Wir interessieren uns dafür, wie Wände im Hinblick auf ihre architektonischen, technologischen und kulturellen Möglichkeiten neu gedacht werden können. In jüngster Zeit gibt es eine Vielzahl von Entwürfen, Experimenten und Entwicklungen, welche die herkömmliche Funktion von Wänden nicht nur konstruktiv sondern auch in ihrer Bedeutung erweitern. Sie gehen weniger vom trennenden Aspekt schlichter Begrenzungsmauern als vielmehr von verbindenden Schichtungen der Wände in einem ökologischen, städtebaulichen und soziokulturellen Sinne aus, während sie deren Eigenschaften, Fähigkeiten und Konstruktionsweisen erneuern.

Wände sind nur scheinbar gewöhnliche Bauteile, sie zeichnen sich durch eine Vielzahl von Potenzialen aus. Wände können tragen, sie können trennen und schützen, sie können aber auch verbinden, Raum und Räume bilden, das Raumklima kontrollieren, Funktionen in sich aufnehmen. Ihre Materialität und ihr Aufbau sind als Struktur, Rhythmus und Tektonik erlebbar. Wände können zur Energieerhaltung und -gewinnung eingesetzt werden und sie werden in jüngster Zeit immer mehr zu dynamisch reagierenden, aktiven Elementen.

Durch technologische Neuerungen und Entwicklungen findet derzeit eine Erweiterung unseres Wandbegriffs statt. *GAM.09* interessieren solche Neukonzeptionen von Wänden sowohl in ihrer Auswirkung auf den architektonischen Raum, wie auch in Bezug auf die sich darin artikulierende Kritik an der überkommenen Funktion von Wänden als architektonischen Grundelementen an den Grenzen eines Gebäudes zwischen innen und außen, deren äußere Gestaltung hinsichtlich Fassaden, Oberflächen und Öffnungen längst eines der klassischen Themen der Architektur ist. Wir suchen Beispiele, in denen Architektinnen und Architekten zu Entwicklern von Wandkonzeptionen werden, die konkret oder im übertragenen Sinne vielschichtig sind und dadurch die Wand nicht nur in ihrer Funktion sondern auch in ihrer räumlichen Wirksamkeit erweitern.

GAM.09 schlägt vor, die traditionelle Trennung zwischen äußerer Form und innerer Funktion von Wänden um eine Perspektive zu ergänzen, die die Wandfunktionen des Tragens, Speicherns und Bewahrens gemeinsam mit Qualitäten des verbindenden Austauschs zwischen innen und außen artikuliert. In dieser integrativen Hinsicht stellt *GAM.09* architektonische Entwürfe vor, die Erfindungen neuer Verfahren mit einer Erprobung ihres Einsatzes kombinieren, um ein klassisches architektonisches Thema wie die Wand und ihre Funktionen als innovatives Feld des Entwurfs und der Analyse zu aktualisieren. Dazu bittet *GAM.09* um Vorschläge für Beiträge, die das architektonische Thema „Walls: Spatial Sequences" in tektonischer, technologischer und kultureller Hinsicht in den Blick nehmen. *GAM.09* lädt Sie ein, ein Abstract (max. 500 Wörter) zum Thema „Walls: Spatial Sequences" bis zum 15. April 2012 einzureichen. Der Abgabetermin für den fertigen Beitrag (Full Paper) ist der 19. August 2012.

http://gam.tugraz.at